W9-CXM-967

Computer Ethics

Also by Tom Forester

The Microelectronics Revolution (ed.) (1980)
The Information Technology Revolution (ed.) (1985)
High-Tech Society: The Story of the Information Technology Revolution (1987)
The Materials Revolution (ed.) (1988)
Computers in the Human Context (ed.) (1989)
Silicon Samurai: How Japan Conquered the World's IT Industry (1993)

Computer Ethics
Cautionary Tales and Ethical Dilemmas in Computing

Second Edition

Tom Forester and Perry Morrison

The MIT Press
Cambridge, Massachusetts
London, England

This book was set in Sabon by .eps Electronic Publishing Services and was printed and bound in the United States of America.

Library of Congress Cataloging-in-Publication Data

Forester, Tom.
  Computer ethics : cautionary tales and ethical dilemmas in
computing / Tom Forester and Perry Morrison.—2nd ed.
    p. cm.
  Includes bibliographical references and index.
  ISBN 0-262-06164-3 (hc).—ISBN 0-262-56073-9 (pbk.)
  1. Electronic data processing—Moral and ethical aspects.
I. Morrison, Perry. II. Title.
QA76.9.M65F67 1994
174′.90904—dc20   93-22874
                                                                  CIP

Contents

Preface and Acknowledgments

The aim of this book is twofold: (1) to describe some of the new problems created for society by computers, and (2) to show how these problems present ethical dilemmas for computer professionals and computer users.

The problems created by computers, in turn, arise from two main sources: from hardware and software *malfunctions* and from *misuse* by human beings. We argue that computer systems have often proved to be insecure, unreliable, and unpredictable and that society has yet to come to terms with the consequences. We also seek to show how society has become newly vulnerable to human misuse of computers in the form of computer crime, software theft, hacking, the creation of viruses, invasions of privacy, and so on.

Computer Ethics has evolved from our previous writings and in particular our experiences teaching two courses on the human and social context of computing to computer science students at Griffith University in Australia. One lesson we quickly learned was that computing students cannot be assumed to possess any awareness of social trends, global problems, or organizational issues. Accordingly, these courses have been reshaped in order to relate more closely to students' career goals by focusing on the ethical dilemmas they will face in their everyday lives as computer professionals.

Many college and university computer science (CS) degree programs are now including or seeking to include an ethics component along the lines of the Social, Ethical and Professional Context (or SP) stream outlined in the recent ACM/IEEE-CS Curriculum Task Force report (reproduced in appendix B). Their plans in the past have been hampered by a lack of suitable teaching texts. *Computer Ethics* has been designed to help fill that gap and to fit squarely into the recommended CS curriculum as one of the nine key areas of a model CS degree. For this reason, we have included numerous up-to-date references as well as hypothetical scenarios and role-playing exercises at the end of the book. The creative teacher should be able to build on these and thus be in a position to deliver a lively and engaging course.

Readers will notice that we have avoided lengthy discussion of philosophical and ethical theory. The reason is that this book is but a first step, with the simple aim of sensitizing undergraduate computing students to ethical issues. It is, as one reviewer of the first edition put it, a "consciousness-raising" exercise, providing a "wake-up call" to students, computer users, and computer professionals. Thus we have placed emphasis on attention-grabbing cases and memorable anecdotes: much can be learned from such cautionary tales, which have been a traditional method of socializing newcomers into professions.

Nor will readers find a detailed account of the legislative positions around the world on the various issues discussed. In each country the legal situation is often complex, confused, and fast-changing—and again this is not the purpose of the book.

Finally, a note on sources. First, we have to acknowledge an enormous debt to Peter G. Neumann, whose "Risks to the Public in Computer Systems" sections in *Software Engineering Notes,* the journal of the Association of Computing Machinery's Special Interest Group on Software (ACM-SIGSOFT), have provided inspiration, amusement, and a vast amount of valuable information. Long may he continue. Second, we have to caution that many of these and other sources are newspaper and media reports, which, like computers, are not always one-hundred percent reliable.

Computer Ethics

1

Introduction: Social, Ethical, and Professional Issues in Computing

Computers are the core technology of our times. They are the new paradigm, the new "common sense." In the comparatively short space of forty years, computers have become central to the operations of industrial societies. Without computers and computer networks, much of manufacturing industry, commerce, transport and distribution, government, the military, health services, education, and research would simply grind to a halt.

Computers are certainly the most important technology to have come along this century, and the current Information Technology Revolution may in time equal or even exceed the Industrial Revolution in terms of social significance. We are still trying to understand the full implications of the computerization that has already taken place in key areas of society such as the workplace. Computers and computer-based information and communication systems will have an even greater impact on our way of life in the next millennium—now just a few years away.

Yet as society becomes more dependent on computers and computer networks, we also become more and more vulnerable to computer malfunctions (usually caused by unreliable software) and to computer misuse—that is, to the misuse of computers and computer networks by human beings. Malfunctioning computers and the misuse of computers have created a whole new range of social problems, such as computer crime, software theft, hacking, the creation of viruses, invasions of privacy, overreliance on intelligent machines, and workplace stress. In turn, each of these problems creates ethical dilemmas for computer professionals and users. Ethical theory and professional codes of ethics can help us resolve these ethical dilemmas to some extent, while computing educators have a special responsibility to try to ensure more ethical behavior among future generations of computer users.

Our Computerized Society

When computers hit the headlines, it usually results in bad publicity for them. When power supplies fail, phone systems go down, air traffic control systems seize up, or traffic lights go on the blink, there is nearly always a spokesperson ready to blame the problem on a luckless computer. When public utilities, credit-checking agencies, the police, tax departments, or motor vehicle license centers make hideous mistakes, they invariably blame it on computer error. When the bank or the airline cannot process our transaction, we're told that "the computer is down" or that "we're having problems with our computer." The poor old computer gets the blame on these and many other occasions, although frequently something else is at fault. Even when the problem is computer-related, the ultimate cause of failure is human error rather than machine error, because humans design the computers and write the software that tells computers what to do.

Computers have been associated with some major blunders in recent times. For instance, the infamous hole in the ozone layer remained undetected for seven years because of a program design error. No less than twenty-two US servicemen died in the early 1980s in five separate crashes of the U.S. Air Force's Blackhawk helicopter as a result of radio interference with its novel, computer-based fly-by-wire system. At least four people died in North America because of computer glitches in the Therac-25 cancer radiotherapy machine, while similar disasters have been reported recently in England and Spain. During the 1991 Gulf war, software failure in the Patriot missile defense system enabled an Iraqi Scud missile to penetrate the U.S. military barracks in Dhahran, killing twenty-eight people, while the notorious trouble with the Hubble space telescope in the same year was exacerbated by a programming error that shut down the onboard computer.[1]

In fact, computers have figured one way or another in almost every famous system failure, from Three Mile Island, Chernobyl, and the Challenger space shuttle disaster, to the Air New Zealand antarctic crash and the downing of the Korean Air Lines flight 007 over Sakhalin Island, not to mention the sinking of HMS Sheffield in the Falklands war and the shooting down of an Iranian airbus by the USS Vincennes over the Persian Gulf. A software bug lay behind the massive New York phone failure of January 1990, which shut down AT&T's phone network and New York's airports for nine hours, while a system design error helped shut down New York's phones for another four hours in September 1991 (key AT&T engineers were away at a seminar on how to cope with emergencies). A whole series of aerospace accidents such as the French, Indian, and Nepalese A320 Airbus disasters, the Bell V-22 Osprey and Northrop YF-23 crashes, and the downing of the Lauda Air Boeing 767 in Thailand has been attributed to unreliable software in computerized fly-by-wire systems. Undeterred, engineers are now developing sail-by-wire navigation systems for ships and drive-by-wire systems for our cars.[2]

Computers and computer networks are vulnerable to physical breaches such as fires, floods, earthquakes, and power cuts—including very short power spikes or voltage sags ("dirty power") that can be enough to knock out a sensitive system. A good example was the fire in the Setagaya telephone office in Tokyo in 1984 that instantly cut 3,000 data and 89,000 telephone lines and resulted in huge losses for Japanese businesses. Communication networks are also vulnerable to inadvertent human or animal intervention. For instance, increasingly popular fiber optic cables, containing thousands of phone circuits, have been devoured by hungry beavers in Missouri, foxes in outback Australia, and sharks and beam-trawling fishermen in the Pacific Ocean. In January 1991, a clumsy New Jersey repair crew sliced through a major optical fiber artery, shutting down New York's phones for a further six hours, while similar breaks have been reported from Chicago, Los Angeles, and Washington D.C. The Federal Aviation Administration recently recorded the shutdown of four major U.S. air traffic control centers. The cause? "Fiber cable cut by farmer burying dead cow," said the official report.[3]

Computers and communication systems are also vulnerable to physical attacks by humans and to software sabotage by outside hackers and inside employees. For example, a saboteur entered telecommunications tunnels in Sydney, Australia, one day in 1987 and carefully severed twenty-four cables, knocking out 35,000 telephone lines in forty Sydney suburbs and bringing down hundreds of computers, automated teller machines (ATMs), and point of sale (POS), telex, and fax terminals with it. Some businesses were put out of action for forty-eight hours as engineers battled to restore services. Had the saboteur not been working with an out-of-date plan, the whole of Australia's telecommunications system might have been blacked out. In Chicago in 1986, a disgruntled employee at Encyclopaedia Brittanica, angry at having been laid off, merely tapped into the encyclopedia's database and made a few alterations to the text being prepared for a new edition of the renowned work—like changing references to Jesus Christ to Allah and inserting the names of company executives in odd positions. As one executive commented, "In the computer age, this is exactly what we have nightmares about."[4]

Our growing dependency on computers has been highlighted further in recent years by such incidents as the theft in the former Soviet Union in 1990 of computer disks containing medical information on some 670,000 people exposed to radiation in the Chernobyl nuclear disaster. The disks were simply wiped and then resold by the teenaged thieves. In 1989, vital information about the infamous Alaskan oil spill was "inadvertently" destroyed at a stroke by an Exxon computer operator. In the same year, U.S. retailer Montgomery Ward allegedly discovered one of its warehouses in California that had been lost for three years because of an error in its master inventory program. Apparently, one day the trucks stopped arriving at the warehouse: nothing came in or went out. But the paychecks were issued on a different system, so for three whole years (so the story goes) the employees went to work every day, moved boxes around, and submitted timecards—without ever telling company headquarters. "It was a bit like a job with the government," said one worker after the blunder had been discovered.[5]

In Amsterdam, Holland, in 1991, the body of an old man who had died six months earlier was found in an apartment by a caretaker who had been concerned about a large pile of mail for him. The man had been something of a recluse, but because his rent, gas, and electricity bills were paid automatically by computer, he wasn't missed. His pension also had been transferred into his bank account every month, so all the relevant authorities assumed that he was still alive. Another particularly disturbing example of computer dependency came from London during the Gulf war, when computer disks containing the Allies' plans for Desert

Storm disappeared, along with a lap-top computer, from a parked car belonging to Wing Commander David Farquhar of the Royal Air Force Strike Command. Luckily for the Allies, the thieves did not recognize the value of the unencrypted data, which did not fall into Iraqi hands. But a court martial for negligence and breach of security awaited Farquhar.[6]

Computers are changing our way of life in all sorts of ways. At work, we may have our performance monitored by computer and our electronic mail read by the boss. It's no good trying to delete embarrassing e-mail statements because someone probably will have a backup copy of what you wrote. This is what happened to White House adviser Colonel Oliver North and to John Poindexter, the former national security adviser to president Ronald Reagan, when they tried to cover up evidence of the Iran-Contra scandal. Poindexter allegedly sat up all night deleting 5,012 e-mail messages, while North destroyed a further 736, but unknown to Poindexter and North the messages were all preserved on backup tapes that were subsequently read by congressional investigators. And if you use a spell-checker or language-corrector in your word processing program, be sure that it doesn't land you in trouble. For example, the Fresno Bee newspaper in California recently had to run a correction that read: "An item in Thursday's Nation Digest about the Massachusetts budget crisis made reference to new taxes that will help 'put Massachusetts back in the African-American.' This item should have read 'put Massachusetts back in the black.'"[7]

Recent government reports have confirmed that our growing dependence on computers leaves society increasingly vulnerable to software bugs, physical accidents, and attacks on critical systems. In 1989, a report to the U.S. Congress from one of its subcommittees, written by James H. Paul and Gregory C. Simon, found that the U.S. government was wasting millions of dollars a year on software that was overdue, inadequate, unsafe, and riddled with bugs. In 1990, the Canadian auditor-general, Ken Dye, warned that most of the Canadian government's computer systems were vulnerable to physical or logical attack: "That's like running a railroad without signals or a busy airport without traffic controls," he said. In 1991, a major report by the System Security Study Committee of the U.S. National Academy of Sciences, published as Computers at Risk, called for improved security, safety, and reliability in computer systems. The report declared that society was becoming more vulnerable to "poor system design, accidents that disable systems, and attacks on computer systems."[8]

Some New Social Problems Created by Computers

Although society as a whole derives benefit from the use of computers and computer networks, computerization has created some serious problems for society that were largely unforeseen.

In this book, we classify the new social problems created by computers into seven main categories: computer crime and the problem of computer security; software theft and the question of intellectual property rights; the new phenomena of hacking and the creation of viruses; computer unreliability and the key question of software quality; data storage and the invasion of privacy; the social implications of artificial intelligence and expert systems; and the many problems associated with workplace computerization.

These new problems have proved to be costly: computer crime costs companies millions of dollars a year, while software producers lose staggering sums as a result of widespread software theft. In recent years, huge amounts of time and money have had to be devoted to repairing the damage to systems caused by the activities of malicious hackers and virus creators. Unreliable hardware and software costs society untold billions every year in terms of downtime, cost overruns, and abandoned systems, while invasions of privacy and database mix-ups have resulted in expensive lawsuits and much individual stress. Sophisticated expert systems lie unused for fear of attracting lawsuits, and workplace stress caused by inappropriate computerization costs society millions in absenteeism, sickness benefits, and reduced productivity.

Computer crime is a growing problem for companies, according to recent reports. Every new technology introduced into society creates new opportunities for crime, and information technology is no exception. A new generation of high-tech criminals is busy stealing data, doctoring data, and threatening to destroy data for monetary gain. New types of fraud made possible by computers include ATM fraud, EFT (electronic funds transfer) fraud, EDI (electronic data interchange) fraud, mobile phone fraud, cable TV fraud, and telemarketing fraud. Desktop printing

(DTP) has even made desktop forgery possible. Perhaps the biggest new crime is phone fraud, which may be costing American companies as much as $2 billion a year. Most analysts think that reported computer crime is just the tip of an iceberg of underground digital deviance that sees criminals and the crime authorities competing to stay one jump ahead of each other.

Software theft or the illegal copying of software is a major problem that is costing software producers an estimated $12 billion dollars a year. Recent cases of software piracy highlight the prevalence of software copying and the worldwide threat posed by organized software pirates. Computer users and software developers tend to have very different ethical positions on the question of copying software, while the law in most countries is confusing and out of date. There is an ongoing debate about whether copyright law or patent law provides the most appropriate protection for software. Meanwhile the legal position in the United States, for example, has been confused further by the widely varying judgments handed down by U.S. courts in recent years. The recent rash of look and feel suits launched by companies such as Lotus and Apple have muddied the waters still further. The central question facing the information technology (IT) industry is how to reward innovation without stifling creativity, but there is no obvious answer to this conundrum and no consensus as to what constitutes ethical practice.

Attacks by hackers and virus creators on computer systems have proved enormously costly to computer operators. In recent cases, hackers have broken into university computers in order to alter exam results, downloaded software worth millions, disrupted the 911 emergency phone system in the United States, stolen credit card numbers, hacked into U.S. military computers and sold the stolen data to the KGB, and blackmailed London banks into employing them as security advisers. Hackers also have planted viruses that have caused computer users untold misery in recent years. Viruses have erased files, damaged disks, and completely shut down systems. For example, the famous Internet worm, let loose by Cornell student Robert Morris in 1988, badly damaged 6,000 systems across the United States. There is ongoing debate about whether hackers can sometimes function as guardians of our civil liberties, but in most countries the response to the hacking craze has been new security measures, new laws such as Britain's Computer Misuse Act

(1990), and new calls for improved network ethics. Peter J. Denning, editor-in-chief of Communications of the ACM, says that we must expect increasing attacks on computers by hackers and virus creators in the years ahead; Professor Lance J. Hoffman has called for all new computers to be fitted with antiviral protection as standard equipment, rather like seatbelts on cars.[9]

Unreliable computers are proving to be a major headache for modern society. Computer crashes or downtime—usually caused by buggy software—are estimated to cost the United States as much as $4 billion a year, according to a recent report. When bug-ridden software has been used to control fly-by-wire aircraft, railroad signals, and ambulance dispatch systems, the cost of unreliable computers sometimes has had to be measured in terms of human lives. Computers tend to be unreliable because they are digital devices prone to total failure and because their complexity ensures that they cannot be tested thoroughly before use. Massive complexity can make computer systems completely unmanageable and can result in huge cost overruns or budget runaways. For example, in 1988 the Bank of America had to abandon an $80 million computer system that failed to work, while in 1992 American Airlines announced a loss of over $100 million on a runaway computer project. The Wessex Regional Health Authority in England scrapped a system in 1990 that had cost $60 million, and Blue Cross & Blue Shield of Massachusetts pulled the plug in 1992 on a project that had cost a staggering $120 million. U.S. Department of Defense runaways are rumored to have easily exceeded these sums. Computer scientists are exploring a variety of ways to improve software quality, but progress with this key problem is slow.[10]

The problem of safeguarding privacy in a society where computers can store, manipulate, and transmit at a stroke vast quantities of information about individuals is proving to be intractable. In recent years, a whole series of database disasters involving mistaken identities, data mix-ups, and doctored data have indicated that we probably place too much faith in information stored on computers. People have had their driver's license and credit records altered or stolen and their lives generally made a misery by inaccurate computer records. There is growing concern about the volume and the quality of the data stored by the FBI's National Crime Information Center (NCIC), the United Kingdom's Police National Computer (PNC), and other national security agencies. (Such concerns even led to a public riot in Switzerland in 1990.) Moreover, new controversies have erupted over the privacy aspects of such practices as calling number identification (CNID) on phone networks, the monitoring of e-mail (by employers such as Nissan and Epson and, it seems, the mayor of Colorado Springs), and the phenomenon of database marketing, which involves the sale of mailing lists and other personal information to junk mailers (in 1990, Lotus and Equifax were forced to drop their Lotus Marketplace: Households, which put on disk personal information about 120 million Americans). Governments around the world are now being pushed into tightening privacy laws.[11]

The arrival of expert systems and primitive forms of artificial intelligence (AI) have generated a number of technical, legal, and ethical problems that have yet to be resolved. Technical problems have seriously slowed progress toward the holy grail of AI, while many are now asking whether computers could ever be trusted to make medical, legal, judicial, political, and administrative judgements. Given what we know about bugs in software, some are saying that it will never be safe to let computers run, for instance, air traffic control systems and nuclear power stations without human expert backup. Legal difficulties associated with product liability laws have meant that nobody dares use many of the expert systems that have been developed. In addition, AI critics are asking serious ethical questions, such as, Is AI a proper goal for humanity? Do we really need to replace humans in so many tasks when there is so much unemployment?[12]

Because paid employment is still central to the lives of most people and, according to the U.S. Bureau of Labor Statistics, about 46 million Americans now work with computers, workplace computerization is clearly an important issue. Indeed, it has proved to be fertile ground for controversies, debates, and choices about the quantity of work available and the quality of working life. While the 1980s did not see massive technological unemployment precisely because of the slow and messy nature of IT implementation, there is now renewed concern that computers are steadily eroding job opportunities in manufacturing and services. Moreover, concern about the impact of computers on the quality of working life has increased with the realization that managers can go in very different directions with the design and implementation of new work systems. Computers have the ability to enhance or degrade the quality of working life, depending upon the route chosen. Computer monitoring of employees has become a controversial issue, as have the alleged health hazards of computer keyboard usage, which has resulted recently in some celebrated RSI (repetitive strain injury) legal suits against employers and computer vendors.[13]

Ethical Dilemmas for Computer Users

Each of the new social problems just outlined generates all sorts of ethical dilemmas for computers users. Some of these dilemmas—such as whether or not to copy software—are entirely new, while others are new versions of old moral issues such as right and wrong, honesty, loyalty, responsibility, confidentiality, trust, accountability, and fairness. Some of these ethical dilemmas are faced by all computer users; others are faced only by computer professionals. But many of these dilemmas constitute new gray areas for which there are few accepted rules or social conventions, let alone established legal case law.

Another way of saying that computers create new versions of old moral issues is to say that information technology transforms the context in which old ethical issues arise and adds interesting new twists to old problems.[14] These issues arise from the fact that computers are machines that control other machines and from the specific, revolutionary characteristics of IT. Thus new storage devices allow us to store massive amounts of information, but they also generate new ethical choices about access to that information and about the use or misuse of that information. Ethical issues concerning privacy, confidentiality, and security thus come to the fore. The arrival of new media such as e-mail, bulletin boards, faxes, mobile phones, and EDI has generated new ethical and legal issues concerning user identity, authenticity, the legal status of such communications, and whether or not free speech protection and/or defamation law applies to them.

IT provides powerful new capabilities such as monitoring, surveillance, data linking, and database searching. These capabilities can be utilized wisely and ethically, or they can be used to create mischief, to spy on people, and to profit from new scams. IT transforms relationships between people, depersonalizing human contact and replacing it with instant, paperless communication. This phenomenon can sometimes lead people into temptation by creating a false sense of reality and by disguising the true nature of their actions, such as breaking into a computer system. IT transforms relationships between individuals and organizations, raising new versions of issues such as accountability and responsibility. Finally, IT unreliability creates new uncertainties and a whole series of ethical choices for those who operate complex systems and those who design and build them. Computer producers and vendors too often neglect to adequately consider the eventual users of their systems, yet they should not escape responsibility for the consequences of their system design.[15]

Under the heading of computer crime and security, a number of ethical issues have been raised—despite the fact that the choice of whether or not to commit a crime should not present a moral dilemma for most people. For example, some have sought to make a distinction between crimes against other persons and so-called victimless crimes against, for example, banks, phone companies, and computer companies. While not wishing to excuse victimless crimes, some have suggested that they somehow be placed in a less serious category, especially when it comes to sentencing. Yet it is hard to accept that a company is any less a victim than an individual when it is deprived of its wealth. Because so many computer criminals appear to be first-time offenders who have fallen victim to temptation, do employers bear any responsibility for misdeeds that have occurred on their premises? And how far should employers or security agencies be allowed to go in their attempts to prevent or detect crime? (Should they be allowed to monitor e-mail or spy on people in toilets, for example?)

The ease with which computer software can be copied presents ethical dilemmas to computer users and professionals almost every day of the year. Some justify the widespread copying of software because everybody else does it or because the cost of well-known software packages is seen as too high. But copying software is a form of stealing and a blatant infringement of the developer's intellectual property rights. In the past, intellectual property such as literary works and mechanical inventions was protected by copyright and patents, but software is a new and unique hybrid. How do we protect the rights of software developers so as to ensure that innovation in the industry continues? What does the responsible computer professional do? Is all copying of software wrong, or are some kinds worse than others? How should the individual user behave when the law is unclear and when people in the industry disagree as to what constitutes ethical practice?

The new phenomena of computer hacking and the creation of computer viruses has raised many unresolved ethical questions. Is hacking merely harmless fun or is it the computer equivalent of burglary, fraud, and theft? When do high-tech high jinks become seriously criminal behavior? Because hacking almost always involves unauthorized access to other people's systems, should all hacking activity be considered unethical? What are we to make of hackers themselves? Are they well-intentioned guardians of our civil liberties and useful amateur security advisers, or are they mixed-up adolescents whose stock in trade is malicious damage and theft? Can the creation of viruses ever be justified in any circumstances? If not, what punishment should be meted out to virus creators? Finally, what should responsible individuals do if they hear of people who are hacking?

The reality of computer unreliability creates many ethical dilemmas, mainly for the computer professionals who are charged with creating and installing systems. Who is responsible when things go wrong? When a system malfunctions or completely crashes because of an error in a computer program, who is to blame—the original programmers, the system designer, the software supplier, or someone else? More to the point, should system suppliers warn users that computer systems are prone to failure, are often too complex to be fully understood, have not been thoroughly tested before sale, and are likely to contain buggy software? Should software producers be made to provide a warranty on software? And to whom should individual computer professionals ultimately be responsible—the companies they work for, their colleagues, the customers, or the wider society?

The recurring issue of privacy confronts computer professionals and users in all sorts of contexts. First, there are general questions, such as what is privacy and how much of it are individuals entitled to, even in today's society. Does individual information stored on databases pose a threat to privacy? What right do governments and commercial organizations have to store personal information on individuals? What steps should be taken to ensure the accuracy of such information? Then there are the dilemmas faced by computer professionals and users over whether or not to use information collected for another purpose, whether to purchase personal information illicitly obtained, whether to link information in disparate databases, and so on. Practically every attempt to improve security (and sometimes even productivity) in organizations involves choices about the degree of privacy to which employees are entitled, while new controversies have arisen over the privacy aspects of e-mail and CNID.

In a sense, the quest for artificial intelligence is one big ethical problem for the computing world because we have yet to determine whether AI is a proper goal—let alone a realistic goal—for humanity. Should computer professionals work on systems and devices that they know will make yet more humans redundant? Should we really be aiming to replace humans in more tasks? Isn't it somehow demeaning to human intelligence to put so much emphasis on making a machine version of it? Perhaps even more to the point, given what we know about computer unreliability, can we afford to trust our lives to artificially intelligent expert systems? What should be the attitude of responsible computer professionals: should they warn users of the risks involved or refuse to work on life-critical applications? Should they refuse to work on the many AI projects funded by the military? Moreover, should institutional users trust computers to make judicial, administrative, and medical judgments when human judgment has often proved to be superior?

Some might think that the workplace does not provide an obviously rich source of ethical dilemmas for computer professionals and users. Yet workplace computerization involves numerous choices for management about the type of system to be implemented, and different systems have radically different impacts on both the quantity and the quality of work. Generally speaking, computers in factories can be used to enhance the quality of working life, to improve job satisfaction, to provide more responsibility, and to upgrade or reskill the workforce; or, they can be used to get rid of as many people as possible and to turn those remaining into deskilled, degraded machine-minders, pressing buttons in a soulless, depersonalized environment. Office computerization can increase stress levels and thus health hazards if the new work process is badly designed or even if the new office furniture and equipment are badly designed. Employee monitoring often makes matters worse, while speed-ups and the creation of excessively repetitive tasks like keying-in data for hours can result in cases of repetitive strain injury. Computer professionals and managers have a responsibility to ensure that these outcomes are avoided.

How Ethical Theory Can Help

"Ethics" has been defined as the code or set of principles by which people live. Ethics is about what is considered to be right and what is considered to be wrong. When people make ethical judgments, they are making prescriptive or normative statements about what ought to be done, not descriptive statements about what is being done.

But when people face ethical dilemmas in their everyday lives, they tend to make very different judgments about what is the right and what is the wrong thing to do. Ensuing discussions between the parties often remain unresolved because individuals find it hard to explain the reasoning behind their subjective, moral judgments. It is virtually impossible to conclude what ought to be the most appropriate behavior. Ethical theory—sometimes referred to as moral philosophy—is the study of the rules or principles that lie behind moral decisions. This theory helps provide us with a rational basis for moral judgments, enables us to classify and compare different ethical positions, and enables people to defend a particular position on a given issue. Thus the use of ethical theory can help us throw some light on the moral dilemmas faced by computer professionals and users and may even go some way toward determining how people ought to behave when using computers.[16]

Classical ethical theories are worth knowing because they provide useful background in some of the terminology, but they have limited relevance to everyday behavior in the IT industry. For example, Plato (429–347 B.C.) talked about the "good life," and much of his life was spent searching for the one good life. He also believed that an action was right or wrong in itself—a so-called objectivist (later, deontological) position. Aristotle (384–322 B.C.), on the other hand, adopted a more relativist and empiricist approach, arguing that there were many good and bad lives and that good lives were happy lives created by practicing "moderation in all things." Epicurus (341–270 B.C.) was the exact opposite, promoting hedonism, or the pursuit of pleasure, as the sole goal of life (although modern hedonists tend to forget that he also warned that too much pleasure was harmful and that the highest form of pleasure was practicing virtue and improving one's mind).

Diogenes (413–323 B.C.) was leader of the cynics, who believed that the world was fundamentally evil. The cynics were antisocial; they shunned public life and led an ascetic, privatized life—rising early, eating frugally, working hard, sleeping rough, and so on. Individual cynics found salvation in themselves and their honest lifestyle, not in worldly possessions. Modern cynics don't necessarily do this, but they are very distrustful of what they see as a thoroughly corrupt world. Finally, the stoics, such as Zeno (ca. 335–263 B.C.) and Epictetus (ca. 55–135 A.D.), were the essential fatalists, arguing that people should learn to accept whatever happened to them and that everything in the world occurs according to a plan that we do not understand. A true stoic believes that there is no such thing as good or evil and seeks to rise above the circumstances of everyday life, rejecting temptations, controlling emotions, and eschewing ambitions.

But probably the three most influential ethical theories of recent times—and the three of most likely relevance for our purposes—are ethical relativism (associated with Spinoza, 1632–1677), utilitarianism (J. S. Mill, 1806–1873) or consequentialism, and Kantianism (Kant, 1724–1804) or deontologism. Ethical relativism, which says that there are no universal moral norms, need not detain us for long, for it offers no guidance as to what is correct behavior. Ethical relativists merely point to the variety of behaviors in different cultures and conclude that the issue of right and wrong is all relative. Ethical relativism is a descriptive account of what is being done rather than a normative theory of what should be done. While it is true that people in different societies have different moralities, this does not prove that one morality might not be the correct one or that one might not constitute the universal moral code. Ethical relativism is not much use when trying to decide what is the right thing to do in today's world of computing.

Consequentialism and deontologism are much more relevant for our purposes. Consequentialism says simply that an action is right or wrong depending upon its consequences, such as its effects on society. Utilitarianism, as outlined by J. S. Mill and Jeremy Bentham, is one form of consequentialism. Its basic principle is that everyone should behave in such a way as to bring about the greatest happiness of the greatest number of people. Utilitarians arrive at this cardinal principle by arguing that happiness is the ultimate good because everything else in life is desired as a means of achieving happiness. Happiness is the ultimate goal of humans, and thus all actions must be evaluated on the basis of whether they increase or decrease human happiness. An action is therefore right or wrong depending upon whether it contributes to the sum total of human happiness.

By contrast, deontologism says that an action is right or wrong in itself. Deontologists stress the intrinsic character of an act and disregard motives or consequences. Thus a deontologist might say that the act of copying software is always wrong, regardless of other considerations, while a utilitarian might say that it was justified if it had a beneficial effect on society as a whole. Deontologists appear to be on particularly strong ground when they state, for example, that killing is wrong no matter what the circumstances, but they are on weaker ground when they say that lying is always wrong. Utilitarians would say that lying can be justified in certain circumstances, as in the case of white lies. On the other hand, utilitarians can find themselves in the position of defending actions that are morally wrong (like lying) or condoning actions that penalize the few in order to benefit the many (such as exploiting labor in a third world manufacturing plant). Consequentialists tend to look at the overall impact on society, whereas deontologists tend to focus on individuals and their rights. Kantians, in particular, argue strongly that people should always be treated as ends and never merely as means.

The distinction between consequentialists and deontologists is quite useful when we consider the ethical issues confronting computer professionals and users.

Ethics and the Computer Professional

Because computing is a relatively new field, the emerging computer profession has had neither the time nor the organizational capability to establish a binding set of moral rules or ethics. Older professions, like medicine and the law, have had centuries to formulate their codes of ethics and professional conduct. And there is another problem, too: the practice of computing, unlike the practice of medicine or the law, goes on outside the profession—this is an open field, with unfenced boundaries.

Computing, with its subdisciplines like software engineering, has not yet emerged as a full-fledged profession. Classic professions involve mental work, a high level of skill, and a lengthy period of training, and they perform some vital service to society—just like computing. But more than that, the classic profession is highly organized, with a central body that admits members only when they have achieved a certain level of skill. Although members have a considerable degree of autonomy, they are expected to exercise their professional judgment within the framework of a set of ethical principles laid down by the profession's central organization. Transgressors can be disciplined or even thrown out of the profession altogether. Some see the development of professions as a sign of a well-ordered, mature society, whereas critics have seen them as little more than self-serving protection rackets (the British author and playwright George Bernard Shaw once described all professions as "a conspiracy against the people").

So what sort of profession is computing? Members of the fledgling computer profession do not yet have the social status of doctors or lawyers. Instead, their status has been likened to that of engineers, who work mostly as employees rather than in their own right, who have esoteric knowledge but quite limited autonomy, and who often work in teams or on small segments of large projects rather than alone. Worryingly, they are often distant from the effects of their work. Yet despite the lower social status of computer professionals, the widespread use of information technology for storing all sorts of vital information puts considerable power into their hands, from the humble operator to the top systems developer. This power has not been sought specifically but arises from the nature of the technology. Computer professionals often find themselves in positions of power over employers, clients, coprofessionals, and the wider public, and this power can be abused easily by those without scruples or those who easily fall victim to temptation.[17]

Computer professionals face all sorts of ethical dilemmas in their everyday work life. First, although they have obligations to their employers, to the customers, to their coprofessionals, and to the general public, these obligations often come into conflict and need to be resolved one way or another. For example, what should be the response of a systems analyst whose employer insists on selling an overengineered, expensive system to gullible customers? Go along with the scam, or tell the customers that they are being duped? Second, almost every day the computer professional is confronted with issues of responsibility, intellectual property, and privacy. Who should take the blame when a system malfunctions or crashes? What attitude should professionals take when someone's intellectual property rights are clearly being infringed? How should they balance the need for greater system security with the right of individuals to privacy?

In an effort to help computer professionals cope with these kinds of conflicts, professional organizations such as the ACM (Association for Computing Machinery), the IEEE (Institute of Electrical and Electronics Engineers), the British Computer Society (BCS), and IFIP (International Federation for Information Processing) have been formulating and revising codes of ethics and professional conduct applicable to the IT industry. One problem with these codes is that they often have consisted mainly of motherhood statements like "I will avoid harm to others" and "I will always be honest and trustworthy." These proclamations could just as easily apply to any profession or walk of life and say nothing of specific relevance to computing. However, the new ACM code (see appendix A) is much improved in this respect in that it talks about specific IT industry responsibilities. A more serious criticism is that these codes contain little in the way of sanctions by which their laudable aims could be enforced. A number of critics have pointed out that these codes have never been used and their language never interpreted. Furthermore, the codes usually have talked purely in terms of individuals being at fault and not whole organizations (although this, too, is addressed to some extent in the new IFIP and ACM codes).[18]

An even more fundamental difficulty with all such codes of ethics is that they don't necessarily do much to make people behave more ethically. The pressure, financial or otherwise, to conform with unethical industry practices is often too great. Thus, in a classic critique of professional ethics, John Ladd argued that attempts to develop professional codes of ethics are not only marked by intellectual and moral confusion (such as describing a code of conduct as ethics), they are also likely to fail. Codes of conduct, he says, are widely disregarded by members of professions. Worthy and inspirational though such codes may be, he says that their existence leads to complacency and to self-congratulation—and maybe even to the cover-up of unethical conduct. "Look, we have a code of ethics," professionals might say, "so everything we do must be ethical." The real objectives of such codes, Ladd says, are to enhance the image of the profession in the outside world and to protect the monopoly of the profession. In other words, they are a bit of window dressing designed to improve the status and the income of members.[19]

Another debate has arisen over suggestions that computer professionals be licensed or certified. Under this proposal, a programmer would have to obtain a certificate of competence before being allowed to work on major projects—especially those involving life-critical systems—and perhaps every computer user would have to obtain a kind of driver's license before being allowed onto the computer networks. Certification of software developers might help reduce software bugs, reduce the risks to the public from malfunctions, and reduce the number of software project runaways. But there would be endless difficulties involved in measuring programming competence, and these problems could perhaps lead to religious wars in the profession![20] Moreover, there is a danger that certification could create a closed shop or craft guild that might exclude talented and innovative newcomers. On the other hand, it seems likely that some sort of certification safeguards will have to be introduced in the future to cover high-risk systems.

The Responsibility of Computing Educators

Recent well-publicized incidents of hacking, virus creation, computer-based fraud, and invasions of privacy have increased the pressure on computing educators to help instil a greater sense of responsibility in today's students. The world of computing has been portrayed in the media as a kind of electronic frontier society where a "shoot from the hip" mentality prevails. It is widely believed that there is far too much computerized anarchy and mayhem.

We believe that computing educators need to do three things. They must encourage tomorrow's computer professionals to behave in a more ethical, responsible manner for the long-term good of the IT industry. They also need to help make students aware of the social problems caused by computers and the social context in which computerization occurs. And they need to sensitize students to the kinds of moral dilemmas they will face in their everyday lives as computer professionals. Many of today's computer science undergraduates will go on to create systems that will have major impacts on people, organizations, and society in general. If those systems are to be successful economically and socially, graduates will need to know the lessons from the computerization story so far, the ethical and social issues involved, and the range of choices available to computer professionals.

The importance of the social, ethical, and professional context of computing was at last officially recognized in the long-awaited 1991 report of the ACM/IEEE-CS Curriculum Task Force, which nominated "Social, Ethical and Professional Context" (or SP) as one of nine key areas of the recommended computer science (CS) curriculum. A comprehensive summary of this important report appears in this book as appendix B. For years, critics complained that most CS curricula paid little or no attention to the social impacts of computing, but now all proposed CS courses going before the joint ACM/IEEE Computer Science Accreditation Board (CSAB) in the United States will have to include an SP (or, more accurately, an SEP) component.

In the report, the task force argues that undergraduate programs should "prepare students to understand the field of computing both as an academic discipline and as a profession within the context of a larger society." Thus graduates should be aware of the history of computing and the economic, scientific, legal, political, and cultural trends that have shaped the discipline over its relatively short life. A key goal, it says, should also be to "expose students to the ethical and societal issues that are associated with the computing field." This goal includes not only maintaining currency with recent technological and theoretical developments but also upholding professional standards and "developing an awareness of one's own strengths and limitations, as well as those of the discipline itself." Students, it says, need to develop "the ability to ask serious questions about the social impact on computing," such as, "Will that product enhance or degrade the quality of life?" and "What will the impact be upon individuals, groups, and institutions?"[21]

However, the task force recommendation that SEP be included as a common requirement of all CS courses (rather than an elective) does not resolve the issue of how it should be taught, and this is a matter for continuing debate. For example, although the task force proposed the inclusion of a stand-alone SEP course, some still argue that SEP issues should be incorporated into all CS courses. Their opponents reply that this approach probably would result in soft SEP material being squeezed in at the end of each semester and dealt with only cursorily because of the pressure to put across so much hard technical material. In addition, many CS teachers have a technical background and are ill-equipped to explain SEP issues or tackle them with the required zeal. A further debate revolves around whether students first should be taught straight ethical theory or whether they first should be sensitized to ethical issues through case studies or cautionary tales. We favor the latter approach.

Some also have argued for a narrower definition of computer ethics, in contrast to the task force report, which recommends that broader social issues be included. For instance, Donald Gotterbarn argues that computer ethics should really be about issues specific to the IT industry and, in particular, about its hallmark activity, the software development process. He rightly points out, for example, that the mere use of a computer in a crime does not necessarily make that particular crime a case for computer ethics, but we argue that there are nevertheless many ethical dilemmas associated with the phenomena of computer-based crime (such as how far we should compromise privacy in order to improve security). Likewise, issues such as the quality of work life and the possible health hazards of video display terminals (VDTs) cannot be relegated as concerns for sociology—as Gotterbarn proposes—because computer professionals are confronted with such issues every time they design a new system.[22] Nor do we find it useful to adopt a two-tier view of computer ethics, with pure computer ethics issues in one basket and issues arising from computer applications in another, because the two are inextricably interlinked.

Finally, Peter G. Neumann has pointed out that we cannot expect the incorporation of computer ethics or SEP into the undergraduate curriculum to be a panacea for all the ills of the IT industry. Of course, the teaching of computer ethics cannot guarantee that students will behave more ethically in the future, just as the adoption of professional codes of ethics and the passing of new laws cannot in themselves transform human behavior.[23] But the point is that we should make the effort. Reducing the incidence of malfunctions and misuse in the IT industry is a massive task. It is a task that requires the deployment of better computer systems, better laws, and better ethics. This book is a modest contribution to that task.

2

Computer Crime

On Christmas Eve, 1987, a twenty-six-year-old clerk at Lloyds Bank in Amsterdam, Frans Noe, ordered that sums of $8.4 million and $6.7 million be transferred via the SWIFT international funds transfer system from the Lloyds branch in New York to an account he had opened with the Swiss Bank Corporation in Zurich. The young Dutchman then flew to Switzerland to collect the money. But because of an unforeseen computer malfunction, the transfer of the $6.7 million failed to go through. Returning after Christmas, fellow employees saw the failed transaction on their screens and reported it. Noe subsequently was arrested and returned to Amsterdam, where he then threatened to leak news of his security breach to the press unless the bank dropped all charges against him. In May 1988, the flying Dutchman was jailed for eighteen months for breaking into a computer system, and his two accomplices got twelve months.[1]

The Rise of the High-Tech Heist

Computers have created opportunities for crime that never existed before. History shows that the growth of crime is strongly related to opportunity and that changes in technology generate both new types of crime and new techniques of detection.[2] Consequently, both criminals and crime-busters compete to stay one jump ahead of each other. The arrival of information technology—and more recently the rapid spread of personal computers and distributed processing—has not only given a new twist to old crimes such as theft, blackmail, forgery, and sabotage, it has also made possible entirely new kinds of crime such as ATM fraud, EFT fraud, EDI fraud, and so on. The huge increase in the number of people with computer skills also means that there are many more potential computer criminals. In a sense, computers are democratizing white-collar crime, because the technology enables even the humblest programmer, operator, or clerk (like Frans Noe) to participate in big-time frauds that were once pretty much the preserve of top management.

SRI International of California has documented more than three thousand computer crimes that have occurred around the world in the past twenty years. They include cases of fraud, theft, espionage, conspiracy, and extortion as well as the theft of hardware and software. A recent British survey found that logical breeches of computer security caused by the activities of fraudsters and hackers (as opposed to physical breaches like fires and floods) were costing U.K. companies £530 million (about $800 million) a year. The head of Interpol's European computer crime group has warned that criminals increasingly are using computers for drug dealing and art and antiques thefts. In his book *Technocrimes: The Computerization of Crime and Terrorism,* August Bequai not only describes how organized crime and the Mafia are using computers for record keeping—not to mention extortion, blackmail, and sabotage—he also suggests that the future of Western society is now threatened by computerized crime and high-tech terrorism.[3]

All over the world, governments have hurried to bring their laws up to date so as to cover crimes associated with computer technology. In Australia, for example, the Crimes Legislation (Amendment) Act of 1989 extended Australian law to cover unauthorized access to data, tampering with data, and the dishonest compilation of data, among other things. In Britain, the Computer Misuse Act of 1990 also made an offence of unauthorized access to computers (whether in furtherance of a crime or not), unauthorized modification of computer material, and malicious damage to computer files. The so-called mad hacker, Nicholas Whiteley, was jailed under the act soon after it was passed, and in another case in 1992 Elaine Borg, computer operator, was charged under the act with attempting to defraud a City of London finance company of no less than half a million pounds (about $750 million).[4]

The arrival of automated teller machines provides a good example of how a new technological device creates new opportunities for fraudulent activity. The number of ATMs in the United States grew from 4,000 to over 50,000 over the decade from 1975 to 1985. The value of transactions is believed to have grown about tenfold, and with it ATM fraud has correspondingly mushroomed into a major growth industry. For instance, in 1989 the U.S. Secret Service seized no less than 7,700 counterfeit ATM cards from one gang of forgers that had already illegally taken between $7 and $14 million in cash from ATMs all over California. In the "phantom withdrawals" scandal in the United Kingdom, British banks and building societies were finally sued in 1992 by hundreds of customers who claimed that they had been wrongly debited throughout the 1980s for withdrawals they did not make. The banks, which lost £166 million (about $250 million) from ATM fraud in 1991 alone, continued to claim that the customers must have withdrawn the money and that phantom withdrawals from their machines were "impossible" (this is always an unwise word to use in computing).[5]

The booming business of long-distance phone fraud is another example. By 1991 call-sell operations running in places such as New York's Grand Central Station and small shops in immigrant neighborhoods of Los Angeles were estimated to be costing major phone users anything between $1 billion and $5 billion a year. Among the victims whose long-distance access codes were stolen and resold were the United Nations bureaucracy, the New York City Council, NASA, IBM, Procter & Gamble, and even the Christian Broadcasting Corporation and the CIA. Most of the stolen calls were made to migrant areas like the Caribbean, Eastern Europe, and the Indian subcontinent and to drug-producing areas in Latin America. Hacking into corporate PBXs via toll-free 800 numbers in order to obtain long-distance calls has become a popular technique of the phone fraudster. Major phone companies, such as AT&T with its NetProtect software, have begun a campaign to crack down on phone fraud, but new scams are appearing all the time.[6]

Other new crimes made possible by IT include credit card fraud, EFT fraud, EDI fraud, mobile phone fraud, cable TV fraud, telemarketing fraud, and desktop forgery. Credit card fraud has grown in parallel with the rapid spread of plastic money. On a number of occasions, fraudsters in the United States have hacked into the systems of credit-checking firms such as TRW and Equifax and have stolen credit card numbers that have then been used to illegally purchase merchandise. And in the United Kingdom, where plastic card fraud has grown rapidly, stolen bank cards have, for example been used to purchase phone calls on the Mercury network, even when the bank account has been closed. EFT fraud has grown with the spread of EFT payment systems, and academics and computer security experts have warned that EDI will provide computer criminals with many fresh opportunities for misdeeds.[7]

Still more opportunities for high-tech high jinks have been provided by cellular mobile telephones: in March 1987, eighteen New Yorkers were arrested on charges of illegally reprogramming memory chips in their mobile phones in order to make calls without being charged for them. The fraud had cost the local mobile phone company about $40,000 per month. It was the first time anyone in the world had been arrested for this type of offence. Commenting on the case, Laurence A. Urgenson, the chief assistant U.S. attorney for the Eastern District of New York, said, "Every new technology carries with it an opportunity to invent a new crime." In 1991 the U.S. Secret Service announced that it had cracked a $100-million-a-year mobile phone racket in New York by distributing a software patch to phone companies and users that blocked no less than 5,000 illegal cellular calls on its first day in use. Agents apparently had purchased an illegal phone, broken into the counterfeit chip, read the microcode, decoded the algorithm at its core, and then written a program that alerted the carrier to unauthorized phone usage.[8]

Ingenious fraudsters also have been busy providing bogus chips to cable TV viewers who prefer not to pay for the service. A thriving black market in pirate descrambler boxes in the United States is believed to be worth $3 billion a year to the manufacturers and to cost cable companies $100 million a year in lost revenue. In 1991 federal agents seized between 20,000 and 40,000 counterfeit boxes in San Francisco and about the same number in Las Vegas. The San Francisco factory was turning out 300 boxes a day. Meanwhile, in New York, American Cablevision formulated a clever sting operation to catch cable TV pirates. First, it sent an "electronic bullet," or zapping software, down the cable to disable the bogus chips, leaving legitimate chips unaffected. When 317 viewers called in to complain that their screens had gone blank, the company helpfully suggested that they bring their boxes in for repair, whereupon the illegal boxes were seized and their owners charged with cable piracy. Some 230 of the 317 pirates rapidly made out of court settlements with American Cablevision.[9]

The arrival of telemarketing has created yet another new crime: telemarketing fraud. What happens is that a telephone salesperson calls a customer and makes an attractive sales pitch. The salesperson then asks for the customer's bank account number and name exactly as it appears on a check. The salesperson then creates a phony magnetically encoded debit draft that contains computer codes telling the bank's computer to automatically transfer money from the customer's account to the crook's account in another bank. The crook then cleans out the customer's account and closes his or her own account. The duped customers only learn of the scam when they receive their monthly bank statements. "It's probably the boldest, most egregious scam that I've ever heard of," Charles Burson, the attorney-general of Tennessee, is quoted as saying. "It is truly cutting-edge criminality."[10]

Telemarketing fraud combines an age-old sales con with desktop forgery—that is, creating bogus documents with the help of new desktop technology such as color copiers, laser printers, and optical scanners. Such documents have already included ID cards, passports, driver's licenses, birth certificates, immigration cards, purchase orders, railroad tickets, letters of reference, drug prescriptions, checks, and even currency. A raid on a house in Vicksburg, Mississippi, in 1990 uncovered a treasure trove of a master desktop forger; another ring in New York was found to be mass producing bogus checks using personal computers. But probably the best example of desktop forgery was the case of Jean Paul Barrett, a convict serving thirty-three years for fraud and forgery in the Pima County jail, Tucson, Arizona. Barrett got out of jail early on 13 December 1991 when a forged fax arrived ordering his release. (He hasn't been seen since.) The U.S. Treasury Department has warned that the problem of desktop forgery will worsen and that anticounterfeiting laws will have to be revised.[11]

The list of amazing new scams made possible by IT is apparently endless. For example, three Woodland Hills, California, men were jailed in 1991 for tampering with an American Airlines computer so as to defraud the company of frequent flyer tickets worth $1.3 million. The crooks had hacked into American Airlines' frequent flyer records and had changed accounts and created fictitious accounts. They then applied for free flights and sold them for a profit or gave them away to family and friends. Earlier, in 1988, a Tulsa, Oklahoma, woman and her father were charged with falsely crediting themselves with fifty million miles on the same American Airlines computer.[12]

Computers have made it easier for criminals to doctor data. For example, in 1991 Emily Fields, a San Francisco police officer, gained access to the police computer and simply cleared a warrant issued against her for nonpayment of $700 worth of traffic citations. Another enterprising Californian couple, Genevieve Pamela Lopez and Donald H. Stables, ran a business cleaning up driving records held at the California Department of Motor Vehicles, where Lopez worked. For a fee of up to $2,500, they would obliterate accident reports, drunk-driving arrests, suspensions, and other driving violations.[13]

Recent reports from the U.S. National Research Council, the OECD (Organization for Economic Cooperation and Development), the U.K. Audit Commission, and many other bodies have repeatedly warned that computer security is far too lax in most companies and government departments. As we move from the mainframe era into the era of networked PCs, they say that security problems will only get worse. Computer security undoubtedly is being improved quite rapidly, but it seems that every time one security loophole is plugged, the computer criminals discover another one. In this endless game of cat and mouse, criminals and security specialists compete to stay one jump ahead of each other. For instance, successive new security devices have been added to credit cards, but every time forgers have found a way of getting around them. Holograms were once thought to be tamper-proof—until forged holograms started appearing around 1990. Now financial institutions are looking to introduce smart cards containing microchips as a way around the problem; but, as we have seen, microchips can be forged, too.

Is Reported Crime the Tip of an Iceberg?

Academics and computer security specialists continue to debate two questions: What exactly is computer crime? and Is the amount of computer crime underreported or overreported? By listing many new scams made possible by IT in the previous section, we have somewhat prejudged the first question. But it is important to know about the definitional debate.

Computer crime generally has been defined as a criminal act that has been committed using a computer as the principal tool. Some have talked in terms of a distinction between computer-related fraud (in which the computer is purely coincidental) and computer-assisted fraud (in which the computer is used to commit the fraud). Some have also distinguished input fraud from output fraud. Others have argued that a true computer fraud is one that could not take place without the use of a computer or that the only true computer fraud is program fraud—that is, one that involves tampering with a program. But most analysts now reject such tight definitions of computer crime and instead count all crimes where a computer has either been the object, subject, or instrument of a crime. For instance, Hugo Cornwall, author of *Datatheft* and *The Hacker's Handbook,* recently wrote, "Most computer crime is ordinary crime which at one stage happens to involve a computer." Very few computer crimes, he says, require a high degree of technical expertise.[14]

Computer crime can take the form of the theft of money (for example, the transfer of payments to the wrong accounts), the theft of information (for example, from files or databases), or the theft of goods (by their diversion to the wrong destination). Two techniques of computer theft are the salami, a program fraud that involves spreading the haul over a large number of transactions like slices of salami (for example, a bank clerk might shave a trivial sum off many customer accounts to make up a large sum in his or her own account) and the Trojan horse, which involves the insertion of false information into a program in order to profit from the outcome (for example, a false instruction to make payments to a bogus company). Theft is undoubtedly the most common form of computer crime: of 191 cases reported to the Australian Computer Abuse Research Bureau (ACARB), for example, 111 involved theft of some kind.[15]

Computer crime can also take the form of unauthorized access or unauthorized use of systems. Such computer break-ins are usually called *hacks* and the perpetrators *hackers* or *crackers* (see chapter 4). Techniques of the hacker include *piggybacking,* which involves riding into a system behind a legitimate user with a password, and *scavenging* for stray data or garbage for clues that might unlock the secrets of a system. Malicious hackers bent on blackmail or sabotage have been known to indulge in *zapping,* which means penetrating a computer by unlocking the master key to its program and then destroying it by activating its own emergency program; unleashing *worms,* or worm programs that delete portions of a computer's memory; and creating *time bombs* and *logic bombs,* which involve the insertion of routines that can be triggered later by the computer's clock or a combination of events. When the bomb goes off, the entire system—perhaps worth millions—will crash; *viruses* are self-replicating programs that can have a similar effect.

Some have argued that the notion of computer crime should be widened to include cases where organizations systematically abuse customers instead of focusing only on cases where individuals steal from—or attempt to steal from—organizations. Two cases that come to mind are the giant company Continental Can, which used a secret computer program to reduce the pension benefits of long-serving employees, and Litton Systems, which rigged its computer billing service in order to overcharge the U.S. government more than $25 million on hundreds of defense contracts.[16] Professor Rob Kling of the University of California, Irvine, suggests that many organizations such as computer vendors systematically abuse consumers as part of day-to-day business practice. Misleading sales pitches, supplying inappropriate hardware and software, overcharging, and questionable service agreements are all too often business as usual in the IT industry. Some newer businesses like the IT business, he says, may be "criminogenic" environments where an ethos of anything goes prevails and where people are almost encouraged to participate in criminal behavior.[17]

Computer crime should not present an ethical dilemma for computer professionals or computer users. Theft is theft and fraud is fraud, and both are generally accepted by our society to be morally wrong. The issues raised by computer crime are empirical and practical rather than moral. Criminal activity is not a new problem, but what is new is that the widespread use of computers has placed great temptation in the hands of ordinary programmers and systems developers—who are often the only persons who know how a particular system works. For a minority of computer professionals, the temptations and opportunities are hard to resist—especially if they see a systematic way to cover up their crimes that makes detection of their crimes difficult or impossible.

Computers also have had the effect of further depersonalizing crime: in explaining their illegal activities, some guilty computer professionals have talked about so-called victimless crimes (for example, against large corporations or banks) as being somehow more acceptable than crimes with human victims. But this is hardly a justification.

Is reported computer crime the tip of an iceberg? Or is there no iceberg of undetected computer crime lurking below the surface of society? The true extent of computer crime is not known, cannot be known, and never will be known. The American Bar Association (ABA), in a major report published in 1984, concluded that losses arising from computer crime sustained by U.S. business and government institutions were "by any measure, huge." Their survey of three hundred top U.S. corporations suggested that annual losses in each company could range from $2 million to as high as $10 million. "If the annual losses attributed to computer crime sustained by this relatively small survey group are conservatively estimated in the range of half a billion dollars, then it takes little imagination to realize the magnitude of the annual losses sustained on a nationwide basis," said the report.[18] More recently, the Cleveland accounting firm Ernst & Whinney estimated that the total losses sustained by U.S. companies amount to between $3 billion and $5 billion a year. Of 240 companies surveyed in 1987, more than half admitted that they had been a victim of computer fraud, while in a further survey in 1989 some 23 percent of respondents said that their organizations had experienced financial losses as a result of computer break-ins in the past two years. A survey of 1,211 organizations by academics Jeffrey A. Hoffer and Detmar W. Straub similarly found that about one in five had suffered losses over a three-year period. But they say that this figure is "undoubtedly an underestimate."[19]

In the United Kingdom, an Audit Commission survey of 1,200 organizations in 1988 found that reported crimes had risen in value from around £1 million in 1981 to around £3 million in 1987. Nine out of ten respondents believed that they had not suffered from computer fraud. Yet a large number of the 118 frauds detected were discovered only by accident. Only 38 of the 118 cases resulted in prosecutions. Another Audit Commission survey of 1,550 organizations in 1991 discovered 180 cases of computer crime that were described as "the tip of an iceberg."

Meanwhile, a 1986 survey of fifty British companies by insurance brokers Hogg Robinson led them to estimate that frauds involving computers were costing U.K. firms £40 million a year. An association of French insurance companies estimated that problems with computer systems were costing French firms about $1.1 billion a year, and 44 percent of this was accounted for by fraudsters, hackers, and disgruntled employees (the remainder was caused by accidents, such as fire, malfunctions, and human error).[20]

More recently, the City of London police surveyed fifty eight leading British financial institutions. Some 59 percent of respondents stated that their firms had been victims of some kind of fraud, with most mentioning computer fraud as showing the biggest increase. Some 23 percent of the 250 delegates at the Computer Security International conference in London also claimed that their organizations had been victims of computer abuse. The largest, most authoritative U.K. survey of computer security, jointly produced by the British governments's Department of Trade and Industry, the National Computing Centre, and the computer company ICL, covering 8,000 companies and published in 1992, concluded that logical breaches of computer security by criminals, hackers, and software errors were costing U.K. firms a staggering £530 million a year. This figure included only the immediate cost of breaches and not the knock-on costs, such as loss of business.[21]

Do these estimates merely represent the tip of an iceberg, as the authors usually claim? Or is the iceberg analogy misleading? Has the real amount of computer crime been exaggerated by a media hungry for sensational stories and by security consultants only too happy to pass on unverified stories and urban folk tales in order to boost business?

There are two main reasons why most experts believe that the actual amount of computer crime is much greater than reported. First, it is likely that many crimes go completely undetected because so many are discovered by accident and because so many are, by their nature, very hard to detect. A 1986 official guide produced for U.S. federal agencies stated that detected computer crimes are less than 1 percent of the total. Two major surveys by management academics found that 41 percent and 32 percent, respectively, of crimes reported were discovered only by accident. Logic seems to dictate that many more computer crimes have occurred but remain undiscovered.[22]

Second, very few computer frauds are made public because companies—especially banks and other financial institutions—are loathe to admit that their security systems are fallible. Publicity of this nature is disastrous public relations, and it could lead to the loss of customer confidence, so companies prefer to cover things up. Hugo Cornwall, in his book *Datatheft,* lists some reasons why nonreporting of computer crime is so widespread: "There is very little benefit to the victim. The law is unlikely to be able to undo the damage caused, the criminal is unlikely to be convicted, much staff time is likely to be tied up assembling evidence (if it can be collected at all), and wider knowledge of the crime is likely to harm the future prospects of the victim organization."[23]

Of those crimes that are detected, only a small percentage arrive in court: for example, a 1986 survey by the Los Angeles–based National Center for Computer Crime Data found that fewer than 100 cases of computer fraud in the United States had been prosecuted in the preceding two years. IBM security analyst Robert Courtney told the U.S. Office of Technology Assessment (OTA) in 1985 that of the 1,406 computer crime cases known to him, 89 percent were never taken to judicial process and convictions were obtained in only 18 percent of the remainder. Detmar W. Straub and William D. Nance found that of 268 discovered computer crime incidents, only 24 (9 percent) were reported to external authorities. Only 10 (4 percent) were prosecuted, and just 7 of the 268 incidents (3 percent) resulted in convictions.[24]

What is therefore clear is that nobody is very clear about the true extent of computer crime—but most analysts who have looked at the problem seem to think that it is large and growing. Even if the percentage of installations affected may be small, the sum involved in the average computer crime is probably much larger than in conventional robberies. According to the FBI, for instance, the average computer crime is worth about $600,000. As to the future, the American Bar Association report concluded, "It would seem beyond dispute that computer crime is today a large and significant problem with enormous potential for becoming even larger and more significant." Hugo Cornwall has written, "Datacrime deserves to be as much a social issue as more traditional areas of 'law and order' such as crimes against the person, crimes against property and the maintenance of public peace."[25]

Targets of the Computer Criminal

Banks and financial companies are major targets for computer criminals. Banks are vulnerable to frauds committed by inside employees and to frauds committed by outsiders playing "vault invaders." Of the computer crimes detected in a British survey by BIS Applied Systems, 37 percent were in the financial sector, while over 50 percent of the crimes by value reported to the Australian Computer Abuse Research Bureau were in banking and finance.[26]

The increased reliance of the financial sector on electronic funds transfer (EFT) systems—it is said that over $200 billion changes hands daily in the New York banks' automated payments system—has greatly increased the opportunities for crime. If the electronic authorization codes used in EFT fall into the wrong hands, huge sums of money can be moved anywhere—including out of the country—in a matter of seconds. For example, in a famous case in 1979, Stanley Mark Rifkin, a computer consultant to the Security Pacific National Bank, visited the bank's wire transfer room where he learned the EFT codes. Later, posing as a branch manager, he phoned the Los Angeles bank and used the codes to transfer money, in amounts of less than $1 million, to a New York bank. Then he instructed the New York bank to send the money—now totaling $10.2 million—to a Swiss bank account. Having flown to Switzerland, he converted the money into diamonds and then returned to the United States. It was only when he boasted openly of his feat that he was caught and convicted.

Probably the largest-ever computer crime involved a foreign exchange contract fraud. In 1987 it became apparent that the Volkswagen (VW) company in West Germany had lost around $260 million in a fraud that took place in 1984. Very little is known about the fraud, except that it entailed tampering with programs and the erasure of tapes. It is also known that VW sacked the head of its foreign exchange department and suspended four others, along with the heads of the financial transfer department and the cash and currency clearing sections.

Some of the biggest frauds ever attempted have involved EFT and banks. In 1988 a huge sum (variously reported to be between $33 and $54 million) was illegally transferred from the Union Bank of Switzerland branch in London to a private bank account in a small Swiss town of Nyon, near Lausanne. The stunt would have succeeded except for a computer glitch at the Swiss end that forced the bank that day to make manual checks of payment instructions that normally would have been processed automatically. Suspicions were aroused and the Swiss police were waiting to pounce on the man who arrived to collect the cash. Further arrests followed. A similar attempt in 1986 to transfer by EFT the sum of $8.5 million from the London branch of the U.S. investment bank Prudential-Bache Securities to another Swiss bank account was foiled after the bank hastily obtained a court injunction in Switzerland to stop the money from being paid. In September 1987 two men admitted conspiracy to defraud in a London court and were sentenced to three years and eighteen months.[27]

In May 1988 seven men were arrested in New York after an attempt to embezzle $70 million by creating phony transactions transferring money out of First National Bank of Chicago accounts of Merrill Lynch, United Airlines, and Brown-Forman. The amounts exceeded the threshold of permissible transactions, but the perpetrators had been able to control the telephone response that requested authorization. The transaction was detected when the Merrill Lynch account became overdrawn. In addition, in July 1989 in Sweden, five men were arrested after attempting to siphon off some $90 million from Swedish banks to Gibraltar via the SWIFT banking network.[28]

Speaking at a British Computer Society Security Committee seminar, Detective-Inspector John Austen of the Computer Crime Unit at New Scotland Yard, London, highlighted the threat to EFT systems from both criminals and terrorists: "EFT now represents 83 percent of the value of all things paid for—money transferred—in Britain. Money, as an invisible export, is a major part of our GNP. Foreign exchange markets in London transfer $200 billion daily using EFT via satellite. The transactions take a very short time, and once complete there is no calling them back. A lot of people are aware of this. And many, both here and abroad, are prepared to steal from EFT systems. The rewards are tremendous. Companies, and even the economies of smaller countries, could be crippled by a sustained hit on EFT systems. Terrorists, such as the Middle East factions, the IRA and the Red Army Faction are particularly aware of this—and they need money. The Red Army Faction has already, unsuccessfully, made moves to intercept EFT in Germany. They and others will try again."[29]

ATM fraud also has become increasingly common in recent years. In 1987, for example, a thirty-five-year-old former ATM repairman, Robert Post, was apprehended after illegally obtaining $86,000 out of New York City ATMs. He spied over customer's shoulders to get their PINs (Personal Identification Numbers), and whenever someone left a receipt, he took it to discover the account number. Then he went home, forged a card using a $1,800 machine he had bought, and returned to the ATM to make withdrawals. He was caught because his encoding of the account number and the PIN, while good enough to work in the machine, was flawed. Manufacturers Hanover managed to program its network to detect the flawed cards and seize them. After capturing two and verifying that they were fake, they reprogrammed the machine to notify security when one was being used and dispatched guards to catch Post. When questioned about his crime, Post said he was not like someone who mugs a customer and steals a card. "I'm a white-collar criminal," he proclaimed, adding that he was surprised that the bank had not offered him a consulting job.[30]

In the United Kingdom, City of London police in 1987 arrested four suspected ATM fraudsters after finding 1,864 cash cards in their possession. Their arrest followed a denial by the major banks that their ATMs posed a security risk after TV viewers had seen a cash card fraud demonstrated on national television. Later a major scandal erupted in the United Kingdom over $250 million worth of so-called phantom withdrawals—cash card withdrawals that the card owners claimed they had not made. In 1992 lawyers acting for the victims finally started filing suits against the banks.[31]

In the United States in 1988, someone successfully used a Security Pacific National Bank master card to steal $237,000, and a plot to bilk Bank of America and other banks on the Plus System of ATMs out of $14 million over one weekend was foiled only at the last minute by an insider tip-off. Police found 7,700 counterfeit ATM cards in the possession of computer programmer Mark Koenig and his four accomplices. In 1992 Syracuse, New York, teenager Curtis Ratcliff hit the jackpot when he shoved a stolen credit card into an ATM and it spit out $20 bills for twenty minutes, until the total reached $5,600. In Ireland in 1991 a gang stole at least $40,000 from ATMs by inserting a gadget featuring double-sided sticky tape into a cash dispenser so that it retained the bank notes. Puzzled users walked away from the machines without their money, and the thieves came along later to remove the gadget and the cash.[32]

From New Zealand came the equally astonishing tale of a schoolboy called Simon who outsmarted a United Building Society ATM by using cardboard from a cornflakes packet to transfer N.Z. $1 million into his account. All the fourteen-year-old did was slip the cardboard into a deposit envelope and insert it into the machine, while punching up $1 million. When Simon checked his account a few days later, he was amazed to find that the $1 million had been credited. So he withdrew $10. When no alarms went off or police appeared, he withdrew another $500, but suddenly got cold feet and put it back again. A few days later, Simon withdrew $1,500, but his nerve failed again and he told one of his teachers, who took him along to the United Building Society for a friendly chat with the manager. His headmaster commented that Simon had not been considered one of the brightest pupils—"at least until now."[33]

But banks are not the only target of computer criminals. Computer thieves also have been attracted to insurance companies, where there is scope for manipulating computers to pay fictitious claims and grant bogus premium refunds. Brokerage houses also have been the focus of computer-based fraud. In 1986 a New York brokerage house decided to speed up the operation of its IBM system at peak hours by switching off the software that recorded information for the audit trail of each transaction. Knowing this, a crafty clerk selflessly volunteered for overtime, during which he sold the stock holdings of many customers and credited the money to twenty-two phony bank accounts he had set up. The money subsequently made its way to Switzerland and the clerk disappeared without trace. To this day, the company has no clear idea of who lost what and has appealed to customers to come forward and provide details of their losses, but one report puts the total cost of the scam at $28.8 million. Another huge securities fraud was uncovered in India in 1992 when it transpired that bankers and brokers had colluded to siphon off a staggering $1.3 billion of public funds in illegal securities transactions in order to play the stock market.[34]

Government departments also have been home to many computer frauds. For example, in a recent case in California, four employees of the Defense Contract Administration Services Region (DCASR) office in El Segundo were accused of having rigged the DCASR computer to issue a check for $9.5 million to one of them individually as payment for a legitimate invoice from a legitimate contractor. A bank officer became suspicious when the person trying to deposit the check wanted $600,000 in cash on the spot, and called in the police. In 1989 Alan N. Scott of Boston was charged with submitting forty-five fraudulent income tax refund claims totalling $325,000 using the IRS's electronic filing system. He had used false names and Social Security numbers and the names of people in prison. In 1991 eighteen Social Security Administration (SSA) employees and private investigators were charged with buying and selling information from SSA and FBI computers.[35]

In the United Kingdom in 1991, a series of computer frauds by government employees was uncovered by the National Audit Office. Department of Employment staff had cashed unemployment benefit checks sent to false addresses, Inland Revenue tax officers had altered friends' tax codes in order to reduce their tax bills, and Post Office employees had dipped into little-used savings accounts. Ministry of Defence computers had been used to divert government equipment, while another government computer had been instructed to issue false driver's licenses. In Australia a major scandal erupted in 1992 when the New South Wales Independent Commission Against Corruption (ICAC) revealed that government employees in many government departments (including the police) had been selling personal information to banks, insurance companies, and private investigators for years and making large sums of money on the side. Even more horrifying was the revelation that a Department of Social Security official had sold the address of a welfare client to a prisoner who needed the information to arrange the contract killing of his former wife.[36]

Phone companies have become prime targets of the high-tech fraudster in recent years, with phone fraud costing U.S. companies and long-distance carriers anything from $1 billion to $5 billion a year. There are signs that the huge problem of call selling is now being brought under control, but hacking into PBXs and voice mail systems in order to obtain free long-distance calls is still a growth industry. The ingenuity of today's high-tech criminals seems limitless: in a recent case in Italy, the Mafia had been selling cheap portable phones that had been reprogrammed so that the buyer paid for all the calls of the seller—until the buyer's first bill arrived. In the United States, a company supplying customer-owned coin-operated telephones to shops and restaurants in New York, Chicago, and Los Angeles had programmed the phones to collect and report the calling card numbers of users, which were then sold to drug dealers who made over $10 million worth of fraudulent calls before the scam was discovered.[37]

Most reported computer crimes involve individuals defrauding organizations, but the latter case is an example of an organization defrauding individuals. One of the largest computer crimes ever discovered involved criminal behavior by a company—an insurance company. From 1965 to 1971, Equity Funding Inc. used its computers to generate thousands of phony insurance policies that later were sold to reinsurance companies for a total of over $27 million. In a more recent case of systematic fraud by a company, Hertz Corporation allegedly overcharged customers who damaged rental cars and were liable for repair charges. Hertz's computers apparently were programmed to generate two estimates: one for the actual repairs at discount rates and one with a higher price that was sent to customers and insurers. According to one report, it is estimated that Hertz may have collected $13 million through this questionable practice.[38]

Computers can be used to steal goods by altering inventories and redirecting items, which can then be sold for cash. Computer records can be doctored to make it seem that goods have been damaged and disposed of, shipped to a customer but returned, or lost. For example, an eighteen-year-old college student, Jerry Schneider, posed as a magazine reporter doing a story on Pacific Telephone's parts distribution system. In this way, Schneider learned that requests for parts came in via touch-tone phones and were delivered to any location. With a foolproof method for convincing the company's computer that his instructions were legitimate internal orders for parts, Schneider collected enormous quantities of telephone parts at specific pick-up points and then sold them through his new company, Creative Telephone. By the time Schneider was turned in by a Creative employee, over $1 million worth of phone equipment had disappeared from Pacific Telephone.[39]

Theft of information stored in computers is another growth industry. In a famous case some years ago, three computer operators attempted to sell *Encyclopaedia Britannica's* list of two million customers to a direct mail company, and in 1984 the Waterford Glass Company in Ireland had twenty-five computer disks stolen that held unique instructions for their glass-cutting machines. These disks probably made their way to counterfeiting factories in the Far East.[40] Many a computer professional has been induced to part with commercial information that has value to a competitor company. Computerized mailing lists or lists of potential or actual customers can change hands for considerable sums of money. Some are acquired legitimately, some are not. Database marketing is a rapidly expanding area, and its growth explains why consumers who have purchased a product or service from company A are then deluged with mail not only from company A but also from companies X, Y, and Z. This increase also explains why the volume of junk mail has grown enormously, particularly to upscale customers or residents of upscale areas, and why postal services are once again becoming profitable—despite the predictions that paperless electronic mail would replace conventional surface mail.

Information technology has given a new twist to old crimes such as blackmail, plagiarism, and sabotage. In the United Kingdom in 1990, a gang of hackers tried to blackmail five London banks after they had broken into the banks' main computers. They demanded substantial sums of money in return for showing the banks how their systems had been penetrated. In 1991 Godfrey Broomes, a computer operator working at the Municipal Mutual insurance company in Hampshire, England, made a copy of the firm's computer files, wiped the originals, and then offered to sell the tapes back to the company for half a million pounds. He was later caught in a police trap. In court he claimed that the company had insulted him by offering him a new employment contract at a substantially reduced rate of pay. In the United States in 1990, freelance journalist Stuart Goldman was charged with hacking into the computer system of Fox Television in New York and Los Angeles in order to steal news stories being worked on by the company's journalists.[41]

Computers can be used to commit sabotage. In 1990 Marshall Williams, a former cost estimator for Southeastern Color Lithographers of Athens, Georgia, was convicted of using the company's computer network to destroy accounting data, including backup copies. The crime allegedly cost the company more than $400,000 in lost business and downtime. A more cunning computer saboteur, Michael John Lauffenburger of San Diego, planted a logic bomb in the mainframe of his employer, defense contractor General Dynamics. Apparently, Lauffenburger had hoped to increase his salary by successfully defusing the logic bomb, which was designed to destroy a database of Atlas rocket components. But someone else was called to do the job, and Lauffenburger was charged with computer sabotage.[42]

In a famous case in 1986, someone entered the Capitol Hill computer systems of two Republican congressmen, Ed Zschau of California and John McCain of Arizona, and destroyed records of letters sent to constituents and mailing lists. One break-in took place over the lunch hour, the other late at night. The police were called, and they recommended better controls in future. But Representative Ed Zshau said, "The entering of my computer was tantamount to someone breaking in to my office, taking my files and burning them . . . the police would be more concerned if this were a physical break-in. Because people don't see the files overturned or a pile of ashes outside the door, it doesn't seem as bad. . . . But it is equally devastating."[43]

Who Are the Computer Criminals and Why Do They Do It?

Who commits computer crimes and what motivates them? From the studies that have been done by computer crime specialists such as Donn Parker of SRI International, Buck BloomBecker, and Hugo Cornwall, a picture has emerged of the typical computer criminal as a loyal, trusted employee, not necessarily possessing great computer expertise, who has been tempted, for instance, by the discovery of flaws in a computer system or loopholes in the controls monitoring his or her activity. Experts on computer fraud attest to the fact that opportunity more than anything else seems to generate this kind of aberrant behavior. The opportunity (and the apparent lack of sanctions) more than anything else seems to lead otherwise honest and loyal employees down the slippery slope from minor misconduct—such as unauthorized use of company computer time—to serious criminal activity.

In a review of the major British studies of computer crime, Keith Hearnden found that the vast majority (80 percent) of crimes involving computers were carried out by employees rather than outsiders. While 25 percent of all crimes were carried out by managers or supervisors and 24 percent by computer staff, a surprising 31 percent were committed by lowly clerks and cashiers who had little in the way of technical skills. Nearly all computer criminals were first-time offenders who were motivated, says Hearnden, by greed, pressing financial worries, and other personal problems such as alcohol or drug dependency. Love and sex could also provide a powerful stimulus. In one case, a twenty-three-year-old male bank clerk became infatuated with a thirty-two-year-old woman. In trying to impress her with expensive gifts, travel, and good living, he spent his way through £23,000 stolen from four bank accounts and covered up the theft by transferring cash through a computer from seventeen other accounts. He then lost £10,000 pounds in casinos while trying to recoup the money. By the time he was finally caught, the woman had deserted him.[44]

There is a commonly held view that the typical computer criminal is a whiz kid, with highly developed computing skills and a compulsive desire to beat the system. But Hearnden shows that the substance for this image is absent: "Not many crimes . . . demonstrate high technical ingenuity on the part of the perpetrator. Most exhibit an opportunistic exploitation of an inherent weakness in the computer system being used." Leslie D. Ball states that most computer criminals "tend to be relatively honest and in a position of trust; few would do anything to harm another human, and most do not consider their crime to be truly dishonest." Hugo Cornwall says we must understand the process by which "nice suburban people with jobs that give them access to sensitive information, systems and data are able to justify to themselves and their friends the committing of certain types of criminal act."[45]

Although the typical computer criminal may not be a whiz kid, there is little doubt that many of the crimes that involve an element of hacking are carried out by young people. For example, U.S. Secret Service agents who smashed a ring of fraudsters in Michigan in 1989 were surprised to discover that the gang was made up largely of teenagers. The gang had penetrated the systems of twenty major companies and had appropriated goods and services worth hundred of thousands of dollars. Some of the teenagers were as young as fourteen and had to be pulled out of eighth grade at school and questioned in the presence of their parents, who were completely unaware of their activities. In Queensland, Australia, parents of boys aged thirteen to sixteen, who attended some of Brisbane's top schools, were amazed to learn that their sons had been operating a racket involving stolen credit card numbers used to purchase expensive cameras, leather jackets, compact-disc players, and rock concert tickets.[46]

British computer crime expert David Davies of the U.K. publication *Computer Law and Security Report* has emphasized the importance of looking at motivation when attempting to understand computer crime. "We tend to think in terms of obvious motives such as direct fraud or malice, and overlook those arising out of the very complex range of human emotions and needs. Employees who would normally stop short of fraud or damaging property can often reconcile their consciences with lesser acts. Similar problems arise when people are made redundant or fear redundancy, or feel under-promoted, overlooked or aggrieved."

Cases cited by Davies included a computer operator having trouble making ends meet who switched circuit boards to reduce efficiency and thus give himself more overtime; a woman sacked for incompetence who programmed the computer to give all the clients the maximum discount and then destroyed all of the original estimates and calculations; a night shift supervisor who discovered his wife was having an affair with someone on the day shift and sabotaged the data center so he would be transferred to day work; and a programmer fired from his job who continued to use his password and access code to amend programs so the system would crash and the woman programmer with whom he was infatuated would call him for advice.[47]

Buck BloomBecker has listed eight motivations that can lie behind computer crimes. Some computer criminals, he says, think of crime as a game and see the computer environment as a kind of "playpen" for their own enjoyment. Others see computer systems as a "land of opportunity" where crime is easy or as a "cookie jar" that will readily solve pressing financial or personal problems. Some see computer and/or communication systems as a kind of "soapbox" for political expression; others see them as a "fairyland" of unreality, a "toolbox" for tackling new crimes or modernizing traditional crimes, or a "magic wand" that can be made to do anything. Finally, crimes involving sabotage are often based on a view that the computer environment is a "battle zone" between management and alienated employees.[48]

Others have surmised that the intellectual challenge of fooling a system plays an important role in motivating individuals to commit computer crimes. Still others have emphasized that computer crimes involve very little physical risk (unlike, for example, a bank hold-up); that computer crimes can be committed alone, without talkative associates, thus further reducing the risk of detection; and that (as in BloomBecker's fairyland) computer crimes can often appear not to be a criminal act—shuffling numbers around in a remote and abstract way is not quite the same as handling gold bars or huge piles of paper money.[49]

There is little doubt that the ethos of certain work environments is conducive to crime. Computer systems in workplaces that engender employee dissatisfaction for any reason must therefore be at risk. One U.S. survey found, for instance, that 63 percent of accountants and 75 percent of computer professionals believed that employees steal because "they feel frustrated or dissatisfied about some aspect of their job." This could be an accurate reflection of the lack of autonomy, minimal job variety, and poor management communications that all too often characterize today's workplaces—including those that have been heavily computerized.[50]

Improving Computer Security

The growth of computer crime calls for new kinds of security measures, measures that can be costly and that can involve the use of computers. But improved security often lags behind the discovery of new crimes; computer security experts are forever trying to shut the stable door after the horse has bolted. Many companies are still extremely lax about computer security, often believing that computer frauds could never happen to them. Market researchers Computer Intelligence estimate that a mere 10 percent of IBM mainframes had data security software in 1982, and this figure had grown to only 35 percent by late 1988. Yet vulnerability to computer break-ins has increased because the operations of so many companies—especially in the service sector—are now entirely dependent on computers.

A good illustration of poor security is provided by the recent case of Herbert Zinn, a seventeen-year-old Chicago high school student who broke into AT&T's computer systems using a personal computer in his bedroom. Some reports say he say he copied software worth $1 million, including material on AT&T computers at military bases. AT&T spokespersons blamed the lapse on employees who had not followed proper security procedures rather than on their security system. Another amazing security blunder occurred at the Rocky Flats, Colorado, nuclear weapons plant in 1991, where top secret bomb designs were left for a week on a VAX computer accessible from the public phone network.[51]

In recent years a whole succession of official reports in the United States and Europe has drawn attention to the perilous state of computer security in most modern organizations. For example, the System Security Study Committee of the U.S. National Research Council published a major report in 1991 that called for the establishment of an Information Security Foundation to tackle what it saw as a critical problem. The U.S. General Accounting Office (GAO) warned of serious technological weaknesses in the security systems protecting the vast network of bank and stock market computers in the United States. In the United Kingdom, successive reports from the Audit Commission slammed British management for being too apathetic about system security. As Peter G. Neumann summarized the situation, "The security provided by many computer systems is fundamentally flawed. In other cases, valid security techniques exist but are not being used properly. Better hardware and software systems are necessary to hinder insider misuse as well as penetrators. People are the ultimate problem. Despite improving technology, serious risks remain."[52]

"The problem with computer security is that everyone talks about it but not enough people do anything about it," says one New York analyst. Military and industrial security are well understood—it is comparatively easy to stop, for example, materials going out of the door—but the need for computer security is less well appreciated, and the task of stopping information from going out the door is much more difficult. A 1988 study by the accountants Coopers and Lybrand found that only one out of a sample of twenty top European companies was "adequately secure." Most computer security experts lay the blame for poor security squarely at the door of top management. Often managers don't understand their computer systems, can't be bothered, don't wish to restrict ease of use, or don't appreciate what their information is worth.

Hugo Cornwall says that too many managers see computer security as an afterthought rather than an intrinsic requirement—as though brakes were considered an optional feature on cars. Few companies carry out a fundamental analysis of the security risks they might face. Many IT managers face an uphill battle to engage the attention of top management in technical problems, and too few companies have a security manager. Security work is also considered dull and boring. In addition, sometimes security products are regarded as modern-day magic talismans that provide an instant solution to all security problems. Improving computer security, Cornwall says, is not purely a technical matter. It's a question of understanding a company's business, its culture, its structure, and its decision-making processes.[53]

Computer security can be greatly improved by the adoption of relatively simple, commonsense measures. Passwords allowing access to systems, for instance, can be made less obvious and memorable by avoiding such passwords as girlfriend's names. Passwords should be issued only to the absolute minimum number of people requiring access. A 1986 survey by British insurance broker Hogg Robinson found that the words chosen for passwords were mostly useless and very easy for colleagues to guess. Top of the list in Britain were "fred" (standing for flipping ridiculous electronic device), "god," "pass" and "genius," while many chose the names of their spouses or family pets. In the United States, apparently, the favorite password is "love," closely followed by "sex."[54]

A growing market is now developing for access control software that closes password loopholes. This software restricts users—individually identified by passwords and codes—to only those files they are authorized to use. Even then, the software permits the users to perform only authorized functions, such as adding or deleting information, and they can no longer browse through parts of the system that they are not entitled to enter. One obvious and major limitation with access control software, however, is that it does not protect a company against frauds committed by inside employees while going about their legitimate tasks.

Many companies are installing dial-back or black box systems to protect their assets. When a user calls into a computer, a black box intercepts the call and asks for a password. The unit then disconnects the call, looks up the password in the directory, and calls the user back at his or her listed telephone number: fraudsters calling from another number will be screened out. A large mainframe may have hundreds of ports of entry from remote stations, and each one has to be protected by these dial-back systems, which can cost many thousands of dollars.

Scrambling devices and encryption software are additional expensive items that scramble messages for transmission so that only the legitimate recipient can understand them. Anyone tapping into a bank's communication lines or eavesdropping on the electromagnetic waves emitted from a computer or piece of electronic equipment, for example, will pick up only a jumbled list of zeros and ones. Encryption devices in the form of DSPs (digital signal processors) are being used increasingly to scramble voice and data messages over telephone networks. Voice encryption is obviously vital in the military and in security agencies. However, even the best encryption codes can be broken, and so the codes have to be changed frequently—every hour, for example. This is what the Pentagon sometimes does with very sensitive information. It is also spending $200 million under its Tempest program to eliminate or muffle electromagnetic signals from machines used by the military, security agencies, and defense contractors.

Audit control software packages are also available that can monitor transactions or the use of a computer. These applications enable auditors to trace and identify any operator who gains access to the system and to tell when this occurs. Audits can also highlight an abnormal number of correction entries, which often indicates the trial-and-error approach of fraudulent activity. But a major problem is that the demand for auditors with computer skills is high and not enough auditors are capable of outsmarting crooked computer personnel. Likewise, more police need to be trained in computer work. Recently, Kenneth Rosenblatt, the deputy district attorney for the County of Santa Clara, capital of California's Silicon Valley, called for the formation of specialized units of computer cops who would specifically target computer crime.[55]

But many argue that improving computer security is a more of a management problem than a technical or policing problem. Careful vetting of employees in the first place can be a great help. Then sensible security procedures, starting with rules for password usage and including sophisticated access control systems, should be formulated and rigidly enforced. Obviously, the latest technology should be used where possible, but it is no guarantee of total security. Ultimately, the best security might be to manage employees more effectively because in the final analysis even the best security systems cannot stop the determined fraudster. Employers must be able to rely on the good will of their employees.

Fighting Crime with Computers

Computers are also being used increasingly in the fight against crime, both conventional crime and computer-based crime. Police forces all over the world are now using lap-top computers, automatic vehicle location (AVL) systems, and computer-aided dispatch (CAD) systems that help them respond more intelligently to emergency calls. A U.S. Treasury system now monitors all bank transactions of $10,000 or more involving cash. A U.K. company has developed software that enables a computer to browse through vast amounts of financial data looking for possible connections that might indicate insider trading or foreign exchange fraud. A similar system is at work on the New York Stock Exchange. A British firm of management consultants used computers to search for illegal multiple share applications made during the U.K. government's privatization program. And an Australian insurance company has developed a system that searches through its claims files attempting to associate random items of information about the company's customers. It is credited with unmasking scores of fraudulent injury claims.[56]

The vast amounts of so-called transactional information—records of phone calls, air travel, credit card purchases, and so on—stored on computers are providing a fertile field for crime busters. The most famous example was the discovery that all the messages passed between Colonel Oliver North and his collaborators in the illegal sale of arms to Iran and the illegal transmission of aid to the Contras in Nicaragua were faithfully recorded on a local area network they used called PROFS (IBM's Professional Office Systems Network). In the United Kingdom in 1992, an elusive kidnapper was finally traced through records of his mobile phone calls; computer monitoring of ticket sales to a U2 concert in Providence, Rhode Island, uncovered a scam whereby extra tickets were being sold to scalpers by an unscrupulous manager. But perhaps the most spectacular example of transactional data nailing a crook was the case in England of John Tanner, who murdered his student girlfriend and hid her body underneath the floorboards of her house. Initially, police treated him as a helpful witness rather than as a suspect, until he told them that they had taken a bus ride together at a time she was already dead. The bus company's computer records showed that only one person got on the bus at the time Tanner claimed.[57]

Another weapon in the fight against crime is *biometrics*, or the digitizing of biological characteristics. These include not only fingerprints, but also voices, the veins of the back of the hand, the pattern of blood vessels in the retina, the wheel patterns of the iris, and—the very latest— lip prints. Police forces all over the world are now using computerized fingerprint identification systems that have a remarkable record of cracking hitherto unsolved cases, while fingerprint scanning devices are now being used to control access to computer rooms, bank vaults, and military bases. So-called smart cards incorporating a fingerprint of the user will probably become common in the next few years. A number of U.S. companies are marketing retinal scanners like the one used in the James Bond 007 film *Never Say Never Again*—only they claim that their products, unlike the one in the film, cannot be fooled.

3

Software Theft

In November 1987, Ming Jyh Hsieh, a thirty-eight-year-old product support engineer, was fired for nonperformance by her employer, the Wollongong Group, a software company of Palo Alto, California. Two months later she was caught downloading Wollongong proprietary software into her home personal computer. Using a secret password and privileges that, surprisingly, were still valid, she spent some eighteen hours over several nights copying vast amounts of her former employer's software. Noticing that someone was logging onto its computers via modem in the middle of the night, the Wollongong Group immediately called the police, who placed a trap-and-trace device on the company's computer phone lines in order to identify the caller. Later, when confronted with evidence, Hsieh confessed. She was arrested and charged with gaining illegal access to Wollongong's computers and stealing millions of dollars worth of software.[1]

The Problem of Software Piracy

Software is the set of instructions that tells a computer what to do. Without software, a computer is just a useless lump of silicon, metal, and plastic. As the cost of computer hardware has declined, the importance of software has increased: software is where the action and the money are these days. The total world market for software is now approaching $100 billion a year.

Partly as a result, copying computer programs, often referred to as software piracy, has become a major growth industry. In schools, colleges, and universities, students duplicate programs for their friends or even for resale, just as you might make copies of videocassette tapes or chapters of this book. Software rental agencies have mushroomed, with no questions asked about what customers do with the software once they get it home. In commerce, industry, education, and even in government departments, there is mounting evidence of the mass copying of software packages, often with the collusion of management. Few individuals can honestly say that they have never used a program for which the developer has not been properly compensated. Software piracy appears to be an endemic social problem that is here to stay.

The U.S.-based Software Publishers' Association (SPA) estimates that software piracy is costing U.S. software producers between $10 billion and $12 billion a year worldwide—part of an estimated $60 to $80 billion a year lost to U.S. companies through the theft of intellectual property of all types. Intellectual property in the form of ideas and innovations in the field of entertainment (records, tapes, and videos), personal consumer goods (watches and handbags), pharmaceuticals (well-known drugs), and computer hardware and software are supposed to be protected by copyrights, patents, and trademarks. But the pirating and counterfeiting of goods is a multi-million-dollar worldwide industry, mainly centered in Asia but with significant activity in Latin America, Eastern Europe, and even in the United States. In a global economy increasingly based on information and technological innovation, the protection of intellectual property has become an important international trade issue. For the computer industry, it is a major headache that ultimately threatens future progress in the industry.[2]

With the growing importance of computer software, producers of software packages have become increasingly concerned about wholesale copying. For example, Lotus claims that over half of its potential sales of 1-2-3 are lost to pirates, at a cost of millions of dollars every year. The U.S.-based Business Software Alliance (BSA) claims that while 40 percent of U.S. software packages sold in the United Sates are illegal copies, this figure rises to over 75 percent in Japan, Germany, Belgium, Holland, and Italy and to 80–90 percent in China, Taiwan, Korea, Spain, Portugal, and Switzerland. An earlier BSA exercise found that while there were 1.5 legitimate software packages sold for every personal computer sold in the United States, in Australia it was 0.82, in France it was a low 0.65, and in Italy it was alleged to be a mere 0.4. One software company spokesman commented that even in comparatively well-behaved countries such as Canada, when you compare the number of PCs sold with the number of legitimate software packages sold, "Two-thirds of the computers must be being used as expensive doorstops."[3]

A dramatic illustration of the pervasiveness of software piracy is provided by the famous Montreal Macintosh case. Richard R. Brandow, a twenty-four-year-old publisher of a Montreal, Canada, computer magazine, and coworker, Pierre M. Zovile, created a benign virus in order to highlight the problem of software piracy. The idea was that when the internal clocks on infected Macintoshes hit 2 March 1988, the first birthday of the Mac II computer, each machine would display an innocuous "universal message of peace to all Macintosh users." But within two months, Brandow says, illegal copying had transferred the virus to no less than 350,000 Macs around the world. And the virus was less than benign: Marc Canter, president of a small Chicago software publisher, found that this universal message of peace caused his computers to crash and infected disks that he had supplied to software producer Aldus Corporation in Seattle. Aldus pulled back the disks, but not before some got to customers.[4]

The history of software theft in the United States goes back to 1964, when Texaco was offered $5 million worth of stolen software. In the United Kingdom there was the famous 1968 case in which the airline management system BOADICEA was copied and offered for sale by employees of the developer, the British Overseas Airways Corporation. The notorious Ward case in 1970 demonstrated how easy it was to steal software down a telephone line. Hugh Jeffrey Ward, a programmer working on a CAD (computer-aided design) package for a Californian computer company, desperately needed a facility to print results neatly on a plotter. Knowing that a good plotter module was available in another company's computer, Ward called the company's computer and requested a listing of the program as well as the punched cards (the method of data input in those days). Unfortunately, the cards were later spotted in his wastebasket and Ward was caught and convicted of theft of a trade secret. He received three years on probation and a $5,000 fine, while the aggrieved company got $300,000 in damages.[5]

Large-scale piracy became common after the arrival of the personal computer and packaged software in the late 1970s. This development put hardware and software into the hands of individuals at reasonable cost for the first time and enabled them to do such things as word processing, ledger accounting, business planning, and mass mailing. Sales of PCs and software packages went hand-in-hand: as PCs proliferated, the demand for useful software soared, and as more software packages like the pioneering VisiCalc became available, the demand for PCs also zoomed. Software became a multi-million-dollar business almost over-night as worldwide sales of software packages leapt from $250 million in 1980 to $2 billion in 1984 and to $8 billion by 1989. A major trend developed toward the integrated software packages we know today that permit the user to perform several different tasks because a number of programs are integrated together on a single storage disk. For example, Lotus's 1-2-3 enables the user to carry out spreadsheet analysis, retrieve data from a database, and display graphic material without having to change disks. Unfortunately, because the original versions of these soft-ware packages were very expensive, the temptation to pirate a copy has proved too much for millions of users and would-be users.

Now there is every indication that software piracy is out of hand. In recent cases, the giant engineering company Davy McKee agreed to pay the SPA $300,000 in an out-of-court settlement after it admitted to the mass copying of software following a SPA raid on its New York offices, and the New York City Council also pleaded guilty to such practices in at least three of its agencies. In 1992 FBI agents raided a computer bulletin board in the Boston area that had been distributing more than two-hundred pirated programs to subscribers in thirty-six U.S. states and eleven foreign countries, including Iraq. The bulletin board, called Davy Jones Locker, was selling pirated versions of costly, sophisticated pro-grams such as AutoCAD, the engineering and design package, and even "beta," or prerelease, versions of well-known programs from Lotus and IBM. Further raids by U.S. marshals in September 1992 at ten sites in California and New Jersey netted $9 million worth of counterfeit com-puter programs. Officers loaded sixteen eighteen-wheeler trucks with the fake software packages and the equipment used in their manufacture, as well as with additional stocks of counterfeit manuals, disks, holograms, and packaging. Included in the haul were more than 150,000 copies of Microsoft's MS-DOS version 5 operating system.[6]

In the United Kingdom, officials from the BSA and the British-based Federation Against Software Theft (FAST) mounted a large-scale raid on the offices of companies in Robert Maxwell's publishing empire and found large numbers of illegal programs. At the headquarters of Mirror Group Newspapers, the raiders found that 80 percent of the software in use was pirated. Meanwhile another British newspaper, The Yorkshire Post, agreed to an out-of-court settlement with FAST after a raid on the paper's offices that had uncovered the widespread use of pirated software.[7]

In an extraordinary long-running case in the United States, a small bankrupt software company, Inslaw Inc. of Washington, D.C., took on the Federal Justice Department for the same offense and initially won a landmark victory in court. In 1982, Inslaw had landed a $10 million contract with the Justice Department to install its PROMIS case-tracking software in the twenty largest federal prosecutors' offices nationwide, plus a version for seventy smaller offices. Inslaw in the meantime allegedly spent more than $8 million enhancing PROMIS on the assumption that it would be able to renegotiate that contract to take account of the extra work done. But once the Justice Department obtained the source code of the enhanced system, it allegedly refused to negotiate new licensing fees, withheld payments of $1.8 million, terminated its contract, and astonishingly went on to pirate a further twenty copies of the new PROMIS. By April 1985 Inslaw was so short of revenue as a result of the Justice Department's behavior that it was forced into bankruptcy.

But owners William and Nancy Hamilton kept fighting, and the case finally ended up in the U.S. District of Columbia bankruptcy court. In February 1988 the court handed down its decision: Inslaw was awarded $6.8 million damages, not including legal fees and "consequential damages" for lost business opportunities, which would be determined at a later trial. Judge George Francis Bason Jr. accused the Justice Department of "trickery, fraud and deceit" in its campaign against Inslaw and warned that similar piracy by a government department would be sternly dealt with. Incredibly, the Inslaw case got to court only because of a loophole in the law; normally, U.S. companies cannot sue the federal government. Inslaw was able to do so only because it was in the midst of Chapter 11 bankruptcy proceedings—a bankruptcy brought about by the actions of a federal government department. And the Inslaw case hasn't gone away. In 1991 Joseph Casolaro, an investigative journalist researching the case for a possible book, was found dead in a West Virginia motel room in strange circumstances, and in 1992 the U.S. House of Representatives Judiciary Committee voted to hold an independent investigation into the ten-year-old affair.[8]

In the Middle East, Latin America, and Eastern Europe, software piracy is part of the way of life. Lotus claims to lose as much as $25 million annually in foregone revenue as a result of rampant copying in the Middle East alone, while in Latin America pirate programs are openly on sale in markets from Peru to Paraguay. In communist Eastern Europe, virtually all software was illegal as a result of Western trade bans, state restrictions on usage, and lack of money. But in the wake of the fall of the Berlin Wall, IBM offered an amnesty to software pirates in the form of a modest fee to legalize all their pirate programs and an exchange service that enabled users to trade in their pirate programs for legitimate copies purchased at a discount. In Australia, an antipiracy campaign by the Business Software Association of Australia (BSAA) began to bear fruit with successful raids on a Sydney-based dealer, Computer Exchange Corporation, and transport giant Mayne Nickless. In a later court settlement, Mayne Nickless agreed to pay sums of money to Lotus and WordPerfect Pacific.[9]

But in Asia copying is king. Most estimates suggest that about 90 percent of all software in China, Taiwan, Thailand, India, and Pakistan has been copied. In Hong Kong, about seven or eight copies of well-known packages are thought to exist for every legitimate copy sold, while the counterfeiting of goods of all kinds is estimated to be worth $1 billion a year to the Singapore economy alone. It is common practice in Asia to purchase a computer complete with a variety of bootlegged programs already installed on the hard disk. Asian companies routinely buy one or two legitimate copies of a piece of software and duplicate hundreds of copies for their employees. Stolen software sells in street markets for a fraction of the normal retail price. Very often bootlegged versions of new packages are available before the packages have been officially released in the Asian market. Most people in Asia see copying software as a legitimate way to cut costs, and antipiracy laws are almost nonexistent. Where such laws do exist, they are rarely enforced and fines are usually minimal.

In China, copying of all Western goods, including software, has been condoned for years by the communist government. The BSA estimates that U.S. software companies lose $400 million a year because of Chinese software piracy. In a recent case, thousands of fake holograms on counterfeit Microsoft software being sold from Taiwan were traced to a Chinese government-owned factory in the special Shenzen economic zone near Hong Kong. In 1991 China announced that it would join the Berne Convention, the international pact governing copyright protection, and in 1992 China agreed to U.S. demands that it outlaw the theft of software when it amended its copyright law. (As a direct result, Microsoft entered the Chinese market for the first time.) But doubts remained about what precisely both moves would mean in real terms.

If mainland China is tops for the quantity of software copied, Taiwan is probably tops for quality. Long known as the counterfeiting capital of the world, Taiwan's capital of Taipei is home to master forgers who apparently are able to produce flawless copies of Western computer manuals, diskettes, packaging, and even licensing agreements that have fooled all but expert company investigators. Taiwan runs a huge balance of payments surplus with the rest of the world—much of it due to piracy—and seems unlikely to take action to curb counterfeiting when it knows that the results are so rewarding. Meanwhile, in Thailand, where an estimated 97 percent of software has been copied, a recent Association of Thai Computer Industry survey put personal computer hardware sales in 1992 at $284 million and software sales at a revealing $9.8 million only.[10]

Revenge of the Nerds? Intellectual Property Rights and the Law

The idea of intellectual property rights has been around since the Middle Ages, and current forms of legal protection have evolved over subsequent centuries. According to the United Nations' Patent Office, the World Intellectual Property Organization (WIPO), intellectual property is defined as the rights to, among other things, the results of intellectual activity in the industrial, scientific, literary, or artistic fields. Generally speaking, copyright law has traditionally protected forms of literary expression, patent law has protected mechanical inventions, and contract law has covered trade secrets. Trademarks also are protected by law.

But computer software is a wholly new kind of entity that presents major new challenges for the law. Chief among these are how we define ownership of this form of intellectual property and how the rights of ownership can and should be protected. Current laws are outdated and confusing: we are not sure whether copyright, patents, or trade secrets apply or should apply to this strange new thing called software. As Pamela Samuelson has argued, digital media such as software have several distinct qualities, such as compactness, plasticity, ease of replication, ease of transmission, and multiple uses. All these properties mean that software presents a challenge to the doctrines of existing intellectual property systems.[11] And as the confusion continues, the gap between legal precedent and everyday behavior on the part of computer professionals and users grows still wider.

Anne W. Branscomb has argued that what suited the age of print and mechanical inventions is proving inadequate in the age of the computer program, the expert system, and the distributed database. Copyright, patents, and contract law worked relatively well in the industrial era, but recently three factors have eroded the effectiveness of these traditional protection mechanisms. First, the development of new information and communications technologies has blurred the boundaries between media. Second, intellectual assets have become increasingly abstract and intangible. Third, the globalization of the world economy has multiplied both the incentives for international violations of intellectual property rights and the economic harm of such violations. Fourth, privatization and the growing trend toward using market mechanisms to gather and disseminate information have disrupted the traditional public infrastructure for sharing intellectual assets. For example, in the United States, Bell Laboratories, federal government agencies, and universities are now turning to patent rights and copyright royalties to recoup their research and development costs. Thus, she says, "at the very moment when information is becoming a valuable commodity, protecting the economic value of intellectual assets is proving more difficult."[12]

U.S. companies filed more than 5,700 intellectual property lawsuits in 1990 (up from 3,800 in 1980). In the same year, no less than 175,000 patents were filed in the United States (up 39 percent over 1985) and a staggering 643,000 copyrights were registered (compared with 401,000 registered over a five-year period in the 1970s). In Japan, the number of patent applications also doubled between 1980 and 1988 (and, incidentally, Texas Instruments was finally awarded a patent on the integrated circuit in Japan—twenty-nine years after it had applied). Protecting intellectual property has become big business for law firms. Some New York law firms now specialize entirely in patent, copyright, and trademark work, while others have employed many more intellectual property experts. Computer companies also retain patent attorneys; IBM tops the list with 140. Some companies, such as Refac Technology, have come into existence purely to pursue lawsuits on behalf of customers or lawsuits concerning rights to technologies they have purchased from their inventors.[13]

One potentially worrying new trend is that big IT companies now tend to see the law as a way of increasing profits rather than as a defensive move to safeguard technology. For example, IBM and Texas Instruments have collected hundreds of millions of dollars from other companies (overwhelmingly Japanese firms, such as Hitachi and Fujitsu) that clearly have infringed their patents and copyrights over the years. These settlements may seem like justice, but some people, such as Mitch Kapor, the former boss of Lotus, have recently warned that litigation is now being used too often as a business tactic rather than as a move of last resort. This trend effectively could mean that wealth in the IT industry in the future will go more to the talkers and arguers than to the innovators and doers—which cannot be a good thing for the long-term interests of the industry.[14]

Among the thousands of lawsuits in the United States over the past decade, the cases involving Lotus Development versus other companies and Apple Computer versus others have been among the most interesting and significant. For example, in the mid 1980s Lotus sued two smaller companies, Paperback Software and Mosaic Software, for copying the "look and feel" of 1-2-3 (Mosaic's program was unashamedly called "Twin"). In turn, Lotus was sued for $100 million by the Software Arts Products Corporation (SAPC), developers of the original VisiCalc program, which claimed that Lotus had copied many of the commands and keystrokes as well as the screen displays of VisiCalc in 1-2-3. SAPC claimed that Lotus founder Mitch Kapor "misappropriated" copyrighted and confidential aspects of the VisiCalc program while he was an employee of the exclusive marketing agent for VisiCalc. SAPC further alleged that later, as a product tester for an advanced version of VisiCalc, Kapor "had access to copyrighted and confidential aspects" of the program. He "deliberately sought to make the 1-2-3 program look and feel like VisiCalc."[15]

SAPC lost, but Lotus won against Paperback in 1990 when U.S. Federal District Court Judge Robert Keeton found that Paperback had unlawfully copied the 1-2-3 method of invoking commands using a command line interface. Days after its victory over Adam Osborne's Paperback, Lotus filed suit against Philippe Kahn's Borland for infringing its copyright on 1-2-3 in Borland's Quattro program. Later, in 1992, Judge Robert Keeton, sitting in Boston, Massachusetts, again found in favor of Lotus by declaring that Quattro had infringed Lotus copyrights. But he also ruled that a further jury trial would be necessary to assess any monetary damages that might be due to Lotus.[16]

Although Lotus (rightly or wrongly) won its major cases, Apple Computer has been less successful in the courts. Apple sued both Microsoft and Hewlett-Packard to prevent them from using a Macintosh-style user interface in their products, although Apple had allegedly borrowed the mouse-and-icons concept from Xerox's Star user interface in the first place. Apple appeared to win a first-round court victory against Microsoft early in 1989, despite Microsoft's attempts to put a brave face on the judgment. Some industry observers warned that a clear victory for Apple in later rounds would put Apple in a commanding position in the marketplace and would drastically reduce both competition and innovation. But this didn't happen. Although U.S. Federal Court Judge Vaughn Walker in San Francisco gave further hope to Apple in some minor rulings in 1991, Apple's main claim that Microsoft had copied the look and feel of the Macintosh interface in its Windows software came crashing down in April 1992 when Judge Walker ruled in favor of Microsoft and rejected Apple's claim for $5.5 billion in damages. In some ways, this judgment appeared to contradict aspects of Judge Keeton's rulings in the Lotus cases.[17]

Meanwhile, Xerox's somewhat belated attempts to gain compensation from Apple for allegedly borrowing the look and feel of Macintosh from Xerox's Star user interface also failed in the courts. Although Xerox appeared to have a strong case for $150 million in damages based on the circumstances at the time (such as Steve Jobs's visit to Xerox's Palo Alto Research Center and his subsequent hiring of Xerox personnel), Apple was able to convince the same Judge Walker that the company had done so much work itself on the Macintosh interface that it was substantially different from the Star interface. In addition, the fact that Xerox had waited many years before claiming it had been badly wronged counted against the company in court. Ironically, while Apple was using the "substantially different" argument against Xerox, in the Microsoft case Apple appeared to be arguing the opposite—that Windows was not substantially different from Macintosh.[18]

Many other intellectual property cases, some more significant than others, have gone through the U.S. courts in recent years. In 1988, for example, Ashton-Tate, then the third-largest producer of PC software in the world, launched a suit against two smaller companies, Fox Software and Santa Cruz Operation, for violating copyright laws supposedly protecting its best-selling dBaseIII database management and development program. Announcing the suit, Ashton-Tate chairman and chief executive Edward Esber said, "The issue is simple: a company like ours spends hundreds of millions of dollars making a brand name and a family of products, and we intend to protect our rights."[19]

In 1991 Wang Laboratories had a major win in its patent infringement suit against Japan's Toshiba and NEC, which both were found to have blatantly copied Wang's single in-line memory module (SIMM) device. Wang followed up with a further suit against NMB and Mitsubishi in 1992. The Japanese firm Hitachi was forced to pay Motorola for copying its popular 68030 microprocessor, and Honeywell collected $96 million from Minolta and $45 million from Nikon in 1992 after the two Japanese camera companies were found guilty of stealing Honeywell's automatic focusing technology in the mid 1980s. Honeywell was also suing Konica, Kyocera, Canon, Matsushita, Premier, and Kodak for the same offense. All of this activity followed U.S. inventor Clay Jacobson's claim that Kawasaki had stolen his designs for the jet-ski.[20]

It Looks and Feels Like the Law Is a Mess

As the previous anecdotes illustrate, the current legal position on software in the United States is very confusing, partly as a result of the seemingly contradictory judgments handed down in recent cases and partly because the U.S. legislature has never made up its collective mind about how to cope with this new thing called software.

The U.S. Copyright Office tentatively began accepting computer programs for registration back in 1964, but for many years the computer industry relied primarily on trade secrets regulations to protect its software. It was not until 1980 that the Copyright Act of 1976 was amended to include software in the form of the Computer Software Copyright Act of 1980. Under this legislation, programs are considered copyrightable as "literary works." Meanwhile, the U.S. Patent Office decided that most computer programs were collections of algorithms (mathematical formulae designed to carry out a specific task or to solve a particular problem) and thus, like other mathematical equations, were excluded from patent protection. Beginning in 1980, the U.S. courts began to steadily extend copyright protection for software—extending it, first, from embracing a program's source code to include the object code. Later, the logic and sequence of the program were also included.

By far the most significant case of this period was Whelan v. Jaslow. In 1986, the Third Circuit Court of Appeals (which covers New Jersey, Pennsylvania, and Delaware) found in favor of the plaintiff, Elaine Whelan, by declaring that copyright protection included the basic structure of a program, its lines of written code, and the nonliteral aspects of a program, such as the screen design and the commands. This decision helped set the scene for the "look and feel" cases launched in the period 1987–1989, which, as we have seen, resulted in victories for Lotus and defeats for Apple and Xerox. But on 23 June 1982, the Second Circuit Court of Appeals in New York handed down a judgment in Computer Associates v. Altai that declared that the basic structure of a program is not copyrightable. As such, this ruling marked a considerable retreat from Whelan v. Jaslow and the prevailing tendency to broaden rather than narrow the coverage of copyright law.[21]

At the same time, the legal waters have been further muddied by the growing tendency of the U.S. Patent Office to issue patents on software, including quite small bits of software. Beginning with a 1983 memorandum from the Patent & Trademark office, computer companies rushed to stake a claim to patents on all kinds of software devices—some innovatory and significant, some quite commonplace and trivial. For example, Teknowledge Inc. received patents on two new artificial intelligence products in 1986, while in 1989 Quarterdeck Office Systems was awarded a patent for Desqview, a Windows-type multitasking operating environment. The patent had been applied for in 1984, the same year that Desqview and Microsoft's Windows package first came on the market. Quarterdeck's persistence was seen as an attempt to get back at Microsoft and to help recoup their $6 million start-up costs, but some industry observers, such as office systems analyst Andrew Seybold, were already warning that such decisions would do great damage to the software industry in the long run.[22]

Cases cited by the critics of software patents include the award to Hayes Microcomputer, the modem maker, of a patent on a program that simply switches a modem from transmit mode to receive mode. Hayes apparently now has the exclusive rights to any program that performs the same function until the year 2002. In another case, Merrill Lynch was awarded a patent on their cash management accounting system, a procedure for moving investment funds between different types of accounts. A federal district court upheld the patentability of the system, even though it accepted that the system was essentially a method of doing business. If the transactions were executable using pencil and paper, the system would not be patentable, but because it made use of a computer, the patent was upheld. The U.S. Patent Office has even awarded patents for other familiar processes, such as generating footnotes and comparing documents. And in 1992 the Patent Office awarded a patent to a company called Arrhythmia Research for the calculations its software performed to analyze electrocardiograms. This award effectively knocked down the final barriers to patenting almost any kind of software. Software developers now live in fear that they will be caught for accidentally using a process that is already patented.[23]

Regardless of widespread industry concerns, the U.S. government, through its Patent Office, is continuing to grant ever-increasing numbers of patents on software. The number of computer-related patent applications doubled between 1987 and 1990. A leading critic of this policy, attorney Brian Kahin, argues that the Patent Office is ill-equipped to make judgments on software patent applications, largely because it does not have enough patent examiners with a deep knowledge of computing. He says that the quality of many of the patents awarded has concerned lawyers and that the spread of patenting to software will place an intolerable cost burden on the software industry. This burden will hit small companies hardest and will also provide a field day for patent lawyers. Most worrying of all, the growth of patenting will slow the pace of innovation in the industry by demoralizing developers. "The software industry was not broke," writes Kahin, "but it is in the process of being 'fixed.'"[24]

What we have, then, is a situation in the United States in which three kinds of law may or may not apply to programs or even to different aspects of a program. In short, the law on intellectual property as it applies to computer software is in a mess. The irony is that while the scope for applying copyright law to software appears to have been narrowed as a result of recent court decisions, the much stronger patent law is being extended to more and more areas. It seems that the basic issues will not be sufficiently resolved until the U.S. Supreme Court makes a final ruling on the matter.

Much the same sort of legal confusion exists in most other leading nations around the world, which are still struggling with their laws in an attempt to take account of the new phenomenon of computer software. In 1985 a joint UNESCO-WIPO conference in Geneva, Switzerland, called to discuss the problem of software piracy, broke up in confusion, with the international delegates coming to no firm conclusions about how to protect programs. Since then, many countries have gone their own way with amendments to their copyright laws. For example, the United Kingdom passed the massive Copyright, Designs and Patents Act in 1988. Germany, France, Spain, Denmark, and Canada have also extended copyright protection to software in recent years.

Australia extended copyright protection to programs as early as 1984, following the case of Apple Computer v. Wombat, in which the Australian company was accused of pirating the operating systems used in Apple's chips. But in 1986, in Apple Computer v. Computer Edge, the Australian High Court held that although source code was deemed to be a literary work and therefore covered by copyright, this protection did not extend to the object code, which was not covered. This ruling created considerable dissatisfaction in the industry, and so a new review of copyright law as it applies to software was launched by the federal Attorney-General's office in 1988 and continued through 1992. In what became the most celebrated, and drawn-out Australian software copyright case, Autodesk v. Autokey Lock, the Australian High Court ruled in February 1992 in favor of Autodesk, thus effectively extending the law of copyright in Australia. The judgment had its supporters and its critics: the latter were particularly vocal in a country where consumers are forced to pay 50–70 percent more for software packages than consumers pay in the United States.[25]

Perhaps the biggest controversy over extending copyright to software occurred in Europe, where the European Community (EC) in Brussels published in 1989 a tough directive that called for complete copyright protection for all software. Critics immediately accused the EC of taking its advice almost wholly from a group of large U.S.-owned computer firms, including IBM, Digital Equipment Corporation, Apple, and Microsoft, which were represented in Brussels by SAGE (the Software Action Group Europe). Pitted against SAGE was ECIS (the European Committee for Interoperable Systems), formed by Italy's Olivetti, France's Bull, Finland's Nokia, and most other nonaligned European computer companies. A fierce battle for the hearts and minds of EC commissioners and parliamentarians ensued, the upshot being that in May 1991 the EC finally adopted a compromise software copyright directive that was much softer than the original proposal. Both sides declared themselves satisfied with the outcome, although most observers seemed to agree that the final directive had moved more in the direction of ECIS than SAGE. But the big worry was that the onset of patenting in the United States and elsewhere in the global marketplace would increase the dominance of large, established computer firms.[26]

Software Piracy and Industry Progress

What, then, is the answer to the software piracy problem? The central dilemma facing lawmakers, the IT industry, and society at large is how to adequately reward innovation without stifling the creativity that has moved the IT revolution forward. This issue is fundamental to the future of the IT industry.

Without adequate legal protection, innovatory individuals and companies might wonder whether the meager rewards for their efforts really justify the time and money expended on original R&D. On the other hand, intellectual property owners might try to stake too large a claim for their innovations in order to squelch new ideas and get the jump on their competitors. This strategy could strengthen the hand of large, established firms over small, entrepreneurial firms, which have been the traditional innovators of the industry. The key question is whether the developmental work justifies the influence innovators may gain over both users and competitors. There is a clear need to strike a balance between the competing interests of these groups as we tread the fine line between piracy and progress.[27]

Mitch Kapor, founder and former chairman of Lotus and now a director of the Electronic Frontier Foundation, argues that any ban on borrowing techniques and ideas from other software developers will strangle creativity in the software business. Tightening copyright law too much and granting patents on software will only serve to increase corporate profits. Many other programmers also argue that software developers should be free to "decompile" the object code of other people's programs—that is, to work backward to the original source—because it is the only way to pick up new programming ideas. Without such freedom, they say, progress in the industry would grind to a halt. In this respect, company programmers often find themselves at odds with company managers and their legal advisers, who are more concerned with profits than technical progress. This difference of focus is also reflected in the split between large companies and small companies on this issue.[28]

What laws, if any, should apply to software? Deborah Johnson and John Snapper rule out trade secrets as a means of protecting software on the grounds that they could apply only to research done under extreme security conditions. The publication of technical results would be restricted and employees would find that they could not change jobs with ease or freely discuss their work with other researchers. These drawbacks, they say, might point in the direction of patent or copyright protection. On the other hand, Paul Marett has argued that contractual relationships rather than copyright law may prove to be more important in the future, at least in the world of electronic publishing, and that we should think in terms of developing an entirely new field of informatics law.[29]

Anne W. Branscomb has argued that because information technology makes a product's form easy to separate from the intellectual assets that go into it, copyright law, with its focus on the expression of an idea rather than on the idea itself, is inappropriate for protecting what is valuable in the new kinds of intellectual property. This view is generally supported by Stuart Hemphill and Paul Marett. Branscomb suggests that a modified form of patent rights—or "soft patents"—with registration procedures, monopoly time limits, and rules for licensing shaped to the realities of the IT industry, may be the answer.[30]

Pamela Samuelson has made a powerful case for using patent law to protect innovation in the computer industry. She says that Whelan v. Jaslow (which, as we saw, favored protecting software by copyright law) was particularly bad news for innovators, and she rejects attempts to modify copyright law or to create new laws treating software as a special case. The existing system of patent law, she says, is still the best vehicle for protecting software. Samuelson argues, in particular, that the look and feel of user interfaces should not be protected by copyright law but by patent law primarily because "it is more consistent with legal tradition."[31]

In complete contrast to those advocating the use of laws and yet more laws to protect software, maverick Massachusetts Institute of Technology programmer Richard Stallman argues that all software should be freely available to be copied. Stallman, who founded the Free Software Foundation in 1985, puts forward a philosophical argument that all information should be free and that "the full fruits of information technology can be realized only when everyone has the freedom and ability to copy and change programs." Stallman argues that programmers should have access to the source code of programs so that they might tinker with it and improve it. Proprietary software obstructs IT progress, he says, and companies should not be allowed to keep their source code secret. He says that too many software developers are merely motivated by greed—unlike Stallman, who distributes software, such as a text editor called EMACS, free. But Stallman is fortunate in that he is financially supported in his work by groups such as the McArthur Foundation; other, more ordinary programmers have to eat.[32]

No doubt this important but complex debate will continue, and while it does, the gap between the law and individual everyday behavior in the real world will remain large and probably grow larger. When asked about their personal copying policy, individuals locate themselves somewhere on a continuum of views ranging from a hard "never copy under any circumstances" position through a soft "sometimes copy in certain circumstances" position to a completely open "copy everything" position of the kind favored by Stallman. Because copying software is so easy and so hard to detect, the issue will, in the final analysis, be determined largely by social attitudes and individual consciences. In this respect, it probably won't matter what new laws are passed. As Anne W. Branscomb has put it, "Although disputes about technology and intellectual property are usually cast in narrow legal terms, they are intimately related to public attitudes. Realistic legal rules depend upon a social consensus about what kind of behaviour is acceptable and what is not."[33] This consensus on software theft seems to be missing at present.

Busting the Pirates

Apart from legal remedies, various technical devices and administrative schemes have been proposed as possible solutions to the problem of software theft. The technical devices, sometimes called "dongles," take the form of programmed chips or electronic locks that are physically attached to a computer; in theory, only those in possession of the correct code or key are able to gain access to the protected program. But clever fraudsters have found ways to reengineer the copy locks and have sold large numbers of lock-breaking devices. Some software companies also have supplied their disks with copy protection devices that allow the disks to be copied only once. But software pirates have found ways of opening and rewriting the files to allow multiple copies to be made.

Among other proposals to cope with the problem of piracy are site-based or company-based licensing schemes, which channel royalties back to the program originators. Another suggestion is to further popularize the concept of shareware, or honorware, by which users are invited to send a donation to the authors named at the beginning of the program. Shareware has become fairly popular in recent years, though users often complain that the range of quality software available as shareware is somewhat limited. The Copyright Clearance Center of Salem, Massachusetts, which collects royalties for magazine and book publishers when their copyrighted material is duplicated by large corporations, has suggested a similar scheme for computer software. Each time a copy of a program is made, the company or the institution would send a royalty payment back to the center, which would collect a commission and pass the rest on to the software supplier.

Despite these suggestions and the efforts of organizations such as the SPA and the BSA, some software companies apparently have thrown in the towel on software copying. In particular, those pursuing the lucrative business computing market say that abandoning protection is the best protection from competitor companies. In 1985 MicroPro International gave up all pretense of protecting its programs, and Microsoft did the same with Word. In 1986 Software Publishing Corporation followed suit, saying, "If you want to get into the corporate market, they won't even look at you if you're copy-protected." Ashton-Tate decided to do likewise, claiming that new legislation around the world now strengthened the hands of software suppliers. The Washington-based Association of Data and Processing Services Organizations (ADAPSO) announced that it was dropping its plans to get software publishers to adopt a voluntary protection standard because it ran against current industry trends. And the small specialist Californian software company Cygnus Support announced that it was giving away its products for nothing, with no restrictions on their reproduction. Although its products (mostly tools for programmers) were free, Cygnus charged for tailoring its programs to customer's needs.[34]

Nevertheless, the battle against piracy seems to be meeting with more success in the 1990s. In the United States, Congress passed the Software Copyright Protection Act in late 1992. The act defines commercial software pirates as individuals who willfully copy software for commercial advantage or for private financial gain. Prison terms of up to five years and fines of up to $250,000 can be imposed on people convicted of making at least ten illegal copies of a software program held under copyright or any combination of programs worth more than $2,500. The act is thus targeted at the professional pirates and users who make multiple copies for employees or friends.[35]

The international battle against the pirates has resulted in a spectacular series of BSA-led raids in recent years in Taiwan, Singapore, Hong Kong, and other Asian nations. In Taiwan, raids in January 1990 netted more than 5,000 counterfeit packages of MS-DOS; 6,000 counterfeit MS-DOS manuals in English, French, and German; and 12,500 disks with bogus

Microsoft labels on them. If sold legitimately by Microsoft, the material would have been worth about $22.5 million. Further raids in October 1990 turned up thousands more items, including the forged holograms previously described that originally had been made in a government factory in China and had come to Taiwan via Hong Kong. In November 1991, a raid on the offices of Taiwan Hoechst found that two-thirds of the software being used on PCs was suspect.[36]

In Singapore, IBM took on six pirate companies and won a landmark victory in the Singapore courts in 1986. In the following year, international pressure—particularly from the United States and the United Kingdom—finally forced Singapore to pass a new Copyright Act, which had been five years in the drafting. It provided for huge fines and jail terms for software pirates. But the act has not put an end to the copying in this booming "little dragon" of Asia. In October 1991, for instance, a BSA-initiated raid on the home of Ong Seow Pheng uncovered a multi-million-dollar business in counterfeit Lotus, Digital, and Novell computer manuals.[37]

In the Crown Colony of Hong Kong, tough new legislation designed to tackle the piracy problem on Kowloon's Golden Mile was passed in 1988. Raids began soon after. For example, in 1989, police busted a huge mail order racket, seizing no less than 109,000 fake manuals, 6,600 bogus disks, and other counterfeit kit from a wooden hut on a remote hillside. The seized material had a total value of $50 million if sold legitimately and a street value in Hong Kong of about $8 million. Further BSA-initiated raids in Malaysia in 1991 uncovered large quantities of pirated software in three computer retailers in the city of Johore Bahru. In India in 1991 a raid on a New Delhi shop turned up 6,000 pirated packages, including the latest version of Microsoft Word, which had not yet reached the official Indian supplier. In South Korea in 1992 five software dealers were arrested after 44,000 pirated disks and 3,000 pirated manuals were seized in a police raid.[38]

Even Italy became the target of a campaign by the BSA, which claimed that organized software piracy in Italian companies was costing the industry $500 million a year. The first lawsuit, filed against Italian chemical giant Montedison, alleged that 100 out of 120 personal computers inspected at the company's Milan headquarters were using illicit copies of Lotus and Ashton-Tate programs. Montedison claimed it had permission to duplicate the software. Pirated programs also turned up at the headquarters of the Lavazza coffee company in Turin and at the Milan offices of Gelme, an alcohol and soft drink distributor.[39]

The BSA has been pursuing its worldwide pirate-busting campaign with a mixture of litigation, lobbying, and education. While it has notched up a number of notable successes with its headline-grabbing raids, its subsequent lawsuits, and its lobbying of governments to bring in new legislation, there are still whole nations such as Thailand, Japan, and China that have so far proved almost impervious to BSA and U.S. government requests that they do more about software piracy. For instance, Japan has successfully built up its huge IT industry over the past thirty years while effectively denying U.S. companies patent or copyright protection on their inventions. Even today, software piracy in Japan is estimated to cost U.S. companies $2.1 billion a year.[40]

Unless more is done to curb software copying, we are likely to see, first, a sharp decline in software production. With the erosion of the potential rewards from software development, programmers are likely to move into other, more lucrative areas of the IT industry. And fewer software producers will mean less innovative software being produced. Second, continued copying may lead to continued rises in software prices. Already, developers have to recoup the anticipated losses from copying by charging more than would be necessary if people did not copy in the first place.

But solving the problem of software theft is no simple matter. Because copying software is so easy and so widespread, the use of the law—whether copyright law, patent law, or whatever—will not in itself be enough. Nor will new technical devices do the trick, because they can usually be circumvented. Therefore, an attempt must be made to change social attitudes and individual consciences. This type of education alone will not solve the problem either, but the effort should be made.

4

Hacking and Viruses

On 27 April 1987, viewers of the Home Box Office (HBO) cable TV channel in the United States witnessed a historically significant event, variously described as the first act of high-tech terrorism or the world's most widely viewed piece of electronic graffiti. On that evening, watchers of HBO's satellite transmission of *The Falcon and the Snowman* saw their screens go blank and the following message appear:

Good Evening HBO from Captain Midnight. $12.95 a month?
No way!
(Show-time/Movie Channel, Beware!).

This transmission lasted for some four minutes. It represented a protest against HBO's decision to scramble its satellite signal so that backyard dish owners were forced to buy or hire decoders in order to view HBO's programs. More significantly—and in a most impressive way—it illustrated the vulnerability of satellites and other communications services to malicious interference.

The search for and apprehension of Captain Midnight took several months and a certain amount of luck. Investigators initially reasoned that the captain had used a commercial satellite uplink facility to overcome HBO's intended signal, but to their dismay, they discovered that there were some 2,000 such facilities. Fortunately for them, only a much smaller number (580) used the kind of character generator that Captain Midnight used to create his text message, and of these only 12 were available that night for jamming purposes. Of the remaining suitable facilities, records showed that they had all been involved in normal activities.

A breakthrough in the case did not occur until a Wisconsin tourist happened to overhear a man talking about the Captain Midnight prank while using a public telephone in Florida. The tourist reported the man's license number, and this information eventually led police to the culprit—John MacDougall, a satellite dish salesman, electronics engineer, and part-time employee at the Central Florida Teleport satellite uplink facility in Ocala. MacDougall was subsequently charged with transmitting without a license and sentenced to one year's probation and a $5,000 fine.[1]

Since the Captain Midnight episode, however, several other instances of uplink video piracy have occurred, including a November 1987 incident in which WGN-TV (Channel 9 in Chicago) was overridden for approximately 15 seconds. That same evening, WTTW (Channel 11 in Chicago) was also overridden by a ninety-second transmission, this time by man in a Max Headroom mask smacking his exposed buttocks with a fly swatter.[2] As a result of these incidents, the U.S. Congress passed a law making satellite hacking a felony, and the first person convicted under that law was Thomas M. Haynie, an employee of the Christian Broadcasting Network, who in 1987 generated a religious message on the Playboy Channel.[3]

Yet the most important aspect of the Captain Midnight hack and other similar incidents is not immediately obvious. MacDougall caused mild annoyance to a large number of viewers and probably, at worst, a severe case of embarrassment to HBO. Yet the fact that this individual was able to broadcast a particular message into the homes of thousands and to take control of a sophisticated satellite transponder demonstrates a much more significant danger. What if, instead of being an angry satellite dish salesman, MacDougall had been an international terrorist and instead of interrupting a movie, he had begun to jam the telephone, facsimile, and data communications of a number of satellites? Further, we know that satellites are directed from the ground by using radio signals to control the functioning of their small maneuvering engines. What if MacDougall or somebody else had used these signals to move the satellite into a decaying orbit or caused it to enter the orbit of another satellite—perhaps a Soviet one—many of which carry small nuclear reactors as a power source?

Even worse, if MacDougall had been an employee of a city traffic authority, could he have used his knowledge of computer systems and traffic control to completely foul up a city's traffic lights during a peak traffic period? One doesn't need much imagination to think of the consequences of such an act for a city, say, the size of Los Angeles. Not only would the traffic snarls take days to untangle, but emergency services (police, fire, ambulance, etc.) would be incapacitated. Maintenance of sewage, lighting, power, and telephones would probably come to a halt, and inevitably there would be fatalities and an enormous insurance bill stemming from the hundreds of wrecked or damaged cars and injured or ill people. More important, the security services would be hard pressed to deal with any additional terrorist acts such as a hijacking or a takeover of the city's water supply.[4]

These kinds of concerns have been echoed in a recent report by the U.S. National Academy of Sciences, which stated that the United States has been "remarkably lucky" with its computer networks and that technically proficient thieves or terrorists could subvert some of the country's most critical computer systems. According to the report, these included telecommunications networks, aviation control systems, and financial systems.[5]

What Is Hacking?

In the media, incidents such as the HBO prank are referred to as "hacking." Yet this term is not easy to define, nor is it a recent phenomenon. According to writers such as Steven Levy, author of *Hackers: Heroes of the Computer Revolution* (New York: Doubleday, 1985), the earliest hackers were students at the Massachusetts Institute of Technology (MIT) in the late 1960s. These hackers specialized in putting together pieces of telephone circuitry and tracing the wiring and switching gear of the MIT network. Next came the phone "phreaks"—epitomized by the famous Captain Crunch (John T. Draper)—who discovered that a breakfast cereal of the same name supplied a toy whistle that generated a tone identical to the one used by the U.S. telephone network to access toll-free services. Eventually, instead of blowing the whistle into a pay phone mouthpiece, Draper and other resourceful individuals developed the "blueboxes," electronic tone generators that could reproduce the full series of tones that the U.S. telephone network used in its call-routing system. With such devices, it was possible to call anywhere in the world for free. But, unfortunately, many "blueboxers" and even the ingenious Captain Crunch himself were convicted on various offenses and enjoyed several stints in jail.

According to Levy, hacking as we understand it—that is, involving the use of computers—began to emerge only with the development of time-shared systems. Hacking then spread quickly once VDTs allowed users to interact with a machine directly rather than through the remote mechanism of card-based batch processing. Yet, even then, hacking referred to a much more noble set of activities than the criminal acts that are described by the term today. Hacking was an elite art practiced by small groups of extremely gifted individuals. It generated its own set of folk heroes, huge rivalries, eccentricities, and cult rituals. But, above all, this early form of hacking was about intellectual challenge and not malicious damage. Levy portrays this period as a sort of golden era of hacking, which mainly took place at two major sites—MIT and Stanford University in California. For most hackers at this time, their chief interest lay in understanding the innards of a system down to the last chip and the last line of the operating system. The software they wrote was for public display, use, and further development and was their major source of self-esteem, challenge, and socialization.

In Levy's view, all of this began to change once huge commercial interests moved into the software industry and flexed their legal and commercial muscles. Suddenly, software was not for public use or refinement. It had become the property of those who had paid for it to be written (and who didn't always appreciate unauthorized revisions), and once this had happened, the golden age came to an end. Intellectual challenge was not enough. Like everywhere else, there was no free lunch in the world of hacking, either. Therefore, to some extent Levy indirectly blames the commercialization of software for the emergence of hacking in its criminal form. Having been introduced to the cut and thrust of the commercial world, the best and brightest may have taken on this different set of values—a set that has been augmented and made more sinister among the current crop of hackers. Then, armed with these different values and goals and empowered by the development of nationwide

Back from the Ashes: The Reemergence of Phone Hacking

In recent years, the merging of the telephone network with computer systems and private PABXs has provided hackers with easier and in some ways more tempting targets. Accessing peoples' voice mail, redirecting calls, and generally fouling up these systems is becoming more and more common.[6]

• From April 1990 the switchboard of Palomar Hospital was intermittently jammed and even disconnected by an individual armed with a common touch-tone phone. The alleged offender, Rick Ivkovich, had operators in tears as he blocked calls to and from the hospital and connected hospital operators to outside lines, including 911 emergency numbers and the county jail.[7]

• In 1991 ten students from the University of Kent, England, admitted in court to making around $1 million worth of calls from six unmodified call boxes.[8]

• Lynne Doucette and a team of seventeen break-in artists defrauded U.S. telephone companies of more than $1.6 million by using other people's credit cards and access codes. Around the same time, an independent attack was made on an office switch that redirected calls from the state parole board office to a New York phone sex line.[9]

U.S. phone companies are responding to the threat from phone hacking and credit card fraud by monitoring overseas calls for suspicious patterns, such as heavy utilization of calls to unusual destinations. If customers agree to pay for these services, the phone companies place ceilings on their liability in the event of an abuse being discovered.[10]

Big losers in PABX fraud have included New York City Human Resources Administration ($704,000), Proctor and Gamble ($300,000), Suitomo Bank ($97,000), Philadelphia Newspapers ($90,000), Tennessee Valley Authority ($65,000), and the Christian Broadcasting Network ($40,000).[11]

networks of computers (the ARPANET being the earliest of these), hackers began to break out of the confines of their local machines and to spread their interests across the United States, even using links to international networks to gain access to systems on the other side of the earth.

Yet, even today, the term "hacking" has a wide range of meanings. To some, to hack is to roughly force a program to work, generally inelegantly. For others, a hack is a clever (generally small) program or program modification that displays unusual insight into a programming language or operating system. On the other hand, any scam or clever manipulation may also be termed a hack. For example, the famous stunt-card "switcheroo" at the 1961 Rose Bowl football game is often referred to as a great hack.[12] In this context, computer viruses (a topic we address shortly) may represent a particular kind of malicious and destructive hack. Many more of us, though, tend to associate the term almost exclusively with attempts to use the telephone network to gain unauthorized access to computer systems and their data (some have preferred to call this cracking). Psychologists, sociologists, and others who concern themselves with the behavioral aspects involved view hacking as mere computer addiction. Those suffering from the malady are regarded as being socially inept and unable to form a peer group through any medium other than that provided by the remoteness and abstraction of computing.

In their book *The Hacker's Dictionary,* authors Guy Steele et al. have outlined at least seven different definitions of a hacker:

1. A person who enjoys learning the details of computer systems and how to stretch their capabilities, as opposed to most users of computers, who prefer to learn only the minimum amount necessary.
2. One who programs enthusiastically or who enjoys programming rather than just theorizing about programming.
3. A person capable of appreciating *hack value.*
4. A person who is good at programming quickly.
5. An expert on a particular program or one who frequently does work using it or on it.
6. An expert of any kind.
7. A malicious inquisitive meddler who tries to discover information by poking around. For example, a *password hacker* is one who tries, possibly by deceptive or illegal means, to discover other peoples' computer passwords. A *network hacker* is one who tries to learn about the computer network (possibly to improve it or possibly to interfere).[13]

It is beyond the scope of this book to provide an exhaustive list of definitions of hacking and their associated behaviors. While we attempt primarily to address those issues that most clearly pertain to ethics, this may involve covering incidents in all of the aforementioned categories. Hence, for our purposes, hacking is any computer-related activity that is not sanctioned or approved of by an employer or owner of a system or network. We must distinguish it, however, from software piracy and computer crime, where the primary issue is the right of information ownership and the use of computer systems to perpetrate what, in any other arena, would simply be regarded as monetary theft or fraud. To some extent, this definition is rather broad and post-hoc. Nevertheless, such a definition provides us with a rich load of cases and events that are very much at the heart of ethical issues in computing.[14]

Why Do Hackers Hack?

There are probably as many answers to the question of why hackers hack as there are different forms of hacking. Clearly, some amount of intellectual challenge may be involved. Rather like solving an elaborate crossword, guessing passwords and inventing means of bypassing file protections pose intriguing problems that some individuals will go to enormous lengths to solve.[15] In other cases, hacking involves acts of vengeance, usually by a disgruntled employee against a former employer. For others, hacking represents a lifestyle that rests upon social inadequacy among otherwise intellectually capable individuals—the so-called computer nerd syndrome, which particularly affects male adolescents between the ages of fourteen and sixteen. These individuals tend to be self-taught, enjoy intellectual games, are not sexually active, and perhaps even neglect personal hygiene.[16] Indeed, a case of "computer psychosis" has even been reported in Copenhagen, Denmark. Apparently the young man concerned became so mesmerized by his computer that he was unable to distinguish between the real world and computer programs; he talked in programming language when carrying out ordinary everyday tasks.[17]

For psychologists such as Sherry Turkle of MIT, hackers are individuals who use computers as substitutes for people because computers don't require the mutuality and complexity that human relationships tend to demand. Other researchers at Carnegie-Mellon University have provided evidence that partially supports this view: Sara Kiesler and her coworkers have investigated the social psychology of computer-mediated communication and found that this medium removes status cues (such as sitting at the head of the table), body language (nods, frowns, etc.), and provides a kind of social anonymity that changes the way people make decisions in groups. Their investigations into computer conferencing and electronic mail showed that group decision-making discussions using this medium exhibited more equal participation and a larger coverage of issues.[18]

However, despite this benefit, the limited bandwidth of the computer screen (i.e., its lack of feedback in the form of body language, etc.) often has caused users to seek substitutes for physical cues. For example, in the absence of any other (nonverbal) mechanisms to communicate their emotions, electronic mail users often substitute depictions of their face to represent how they are feeling or how their message should be interpreted. The following keyboard characters are often used to represent a smile, a wink, and a sad face respectively (view them sideways):

|:-) |;-) |:-(

Hence, the form of communication that computers require, even when communicating with other human beings, may be attractive to those who feel less competent in face-to-face settings, where the subtleties of voice, dress, mannerisms, and vocabulary are mixed in complex ways. Those who are less skilled in dealing with these sources of information therefore may retreat to more concrete and anonymous forms of interaction with a machine, while those who are limited by these communication modes attempt to extend them to incorporate more naturalistic features of communication when dealing remotely with other human beings.

In contrast to this, other commentators, such as Professor Marvin Minsky of MIT, have argued that there is nothing very special about hackers: they are simply people with a particular obsession that is no different from that of old-style "radio hams" or of those addicted to certain sports, hobbies, cars, or any other popular kind of fascination.[19]

Yet this latter view ignores a very important difference between, say, an addiction to TV sports and an addiction to computers, particularly if the latter takes a malicious form. The amount of damage the TV sports enthusiast can cause is likely to be minimal, whereas hacking in its most malicious forms retains the potential to cause massive damage and perhaps even loss of life. The hypothetical scenarios presented in the introduction to this chapter depict some quite feasible applications of malicious hacking. Indeed, the power that we invest in computer systems sets them apart from conventional systems. This capability, allied with the remote and abstract nature of computing, provides the potential for individuals to cause massive damage with little understanding of the enormity of their acts, because the consequences are not fed back to the perpetrators in any meaningful way—and especially not in any form that emphasizes human costs.

Although this fact may contradict popular stereotypes about hackers, by far the greatest amount of hacking involves very little intellectual challenge or great intellectual ability.[20] Certainly, some system penetrations or hacks display incredible ingenuity. But, for the most part, hacking relies on some basic principles: excessive determination on the part of the hacker and reliance on human fallibility. For example, when faced with a new unpenetrated system, the most common form of attack is to guess passwords, because there is an amazing lack of variation in the kinds of passwords that users choose.

In addition, many systems have guest accounts that are used for display purposes, and these often have the log-in name "guest" with the same word used as a password as well. To assist their chances of penetrating a system, hackers will often scan the waste baskets of computer centers looking for password clues, or they may attend computer exhibitions hoping to look over the shoulder of someone logging on to a remote system. The details of successful or partially successful penetrations are often listed on computer bulletin boards (electronic notice boards for posting and circulating information), and this information allows other hackers to further penetrate a system or to cooperate in exhausting the possible mechanisms for unauthorized entry.

Most hackers use only a small suite of equipment: generally a modem, a personal computer (PC), and some communications software. The modem converts digital pulses from the computer into analog (continuous) signals of the kind that the telephone network uses. Once on the telephone network, the PC is able to communicate with almost any machine that has a dial-in line—that is, a phone line that also has a modem connected to it. Once the hacker's modem has connected to the target machine's modem, both devices will convert the analog phone signals back to digital ones and allow communication to proceed. Generally, the communications software that the hacker uses provides high quality emulation of a range of popular terminal types (such as DEC's VT52 or VT100), and sometimes such packages have a number of built-in features that aid the hacker.

For example, some communications packages autodial telephone numbers within a particular numeric range. Thus, while the hackers sleep, watch TV, or whatever, their computers can target a particular region or suburb (where a large computer installation is believed to exist) by dialing all the numbers in that region until a computer is identified. Undoubtedly, a large number of these calls will be answered by humans or facsimile machines, but every so often the carrier tone of a computer's modem will be identified and the hacker can later begin work on gaining access to that system. Furthermore, if the calls are charged to a stolen credit card number or a telephone account (such numbers are freely circulated on many hacker bulletin boards), the hacker can make thousands of calls at no personal cost.

Yet, apart from guessing passwords, there are very few ways in which a hacker can penetrate a system from the outside—although the stereotyped passwords that many people use often maximize a hacker's chances of discovering a legitimate user name and password combination. Despite such flukes, most system penetrations are abetted by some form of inside assistance.

For example, a common trap in university computer laboratories is to leave a terminal switched on, waiting for an unwary user to log on to the system. In some cases, the terminal may still be running a program from the previous user that will simulate a log-on procedure, thereby capturing the user's log-on name and password. The log-on procedure will then abort with the usual failure message, and normally such users will assume that they made an error when typing in their password and will try again. Unfortunately for these users, although the terminal appeared to be idle, the program already running on it will have captured their log-on details and then shut down, so that the real system log-on procedure appears. Given the closeness of this sequence of events to very common log-on errors (everyone at some stage makes mistakes in logging on) and given some amount of naiveté, in most instances it is unlikely that many users would even suspect that they have been duped. Then, using the ill-gotten log-on name and password, the hacker can enter the system, thereby gaining full access to the data and programs of the legitimate user.

Indeed, some insider knowledge or partial access has proved to be an important part of the most spectacular break-ins that have occurred in recent years. For example, in 1986 a series of break-ins occurred at Stanford University in California. These were made possible by certain features of the UNIX operating system (one of the most popular operating systems in academic computing) as well as by the laxness of the systems programmers administering these systems.[21] The weaknesses included the networking features of certain versions of UNIX and the fact that this operating system will often allow users to log on using a guest account (usually with the same password, "guest"). Once into the first system, hackers were able to impersonate other users (again, knowing a couple of the classic weaknesses of UNIX) and gain access to other machines in the network that these same users had legitimate access to. The well-publicized hack carried out by Mathias Speer in 1988, in which he penetrated dozens of computers and networks across the world, also used many of these techniques to cross from machine to machine and from network to network.

In other cases, system and network inadequacies can sometimes be exploited to obtain access. For example, a persistent hacker sometimes can grab a line with legitimate privileges after a legitimate user has logged out. This can happen if the log-out sequence has not yet completed, so that the line the legitimate user has relinquished has not yet been hung up. If the hacker happens to log onto the system in those few microseconds, it is sometimes possible to grab the line and job of the legitimate user, who, more often than not, is preparing to walk away from the terminal.[22]

For those who are interested in further details of the techniques that hackers use, a particularly clear and comprehensive guide can be found in Hugo Cornwall's book, *Hacker's Handbook III* (Century, London, 1988). Cornwall not only provides a potted history of hacking in the United Kingdom but also describes the principles of digital communication, radio transmissions, and datastreams. Another book that had a wide impact was Bill Landreth's *Out of the Inner Circle* (Microsoft Press, Bellevue, WA, 1985). Landreth was a key figure in the legendary hacker group known as the Inner Circle. Some press articles have reported Landreth's disappearance, amid rumors that he planned to commit suicide on his twenty-second birthday and fears that others in the Inner Circle were preparing to get their revenge on Landreth because he allegedly broke their code of silence.[23]

Hackers: Criminals or Modern Robin Hoods?

The mass media has tended to sensationalize hacking while soundly condemning it. But there are other points of view: for example, in many instances the breaching of systems can provide more effective security in future, so that other (presumably less well-intentioned hackers) are prevented from causing real harm.[24] A good illustration of this was the penetration of British Telecom's electronic mail system in 1984 by Steven Gold and Robert Schifreen, who left a rude message in the Duke of Edinburgh's account. This incident attracted enormous publicity and led directly to improved security arrangements for the whole of the Prestel system. Gold and Schifreen, therefore, were extremely indignant at being treated as criminals, and their attitude illustrates once again the discrepancy between what the law considers to be criminal behavior and how hackers perceive themselves. Although Gold and Schifreen were convicted under the Forgery Act and fined £2,350, an appeal saw the charges quashed. It was argued that because the hackers had caused no damage and had not defrauded anyone, they could not be held guilty of an offense.[25]

More recently, the U.K.-based National Westminster Bank and the merchant bank S. G. Warburg met with a number of hackers to discuss arrangements for these computer experts to test the banks' security systems. Using the American idea of a "tiger team"—putting hackers in a controlled environment and pitting them against the existing security—the banks hoped to identify their weaknesses and also gain inside information from the hackers about what was happening in the hacking community and where potential threats might come from.[26]

We might ask ourselves whether, for the sake of balance, a truly democratic society should possess a core of technically gifted but recalcitrant people. Given that more and more information about individuals is now being stored on computers, often without their knowledge or consent, is it not reassuring that some citizens are able to penetrate these databases to find out what is going on? Thus, it could be argued that hackers represent one way in which we can help avoid the creation of a more centralized, even totalitarian, government. This is one scenario that hackers openly entertain. Indeed, we now know that at the time of the Chernobyl disaster, hackers from the West German Chaos Computer

Club released more information to the public about developments than did the West German government. All of this information was gained by illegal break-ins carried out in government computer installations.

Given this background and the possibility of terrorist acts becoming increasingly technologically sophisticated, perhaps we also can look to hackers as a resource to be used to foil such acts and to improve our existing security arrangements. To some extent this development is already happening: in the United States, convicted hackers are regularly approached by security and intelligence organizations with offers to join them in return for amelioration or suspension of sentence. Other hackers have used their notoriety to establish computer security firms and to turn their covertly gained knowledge to the benefit of commercial and public institutions.[27]

Perhaps we should recognize that in a fair and open society there is a tension between the capabilities of government and the capabilities of individuals and groups of concerned citizens. As the communications theorist Harold Innes stated in the 1930s, in terms of information control, there is a constant struggle between centralizing and decentralizing forces. Clearly, total centralization of information poses significant problems for the rights of individuals and for the proper conduct of a democratic government.

On the other hand, total decentralization of information resources can lead to gross inefficiencies and even to the denial of services or aberrations in the quality of services provided by government. As long as this tension exists and as long as things do not become unbalanced, we can remain reasonably assured that the society we live in and the governments we elect are fairly effective and equitable. Perhaps, with the advent of digital computers and telecommunications, hacking represents an expansion of this struggle into a different domain.

Admittedly, hacking has the potential to cause enormous harm by utilizing resources that have tremendous power. Yet we should not forget that there are other, equally powerful—and much older—ways in which similar powers can be unleashed. Leaks to the press, espionage of all kinds, and high-quality investigative journalism (such as that which uncovered Watergate and the Iran-Contra affair) have the power to break a government's control over the flow of information to the public and can even destroy corporations or governments that have been shown to be guilty of unethical or criminal acts.

Perhaps, therefore, the hallmark of a democracy is its capacity to tolerate people of all kinds, from different ethnic backgrounds, cultural beliefs, and religions, as well as those with radically opposing political views. It remains to be seen whether hacking in all its forms will be banned as a criminal offense in most modern democracies or whether some forms of it will be tolerated. From an ethical perspective, is the outlawing of hacking equivalent to criminalizing investigative journalism because journalists have been known to bribe officials or to obtain information unlawfully? As always, a balance must be struck between the ethical difficulties that are attached to activities such as investigative journalism and hacking and the greater public good that may (or may not) arise from them.

Indeed, to complete the analogy, we should bear in mind that a great deal of journalism is merely malicious muckraking that can damage a government or a company much more deeply than can some simple kinds of hacking. On the other hand, we need the muckrakers: the press is the principal institution that most democracies rely upon to ensure that the people are informed and that citizens remain aware of what is being done in their name.

The Hacker Crackdown

If any trend is evident in the world of hacking—apart from its increasing incidence—then it seems to involve the creation of stiffer penalties for hacking and a tighter legal framework classifying hacking as criminal behavior. For example, in August 1990, the United Kingdom introduced the Computer Misuse Act and identified three new offenses:

1. Unauthorized access: entry to a computer system knowing that the entry is unauthorized (six months' jail term).
2. Unauthorized access in furtherance of a more serious crime, punishable by up to five years imprisonment.
3. Unauthorized modification of computer material (viruses, trojan horses, malicious damage to files, etc.), punishable by up to five years imprisonment.[28]

The first person to be jailed under this legislation was Nicholas Whiteley (the so-called Mad Hacker). Whiteley, then a twenty-one-year-old computer operator was sentenced to a four-month jail term with a further eight-month suspended sentence.[29]

Elsewhere, similar calls for a crackdown on hacking have reached the popular press from concerned computing professionals or victims of hacking activity, and the number of prosecutions and convictions appears to be on the increase. In Pennsylvania, two men were charged with theft of service, unlawful computer use, and criminal conspiracy over the use of university computer facilities.[30] In Australia, three men are currently under investigation for their role in accessing the computers of NASA, the Smithsonian Institution, Melbourne University, and universities in the United States and Europe. As part of their hacking spree, the men allegedly accessed the computer of Clifford Stoll, the Harvard University astronomer who played a key role in tracking down a group of German hackers in search of top-secret data and files. Stoll published an account of this investigation in his book *The Cuckoo's Egg,* and the Australians apparently left a message for Stoll: "Now the cuckoo has egg on his face."[31] However, the consequences for the accused hackers could be very serious. For illegal use of Australian government computers alone, they face a possible ten-year jail sentence.[32]

In July 1992 U.S. federal agents indicted five members of the group of computer crackers known as the Masters of Disaster (MOD). The gang members—who called themselves Phiber Optic, Corrupt, Outlaw, Acid Phreak, and Scorpion—were arrested on eleven charges, including conspiracy, wire fraud, unauthorized access to computers, unauthorized possession of access devices, and interception of electronic communications. In sum, the charges allege that the group broke into telephone switching computers of several Bell systems and engaged in phone phreaking and computer tampering. It is alleged that the defendants gained access to Bell Tymenet computers and intercepted data communications on a network owned by the Bank of America. In addition, it is alleged that the gang accessed credit reporting services such as TRW, Trans Union, and Information America.[33]

Hacker cooperation seems unaffected by distance. In one noteworthy case, an eighteen-year-old Israeli and a twenty-four-year-old man from

Colorado jointly penetrated NASA and U.S. Defence Department computers during the Desert Storm Gulf war operation. Of even greater interest than the distance involved was the sophistication of the Israeli teenager's phone phreaking equipment and the evidence of his involvement in an international credit card forgery ring.[34]

In mid 1991 Scotland Yard announced that it had cracked the world's largest (a term they left undefined) computer hacking ring. Karl Strickland, an eighteen-year-old computer programmer from Liverpool; Neil Woods, twenty-three and unemployed; and Paul Bedworth, a seventeen-year-old student from Yorkshire, were charged under the Computer Misuse Act with offenses in at least nine countries that included making financially devastating alterations to computers at Edinburgh, Lancaster, Bath, London, Strathclyde, and Oxford universities. Scotland Yard revealed that the investigation involved eight police forces and a surveillance team from British Telecom and that it cost U.K. and European companies millions of pounds.[35]

But perhaps the clearest indication of a new hard-line approach to hacking occurred in 1990 when U.S. Secret Service agents instigated a national computer fraud investigation known as Operation Sundevil. This operation involved 150 agents simultaneously executing 28 search warrants on 16 U.S. citizens and the seizure of 42 computer systems, including 23,000 computer disks.[36] However, by mid 1991 it became clear that the operation had produced only one indictment as a result of a combination of lack of evidence and lack of the high-tech savvy needed for present gumshoe law enforcement officers to find such evidence.[37] Two of the most publicized victims of Operation Sundevil included Craig Neidorf and Steve Jackson of Steve Jackson Games, both of whom had systems and computer-related property seized by the Secret Service as a result of various charges involving wire fraud, computer fraud, and interstate transportation of stolen property. Eventually Neidorf stood trial but was acquitted, although he was forced to bear the $100,000 in costs incurred in making his defence.[38]

Yet, in contrast to these growing demands to bring hackers to account, a number of commentators have argued that these law enforcement efforts are misplaced. The threat from hackers, they argue, is overblown, and the major threat to computer installations remains what it always has been—not outside intruders, but inside employees.[39] Sociologist

Worms, Trojan Horses, and Bombs

New terms are entering the nomenclature of computing, many of them borrowed from other domains and many of them with sinister connotations. The following definitions may assist the reader in identifying the differences and similarities among some of these terms.

Trojan Horse A program that allows access to an already-penetrated system—for example, by establishing a new account with superuser privileges. This tactic helps avoid overuse of the system manager's (superuser) account, which may show up on system statistics. It can also refer to a program that gathers the log-ins and passwords of legitimate users so that those who already have penetrated a system can log in under a wider variety of accounts. Sometimes confused with a "trap door," which is generally a secret entry that system designers build into their systems so that once they have left, they may gain access at any time without fear of discovery. The principle of the Trojan horse relies upon successful penetration and creation of alternative entry paths.

Logic Bomb or Time Bomb A program that is triggered to act upon detecting a certain sequence of events or after a particular period of time has elapsed. For example, a popular form of logic bomb monitors employment files and initiates system damage (such as erasure of hard disks or secret corruption of key programs) once the programmer's employment has been terminated. A simple variation on the theme is a logic bomb virus—that is, a virus that begins to replicate and destroy a system once triggered by a time lapse, a set of preprogrammed conditions coming into existence, or remote control using the appropriate password.

Virus A self-replicating program that causes damage—generally hard disk erasure or file corruption—and infects other programs, floppy disks, or hard disks by copying itself onto them (particularly onto components of the operating system or boot sectors of a disk). Viruses use a variety of strategies to avoid detection. Some are harmless, merely informing users that their systems have been infected without destroying components of the systems. Most are not benign, and identification of their creators can be virtually impossible, although some have been quite prepared to identify themselves.

Vaccine or Disinfectant A program that searches for viruses and notifies the user that a form of virus has been detected in the system. Some are general-purpose programs that search for a wide range of viruses, while others are more restricted and are capable only of identifying a particular virus type. Some are capable of eradicating the virus, but there are relatively few such programs. Other forms of virus protection include isolation of the infected system(s), use of nonwritable system disks so that viruses cannot copy themselves there, and trying out unknown software (particularly public domain software downloaded from bulletin boards) on a minimal, isolated system.

Worm   A self-replicating program that infects idle workstations or terminals on a network. The earliest worms were exploratory programs that
demonstrated the concept itself and were generally not destructive, although they often replicated to the point at which a network would
collapse. The latter phenomenon was used to good effect as the basis of
the science fiction book, *Shockwave Rider* by John Brunner (Ballantine,
New York, 1975). Worms tend to exist in memory and are not permanent,
whereas viruses tend to reside on disk where they are permanent until
eradicated. In addition, worms are network-oriented, with segments of the
worm inhabiting different machines and being cognizant of the existence
of other segments in other nodes of the network. Worms actively seek out
idle machines and retreat when machine load increases. Viruses (at present)
have none of these capabilities.

Tempest   A term that refers to the electronic emissions that computers
generate as they work. With the right equipment, these transmissions can
be monitored, stored, and analyzed to help discover what the computer is
doing. As would be expected, most security agencies throughout the world
are interested in this phenomenon, but up to now it has not been the
mechanism for any known hack. But given time, who knows?

Richard Hollinger argues that hackers are simply the easiest target:
isolated individuals pitted against massive corporate and government
interests forced into a judicial system that finds it difficult to understand
the offense, let alone make judgments on it. Yet, faced with the need to
be seen to be doing something against the tide of "computer related
criminal activities," law enforcement officials find hackers easy, high-
profile targets compared to the hidden, often forgiven, or paid off inside
computer criminals.[40]

The Virus Invasion

Software viruses are the most recent computer phenomenon to hit the
headlines. Hardly a day goes by without reports of new viruses or
accounts of a virus attacks that have resulted in the destruction of data
and the shutdown of networks.

   Yet the concept of a virus is not altogether new. Its precursor—the
worm—was created in the early 1980s, when computer scientists John
Schoch and Jon Hupp devised a program that would spread from machine to machine, steadily occupying the idle resources of the Xerox Palo

Alto Research Center's network.[41] These early worms were fairly harmless and were released only at night when network traffic was low and the machines were unlikely to be used in any case. Whatever maliciousness was embedded in worm-type programs lay in their tendency to consume resources—particularly memory—until a system or network collapsed. Nevertheless, worms almost never caused any permanent damage. To rid a machine or network of a worm, all one had to do was to restart the machine or reboot the network.

The conceptualization and development of viruses had a longer gestation period. Other precursors to the virus included a number of experimental computer games, including the game program known as Core Wars.[42] This game operates by setting aside an area of machine memory (which in the earliest days of computing was often called the core) as a battleground for programs to compete for territory and to attempt to destroy each other. In order to understand how Core Wars works and its relationship to the virus concept, we need to understand a little about the structure and nature of computer memory and Core Wars programs themselves.

To begin with, computer memory can be regarded as a series of pigeonholes or boxes in which an instruction, some data, or another memory address can be located. The following schematics represent a typical Core Wars battle:

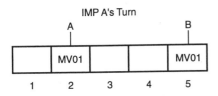

The letters A and B identify the location of the two combatants. The contents of address 2 in the preceding schematic is a machine code instruction that is a Core Wars program called IMP. Address 5 also contains an IMP program—the first IMP's adversary. (There are many kinds of Core Wars programs; IMP is among the simplest, but also one of the most powerful.) The battle proceeds like this: it is IMP A's turn and its program is executed; MV01 (the IMP program) means "move the contents of an address that is 0 addresses away (that is, the current address, address 2) into an address that is 1 address away" (that is, address 3). Essentially, this instruction copies the contents of address 2 (the IMP program) to address 3. In other words, IMP A has replicated itself.

When this has been done and it is IMP B's turn, IMP A has copied itself to address 3 and IMP B moves to address 4 (by executing its own program). This state of affairs is represented below:

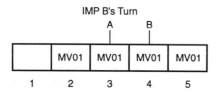

When it is IMP A's turn again, it already occupies address 3 (as well as its prior addresses), while IMP B occupies addresses 4 and 5. On IMP A's second turn (which we need not show here), it copies itself into address 4 (again by executing its MV01 instruction) which is where the current IMP B resides. Hence, by overwriting IMP B, IMP A has won this battle.

The bulk of Core Wars programs (and battles) are not this simple. Many of the more complex programs have facilities for repairing themselves, for totally relocating themselves in memory (i.e., evading enemy programs), and can even detect the approach of other programs by having sentinels. What is most important about Core Wars, however, and indeed this whole genre of game programs, such as the games LIFE and Wa-Tor (both games that demonstrate the evolution of "life forms" in a computer-generated environment), is their common notion of reproduction in a computer-based system.

This concept of a program reproducing itself began to fascinate many people and, in particular, the notion that a program could spread itself beyond the boundaries of a single machine or network attracted a growing interest. The acknowledged originators of the virus concept were Fred Cohen and Len Adleman (who conceived of the term *virus*). At a computer security conference sponsored by the International Federation of

Information Processing (IFIP) in 1984, they publicly announced the results of a range of experiments they had conducted using viruses to infect a range of different networks and host machines.[43] Their experiments showed how easily isolated machines and even whole networks could succumb to simple viral forms. In fact, their experiments were so successful that they often were banned from carrying out further experiments by the administrators of various systems. Yet, despite this and other public warnings of the future threat of software viruses, the first viral epidemics took much of the computing world by surprise.[44]

By far the most obvious (and common) way to virally infect a system is to piggyback a virus onto bona fide programs so that it can be transported on storage media such as tapes, floppy disks, and hard disks. In addition, a virus can be transported via network links and electronic mail. So long as the virus either appears to be a legitimate program or is capable of attaching itself to legitimate programs (such as the operating system), then its spread to other system users and countries can be almost assured. It should be noted, though, that although most of the current crop of viruses is maliciously destructive, a number of viruses have been released that are quite harmless; these usually inform the user that the virus has only occupied a few bytes of disk space. More common viruses tend to erase the entire contents of a user's hard disk or else corrupt programs and data to the point where they are irretrievably damaged and quite useless.

Perhaps the most widely reported virus attack occurred in October 1987, when large numbers of microcomputer users throughout the United States began to report problems with their data disks. A quick inspection of the volume labels of these disks (a volume label is a user-supplied name for the disk—such as "cash flow figures") showed that they all possessed the same volume label: "© Brain." For these reasons, the identified virus is often referred to as the Brain virus or as the Pakistani Brain virus after the authors' Pakistan address, which is revealed if the boot sector of the disk is inspected. Although this virus caused some loss, procedures were soon implemented that effectively eliminated the virus. These included using only system disks that were write-protected so that the virus could not copy itself from one system disk to another, as well as programs that identified an infected disk and rewrote the boot sector so that the virus was destroyed.[45]

Shortly before Thanksgiving 1987, a further virus was discovered at Lehigh University in Bethlehem, Pasadena (and hence called the Lehigh virus). This virus appeared to be particularly malicious in that it totally destroyed a disk's contents once the disk had been copied four times. Unlike the Brain virus, which spread when an infected disk was totally copied, the Lehigh virus was much more virulent and intelligent. Once it had infected a disk, this virus checked all other disks inserted into the machine. If they were bootable (that is, if they carried a copy of the operating system on them), the virus then checked whether the disk was already infected; if it wasn't, the virus copied itself onto the new disk. Fortunately, the same kinds of countermeasures that were effective against the Brain virus were also effective against the Lehigh virus, and it now appears to have been eradicated.[46]

And in yet another incident, Israeli PCs showed signs of viral infection in December 1987, when programs that had been run thousands of times without incident suddenly became too large to fit within available memory. This virus, which was disassembled by computer scientists at the Hebrew University of Jerusalem, exhibited a somewhat different modus operandi. It appeared to work by copying itself into memory and then attaching itself to any other program that the user might subsequently execute. The author of this virus also had been clever enough to program the virus so that it exhibited different effects over several months (almost a form of time bomb). In 1988 the virus would wait thirty minutes after the machine had been booted up, then it would slow the machine down by a factor of around five, and portions of the screen would be uncontrollably scrolled. More important, though, if the date was Friday the 13th (any Friday the 13th after 1987), any program that was executed was erased from the disk. It was soon found that the virus was extremely widespread in both the Jerusalem and Haifa areas, with an estimated infection base of between 10,000 and 20,000 disks. But, once again, antiviral software was written to identify infected files and kill the virus, while another program was written to act as a sentinel, warning users if an attempt had been made to infect their disks.[47]

Since the late 1980s hundreds of viruses have been created and have caused varying amounts of damage around the world. In 1990 it was even reported that 10 percent of the computers in China had been affected by only three strains of virus.[48] Now internationally recognized virus guru John McAfee has placed the number of different viruses at more than 1,200, with 10 to 15 new strains being found each week.[49] And perhaps the worst offenders are former Eastern Bloc programmers; some Russian experts estimate that there are 300–400 Russian strains alone.[50] Many of these viruses are variations on a theme in the sense that they rely on well-understood techniques for propagating themselves and infecting systems. However, new vaccine techniques are constantly being developed, and the vaccine development industry becomes more lucrative every year as its software products attempt to immunize systems from large-scale data loss to the annoying refrains of Barry Manilow hits. Yes, the Barry Manilow virus plays "Mandy" and "Copacabana" in endless succession![51]

Unfortunately, not all self-replicating software is so innocuous. In November 1988, a twenty-three-year-old Cornell University computer science student, Robert Morris, devised a worm program that crippled the network connecting MIT, the RAND Corporation, NASA's Ames Research Center, and other American universities. This virus was said to have spread to 6,000 machines before being detected. In June 1989 Morris was suspended from college after having been found guilty of violating the university's code of academic integrity. The FBI also carried a six-month investigation into this remarkable virus attack, and Morris was later charged under the Computer Fraud and Abuse Act of 1986 with unauthorized access to government computers.[52]

Eventually, Morris was convicted, sentenced to four hundred hours of community service, and also fined $10,000.[53] But despite the fate of Morris, other Cornell students since have been accused of using computer viruses to cause malicious damage. For example, in February 1992 sophomores David Blumenthal and Mark Pilgrim were accused of implanting infected game programs into a Stanford University public computer archive.[54]

Conceptually speaking, it is possible for viruses and worms to achieve much more sophisticated disruption than the cases reported so far, and it is quite likely that the next generation of software viruses will exhibit a quantum jump in intelligence and destructiveness. For example, it might be possible to develop a virus that only affects a particular user on a particular network. In other words, given sufficient technical expertise, instead of affecting all users, the virus would wait until a particular user ID executed an infected program. Then the virus would copy itself into the disk area of that user and begin to wreak havoc.

Alternatively, viruses may have a range of effects that they carry out on a random schedule, such as slowing a system down, deleting electronic mail, fuzzing the screen (which almost certainly would be attributed to a hardware problem), and encrypting files with a randomly selected encryption key (this would effectively deny users access to their own files until the key was discovered—an almost impossible task). Such strategies would delay the identification of a viral infection for an extended period, because the set of symptoms would be large and extremely variable.

At least one recent virus appears to use such a strategy. The Twelve Nasty Tricks virus generates a random number to determine which of twelve different actions to take. Its repertoire includes a low-level format of a PC's hard disk, reversing upper and lower characters in print output, eliminating the printers' line feed, blanking out the monitor, and affecting the computer's clock.[55]

Even more worrying is the fact that commercially distributed software has been contaminated by viruses. In one well-publicized case, desktop publishing specialist Aldus shipped several thousand shrink-wrapped disks that were infected with the Peace virus.[56] The concern generated by the advent of increasingly sophisticated and powerful viruses has prompted some notable members of the computing community to call for new computers to be fitted with antiviral protection (both in software and hardware) as a standard feature.[57]

The next generation of viruses probably will be more selective, not only in whom they act upon and in the acts they carry out, but also in their objectives. This prospect raises a number of interesting questions and hypothetical scenarios. For example, could viruses be used for espionage purposes, not only infiltrating an enemy's machines to delete their files but gathering intelligence data that would be mailed back (electronically) or eventually gathered as versions of the virus filter back to the virus authors? Could viruses become another facet of military capabilities in much the same way that research into cryptography currently is? (A science fiction book has encapsulated this theme. *Softwar: La Guerre Douce* by French authors Thierry Breton and Denis Beneich depicts this scenario in pre-Glasnost days.) Given the remarkable swiftness with which new viruses appear to spread around the world, their potential uses as a weapon should not be underestimated.[58]

Such speculation seems to have some foundation from reports emerging out of the Gulf war. Citing a new book, *Triumph without Victory: The Unreported History of the Persian Gulf War*, U.S. *News and World Report* writer Philip R. Karn claimed that U.S. intelligence agents placed a virus in one of the microchips used in a model of printer and shipped it to Baghdad via Amman—apparently with devastating effects.[59] Other reports indicate that the United States Army is very interested in the possibilities of computer viruses and has even awarded a $50,000 preliminary study to a company known as Software and Electrical Engineering.[60]

Some other developments also suggest that virus warfare is not mere speculation. Already, the analogy of a computer system as an organism and a virus as an infection has been extended to incorporate the development of virus-killing programs called *vaccines*. These programs look for virus symptoms and notify users that their systems have been infected. Some of the better vaccines seek out the virus and kill it by repairing infected files. Furthermore, just as we would expect to eliminate a virus in humans by the use of quarantine procedures, when dealing with infected systems and media these procedures work equally well.

But for many virus attacks the only solution—provided that a vaccine doesn't work—is to erase the hard disk as well as any other media (tapes, floppy disks) that might have come into contact with the virus (almost like burning linen and other possibly infected items). Then, clean copies of the system and backup disks are reloaded onto the hard disk. Until this is done, the computer should not be used for any other purpose and the trading of storage media is extremely unwise.

Yet perhaps the best form of defense against viruses is to make them much more difficult to write. Some experts have argued that the way to do this is to place the operating system on a read-only disk or in ROM (read-only memory composed of chips, which cannot be altered and hence infected). Other procedures include carrying out parity checks on software (basically an arithmetic calculation, such as an addition, on a file; if the calculation yields the correct result, it is unlikely that the file has been tampered with); making each copy of an operating system different in its physical layout (that is, its pattern of storage on disk); and, whenever one uses a disk for the first time, making sure that the operating system on disk matches that in memory.[61]

Because of the risks that virus attacks pose to the knowledge assets of large companies and corporations, and because of their lack of experience in dealing with them, a number of security firms and consulting companies have sprung up to exploit this rich commercial niche.[62] Furthermore, the development of hardware forms of viruses has fueled the demand for such firms, particularly since the discovery of the device known as Big Red. This small electronic gadget is surreptitiously installed in a computer installation by an insider or commercial saboteur. Like software viruses, this device is parasitic in that it interfaces with the host computer's operating system and converts encrypted files into "invisible" ones that can be inspected easily by other users, if they know where the files are and what to look for. At least fifty Big Reds have been found in the United States, the United Kingdom, and Australia in banking and transaction-handling systems.[63]

Unfortunately, like system penetrations and computer crimes, it is often difficult to gather data on the incidence of virus attacks because these may have important consequences for share prices and investor confidence. However, a recent survey of 600 U.S. and Canadian companies and government agencies revealed that 63 percent of them had experienced at least one virus in 1991, compared to only 25 percent in 1990. Furthermore, 40 percent of these institutions had at least one virus incident in the last quarter of 1991, with networks being the most common form of propagation.[64] Other independent surveys by Coopers & Lybrand Deloitte suggest that of the top 500 U.K. companies, 24 percent had suffered a virus attack in the last three years.[65] The U.S. National Security Agency has revealed that two-thirds of the companies it surveyed had reported at least one virus in their computers and that 10 percent of the 600 government agencies and businesses it polled had experienced an attack sufficient to shut down twenty-five or more computers.[66]

But perhaps even more worrying is the effect that viruses may have on large, extremely complex, and potentially dangerous systems, such as those that manage air traffic control systems, hydroelectric dams, and nuclear plants. Already at least one nuclear power plant has been affected by the introduction of a computer virus. In early 1992 an employee of the atomic power plant in Ignalina, Lithuania, infected his system in the hope that he would be paid handsomely to fix the damage. As a result of the incident, both reactors were shut down and the Swedish government announced that it would pay to correct the twenty "small problems" that had emerged.[67]

Other potentially life-threatening virus attacks include infections in three Michigan hospitals that delayed patient diagnosis and threatened data loss and even a mix-up of patient records.[68] And like any powerful technology, viruses have been used by the mentally unbalanced to cause monumental harm. Perhaps the most serious case involved Dr. Joseph Popp, an AIDS researcher who had worked in Africa for ten years, who distributed 20,000 infected computer disks labeled "AIDS Information" to organizations obtained from an AIDS-related mailing list. Unfortunately, Popp's mental state deteriorated to such an extent that he was unable to stand trial for his offenses.[69] These and other incidents have prompted calls for both preventive measures and highly responsive emergency teams who can act quickly to limit the viral damage caused to sensitive systems. One example of this is the U.S. Defense Department's initiative in creating Computer Emergency Response Teams (CERTs) to fight viruses and other computer-based security threats.[70]

Ethical Issues Arising from Hacking

Some of the ethical difficulties associated with hacking and viruses are already quite well known, while other, more hypothetical, ones have yet to emerge. With regard to hacking or system penetration, the legal position in different countries is often confusing and is sometimes contradictory. But the central issues involved in hacking remain almost universal.

When a hacker gains access to a system and rummages around in a company's files without altering anything, what damage has been caused? Has the hacker simply stolen a few cents worth of electricity? Indeed, if the hacker informs a company of its lax security procedures, is he or she creating a public benefit by performing a service that the company otherwise might have to pay for? In some countries, such as Canada, it is not an offense to walk into somebody's residence, look around, and leave, as long as nothing has been altered or damaged. Can a hacker's walk through a system be considered in similar terms?

Unfortunately, the legal basis applied to system break-ins languishes in the dark ages of real locks and doors and physical forms of information such as blueprints and contracts. Equally, the law as it applies to breaking and entering—the destruction of physical locks—and the theft of information in paper form is a poor analogy when applied to the electronic locks that modems and password systems provide and the highly mutable forms of information that computer files represent. After all, when one breaks into a system, nothing has been broken at all; hence, there is no obvious intent to cause harm. When a file has been copied or selectively viewed, what has been stolen? The information is still there. And if one happens to try out a few programs while browsing through a system, is this almost analogous to seeing someone's bicycle, riding it for a while, and then putting it back? Again, what harm has been caused, what crime has been committed? In the eyes of many hackers, only in the most trivial sense could this kind of use be considered unlawful.

On the other hand, where malicious damage of information does occur (such as the destruction of patients' records in a health administration system), then a form of criminal act clearly has occurred. The problem lies in determining the extent of the damage and the degree to which the act was premeditated. Unfortunately, in a complex and perhaps poorly understood computer system, it is quite easy to cause unintentional damage, yet it is extremely difficult to determine the extent to which the act was maliciously premeditated. In addition, for those figuring out a system for the first time, it is difficult to estimate the consequences of some acts or the extent to which a command sequence may alter the functionality of a system. Is this an example of ignorance of the law and is it equally unacceptable as a defense?

Perhaps what is central to the ethical debate regarding hacker behavior is the different conceptualizations of systems by their owners and by would-be hackers. For system owners, the system is their property (as suggested by the legal framework)—physical, touchable collections of central processors and disk drives—bought, paid for, and maintained for the use of authorized individuals to carry out authorized functions for the company's benefit. Any unauthorized person or even an authorized person who uses the system for unauthorized purposes is therefore guilty of a form of unlawful use—a criminal act in the eyes of the owners. For hackers, however, a system is an abstract resource at the end of a telephone line. It is a challenging talisman, an instrument they can borrow for a while and then return, probably without any damage done and without anybody being the wiser.

We enter a different arena, however, when we encounter acts of theft and willful damage. Clearly, the theft of credit card numbers and their circulation to other hackers are criminal acts, as is their use to obtain free telephone calls or to charge other goods and services. The destruction of information or its intentional alteration on a computer system can be regarded in similar terms. Yet, to return to our earlier point, should we regard browsing through a system as a criminal act? Perhaps the answer depends upon the nature of the information and who owns it. Undoubtedly, the operators of a military installation would prosecute over any unauthorized access, even if the system were concerned with the control of the army's laundry requirements. The government and the military have the right to deny access to certain information if they believe that it is central to the nation's defense or to its continued good government. Yet, is a laundry service central to national security or good government? Once again, we encounter a very familiar dilemma: who owns this information and who should or shouldn't have access to it?

In the private sector, we might even ask, What right does a company have to hold information on individuals and what right does it have to deny individuals access to that information? For example, many commercial institutions tap into databases that hold the credit ratings of hundreds of thousands of people. The providers of these databases have collected information from a huge range of sources and organized it so that it constitutes a history and an assessment of our trustworthiness as debtors. Who gave these companies the right to gather such information? Who gave them the right to sell it (which they do, along with subscription lists, names, and addresses)? What limits are there on the consequences of this information for the quality of our lives? What rights should we have to ensure that our particulars are correct? Suppose that a hacker penetrates a system to correct the records of those who have been denied correction of incorrect data. Which of these entities—the database owners or the hacker—has committed the greatest ethical error? Or are both equally guilty?

Perhaps the final issue is that concerning information ownership: Should information about me be owned by me? Or should I, as a database operator, own any information that I have paid to have gathered and stored? On the other hand, given that the storage of information is so pervasive and that the functioning of our modern society relies upon computer-based data storage, does the public have the right to demand absolute security in these systems? Finally, should some hackers be regarded as our unofficial investigative journalists—finding out who holds what information on whom and for what purpose; checking whether corporations are adhering to the data protection laws; and exposing flagrant abuses that the government cannot or will not terminate?

Many organizations in modern society claim to possess rights to the gathering and maintenance of information and its application in the form of computer-based information systems. In addition, apart from the dangers of the centralization of government power and authority, the centralization of information in powerful computer systems increases their influence in running our societies and, in turn, makes us more reliant upon them, thereby increasing their influence even further. In this milieux, the hacker represents a dangerous threat. Yet, like the corporations and institutions hackers act against, they also claim certain rights in terms of information access and ownership.

For many commentators, these issues should be resolved in the legal domain by determining the rights and responsibilities of information holders and the legal status of information and information systems. But such an approach may be too limited. Hacker activities can be deterred not only by punitive legislation but by making systems secure in the first place; that is, by making them secure in their design, in their technological implementation, and in the procedures and practices that are used in running them. And, in turn, that protection also implies inculcating security habits among employees and system managers.

There is an important role for ethics education in clearly identifying unethical practices and areas of ethical conflict. Unfortunately, the abstract nature of computing often removes it from its real-life consequences, and what appears to some to be an innocent act can cause untold harm if it goes wrong. By increasing the sensitivity of computing professionals and students to the ethical implications of their conduct, the amount of hacking might be reduced. This three-pronged approach of revising existing laws, building and running more secure systems, and sensitizing individuals to ethical issues has been advocated in more recent writings by Peter Denning and other authorities.[71] Even representatives of IBM have spoken of the limitations of technical measures against hacking and viruses and have suggested that the greatest gains might be made in simply convincing people that high-tech high-jinks are wrong.[72]

5
Unreliable Computers

The Titanic Effect: The severity with which a system fails is directly proportional to the intensity of the designer's belief that it cannot.

In 1992 a British hospital spokesperson admitted that, over a ten-year period, almost 1,000 cancer patients had been given radiation therapy that was up to 30 percent below the proper dosages because of an undetected programming error. The 989 patients treated at the hospital in Stoke-on-Trent were undergoing therapy for cancer of the bladder, pelvis, lung, and throat. They were undertreated because some computer software contained an unnecessary correction factor. Although officials denied that the error had a "deleterious effect," only 447 of the 989 patients treated were still alive. Such apparent confidence seemed somewhat misplaced given the poor survival rate.[1]

In another well-known incident, computer error led to the overdosing of patients undergoing radiation treatment. This happened when two computerized Therac-25 X-ray machines malfunctioned over a period of several months, killing one person, badly burning others, and leaving yet others with partial paralysis.[2] The malfunctions occurred in 1985 and 1986 at the East Texas Cancer Center in Tyler, Texas, and at the Kennestone Regional Oncology Center in Marietta, Galveston. A subtle software error caused some body areas to receive between 17,000 and 25,000 rads, when research has shown that doses as low as 1,000 rads delivered to the whole body can be fatal. Typical therapeutic doses to small areas of the body range from between 4,000 and 6,000 rads delivered in twenty or thirty treatments over a month or more.[3]

Many Information Systems Are Failures

Although these therapeutic calamities are alarming and the loss of life deplorable, they are relatively trivial compared to the potential risks we incur by entrusting complex tasks and heavy responsibilities to computer systems in many other applications. For instance, computer systems in one form or another are now indispensable in air traffic control, medicine, nuclear power stations, toxic chemical plants, spacecraft, missiles, ships, tanks, and other weapons systems, as well as in the maintenance of our financial systems, stock markets, and communications services. Even in these often life-critical applications, it is apparent that the reliability of computer systems is less than what we would hope. In many instances, "system failure" is really a euphemism for disaster and/or substantial loss of life.

Computer scientist Peter Mellor defines reliability in a computer system as the probability that it will not fail during a given period of operation under given conditions. For example, measures of reliability can include the number of failures per unit of operating time and the expected length of time that a system will operate without failing. Like many computer scientists, he advocates the application of statistical principles to software quality so that, for example, it may be more acceptable to have many infrequent bugs than a small number of very frequent ones.[4] However, systems can fail not only in operation but at various stages in their design and development.

Indeed, failures in computer system development and use are not just commonplace: more often than not, they are the rule. According to one U.S. survey, an astonishing 75 percent of all system development undertaken is either never completed or not used even if it is completed.[5] Some writers have identified a crisis in system development that is demonstrated by the finding that 70 percent of the work on software projects is generally directed to maintenance after the system has been verified and commissioned for use.[6] Other figures seem to confirm this: a study by the U.S. government's General Accounting Office showed that, of nine federal software projects that cost a total $6.8 million, projects worth $3.2 million (47 percent of the total by value) were delivered but not used, $2.0 million worth were paid for but not delivered, $1.3 million worth were abandoned or reworked, and just $200,000 worth were used after substantial modification. Incredibly, just one project worth less than $100,000 was used as delivered by the developer.[7] Recent reports from Logica and Price Waterhouse have also indicated that poor software quality costs the United Kingdom about $900 million per year.[8] A more extensive study of Fortune 1000 companies in 1991 by the research corporation FIND-SVP of New York estimated that computer downtime costs U.S. businesses some $4 billion a year.[9]

Even more worrying than the level of unreliability in existing systems is the growing number that never make it into service—despite millions of dollars spent in development costs. In 1992 American Airlines canceled a new airline, hotel, and car reservation system after spending $109 million on its development. The United Kingdom's Wessex Regional Health Authority spent £43 million on a system that never worked and was finally scrapped in 1990. Even smaller systems, such as Philadelphia's Finance Department system, had to be scrapped after four years of development and $4 million in costs. In Australia, the Westpac Banking Corporation sank more than $100 million into an abortive system called CS90. Yet this loss pales into insignificance beside the comprehensive failure of the U.S. Defense Department's Advanced Logistics System at a cost of $217 million.[10] Given these illustrations, one wonders how many more large-scale development failures have been covered up by anxious boards and shareholders. What proportion of the $450 billion projected to be spent worldwide on software development in 1995 will end up as money down the drain?[11]

When complex systems do manage to establish good performance records, occasional failures can still be catastrophic because of our dependence on them. For instance, the failure of a single postal banking center in Sendai, Japan, affected 1,200 post offices, 1,300 automatic teller machines, and 3,000 transaction machines used by counter clerks.[12] On 15 January 1990, the AT&T long distance network suffered a nationwide blockage on long distance calls for eleven hours. Ironically, a new recovery algorithm caused telephone exchanges to crash in a chain reaction across the network.[13] And on 5 September 1992, five British Telecom exchanges crashed, leaving thousands of subscribers without service for up to eight hours.[14]

Yet unreliability in operation is not the only point of failure for complex computer systems. Systems can fail at a number of levels, from the failure to meet the users' requirements to massive budget blow-outs and lack of use by the system's eventual purchasers. An extended discussion of the different types of failures and their underlying causes is beyond the scope of this book, but the interested reader can pursue these issues further in the literature available on this topic.[15] Nevertheless, even without such preparation, much can be gained from a casual survey of some classic system failures, since many ethics-relevant issues can be found here.

For example, in October 1960, computers of the Ballistic Missile Early Warning System at Thule initiated a nuclear alert after the rise of the moon above the horizon was interpreted as a nuclear attack.[16] In other cases involving this same system, a flock of geese was thought to be a group of inbound nuclear missiles, and in June 1980, within the space of four days, a faulty multiplexer chip at NORAD twice scrambled B-52 bombers and simulated most of the initial characteristics of a nuclear attack.[17]

More recently, in the Persian Gulf, a U.S. guided missile cruiser, the USS *Vincennes,* shot down an Iranian Airbus and caused the loss of 290 civilian lives. As a result, much criticism was leveled at the capabilities of the Aegis fleet defense system—the constellation of radar, computers, and missiles that carried out the attack. However, the record shows that the Aegis system had been soundly condemned by its critics long before it was installed on U.S. Navy ships at a cost of around $1.2 billion per unit. Both Mary Kaldor and defense journalists James Coates and Michael Kilian had pointed out that Aegis passed its capability trials by being deployed in a New Jersey cornfield.[18] Yet one would not unreasonably think that a dry agricultural plot would bear little resemblance to a naval environment, with its inclement weather, rolling swells, corrosive conditions, and temperature extremes.

Aegis is a battle management system for the coordinated defense of U.S. Navy battle groups. It is designed to track hundreds of airborne objects in a 300-kilometer radius and to allocate sufficient weapons to simultaneously destroy up to twenty targets with its array of missiles. The system integrates phased-array radars (a quantum improvement on the rotating mechanical radars we normally visualize) with complex software that matches potential targets with a threat library, assesses threat values, and assigns weapons systems accordingly. Although Aegis is designed to deal with up to twenty targets simultaneously, its first operational test in April 1983 showed that, even when presented with only three targets at a time, Aegis failed to shoot down six out of seventeen targets because of software failures.[19]

It is difficult to determine how much of the Airbus tragedy can be attributed to computer error or to human error (or a combination of both). Indeed, given present security arrangements the full story may never be known. Nevertheless, it is disturbing to note that a system such as Aegis can have such a checkered development history, be subjected to suspect testing and validation procedures, and finally figure in a major aviation mix-up resulting in huge loss of life. As many commentators have noted, if Aegis cannot discriminate between a civilian airliner and a modern fighter plane at a range of twelve miles (well within visual range), then what chance does it have in more complex scenarios where discrimination must be much finer? More recent analyses of the Iranian Airbus incident have shown that deficiencies in the human interface of the Aegis system were significant contributory factors to the disaster. Replays of the system's tapes show that the A-320 was on schedule and on course, but the manner in which the system displayed information was inadequate in the context of a time-critical, highly charged combat-decision scenario.[20]

Another controversial shoot-down incident involved the performance of U.S. Patriot missile systems against Iraqi Scud ballistic missiles in the Persian Gulf war. Despite the U.S. Army's self-congratulatory declaration that the Patriot was a resounding success (an 80 percent success rate was claimed), civilian reanalysis of the videotapes showed that Patriots killed a mere 10 percent of the eighty Scud warheads. The situation was complicated by the fact that many of the Scuds broke up on reentering the atmosphere and created unintended radar decoys that helped to confuse the Patriots. In some cases, the intercepting missiles missed their targets by up to a kilometer. In addition, the Patriot system was designed to shoot down aircraft—not incoming ballistic missiles travelling at Mach 4 at very steep angles of approach—and it was never intended to be left running continuously for days at a stretch. However, because of the need to protect the Allied air bases, Patriot crews were forced to do this, and the internal clock of the systems drifted, thereby contributing to the inaccuracy of the interceptions.[21]

An interesting aside to the Patriot's wandering clock problem is its deep hardware history. The timing hardware was developed in the 1960s using a twenty-four-bit digital clock that was thought to be more than adequate for the task at hand. However, the limitations of the twenty-four-bit register meant that the clock would drift from real time by about a third of a second every hundred hours of operation. On 25 February 1991, a Patriot battery on the outskirts of Dhahran, Saudi Arabia, had been operational for more than 100 hours without being shut down to resynchronize the clock: the missile's resulting clock error was sufficient to miss the Scud by five hundred meters and allow the Iraqi weapon to impact and kill twenty-eight U.S. servicemen.[22]

Even in less critical applications, old hardware and software still abounds, making it difficult for vendors to provide upgrades compatible with ancient but important pieces of software and hardware. This problem further erodes the reliability of computer systems, as patchworks of old and new code run on both modern work stations and monolithic mainframes connected by gleaming new fiber optic networks.

Military case studies such as the Patriot missile provide rich sources of information on computer unreliability, but system failures can occur in all areas of society and can involve most aspects of our lives. Even a humble fishing boat can fall prey to computer foul-ups. For example, in August 1992, a huge fish-processing ship, the *Dona Karen Marie,* was attempting to dock in Seattle when it began listing to the left. After an engineer came to fix the problem, the ship leveled, then listed to the right—straight into the United Marine Marketing dry dock. A computer controlling the ballast pumps simply swooshed water from one side to the other, and for several weeks the vessel sat, four stories high at a thirty-degree angle, while engineers figured out what had gone wrong.[23]

When a Crash Really Can Be a Crash

Since 1982 twenty-two U.S. servicemen have died in five separate crashes of the U.S. Air Force's sophisticated UH-60 Blackhawk utility helicopter. On each occasion the machines either have spun out of control or nose-dived into the ground. Yet it was only in November 1987, after this series of mysterious crashes had been thoroughly investigated, that air force officials finally admitted that the UH-60 was inherently susceptible to radio interference in its computer-based fly-by-wire control system and that modifications to the aircraft would be needed.[24]

Similar fly-by-wire systems exist in the European A320 Airbus as well as other modern airplanes. Essentially, fly-by-wire systems work by eliminating the mechanical linkages between the pilots' controls and the control surfaces on the wings and the tailplane (or, in the case of helicopters, the main rotor and the tail rotor). In other words, a pilot's analog control movements on the joystick or control column are converted to digital pulses that, in turn, drive servo motors and other power systems that move the ailerons, rudder, and elevators. In effect, pilots in these aircraft no longer have a physical link connecting their controls with the control surfaces. Instead, onboard computers interpret control movements and relay this interpretation to the activating units.

In the case of the Blackhawk, inadequate shielding in some of the logic modules involved in the fly-by-wire system allowed electronic smog in the form of microwave and other radio transmissions to affect the onboard computer system. Because of this, the computer would sometimes send spurious signals to the hydraulic system, thereby bringing about an uncontrollable nose-dive.

Similar fears are held over an effect known as HERO (hazards of electromagnetic radiation to ordnance). The problem is that the modern electronic battlefield generates so many electronic emissions that electronically detonated munitions (aircraft ejector seats, flare canisters, bomb ejector racks, artillery rounds) can be accidentally detonated. These emissions can even interfere with aircraft controls, thereby putting the craft into unintentional maneuvers. HERO has been blamed for at least twenty-five accidents and the loss of a U.S. aircraft in the 1986 air raid on Tripoli, Libya. In that raid, many unintended bomb hits were registered, while at least seven of the surviving thirty-two aircraft were unable to deliver their bombs—mainly because of the electronic blizzard that U.S. jammers and radars generated.[25]

In the civilian world, when aviation computers such as air traffic control systems fail, they too can cause widespread problems. For example, on Saturday, 6 August 1988, one of the busiest days of the year, Heathrow airport, London, was due to handle 830 takeoffs and landings, but the air traffic control system failed. Despite the employment of seventy full-time specialists to keep the computer running and to update its software, in the twelve months to April 1988 there were five similar software failures.[26] And, of course, Heathrow's situation is not unique: its computers use a traffic control system known as the National Airspace Package, which consists of around a million lines of program code that took approximately 1,600 worker-years to write and 500 worker-years to further develop. Yet despite this massive amount of effort, which was made more complicated by the system's conversion from U.S. air traffic control requirements to British ones, the system's performance is far from satisfactory.

An even more potentially dangerous failure occurred on 23 August 1987, when the National Air Traffic Services' Oceanic Centre at Prestwick in Scotland found that their Flight Processing System, the computer that controls the bulk of transatlantic flights, had crashed. It was the ninth serious breakdown of the system, which had experienced minor failures every other day since its commission earlier in the year. The new computer system is totally electronic and does not make provision for the printed cardboard strips that controllers like to use as a manual backup procedure. The system crashed at 11:30 A.M., and by midafternoon Heathrow, Paris, Frankfurt, Zurich, and other major European airports had begun to run out of parking space for delayed aircraft, many with passengers onboard. The Oceanic controllers were forced to telephone nearby air traffic control centers to discover which airliners had been handed over to which facilities and to find out which aircraft were still supposedly under their control. A senior controller was reported as saying, "They wonder why we have so little confidence in our top management when they give us tools like this—aeroplanes have to have duplicated or even triplicated systems as backup, but the same safety rules clearly do not apply to our equipment. These continual failures are the basic ingredients of a mid-air disaster."[27]

In August 1992, it was revealed that an $810 million program to install updated radar systems at Canada's major airports had been stalled by stubborn software bugs. The system had crashed repeatedly in tests and in use. Controllers in Montreal, for example, were left without radar for fifteen minutes. In addition to other problems, the software exchanges the radar identification tags whenever two aircraft are in close proximity and even shows jets flying backward.[28] Other reports from O'Hare International Airport in Chicago indicate that their radar systems began malfunctioning for several months in late 1991. Planes disappeared off the screens while ghost images appeared and disappeared for between two and fifteen seconds.[29] Controllers also reported double images— thought to be partly caused by the emissions of the new Traffic Alert Collision Avoidance System (T-CAS), an initiative designed to prevent midair collisions. Already, though, the T-CAS system appears to be proving itself; it prevented a collision between three passenger jets near Midway airport in October 1991 after an error by air traffic controllers.[30]

Other examples from the world of aviation show how reliant humans become upon automation when it is provided. A good example happened on 11 August 1987, when a Concorde landed at JFK International airport and blew five tires. Two engines were later replaced because of fears that they had ingested debris from the runway, but the main cause was the pilot's reliance on the antiskid braking system that was not operational on the secondary hydraulic system. The primary hydraulic system had failed, and it appears the pilots assumed the secondary system also had the antiskid feature.[31] An even more fascinating illustration of humans blindly relying on computers occurred when two RAF Tornado fighters collided in August 1988 over the village of Millburn in Cumbria, England. Incredibly, both aircraft—from different airfields—had loaded the same preprogrammed inertial guidance tape into their computers so that they arrived at the same point from opposite directions.[32]

Banking Blunders

Other system failures, although perhaps less threatening to human life, illustrate the extent to which the lifeblood of our economies—cash and capital—have become controlled by complex systems that border on the limits of our understanding.

A good illustration is what happened on the morning of Thursday, 20 November 1985, when more than 32,000 government securities trans- actions were waiting to be processed at the Bank of New York, New York. At 10 A.M., the bank's computer systems began to corrupt these transactions by overwriting records. As a consequence, it was impossible for the bank to determine which customers should be charged for which securities and for what amount. Meanwhile, the New York Federal Reserve Bank continued to deliver securities to the Bank of New York and to debit its cash account. At the close of business that day, the bank was $32 billion overdrawn with the Federal Reserve, and despite half-successful efforts to patch up the program, by 1:30 A.M. the next day the Bank of New York was still overdrawn by some $23.4 billion. Frantically, the bank borrowed to help cover its deficit, using its total asset base as collateral. By late Friday morning, the software had been fixed and processing restarted. However, this fiasco cost the bank $5 million in interest for its overnight loans, and it also shattered dealer confidence. As has been noted by Hopcroft and Krafft, it was fortunate that an error of this sort did not coincide with the October 1987 Wall Street crash, because the drain on the Federal Reserve and the effect on investor confidence could have been even more disastrous.[33]

A similarly incredible case occurred in the appropriately named British system known as CHAPS. These CHAPS (clearing house automated payment system), it seems, were very generous in that they accidentally transferred £2 billion (more than $3 billion) in just over thirty minutes. The error was due to a software flaw that allowed the clearing house system to choose its own payment dates. CHAPS has fourteen member banks, including the Bank of England, and funds transferred on the system are guaranteed payments that are technically irretrievable. Yet even if the funds were fully retrieved (at last report they weren't), the daily interest bill on the lost funds would be more than $1 million per day.[34]

Despite these frightening foul-ups, the financial systems of the world are charging headlong into vast communications networks with high levels of computer control and automation. In June 1992 Reuters and the two major Chicago commodities exchanges launched a system called Globex, a twenty-four-hour electronic trading system for futures and option contracts. Eventually it and similar systems will be able to handle stocks, bonds, and any other trades, virtually eliminating the need for trading floors in New York and other financial capitals. Much of the pressure forcing these developments comes from competitors; others would gladly take the ball into their court and develop twenty-four-hour exchanges if they had the know-how and the capital to do so.

However, these developments are not without their critics. The shock of the 1987 crash is still reverberating, especially with the growing acknowledgment of the role of programmed trading and computerized stop-loss loss orders in generating a chain reaction of selling. Instantaneous electronic trading on a global scale could eliminate even the weekend and overnight trading closures that acted as partial circuit breakers in the 1987 collapse. And the absence of human intervention and judgment could create a system so volatile that minor computer glitches could be interpreted as bad news, sending stock prices plummeting or surging to unrealistic and dangerous heights.

Already the computerized Toronto Stock Exchange (TSE) has experienced a major breakdown. In March 1992 a software problem scrambled information, recorded wildly inaccurate stock prices, and failed to print tickets to confirm trades. In solving these problems, TSE consultants face the familiar problem of dealing with a patchwork of different software and hardware, with no idea of what was done by the creators of the system eight years ago. As investment expert Albert Sindlinger puts it, "If the past is any indication of what computers will do to markets in the future, then we may all be in big trouble."[35]

More Great Software Disasters

If one has a black sense of humor, then case studies of software problems can be a definite source of amusement—such as the inertial guidance system of the F-16 fighter that, in simulation, caused the aircraft to become inverted whenever it crossed the Equator or the loss of the twelfth F/A-18 prototype when its software refused its pilot the control authority he needed to recover from a spin. In another military incident, an F/A-18 attempted to launch a wing-tip-mounted missile, but although the weapons system ignited the missile correctly, it closed the restraining clamp on the wingtip before the missile had generated sufficient thrust to move. Thus the pilot found an extra three-thousand pounds of thrust on one wingtip and was about to eject after dropping 20,000 feet when control was finally recovered.[36] Then there was the case of former President Reagan's E-4B aircraft (a modified 747), whose electronic emissions were alleged to have closed thousands of remotely controlled garage doors in California whenever it operated from March Air Force Base, about ten miles south of San Bernadino.[37]

However, it would be a mistake to assume that computer failures only occur in supersophisticated military or aerospace applications. As digital technology infiltrates almost all aspects of our lives, even the humble automobile, our involvement in mystifying technological failure becomes more common. The Audi 5000 was a case in point. At least 250 incidents involving this car—including two deaths—cast suspicion upon its computer-controlled systems. Essentially, the problem appeared to lie in the idle stabilizer, which was responsible for ensuring a minimum fuel flow to the engine when the brakes were applied. In one case, a boy was opening a garage door for his mother when she applied the brake and shifted the automatic transmission into forward gear. The car then accelerated rapidly, punching the boy through the garage door and crushing him against the rear wall. The rate of acceleration was so great that a large skid mark was left behind, and even after impact the wheels continued to spin at high speed.

Despite Audi's dismissal of the problem, a group of owners allegedly was able to demonstrate that the accelerator pedal moved downward when the car was placed into gear. Yet in March 1989, a U.S. National Highway Traffic Safety Administration (NHTSA) report ruled out mechanical defects as the cause of sudden acceleration in Audis and other cars. The NHTSA said that the most likely cause was drivers' stepping on the gas pedal instead of the brakes. However, some safety experts disagreed with the report's findings, and Audi increased its reserve for U.S. liability claims to $105 million.

In other well-known foul-ups, the loss of the *Mariner 18* space probe was found to be due to a one-line error in a crucial program, while the *Gemini V* capsule splashed down one hundred miles off target because the programmers who wrote the inertial guidance system failed to take into account the rotation of the earth around the sun. The U.S. Navy has also admitted that during an exercise off San Francisco, a computer glitch caused a guided missile frigate's three-inch guns to fire a shell in the opposite direction from that intended. The shell missed a merchant ship by about nine miles.[38]

To illustrate the fact that even a nation's best minds can be defeated by computer-based system failures, the *San Francisco Chronicle* of 13 September 1988 reported that the $115 million Stanford Linear Collider (a huge device for studying elementary particle physics) had to be shut down after several months of work had failed to make it run properly. Basically, the problem was that, despite the efforts of a hundred scientists and technicians, the system was so complex that it proved impossible to keep enough of its components or computers working long enough to get any results. No wonder that the U.S. House of Representatives recently baulked at the $8.3 billion price tag for more atom-smashing research.[39]

The U.S.S.R. also suffered from software snafus in space. In 1988, the *Phobos I* spacecraft was lost after Soviet ground controllers reprogrammed the craft by beaming up a twenty- to thirty-page message. Unfortunately, the program contained an error that caused the vehicle to point its solar panels in the wrong direction—away from the sun—and eventually the spacecraft lost power and was abandoned. A similar problem cost the Soviets a major space victory when their *Mars 1* space probe failed to leave earth orbit and was renamed *Cosmos-419*. The probe was originally designed to be Mars's first artificial satellite and was intended to beat the *Mariner-9* vehicle to the red planet because of its lighter weight and consequent speed. However, programmers entered an incorrect code into its onboard computer that left it stranded in orbit around the earth.[40]

Software failures aren't limited to exotic systems. They happen to ordinary people doing ordinary things. In 1980 a man undergoing microwave arthritis therapy was killed when the therapy reprogrammed his pacemaker. It also has been reported that another man was severely affected when his pacemaker was reprogrammed by interference from an antitheft device in a store. He subsequently died as a result of the trauma.[41] In other computer-related medical incidents, an infusion pump for insulin had a software problem that caused insulin or dextrose to be delivered at incorrect rates; a reprogrammable pacemaker locked up in a doctor's office while it was being reset by an external programming device, but luckily, the patient was revived; and a patient monitoring system was recalled after it was discovered that it incorrectly matched patients' names and data.[42]

But perhaps the biggest health-related foul-up of recent years was the collapse of London's computerized ambulance dispatch system. On 26 October 1992 the system went live without manual backup, despite repeated problems when it had been introduced in northeast London earlier in the year. After the system received 2,900 emergency calls—600 more than on a normal day—it sent several ambulances to the same request, diverting them from other emergencies. Following a thirty-six-hour breakdown, health service unions claimed that in ten to twenty cases people may have died because of delays in ambulances reaching them. One involved a two-year-old child who went into convulsions and another a boy of fourteen who died from an asthma attack. At least one nonfatal case had to wait eleven hours before an ambulance arrived. All of this resulted in the forced resignation of the chief of the London Ambulance Service.[43]

Not only can software inadequacies have a detrimental effect on the health of individuals, it may one day be accepted that one particular software problem affected the health and lifestyle of every person on earth. Limitations in the programs on NASA observation satellites used during the 1970s and 1980s caused these programs to reject the ozone readings they were registering at the time. Because the readings were so low, they were regarded as spurious. In other words, deviations from established normal levels were so extreme that they were assumed to be errors. Only after British scientists using ground-based instruments reported a decline in ozone levels did NASA scientists reprocess data going back to 1979 and confirm the British findings.[44]

Computer foul-ups have been known to severely reduce the quality of life of individuals. For example, in an article in *The Los Angeles Times* of 24 May 1986, an individual by the name of Foreman Brown provided a testimonial that was both amusing and horrifying:

I first became aware of my death last May when my checks began to bounce. Never having experienced bouncing checks before, and knowing that I had quite a respectable balance at the bank, I was both shocked and angry. When I examined the returned checks and found, stamped over my signature on each of them, in red ink, "Deceased," I was mystified. Then, when one of the recipients of my checks, a utility company, demanded that I appear in person, cash in hand, plus $10 for their trouble—*their* trouble—I was shocked, angry and mystified. I wondered just how they expected us deceased to acquiesce.

Eventually, Brown went to the bank to inquire but received little in the way of explanation except that it was somehow the computer's fault. Next month, his Social Security payment was not credited to his account: it appeared that the problem with the bank had affected the Social Security system as well. Even after it appeared that the mess had been sorted out, Brown reported that his physician was unable to bill Medi-

Warranties and Disclaimers

Given the incidence of faulty software and of system failure in general, perhaps it is not surprising that software developers rarely provide their clients or purchasers with warranties of any substance. Indeed, if one compares this situation with that of almost any other form of purchased goods, it is difficult not to be amused and perhaps even incredulous. While refrigerators, cars, washing machines, and computer hardware are sold with worthwhile guarantees of quality and workmanship, the same cannot be said of software. The following disclaimers provide a clear picture of the faith (or lack thereof) that software developers have in the products that they produce and market:

Cosmotronic Software Unlimited Inc. does not warrant the functions contained in the program will meet your requirements or that the operation of the program will be uninterrupted or error-free.

However, Cosmotronic Software Unlimited Inc. warrants the diskette(s) on which the program is furnished to be of black color and square shape under normal use for a period of ninety (90) days from the date of purchase

Note: In no event will Cosmotronic Software Unlimited Inc. or its distributors and their dealers be liable to you for any damages, including any lost profit, lost savings, lost patience or other incidental or consequential damage.

We don't claim Interactive EasyFlow is good for anything—if you think it is, great, but it's up to you to decide. If Interactive EasyFlow doesn't work: tough. If you lose a million because Interactive EasyFlow messes up, it's you that's out of the million, not us. If you don't like this disclaimer: tough. We reserve the right to do the absolute minimum provided by law, up to and including nothing.

This is basically the same disclaimer that comes with all software packages, but ours is in plain English and theirs is in legalese.

We didn't really want to include a disclaimer at all, but our lawyers insisted. We tried to ignore them, but they threatened us with the shark attack at which point we relented.[45]

Another extraordinary aspect of software marketing is the fact that the user generally pays for software updates. In other words, even if the product is faulty or needs amendment, the user pays the software supplier to provide more correct versions.

care because Medicare's computers indicated that the service was performed six months after the patient had deceased.

This example shows how an individuals' rights and privacy can be violated and how extensive our reliance on computer systems really is. However, it is also a very useful illustration of how tightly coupled or interdependent our systems are: a bank's mistake feeds into the Social Security network and eventually into medical insurance systems. Even more noteworthy, however, is how resistant these systems are to correction and how persistent problems remain even after they have been identified. Although it is unclear in the Brown case whether the root of the error lay in inadequate software or in operator error, the fact that a number of sophisticated systems did not independently verify the date, location, or cause of the alleged death indicates that their design and operational procedures were grossly inadequate.

Why Are Complex Systems So Unreliable?

The issue of computer unreliability and its disastrous consequences begs several questions, most of which have ethical aspects to them. Some of these questions are, Why can't we build computer systems with the same inherent reliability that we find in other designed artifacts such as bridges and buildings? Why isn't software guaranteed in the same way that other purchased goods are? Why does so much shoddy software exist and how can so much of it appear in important systems? Should we entrust responsibility for the conduct of nuclear war, the control of massive energy sources, and even national (and international) economies to computer systems that are less than totally reliable?

The answers to such questions highlight the present plight of computer professionals and the realistic role they may be expected to play in the development of reliable computer systems. In other words, the ethical dimensions of computer reliability are to some extent bound up with the nature of computers and software and the complexity of such systems. To a large degree, the behavior of existing complex systems is at the outer edge of our intellectual understanding, so that our ability to know or predict all the possible states (including error states) that a system might take is severely restricted.

A quick calculation provides some powerful support for this assertion. For example, suppose that a system is designed to monitor 100 binary signals in order to determine the performance of a particular industrial complex—say, a nuclear power station. This amount of monitoring certainly is not excessive given the huge numbers of values, pressure pumps, and switches that must be used to keep the behavior of such systems within tolerable limits. Given these 100 different signal sources, there are 2^{100} or 1.27×10^{30} possible combinations of signal inputs. The path that such a program follows depends upon the combinations of signals it receives in any given time period (signal values might be read or updated, say, every few milliseconds). That is, if a particular combination of signals is registered, a particular part of the program will be executed, while other, different parts of the program may be executed for other input patterns. Given the large number of such subroutines in a program of this scale, there may be at least 10,000 (10^4) or more possible paths through it. Thus, the system can exist in at least 1.27×10^{34} possible states, any one of which could cause the software to fail or return information that is wrong.

If one wanted to empirically test such a program to identify incorrect states and then to correct them, and if one could do this automatically at a rate of, say, 100 per second (which is, incidentally, far beyond present capabilities), then the software testers would need some 4×10^{24} years to exhaustively test the array of possible states that this piece of software might conceivably take. Unfortunately, such a figure is many times the life of the universe.[46] Furthermore, some of these states will involve error recovery subroutines (modules that have been designed to identify errors and overcome them), and for testing, these subroutines generally are triggered by modifying the program to simulate an error state. However, these modifications in themselves can create new bugs. Indeed, Adams has estimated that 15 to 20 percent of attempts to remove program errors tend to introduce one or more new errors.[47]

To rub even more salt into the wound, it is now accepted that for programs with between 100,000 and 2 million lines of code, the chances of introducing a severe error during the correction of original errors is so large that only a small fraction of the original errors should be corrected. In other words, it is sometimes better to be aware of an error and to work around it by informing users of particular circumstances that will trigger it rather than take the chance of creating even more bugs by tampering with the program.[48] As a result, honest programmers generally admit that it is impossible for them to write a program for nontrivial software that they can guarantee to be bug-free. This principle is even more true of sophisticated software such as compilers and operating systems. The software on board the space shuttle, for example, contains 25,600,000 lines of code and required 22,096 man-years to develop at a cost of $1.2 billion. Even Citibank's automatic tellers contain 780,000 lines of code, not to mention the common IBM checkout scanner with 90,000.[49]

It is only when we consider safety-critical systems, however, that the enormity of the software reliability problem becomes apparent. Recently, a number of concerns have been raised about the adequacy of the systems controlling nuclear power stations and industrial plants. In 1990 a computer software error released thousands of gallons of radioactive water at the Bruce nuclear power station. British Nuclear Fuels admitted in 1991 that the software controlling its Sellafield reprocessing plant had around 2,400 faults in its first versions and that a software error had accidentally opened radiation safety doors while highly radioactive material was still inside. Finally, there have been calls for the scrapping of the software running Britain's Sizewell B nuclear reactor because the software is too complex.[50]

So what does all this imply? Because of these realities, are programmers free of obligation in the event of a substantial system failure? If such a system (say a robot) kills someone, is the programmer a murderer? If a patient dies on an operating table because software running the life support equipment fails, is the programmer guilty of manslaughter or malpractice? Would providing a disclaimer or informing the surgeon of potential configurations that could cause problems excuse the programmer? Or is the programmer guilty simply for providing a system that (both theoretically and practically) could not be guaranteed for application in a life-critical situation? After all, if a manufacturer of heart pacemakers knowingly supplied defective equipment, surely it would be required to answer in court.

These issues involve the area of software engineering, which is, if you like, computer science's attempt to answer the problem of reliability by developing new intellectual tools for the design and development of software. At this stage, too, it is probably helpful if we abandon the distinction between hardware and software because, in many instances, the line dividing them is already very gray. Software becomes hardware when it is burned into read-only memories (ROMs), and is "firmware" when it is encoded as electronically erasable reprogrammable ROMs (EEPROMs). Moreover, although the interaction of problems at the physical level of hardware (voltage spikes, short circuits, cracked joints, poor connections, overheating, etc.) combines with those at the abstract level of software to produce problems that are greater (and more interesting) than the sum of either of these parts, it is essentially the abstract nature of software and the intellectual problems we have in dealing with it that provides us with most difficulty.

What Are Computer Scientists Doing about It?

We have been fairly critical of software engineers and the systems they create. It would be unfair of us, however, if we did not present their side of the story and the peculiar circumstances they find themselves in when designing the abstract artifacts that are computer systems.

It would also be irresponsible if we did not take account of the environments that software engineers must work in. A noteworthy case in this regard is the apparent persecution of Sylvia Robins, who began work on the space shuttle program as a software engineer shortly after the *Challenger* disaster. This employment involved working with Unisys and Rockwell on the software for the onboard flight management system—an experience that since has caused her to sue these companies for $5.2 million in damages for wrongful dismissal and harassment. Robins claims that the software controlling the shuttle was never properly checked and, indeed, was untestable, with modifications not properly verified and not even documented. Her efforts to remedy this lapse led to intimidation and harassment that eventually brought about her physical collapse and dismissal from her job.

The Robins case illustrates that software engineers often can fall prey to the pressures of a commercial environment that may force them to skimp in applying rigorous methods to their software. Yet, as we shall see, these same methods have severe limitations as well, many of which stem from the nature of digital computers and binary logic.

Essentially, digital computers are discrete state devices—that is, they use digital (binary) representations of data (in memory, on tape, or on disk or other media) and instructions (i.e., a program)—so that a computer program can effectively exist in literally millions or even billions of different states. Thus, every change in a variable's value (and some programs contain thousands of variables with thousands of possible values) effectively alters the system's state. Every input or output, disk access, print request, modem connection, or calculation (indeed, anything that the system can engage in) alters the state in which the system exists. Multiply all of these and other relevant factors (time of day, load on system, combination of jobs in progress, etc.) by each other and you have effectively calculated the number of possible states of the system. Our earlier example illustrated the difficulty of exhaustively testing the correctness of all such states, even for programs of modest size. For most complex systems, it is impractical to list all of the possible variables that may cause a state change, and even if it were possible to calculate, the number describing the total set of states generally would be so large that it would be on the verge of meaninglessness.

The problem with finite state machines such as digital computers is that each of these states represents a potential error point. Unlike an analog system such as a simple thermostat or bimetallic strip, these states are discrete: you are either in a particular state or you are in another state. Analog systems in contrast have an infinite number of states—they are continuous—in that, say, a bimetallic strip used in a thermostat can take on an infinite number of positions within a certain range, just as a ruler has an infinite number of points. The real difference, however, is that while the continuous movement of the bimetallic strip is unlikely to fail catastrophically, our discrete state machine on the other hand can fail catastrophically because the execution of each state depends on the previous state being correct or achieving the computational goal that the programmer hopes to achieve. If the previous state is not correct or even prevents the next instruction from being executed, then the program will malfunction. When the program stops or behaves erratically, this failure is referred to as a *discontinuity*—a departure from what was otherwise predictable behavior (and the mathematics that describes digital computers is referred to as discontinuous mathematics).

In general, analog systems like thermostats or a tuning knob on a radio tend to have few or no discontinuities. In other words, it is unlikely that you will ever encounter a situation in which they will be working perfectly and then reach a point where they behave aberrantly or fail totally. Analog systems do not depend upon the correctness of the previous state; indeed, states have little direct relationship to their functioning. These systems can best be described by continuous functions or curves, and these curves have a great deal of predictability embedded within them. For example, we can follow the performance curve of an analog device and predict how it will function at particular levels. Essentially, this is how we construct buildings. We know the properties of steel and other materials because they, too, can be mostly described by continuous functions. Steel, for example, will take increasing loads and exhibit stress in an extremely predictable way until it reaches the point at which it fails. These mathematical tools help us to make very accurate predictions about the behavior of analog systems and, what is more, we can build a "fudge factor" or safety margin into our computations and predictions so that the resultant design is overengineered for robustness.

With large discrete state systems, however, and even in quite simple ones, this is not the case. A simple analog system such as a thermostat may not function correctly—it may change too quickly or too slowly, for example—but it rarely will fail totally unless it suffers a very obvious fault such as a loss of power or breakage of a component. A computer program performing the same function, on the other hand, could quite easily fail catastrophically and in a surprisingly large variety of ways. In such a system, in order to measure temperature values, a device known as an analog-to-digital converter converts the room's temperature value at a particular time into a numeric value. This numeric value is then compared to the required temperature and depending upon whether the actual temperature value is high or low or about right, an instruction is sent to the heating unit to turn on, turn off, or remain as it is. In achieving this, a large number of states will be executed according to the algorithm or procedure that the programmer has devised to achieve the task, and each state represents a potential point at which the program could stop or begin to behave unpredictably. Finding the particular state that caused such a problem can take some time because of the sheer number of states. The conditions that existed at the time of the problem (which is essentially the error state) have to be replicated so that the error can manifest itself again and be identified.

Our discussion up to this point may appear to paint a rather grim picture of digital computation, yet a moment's thought should convince us that its weakness is also its source of strength. With digital representation, we can represent almost anything from, say, a real-time graphic simulation of aircraft flight to a 3-D map of Mars. Indeed, it is conceivable that we could take a photograph of deep space, digitize it, apply some mathematical formula that would convert its digital form into an appropriate range of musical notes, and play the resultant music—or we could even use the data to drive a laser beam in the production of a hologram. This is the essence of digital computation: the ability to represent abstract or physical qualities and to manipulate them in powerful ways. It is also the reason why we are able to understand and manipulate theories and environments that are beyond our immediate perception or that are so abstract that they can have no physical analogs. For these reasons, despite the obvious difficulties we have in building reliable, complex systems, digital computation cannot be discarded, even if it were possible for us to physically run the world without machines of this kind. Indeed, much of software engineering in its most modern forms concerns itself with methods and techniques for making software more reliable, useful, and trustworthy. Most of this work can be grouped around a number of rubrics.

The first area of structured programming stems from criticisms of the spaghetti-like code that programmers tended to produce using the earliest high-level languages, such as FORTRAN and COBOL. More recent languages, by their design, impose structure and modularity as well as information hiding, so that individual programmers on a large project need not concentrate on minute details that are more properly the concern of the project manager or those overseeing the production of the software. Other languages such as Ada—a much-touted solution to the software problems of the U.S. Defense Department—are much more restrictive: by limiting the freedom of the programmer, they help to limit improper coding practices. This drive to produce more powerful, usable programming languages still continues, but some critics are doubtful that it will produce improvements of the magnitude needed in software engineering if reliable programs are to be produced regularly.

A more recent development in devising better programs is object-oriented programming, or OOP. The essential advantage of OOP is its use of greater abstraction in creating programs and program elements. That is, by defining certain properties that different parts of a program inherit, it is possible to construct new objects that share well-defined and well-behaved properties. For example, in creating, say, aircraft instruments, we know that most of them will share certain properties such as a round dial, calibration of the dial in some units, hands to indicate a reading, and so on. By predefining these properties and including them as needed in new instruments, a great deal of drudgery has been eliminated, a better conceptual handle has been created for the programmer, and the structure of the software is clearer because a huge amount of detail has been sidelined into objects that are logically separate. In addition, large-scale modification is easier to carry out for these same reasons.[51]

A second research domain lies in the area of program verification and derivation. This field is concerned with mathematical techniques for proving programs correct once they have been written (verification) or showing programs to be correct in the process of building them (derivation). Unfortunately, these techniques are not yet able to handle programs even of modest size, let alone those demanded by most commercial applications or by megaprojects such as the Strategic Defense Initiative.[52] Furthermore, even the most correct of programs still can be shown to be unsatisfactory or even useless if it fails to meet the needs of the individual user or organization. No mathematical technique can tell us if we have encapsulated the users' needs adequately or indeed if we have probed deeply enough to discover what they are.

Another partial answer to the problems of software engineering lies in the development of programming environments. These essentially are operating systems and collections of software tools that aid programmers by providing flexible and powerful ways of managing much of the complexity of software development. Hence, environments such as UNIX provide powerful facilities for managing different program versions, updating all files affected by a modification, sophisticated bug identification, and so on. Yet, again, although these environments are a significant advance in handling the drudgery and complexity of software development, they, too, do not approach the magnitude of the improvements that are required if software is to meet the standards of reliability that we have come to expect in other areas of engineering.

A fourth solution lies in extensive and very expensive debugging, quality control testing, and product proving. For example, the latest version of the popular Lotus 1-2-3 spreadsheet program required 263 man-years to develop, and Lotus spent an additional $15 million testing the software on a huge range of PC compatibles.[53] However, as noted earlier, exhaustive testing of large programs (even this microcomputer program has 400,000 lines of code) cannot eliminate all bugs because of the sheer combinational complexities involved. There is always the chance of new bugs appearing.

One report claims that a particular computer installation avoided all updates to its system because of the inevitable software problems they introduced. By sticking to the same, ancient version of the software, the site eventually managed four years of failure-free running. Yet, at the end of that period, a new and very serious bug was discovered that had lain dormant for all those years. In one extensively used operating system, over 30 percent of all bugs reported would have caused a failure on average only once every 5,000 years of operation.[54]

Exhaustive testing is by no means cheap. NASA estimates that it spent around $500 million in testing its space shuttle software, or about $1,000 per line of code tested. However, better quality is certainly achievable: Tokyo's bullet train has had nineteen years of virtually error-free operation—due in part to the application of Japanese manufacturing techniques to the process of software production. The developer of the software, Hitachi, relies upon tried and tested software modules and heavy monitoring of programmers in an assembly-line situation.[55]

Lastly, the human management aspects of software development also have been tackled, and a large variety of methodologies and project management practices have come into vogue. The assumptions underlying these methodologies are that by appropriately managing and controlling the software development process in its human-organizational forms (specifying client need, prototyping documentation, further client consultation, testing, and debugging, etc.) a higher quality product can be delivered more reliably.[56]

Whether such hopes will ever be realized remains uncertain. But there are clear signs that the software community is becoming sensitive to the possibility of a public backlash if computers continue to be involved in serious failures, particularly those that may involve large-scale loss of life and property. What is perhaps most feared by computing professionals is a generalized call for the licensing of programmers and the registration of their professional competence through an examination system—something that may be about to happen in at least one U.S. state.[57] Partly because of these concerns, a greater recognition of the peculiar properties of software is emerging and better practices for the production of software are being adopted, with strong backing from the military in particular.[58]

We are forced to conclude that the construction of software is a complex and difficult process and that existing techniques do not provide software of assured quality and reliability. In the case of large, complex systems to which we entrust major responsibilities and sometimes awesome energies, this conclusion is hardly reassuring.

Furthermore, given the evidence we have presented here, it is clear that several ethical issues arise: in circumstances in which software engineers are asked to build systems of this sort, should they be more honest about their limitations? If it is possible that a system might not work at all, should computer professionals accept funding for its R&D? If it is theoretically impossible to demonstrate the correctness of a program and the program causes catastrophic loss, is the programmer immune from an ethical obligation? What is the ethical status of existing warranties and disclaimers?

These are the kinds of questions that all of us, computer professionals and lay persons alike, need to address in considering the proper role of computers in our lives and the responsibilities and obligations that should be imparted to those whom we employ to construct them.

6

The Invasion of Privacy

A few days before Christmas 1988, U.S. Customs officials at Los Angeles International Airport ran a routine check of passengers on a TWA flight from London and scored a hit on a Richard Lawrence Sklar, a fugitive wanted for his part in an Arizona real estate scam. As part of standard procedure, Customs confirmed his birth date, height, weight, eye and hair color and promptly arrested him. Over the next two days, the fifty-eight-year-old passenger was strip searched, moved from one holding cell to another, and handcuffed to several violent offenders. The only problem was that the authorities had the wrong man. This Sklar was a professor of political science at the University of California, Los Angeles, and had been fingerprinted three times in twelve years for the crimes of an impostor whose records remained buried along with 19 million other computer files in the National Crime Information Center.[1]

The Sklar case is a dramatic illustration of the impact that databases and computer-based information of all kinds can have on innocent people's lives. It also suggests that the considerable faith we place in computer-based records may be unjustified. We encounter a number of such incidents in this chapter, but what we must bear in mind from the outset is that many computer privacy issues may be understood as power issues arising from the capabilities of computers and their potential to affect the lives of individuals.[2] For example, balancing the needs for privacy and security may be difficult to achieve, because conflicts exist between the needs and expectations of the individual and the obligations and roles of the organizations and agencies that perform key functions in any complex technological society.

Therefore, this chapter is really about balance and how it is maintained in the kind of society that the Western democracies have constructed.

Through this lens, the fundamental ethical issues associated with privacy, surveillance, and democracy are viewed.

Database Disasters

Computer databases have been responsible for some terrible blunders. Houston schoolteacher Darlene Alexander believed that she had a respectable credit record until she applied for a $75,000 mortgage and the lender informed her that she had accumulated too much debt to be considered. Her records showed outstanding accounts with American Express, MasterCard, and Visa and a $22,800 loan for a Chevrolet Camaro. Unfortunately, none of the accounts were hers, and she owned outright a 1983 Datsun. Alexander had become a victim of the so-called credit doctors, people who steal good credit histories and then sell them to those who have accumulated atrocious credit histories. An impostor had opened accounts in her name and had taken out loans, with the result that Alexander is now stuck with a poor lending history and has little chance of gaining credit for a home purchase or other important purposes.

In many ways, the modus operandi of credit doctors is very similar to that of the most malicious kinds of hackers. Generally, credit doctors work by bribing credit agency employees to reveal the passwords to their systems. Then, logging in with a personal computer, they search for someone with the same name as their client who happens to have a good credit history. Having found their victim, the credit doctors copy the information associated with this person (including the all-important Social Security number) and supply it to their client. The client now has instant, easy credit. But what makes credit doctoring even more attractive is that the offense generally will not be discovered until the real owner of the identity happens to make an inquiry—usually as a result of too much accumulated debt. By that time, the credit doctors already will have supplied their clients with another illicitly gained line of credit.[3]

In another incident, American Express contacted one of its members to express concern that he might not be able to pay his account. American Express had accessed this man's checking account to discover that he had less money than they were owed. As a result, the company deactivated his card. The fine print of the American Express application form reserves the right to access a member's account in order to determine if the member has the capacity to pay.[4]

A further example of a database dust-up severely affected the life of Michael DuCross, a Canadian-born Indian living in Huntington Beach, California. At around 9:00 P.M. on 24 March 1980, DuCross drove to a local supermarket and was stopped by a police patrol car after he had made an illegal left turn. The policeman took down DuCross's name and driver's license number and asked for a check of identity using his two-way radio. The request went to Sacramento, the state's capital, and then was sent 3,000 miles east to the FBI's National Crime Information Center (NCIC) in Washington. These records indicated that DuCross was wanted by the federal government for going AWOL from the Marine Corps at Christmas 1969. Based on that information, and despite his protestations of innocence, DuCross was taken to the brig at Camp Pendleton, California. Five months later, the charges were dropped after it was discovered that DuCross had never gone AWOL. He had left the Marine Corps voluntarily in 1969 under a special discharge program for resident aliens. Again, the faith placed in the accuracy of computer-based records appears to have been totally misplaced: the victim, Michael DuCross, lost five months of his life because of blatant database mismanagement.[5]

Another instance of misplaced trust in the adequacy of computer-based records is provided by the experience of a U.S. citizen whose wallet was stolen by a criminal who subsequently adopted his identity. The thief was later involved in a robbery involving murder, and through the circumstances of the case, his adopted identity became known to the Los Angeles Police Department. This information was duly stored in their database, and when the legitimate owner of the identity was stopped for a routine traffic violation, the computer indicated that he was a prime murder suspect and he was immediately arrested. As might be expected, he spent a few days in jail before the full details were revealed.

At first sight, this incident might be regarded as a tolerable error. However, even after the confusion of identities had been discovered, this individual was arrested five times in fourteen months on the basis of the same incorrect data records. After extensive frustration, he managed to obtain a letter from the local chief of police indicating that he was not a real murder suspect and that the database records were wrong. Yet,

Dirty Harry with a Database

On Friday, 9 November 1979, three young Frenchmen filled their car with gasoline at a service station in Etampes, a small town near Paris. The owner of the service station noticed that the license plate was patched together with pieces of tape and became suspicious, especially after the check they offered had a scrawled signature on its face. He took a note of the license number and contacted the police after the men had left.

A routine interrogation of their database revealed to police that the car had been stolen, and a patrol car was dispatched to intercept. They caught up with the young men while their car was stopped at traffic lights: two officers in plain clothes jumped out, one holding a machine gun, the other a .357 magnum revolver. The only uniformed officer remained in the car.

Although the precise sequence of the subsequent events is still not clear, it is known that the officer with the magnum revolver opened fire on the trio; the bullet pierced the windscreen and hit one of the young men just under the nose. The other two men were then informed that their assailants were police (not gangsters), and they were handcuffed while an ambulance came to assist their injured friend.

Later investigations placed the whole matter in a quite different light. One of the three men had purchased the car, quite legally, ten days before. It was true that the car had once been stolen, but that was in 1976 and it had been recovered by the insurance company, which had then sold it to the firm from which the man later legally bought it. The primary cause of this incident was a failure to update the computer file covering the vehicle so that changes in status and ownership were accurately represented. Unfortunately, at the time of interrogation, police records still labeled the vehicle as stolen, and police reacted as if they were dealing with potentially dangerous criminals.[6]

although the letter was sufficient for the local situation, experience soon showed that it held little weight when he traveled out of state. Only after a protracted court battle (and a $55,000 financial settlement) was the record finally expunged.[7]

Of course, the majority of database errors are not as devastating as this—they just produce hardship and frustration. Yet the frequency with which such hardship and frustration occurs is increasing given the rapid penetration of database services into more domestic areas of our lives. For example, in 1977, Harvey Saltz, a former Los Angeles district attorney, formed UD Registry Inc., which provides landlords with information about prospective tenants. Saltz's company takes information from legal suits filed by landlords against tenants, and 1,900 landlords (at the last count) pay him an annual fee to identify potential tenants who have been sued by landlords in the past.

On the face of it, this precaution seems reasonable for landlords to take. However, anyone who has ever attempted to find rented accommodation and has been puzzled by rejection could gain some insight from the case of Barbara Ward, a resident of Los Angeles. In 1972 she rented an apartment and found that it was infested with cockroaches and rodents. When her landlord refused to deal with the infestation, Ward gave him thirty days' notice and he countered with an eviction notice. Ward went to court with documentary evidence in the form of county health records, but the landlord failed to show. The case was dropped, but a few years later, Ward was refused accommodation by several landlords because her listing in Harvey Saltz's UD Registry computer showed that she had once been served with an eviction notice. Unfortunately for Ward, she was not aware of UD Registry's existence, let alone the fact that it had generated and was perpetuating incomplete information about her tenancy history.[8]

Recently it was also revealed that the Employer's Information Service based in Gretna, Louisiana, had created a massive data bank on workers who reported injuries on the job. For a fee, employers can request a report on prospective employees, including a history of prior job injuries and a record of worker's compensation claims and lawsuits. To prevent being added to other data banks, workers in Idaho are suing that state's industrial commission to prevent it from releasing such records.[9]

Perhaps one of the best-known cases of the cumulative and distorting effects of storing personal data can be found in *The File* by Peter Kimball, a former professor of journalism at Columbia University. When released under the Freedom of Information Act, Kimball's personal file at the FBI revealed that for more than thirty years he had been classified as an undesirable citizen and a communist sympathizer—and one who was "too clever" to be found holding a party card. This classification resulted from the combination and embellishment of two incidents early in his life. The first occurred when he applied for a government position shortly after his release from the Marine Corps at the end of World War II. One of the referees he nominated very briefly had questioned his political views, but that same referee made no mention of communism or of any other school or flavor of political thought. The second event was his rejection of the government position after it had been offered so that he could take a more promising position with a leading American newspaper. In his book, Kimball shows how, over a thirty-year period, these events and subsequent inquiries to elucidate the reasons for his rejection of the position were combined and magnified to the extent that his file received the attention of J. Edgar Hoover and his later applications for senior government posts, academic appointments, and even passports were substantially affected.

Kimball's book provides an interesting account of an individual's protracted and ultimately futile struggle with bureaucratic indifference and inertia. In particular, it details how the quizzical comment of an elderly right-wing referee could snowball into a massive document proclaiming Kimball to be a "dangerous national security risk of doubtful loyalty to the U.S. government and institutions." Subsequent discussions with those individuals who allegedly were interviewed by the FBI revealed that there had been deliberate distortion or suppression of individuals' testimonials and other evidence in order to preserve the file's early and presumably unalterable theme. More importantly, Kimball had never been informed that such allegations were being made against him, let alone given the opportunity to publicly defend himself.[10]

Although the Kimball case relates to the days when record keeping was based on physical rather than computer-based files, its implications are perhaps even more sinister given the ease with which widespread computer-based surveillance and high-technology intelligence gathering can be carried out. Furthermore, although the technological capabilities to gather awesome amounts of personal information have increased exponentially in recent decades, the abilities of humans to judge the worth and the validity of such data (as compared to information) have not improved at all.

This, therefore, is one of the greatest dangers associated with the application of technology to covert intelligence and population surveillance: Although the apparent accuracy and sophistication of the new technologies lend an aura of correctness to the data gathered, ultimately human beings have to make judgments based on the data, and this process is based upon prejudices, prior assumptions, and personal inter-

Privacy Potshots

- Martin Lee Dement spent two years in Los Angeles County jail because of botched use of the California Automated Latent Print System that identifies suspects' fingerprints. Manual checks of another suspect's fingerprints finally cleared him.
- Joseph O. Robertson was arrested, extradited, and confined to a state mental facility for seventeen months despite available mug shots and fingerprints that indicated his innocence.
- Sheila Jackson Stossier was arrested and jailed because of an NCIC match on a warrant for a Shirley Jackson.
- Despite being six inches different in height, having a different birthday, and differing by seventy pounds in weight from the culprit, one Shirley Jones was arrested while the real suspect was already in jail.
- New York residents Anne Marie O'Connor and Ann Marie O'Connor shared the same Social Security number, appearance, and birthday. The confusion was revealed only after a tax investigation was launched on back taxes from their combined incomes.
- Two James Edward Taylors in New York shared the same birthday, birth state, and Social Security number. Although detected in 1965, the error remained uncorrected in 1973.
- Actress Rebecca Schaeffer was murdered by an obsessed fan who obtained her home address from the California Department of Motor Vehicles.
- The FBI's Library Lending Project was an attempt to track the library usage habits of foreign nationals.
- Roberto Hernandez was held three times between 1985 and 1989 as a suspect in a 1985 residential burglary. Authorities confused him with another Roberto Hernandez identified by the NCIC. Both men have the same height, weight, hair and eye color, tattoos on their left arm, and birthday, and their Social Security numbers differ by only one digit.[11]

pretations. We cannot ask machines to identify conspiracy, even if they could gather data and store it with unerring accuracy (which they don't). These judgments are human judgments: Is a reader of communist literature a communist or simply a scholar? Is an observer of military aircraft an enthusiast or a low-level espionage threat? Of course, given what we understand about the unreliability of computer systems in other contexts, the problems of data accuracy, completeness, and relevance merely compound the difficulties attached to the storage and processing of personal information by the application of computer systems.

The Information Mosaic

Data is more than just the lifeblood of information societies. It is the basis of a complex web of data dependencies and symbiotic relationships. In such societies, the information output of many data collection and analysis processes is restructured to become the input of even higher processes. For example, retail purchase records may become input for mail order companies, while their sales patterns in turn might be input for regional magazine and TV advertisers, and so on. Just recently, American Express admitted to its 25 million card holders that for years it had been sorting their transaction records by spending patterns and then renting their name and address lists to organizations ranging from stores to insurers.[12] These complex relationships among data collectors, consumers, and reprocessors have formed an information ecology that upwardly refines information until the largest organisms at the top of the food chain—large corporations and government bodies—can use it to make strategic decisions about individuals, neighborhoods, communities, and even entire segments of society.

But for these webs of input and output to occur, the base of the food web—the raw data—must be available, recent, and in a usable form. And whether we are aware of it or not, whether we like it or not, anyone functioning in a modern society inevitably generates a trail of information that acts as the plankton of this complex information ecology. To get a driver's license, a mortgage, or a credit card, to be admitted to a hospital or to register the warranty on a new purchase, people in the United States routinely fill out forms providing a wealth of facts about themselves. Little of it remains confidential. Even U.S. government agencies plug into commercial databases to make decisions about eligibility for health care benefits and Social Security. Personal finances, medical histories, purchasing habits, and more are raked in by data companies. These firms in turn combine the records with information drawn from other sources—for instance from state governments that sell lists of driver's licenses—to draw a clearer picture, or mosaic if you will, of an individual or household. These repackaged mosaics, including errors and inaccuracies, are then sold to government agencies, mortgage lenders, retailers, small businesses, marketers, and insurers. The result is a billion-dollar-a-year industry that adds little to export performance, national productivity, or GDP.[13]

The major players in this commercial information ecology are the three giant credit bureaus: TRW, Equifax, and Trans Union, plus about 450 smaller outfits. Every month the big three purchase computer records, mostly from banks and retailers, that detail the financial activity of virtually every adult American. Indeed, both TRW and Equifax are each estimated to have about 150 million individual files. Clearly outclassed by the volume of this data, many smaller competitors try to enhance their profits by resorting to questionable practices. Some smaller firms, for example, have been known to sell the location of nearly every U.S. household with a newborn child. Others have shown a propensity to sell any kind of information to anyone willing to pay for it—including private investigators, debt collectors, and jealous husbands. TRW was heavily criticized for storing erroneous tax delinquency data on residents of Norwich, Connecticut, an incident that confirmed for many how lax TRW's verification procedures are.[14]

But perhaps the major enduring problem experienced with commercial information bureaus (as with almost any large database) is the difficulty in detecting incorrect information. Beyond that, there is the problem of implementing appropriate procedures for its correction. As one would expect, the larger bureaus argue that their services are critical to the operation of the credit card and loan industries, but critics have had no difficulty in establishing the widespread existence of chronic, uncorrected errors and dated information. In 1991, the Consumers Union reported that nearly half of the credit reports it studied from the nation's largest credit bureaus contained some inaccuracies. Even the credit bureaus admit that, of the 9 million credit reports requested annually by consumers, 3 million request verification or updating of information in the file. According to some reports, as much as 30 to 40 percent of the information contained in the databases of the big three is inaccurate. Even the Texas attorney general's office has stated that it receives more complaints about TRW than any other ongoing business.[15]

This issue of faulty reporting finally came to a head in July 1991 when the attorneys general of six states—Alabama, California, Idaho, Michigan, New York, and Texas—brought suits against TRW's credit agency

How to Get a New Mortgage, New Wife, and Relocate out of State—without Really Trying

In June 1991 Robert J. Corbey applied for a $2,000 loan to put vinyl siding on his Aspen Hill, Maryland, home. To his amazement, his lender refused, citing unpaid mortgage bills on two homes in Virginia and an Internal Revenue Service lien against him and his wife, Ann. However, Corbey had paid his thirty-year mortgage, had never lived in Virginia, and had never been married to anyone named Ann. Computer records at Equifax had confused him with another Robert Corbey, and it took more than eight months for the confusion to be cleared up.

Clearly, Corbey was lucky in that he had plenty of evidence to back him up and the issue of a $2,000 loan did not compare to, say, failing a job interview over a poor credit history. Needless to say, that, too, easily could have happened.[16]

White Line Fever

James Russell Wiggins thought he had finally made it. In 1989 the thirty-six-year-old father of four landed a $70,000-a-year sales job at District Cablevision in Washington, D.C. But six weeks later, a routine background check showed that Wiggins had been convicted of cocaine possession. Because he hadn't told Cablevision about it, he was fired. But Wiggins said he had never been before a judge in his life and the record was wrong. It turned out that Equifax had goofed by pulling the criminal record of James Ray Wiggins and folding the disparate files together to provide a mosaic that was not only wrong but very damaging to the career and livelihood of an innocent person. Wiggin's only crime was to have generated data in a data-gathering society.[17]

operations that accused it of violating consumer privacy and failing to correct serious reporting errors. Eventually, the case swelled to include nine states and the Federal Trade Commission. In retaliation, TRW filed countersuits in federal court and argued that the federal Fair Credit Reporting Act of 1970 supersedes state law. Eventually though, TRW bowed to the weight of adverse opinion and announced that it would supply consumers on request with free copies of their credit files (instead of charging twenty dollars per copy).[18]

In addition to notifying consumers of their rights to dispute information and to tell them on request about other companies to whom the credit reports have been sold, TRW also agreed to adopt procedures to prevent data mix-ups, review within thirty days any disputed information and delete any that cannot be confirmed within thirty days, delete any disputed information when the consumer presents relevant documentation, and implement procedures to prevent reappearance of seriously derogatory information that has been deleted following a complaint.[19]

But despite this continued pressure on credit reporting agencies and information bureaus, there is much to remain concerned about. The U.S. House of Representatives now has before it legislation that would require written agreement from consumers before information about them is released by a bank, credit bureau, or other institution. However, given the amount and frequency of information sharing, recycling, and repackaging that occurs in the information ecology, it is not difficult to imagine each such transaction generating yet another document for endorsement. Nor do these or any other proposed measures deal with the multitude of fragmented data snapshots that in themselves are not worthy of legislation but that can be combined to yield much greater value and also have potential for error and abuse.

Instead, what appears to be one of the most effective strategies for crippling emerging privacy threats is the swift and massive expression of public sentiment. In 1991 30,000 complaints were received by Lotus Development Corporation against its proposed *Lotus Marketplace: Households* database. This product was to have contained a vast amount of data on 120 million Americans, including their names, addresses, estimated incomes, consumer preferences, and other personal details—all of it supplied by Equifax Inc. In effect, anyone with a suitable PC could purchase a copy for $695 and utilize the information for whatever purpose. For example, searching for the names and addresses of single women over seventy years of age living in a specific area would provide a comprehensive list for the inquiring burglar. Even more disturbing, it was soon discovered that individuals wanting to be removed from the database had to supply only their Social Security number—blatant evidence that the data was keyed to the SSN, with all the known problems that the SSN has as an identifier and target of abuse and error.[20]

Intense opposition soon was orchestrated by Computer Professionals for Social Responsibility and other groups. Faxes, e-mail messages, letters, and phone calls continued to pour in until even Lotus could see the

Sick Data

> Information on MIB (formerly Medical Information Bureau of Brookline, Massachusetts) is difficult to find, yet its databases are used to fulfill 15,000 medical information requests every year. Unfortunately, in the United States, a person applying for life insurance enjoys none of the (meager) privacy rights and protections of a person applying for credit. Insurance companies are under no obligation to reveal the basis of their decisions, so individuals who are denied coverage have no way of knowing if the decision is legitimate or based on an erroneous record that will follow them from insurer to insurer for the rest of their lives.
>
> In one case, a clerical error caused a woman's records at MIB to state that she carried the HIV virus. It was only after unusual intervention by the state regulatory board (because the woman worked for a physician) that the records were corrected.
>
> Given the growing interest of the insurance industry in recording genetic defects and other newly revealed medical information, one wonders how much further scope there will be for such errors and what their effects will be on people's lives.[22]

writing on the wall, even though it protested to the end that the product and the technology had been misunderstood by the public. However, a parallel product, *Lotus Marketplace: Businesses,* will proceed because its data on 7 million U.S. businesses did not attract the same level of criticism. It will be marketed by a spinoff company, Marketplace Information Corp.[21]

The Number of the Beast: Calling Number Identification

Not all privacy issues stem from information threads being woven together by huge mainframes in air-conditioned offices. Some of them involve familiar domestic appliances such as the telephone. The most recent controversy surrounding this nineteenth-century device is the development of CNID (calling number identification) or "caller ID," as it is commonly known. In simple terms, caller ID is a phone service that allows you to see the number of the person calling you before you pick up the phone.

This capability has generated much heated debate, with opposing camps differing over which party should be protected from it. Those in favor say that caller ID can inhibit obscene and prank callers and discourage false alarms to the police, the fire service, and ambulance services. Opponents argue that revealing people's unlisted numbers not only makes that service a contradiction but potentially could be dangerous to people in threatening situations—those protecting not just their privacy but their lives. At a more mundane level, opponents feel that a casual inquiry to a local store shouldn't result in weeks of badgering by high-pressure salespeople. But the parties are more evenly divided over calling in sick while displaying the number of the local video store.

This degree of concern and the parallels between caller ID and call tracing have led to some fiery debates in the state legislatures. Pennsylvania, for example, found that the service violates state constitutional privacy rights. Around fifteen states may restrict caller ID under wiretap legislation that currently covers call tracing devices, although there is growing confidence that caller ID may be granted federal exemption from this legislation.

As a compromise, some commentators have suggested providing per-call or per-line blocking to consumers, so that those who don't want their phone number to precede every call they make can block the display. But, understandably, telephone companies oppose the provision of blocking because it could erode the attractiveness of the service. After all, what's the point of caller ID if the heavy breathers are first in line for per-call blocking? However, determined heavy breathers can always call from a public phone booth, so caller ID is certainly no panacea in itself. Finally, if caller ID is intended to screen us from telemarketers, annoying relatives, or people we don't wish to talk to, then an answering machine may be a better option—and besides, it's cheaper.[23]

In Australia and in Britain, caller ID has aroused similar concerns. The Data Protection Registrar in the United Kingdom is making moves toward allowing per-call blocking on caller ID, and Australia is thinking along similar lines. But for most countries, the possible efficiency gains are propelling caller ID into realization. Banks, telephone companies, and other large commercial enterprises can use the displayed telephone number to immediately access their records and to provide prompt service to customers. In addition, business can better protect themselves from telephone fraud and false orders as well as improve the service of their personnel. Even computer hacking might be curtailed by recording the numbers of unsuccessful log-ins via modem.[24]

Privacy Legislation

Most countries have come to terms with the need to treat information as property, as evidenced by the array of patent and copyright protection laws now in existence. The extension of legal powers to cover personal information is also occurring, especially now that the number of private organizations or companies holding such information is growing exponentially.

In the United Kingdom, the Data Protection Act of 1984 provides individuals with a number of safeguards against abuse of personal information contained in databases. Individuals are able to apply for a copy of all data stored on computer that relates to them. They can also insist on that information being corrected if it is wrong or out of date. The act even makes provision for compensation for financial loss or physical injury that occurs as a result of data that is inaccurate, lost, destroyed, or disclosed without authority. However, some exceptions fall outside the scope of the act, including manually held as opposed to electronically stored records and any records held for the purposes of guarding national security, preventing or detecting crime, prosecuting offenders, or collecting taxes. Other exceptions include files relating to judicial appointments and medical records that a doctor may feel could seriously damage a patient's health if disclosed.

Of course, legislation cannot be of real use unless it has some penalties attached: the legal teeth of the act therefore lie with the Data Protection Registrar, the individual responsible for the maintenance of the register of data collectors and processors. Under the provisions of the act, if an individual or organization is involved in the routine processing of personal data, then it is a criminal offense for the data handlers not to register themselves and the relevant details of the kind of data they maintain and the purposes to which it is put. It is also a criminal offense for a company or an individual data user to use that data in any way not stated in the register entry. Furthermore, if there is a breach of the act or its principles, citizens can complain to the registrar or pursue a claim in the courts. In such circumstances, the registrar either may try for a mediated solution or else may issue enforcement notices. These notices require data users to take specified action to comply with the law, and failure to do so is regarded as a criminal act. The registrar is also empowered to issue a notice removing users from the register, thereby preventing them from legally processing their data. Of course, as would be expected, an appeal procedure can be invoked against all such judgments.[25]

Much of the thrust behind the implementation of the Data Protection Act in the United Kingdom came not from a desire to protect individuals but from the need for the United Kingdom to conform to European Community (EC) guidelines on databases and data flows. Failure to comply could have been a major stumbling block to trade. However, there were other influences and precursors to these developments. For instance, European countries had been strongly influenced by two publications: the first of these, *Guidelines on the Protection and Privacy of Transborder Flows of Personal Data,* published by the OECD in 1980, was adopted by all twenty-four OECD member countries; the second, the Council of Europe's *Convention for the Protection of Individuals with Regard to Automatic Processing of Personal Data,* which came into effect on 1 October 1985, was signed by eighteen countries and ratified by a further seven. Although the OECD *Guidelines* have no legal force attached to them, the European *Convention* is legally binding upon member states that have ratified it.[26]

The data privacy principles set out in the *Guidelines* are

• The collection and limitation principle. Data can only be obtained by lawful means and with the data subject's knowledge or consent.

• The data quality principle. Data collectors may only collect data relevant to their purposes, and such data must be kept up to date, accurate, and complete.

• The purpose specification principle. At the time of collection, the purposes to which the data will be applied must be disclosed to the data subject, and the data will not be used for purposes beyond this.

• The use limitation principle. The data is not to be disclosed by the collector to outsiders without the consent of the data subject unless the law otherwise requires it.

• The security safeguards principle. Data collectors must take reasonable precautions against loss, destruction, or unauthorized use, modification, or disclosure.

• The openness principle. Data subjects should be able to determine the whereabouts, use, and purpose of personal data relating to them.

• The individual participation principle. Data subjects have the right to inspect any data concerning themselves as well as the right to challenge the accuracy of such data and have it rectified or erased by the collector.
• The accountability principle. The data collector is accountable to the data subject in complying with the above principles.

Although the U.K. Data Protection Act is in accord with these principles and on the face of it appears admirably responsible in terms of the protection of individuals, some damaging accounts of its practicalities have emerged. For example, journalist Duncan Campbell recounts his efforts to utilize the protective mechanisms contained in the act. With the aim of obtaining details of his record on the Police National Computer (PNC), he began by searching for a copy of the Data Protection Register, a list of all computer systems registered under the U.K. Data Protection Act. Although a copy is supposed to be located in every public library, Campbell found that most libraries had never heard of it. When he finally found a copy, the librarian was extremely reluctant to let him see it. With some perseverance, however, Campbell managed to find out which systems composed the PNC network and lodged queries with each of these five systems—at a cost of ten pounds per request. Furthermore, the request forms required several personal (and apparently irrelevant) questions to be answered, and the replies appeared only after forty days, the maximum delay permissible under the legislation.[27]

Other commentators have expressed concern that the Data Protection Act is a paper tiger that doesn't work. New demands are being made for tighter legislation that can be enforced more rigorously. And small wonder, given recent revelations of improper use by the British police of the PNC, including instances of police using the system to trace the number plates of national lottery winners, checking the movements of their spouses and the backgrounds of their childrens' friends, and obtaining data on homosexuals for sale to other homosexuals. The pressure group Liberty also claims that 70,000 people in the United Kingdom are unlawfully held in the "under surveillance" section of the PNC even though they have no criminal record.[28]

On a more optimistic note, some evidence suggests that the message of the *Guidelines* and the European *Convention* has filtered down to private corporations. For example, IBM and Bank of America have developed and published rules that conform to these principles. But the

U.S. legislature is only just beginning to come to terms with the complexities of new technologies coexisting with ancient legislation based on inadequate and dated precedents. Aside from recent controls on the nation's three major credit bureaus, a bill introduced in the House of Representatives in 1991 aimed to create a new Federal Data Protection Board, while another focused on the widespread use of the Social Security number to link disparate private and government database records—and as a routine instrument of fraud. Still other legal issues have emerged concerning the U.S. government's rights of search and seizure in suspected hacking cases in which analogies have been drawn between a computer bulletin board and a conventional printing press.[29]

The National Security Agency: Big Brother Is Watching You

For many civil liberties campaigners, the U.S. National Security Agency (NSA) is the epitome of what we have most to fear in terms of the invasion of individuals' privacy and the covert control of peoples' lives. The responsibilities and limitations of the NSA have never been clearly defined by the U.S. Congress, and since its establishment by President Truman in 1952, it has operated solely on the basis of a series of White House directives. This agency has a budget that is some five to six times that of the CIA and is reputed to have the most sophisticated and awesome computing capability of any single existing organization—enough to intercept and analyze perhaps 70 percent of all telephone, telex, data, and radio transmissions generated on earth. In 1971 the agency decided it needed a high-temperature incinerator to dispose of the masses of printouts and secret documents that it generated every day in the course of its activities. The specification required that the unit be capable of destroying at least six tons an hour and not less than thirty-six tons in any eight-hour shift—such is the size and extent of the agency's activities.[30]

Of course, the NSA was not created in some political or social vacuum. Like a number of other intelligence agencies in the United States, it emerged as a response to perceived threats and social circumstances that alarmed governments of the day. For example, during the Kennedy administration, far-reaching efforts were initiated to keep track of civil rights activists such as Martin Luther King, members of Congress such as Abner Mikva, and members of civil liberties organizations such as the American Civil Liberties Union, the American Friends Services Committee, and the National Association for the Advancement of Colored Peoples (NAACP). During the Johnson administration, concern about race riots, civil rights demonstrations, and antiwar protests prompted the president to order the army to increase its surveillance activities, thereby creating files on about 100,000 individuals and a vast number of organizations. Richard Nixon was accused of having violated the law by obtaining the computerized tax files of his political enemies, but he was unsuccessful in his attempts to require all television sets sold in the United States to be equipped with a device that would allow them to be turned on from a central location.[31]

In 1967 the FBI established the National Crime Information Center (NCIC) to maintain computer-based files on missing persons, warrants, stolen property, securities, criminal histories, and registered property (guns, vehicles, etc.). With an annual operating budget of approximately $6 million, NCIC houses some 8 million individual dossiers (that is, on one in every thirty Americans), and this number is expected to grow to encompass records on 90 percent of all U.S. residents with arrest records—or as many as 35 million people, approximately 40 percent of the U.S. labor force. About 64,000 federal, state, and local police agencies have authority to access NCIC data via one of the 17,000 terminals now linked to the center.[32]

As recently as 1992, the FBI requested that it be given authority to set technical standards for the computer and communications industry. This step would enhance the FBI's ability to intercept communications by mandating that every communication system in the United States have a built in remote monitoring capability to make wiretaps easier. The proposal covered all communication equipment from office phones to advanced computer networks, with fines for noncompliance up to $10,000 per day. As one might expect, leading phone companies and computer manufacturers such as AT&T, IBM, and Digital Equipment Corporation and Computer Professionals for Social Responsibility opposed the proposal.[33] Once more, this case illustrates the classic tug of war between the perceived role of the state to preserve law, order, and national security and the rights of individuals to fundamental democratic freedoms.

A good example of the instability of this democratic tightrope is the NSA's involvement with the establishment of encryption standards. Encryption—or, more properly, cryptography—is the science of codes and code breaking. Because of the sensitivity of many financial transactions and other data communications, encryption is becoming an increasingly favored precaution. With encryption, even if a transmission is tapped or illicitly recorded, decoding the message is so computationally demanding that only the most skilled of individuals with the best of computing facilities could hope to do so within a reasonable period of time.

During the establishment of the Data Encryption Standard (DES)—a set of universally acceptable conventions for encryption—the NSA lobbied strongly inside the International Standards Organization (ISO) to have the DES disapproved. The most popular interpretation of this act is that widespread standardization of encryption and its concomitant routine use would make it substantially more difficult for the NSA to monitor overseas voice and data communications. Similarly, in the early 1980s several major banks and financial institutions in the United States met to determine characteristics of encryption keys (the number sequences used to decode encrypted messages) that were of prodigious length (some fifty to one hundred digits long). Once more, the NSA successfully exerted enormous pressure on these bodies to drop the proposal, again for very obvious reasons. Encryption keys of this length would have meant that messages probably would require three to four days to break using the existing facilities of the NSA; obviously, this obstacle would have placed the agency in extreme difficulties if it wished to monitor such transactions. Even worse, it would have become a nightmare for the organization if such practices caught on and became commonplace.[34]

Yet it appears that the saga of the NSA and its alleged interference in encryption standards has not ended. The development and popularization of public key cryptography (PKC)—so called trap door encryption—has made it possible for almost anyone (even the humble PC user) to encrypt messages so that they become uncrackable for all practical purposes. And clearly, the possibility of any PC user, drug dealer, terrorist, or spy being able to defeat the power of the NSA with a humble MS-DOS machine is a bitter pill for a federal agency to swallow. The power of

PKC comes from its ability to use two keys: one that encrypts and one that decrypts. But only public distribution of the encryption key is allowed. This means that I can create encryption and decryption keys and publicly display, mail, or broadcast the encryption key to anyone, because possession of the public key merely allows the owner to encrypt messages, not decrypt them. Once the exchange is made to a confederate, that person can then encrypt, say, the keys to another encryption scheme and because only I possess the matching decryption key to this message, only I can obtain the keys. Hence, a virtually foolproof method of encrypting messages and distributing their keys has been established, and communication can proceed in absolute privacy.[35]

In addition, PKC has the unusual property of allowing public key owners to verify the source of a message (a so-called digital signature) without being able to read its contents. It is here (in the standards for the digital signature) that some commentators have alleged interference by the NSA. For many experts in the field, the public key algorithm of choice is the RSA technique, which was devised in 1978 by three scientists at MIT. However, rather than adopt RSA, which has a patent in effect, the NSA recommended in 1991 that the National Institute of Standards and Technology (NIST) adopt a technique developed by NSA—a public key technique known as the Digital Signature Standard (DSS). As a result of protests, the NSA modified the standard to accommodate 1024-bit keys rather than 512, but this concession still has not satisfied some experts, who criticize the DSS's inability to be used for encryption (rather than just digital signature verification) and hence its capacity for use in distributing encryption keys.[36]

Despite these alarming developments, in many circumstances the need for surveillance appears patently obvious and totally warranted. For example, in the war against drugs and terrorism, the application of sophisticated technology seems to be an appropriate and much-needed source of countermeasures. In accordance with this, the U.S. Defense Advanced Research Projects Agency (DARPA) is now involved in a multi-million-dollar program to apply artificial intelligence and parallel-processing techniques to the detection and elimination of drug-related criminal activities. These initiatives will involve tracking currency, cargo shipments, and telephone usage so that subtle but telltale patterns are revealed to investigating authorities. By tracing serial numbers of cash and by monitoring the movements of container shipments, DARPA also hopes that almost real-time control and detection of narcotics activities can be provided.[37]

Yet while almost all of us would like to see the drug trade and its social destructiveness ended, we might not appreciate such technologies being applied to our everyday lives—and this is the practical implication behind such moves. After all, what distinguishes your telephone from that used by a drug dealer? What differentiates your bank account from the slush fund of a narcotics racket? Given these problems, several pertinent questions come to mind: Are the costs to privacy greater than the benefits of squeezing drug trafficking out of existence? Is the damage visible on the streets preferable to the invisible, secret damage that surveillance could bring to society and its freedoms? Might we conclude that the drug rackets, just like the oldest profession, can never be eliminated?

The collective response of the drug barons might be to counter with high-technology foils of their own: scramblers, encryption devices, and so on. After all, drug syndicates already use some of the best and most sophisticated equipment, and wrecking a brand-new aircraft or two is a negligible business cost given the incredible profits that can be made from narcotics trading. Furthermore, with huge amounts of money for the taking what defense can high technology offer to the ancient art of bribery and corruption? What point is there in creating elaborate technological surveillance systems if their locks, keys, and blueprints already have been sold? And if this result is the most we can hope for from using high technology to combat the drug problem, why should we accept the destruction of privacy that it may bring?

In a further instance of the NSA pursuing its perceived role with some degree of overenthusiasm, a recent report claims that the National Computer Security Center (a division of the NSA) contacted researchers at Purdue University, Indiana, and asked them to remove information from campus computers showing the internal workings of Robert Morris's Internet worm program (see chapter 4). Ostensibly, the NCSC's concerns stemmed from the belief that not all sites had corrected the security problems that the worm program relied upon and exploited. Some computer security experts, however, said that the NSA was more concerned with preventing the dissemination of such techniques and their potential exploitation in system break-ins.[38]

Yet the role of the NSA in attempting to restrict the flow of information (of all kinds) goes much deeper than this. For example, in 1984 President Reagan signed an executive order for the NSA (National Security Decision Directive 145) that describes information contained in databases as part of a mosaic in which individual pieces are innocuous but, when aggregated, allow a more complete picture to appear. This notion of an information mosaic has had far-reaching consequences that are only now beginning to be felt.

Perhaps the most often cited example is the publication of the blueprint for an H-bomb in a 1979 edition of *The Progressive* magazine. All the information contained in the article was gleaned from unclassified data scattered throughout various scientific journals. Under the influence of the mosaic concept, the then director of the NSA, Admiral John Poindexter, moved to restrict unclassified information affecting not only national security but also "other government interests," including "government or government-derived economic, human, financial, industrial, agricultural, technological and law-enforcement information." Because of its calls for "a comprehensive and co-ordinated approach" to restricting foreign access to all telecommunications and automated information systems, Poindexter's directive prompted fears that U.S. intelligence agencies would monitor virtually all computerized databases and information systems in the United States. The White House eventually withdrew the notice in 1987 under pressure from Congress, but the underlying policy, as set out in NSDD 145, is still in place.[39]

Surveillance Societies

While most Western governments are sensitive to being labeled Big Brother, in Asia there appear to be no qualms about embracing the Orwellian concept. Recently it was reported that the Thai government had inaugurated a centralized database system in order to track and to cross-reference vital information on each of its 55 million citizens. The system includes a population identification number (PIN) with a computer-readable ID card with photo, name, address, height, thumbprint, parent's names, marital status, children's names, education, occupation, income, nationality, religion, tax return, and criminal record (if any). Among other aims, the card is designed to track voting patterns, domestic and foreign travel, and social welfare. The Thai system is likely to become the largest government database in the world. In the private sector, only the Church of Jesus Christ of Latter-Day Saints (the Mormon Church) has a larger one. Even more worrying, the second annual Computerworld-Smithsonian Award for innovative information technology in the governmental sector was awarded to the Thailand Ministry of Interior, and two of the three panel judges have major computer responsibilities in the U.S. government.[40]

Other developing nations also have shown a penchant for applying computer-based systems in registering their citizens and monitoring their activities. Indonesia and the Philippines are considering adopting the Thai system with all its possibilities for cross-matching. Until quite recently, the white-ruled government of South Africa used pass card and fingerprint systems—running on IBM and British ICL computers—to enforce travel restrictions on the black majority. Today, Israel uses a work permit card system, running on U.S. equipment, to monitor the movements of Palestinians living in the occupied territories. Guatemala, with its nightly death squads, purchased Israeli surveillance software in the 1980s, and one of the Asian tiger economies, Taiwan, is planning its own "residential information system."

The government of the Republic of Singapore has committed itself to a road tax system that works by monitoring car locations and levying an appropriate fee for road usage. Although the intention of the system is to control traffic congestion, it is not yet clear what kind of information will be logged and how accurate it will be. However, imaginative counterterrorist forces in places such as Northern Ireland perhaps could be forgiven for thinking that such a system could lighten their workload of tailing cars, observing houses, and using helicopters to pick out number plates.

Yet, even established democracies such as Australia have experienced a savage tug of war over government plans to tag its citizens and more closely monitor their activities. After its failure to introduce a national ID card system in 1988, the Australian government expanded its tax file numbering system so that many government and commercial interactions could not proceed without it. Now the attorney general's department is trying out a Law Enforcement Access Network (LEAN) with six federal agencies plugged into it, including the Tax Office, the Department of Social Security, and the Australian Federal Police. The aim is to match and compare diverse data sources, such as profits reported to the Tax Office and listed property transactions or above- average property ownership with lists of suspected drug traffickers.[42]

Some commentators have suggested that the LEAN system would incorporate Telecom's Yellow and White Pages (already available on CD-ROM); printed electoral rolls; drivers license and motor registration records; births, deaths, and marriage registry records; and perhaps even records from public utilities. Yet even without the LEAN system, existing government databases have created cause for concern. For example, pensioners and the unemployed claiming pharmaceutical benefits must present a Medicare card. Although the system is designed to control fraud and abuse in the health system, opponents have argued that the stored data also can be cross-referenced with employment, social security, and tax records.[43]

More recently, the LEAN system has come under renewed attack. In 1992 international privacy experts and advocates expressed their extreme concern that a stable democracy such as Australia—a nation that has never suffered a military invasion, civil war, revolution, or even a political assassination—should be on the verge of implementing comprehensive databases that contravene international guidelines and requirements. At a Washington meeting of Privacy International, thirty-five international privacy figures criticized the LEAN system, the lack of any prior consultative process, its breadth of intended usage, and the contention that no privacy issues are involved in relation to publicly available information.

In the United States, some commentators have highlighted the adoption of optical character recognition (OCR) technology in the U.S. Postal Service and the possibilities for scanning envelopes to generate lists of correspondents so as to create a communications matrix. This step would be especially easy when an envelope also has a return address.[44]

But perhaps what is most disturbing about the growing trend for governments to introduce databases of different sorts is that most of these proposals have laudable aims in mind. For example, the U.K.

Department of Health was keen to introduce a clinical memory card that would store patients' histories, drug allergies, and so on. All of this information would be enormously useful in the event of an emergency and could eliminate overlapping, inefficient record systems and replace them with a centralized database. However, a trial of smart card technology by the department revealed too many teething problems, and the department has opted instead for a series of "niche" cards for diabetics, pregnant women, and others.[45]

In France, a country that has never been noted for privacy abuses, 20,000 citizens rioted in 1990 in protest at the discovery of 900,000 government files that had been compiled in an effort to combat terrorism. Despite these difficulties, as the European Community lurches toward unification, various proposals are being put forward for sharing information internationally—including a data-sharing arrangement between police forces. A network known as the Schengen Information System has been proposed by France, Germany, and the Benelux countries and could provide police with data on 320 million people across Europe. Other writers have argued that the introduction of an ID card system in Britain is inevitable. Indeed, compulsory card systems already operate in Belgium, Greece, Germany, Italy, Luxembourg, Portugal, and Spain, and the advocates of the British scheme are harping upon the social benefits and administrative efficiency that it would provide.[46]

More than anything else, what emerges from such debates is the pressing need for modern societies to decide what forms of data collection are necessary and what are unnecessary intrusions on individual privacy. In the absence of a consensus, we are left with technological capabilities coupled with simple, instrumental ends that could have dangerous repercussions for the way that societies function and for the quality of life of their citizens.[47]

Just When You Thought No One Was Listening

It is a mistake to believe that the only threat to privacy lies in the databases of supersecret intelligence agencies, the police, and other authorities. Surveillance technologies are also available to those with sufficient need and sufficient funds to purchase them. For example, microphone transmitters these days can be as small as a pin head and can be embedded almost anywhere. Some do not need wires for transmissions—they send out microwave signals that can be read by equipment outside the building. They can be turned on and off by remote control or set to be activated by heat, radiation, the vibrations of a voice, body movement, or pressure. A bug located in a chair, for example, can be programmed to turn itself on whenever someone sits down. Bugs also can be hidden in typewriters and computer keyboards to pick up and transmit the electronic signals given off by each key so that the eavesdropper can watch as the message is keyed in. Other techniques include camouflaging bugs by incorporating them into everyday objects such as a pack of cigarettes, an electrical plug, or—in the case of one home-made device—even an olive.

One way to make bugs harder to detect is to design them so that they transmit along frequencies that are very close to those used by standard radio or TV broadcasts. Another method is called frequency hopping. With this technique, the bug transmits using a preset sequence of frequencies—often for only a few milliseconds on each frequency—and a "frequency agile" receiver, also attuned to this sequence, picks up the transmissions in a perfectly synchronized fashion. Yet the hardest bugs to detect are those that do not transmit through the air. Instead, they transmit using any available metallic medium: a power cable, an air-conditioning vent, or even metallic paint. A listening post somewhere outside the building then plugs in and monitors whatever the bug relays. Finally, the familiar Hollywood countermeasure of turning on the shower, radio, and faucets to provide a noisy background to defeat bugs is a thing of the past. Sophisticated electronic filters now can remove almost all extraneous noise and produce a clear untainted voice signal.

Closer to home, it seems that even commonplace technologies are being recruited to fulfil surveillance roles. For example, many telephone answering machines can be programmed to enter a listening mode that allows the owners to hear conversations occurring in their own office or home. Even ordinary telephone, video, and fax technologies have been combined to enable monitoring cameras to fax images to remote locations. Mobile phone conversations also have been recorded; former U.S. Vice President Dan Quayle, Prince Charles, and Princess Diana allegedly have been recent victims. Similarly, cordless phones can be overheard by any radio capable of listening into medium wave.[48]

More exotic methods of surveillance allow eavesdroppers to monitor computers as they work. The electromagnetic transmissions emitted by chips and cathode ray tubes, a phenomenon known as tempest, can be recorded some distance away from the machine for later analysis. The only known precaution against this kind of interception is the use of specially designed and prohibitively expensive shielding. Another exotic surveillance technique uses laser beams that are aimed against a window or any surface that can vibrate slightly from the impact of sound waves. The laser beam is affected by the minute vibrations caused by voices, and these can be decoded by appropriate ancillary equipment. Even the humble dairy cow may be monitored by an implanted silicon chip so that production data can be tallied by European Community authorities keen to check on subsidy fraud. The same EC committee is also considering satellite monitoring of crop production to check on its farmers.[49]

However, we don't need to look for industrial espionage, cloak-and-dagger experts, and switched-on private eyes in order to find evidence of high-technology surveillance. Although we might immediately associate surveillance with bugging devices and sophisticated electronics, employers, with the computer systems we are familiar with, are also involved in surveillance of their own employees. Indeed, some reports have indicated that up to 26 million Americans are having their work tracked electronically and up to 10 million have their pay based on computer evaluations.

At Pacific SouthWest Airlines offices in San Diego and Reno, the main computer records exactly how long each of their 400 reservation clerks spends on every call and how much time passes before each picks up the next one. Workers earn negative points for such infractions as repeatedly spending more than the average 109 seconds handling a call and taking more than 12 minutes in bathroom trips beyond the total one-hour allocation they have for lunch and coffee breaks. If employees accrue more than 37 points in any single year, they can lose their jobs. One employee of fourteen years' standing, Judy Alexander, took disability leave after compiling 24 demerit points and complaining that "you're a nervous wreck. The stress is incredible." Indeed, increased stress levels caused by employee monitoring have been reported by many studies, with headaches, back pain, fatigue, soreness, and anxiety levels all climbing. Pacific SouthWest defends the system by arguing that it's a productivity booster and that it's no more severe than the monitoring that occurs in other airlines.[50]

Supporters of computer monitoring argue that it provides incentives for employees and rewards individuals for true merit and effort. They also point out that what is measured is factual and concrete and that workers tend to favor such systems because they've seen too many cases of the wrong people being promoted for the wrong reasons. With the facts that the computer gathers, diligent workers can legitimately argue for better pay and conditions without being subjected to personal biases. Furthermore, these systems can help eliminate rampant waste by detecting employees making long-distance private calls or a work team carrying the load for an unproductive team member or by identifying the theft of materials by matching the stock used with the amount processed by line workers, and so on. Finally, monitoring on a computer network can assist in troubleshooting and fine-tuning of a system, as well as streamlining job design and fairly apportioning workloads.[51]

On the other hand, there is also the danger of turning workers into paid battery hens by denying them job satisfaction and eliminating the human element from their work. For example, although reservation clerks may be given an incentive to process more calls when they are being monitored, the system also may eliminate any human spontaneity or friendliness in their communication. Surely this factor is as important in return business as prompt and efficient handling? Similarly, workers may become sufficiently aggravated to devise ways to beat the system, as workers in one factory did by leaving their machine tools running while they had their coffee breaks. Unfortunately, the computer detected differences in the amount of power used, and managers caught on to the scam. However, the point surely is that such adversarial circumstances are best avoided and that a constant battle between the employees and the system is, in the long run, mutually disadvantageous.

Once again, we are faced with a question of balance between the rights and expectations of the individual versus the obligations and objectives of the group—but this time the group is employers. However, sometimes our responsibilities lie with the system and its continued health. For example, the 1980s left a legacy of Wall Street insider-trading scandals, and now Wall Street has had to invest in surveillance technology that is designed to detect aberrant trading patterns.[52]

Clearly, profits are important to the continued functioning of capitalist societies, and profit depends on competitiveness. However, how far we are willing to proceed in the pursuit of competitiveness and profitability is a matter of judgment. For example, the use of cheap child labor was once regarded as a sensible business strategy, but now our ethical sense and labor protection laws prohibit this practice. It remains to be seen in which direction our ethical intuitions will take us in determining the quality of future employment. Can we all expect to be monitored in the interests of profit and accountability, or will we see a renewed interest in designing jobs for people?

In addition, we need to ask what kind of precedent computer-based monitoring of employees will set for other invasive practices. For example, similar arguments can be marshaled for compulsory drug-testing of key personnel such as pilots, train drivers, plant operators, and so on.[53] If these people have the potential to accidentally kill thousands, then do we not have the right to ensure that they are in a fit state to work? On the other hand, why not also monitor the alcohol purchases of convicted drunk drivers? And after that . . . Perhaps this is the most contentious aspect of any form of computer-based monitoring: it is not so much the harm it currently may be causing, but what it represents—a yawning Pandora's box of things to come. We return to the question of computer monitoring in chapter 8.

Privacy and the Instrumentalism of Efficiency

The major benefit of computers in most commercial and real-life applications lies in their simple, time-honored capacity to endlessly perform routine functions quickly. Despite the hoopla about new forms of analysis, new applications on spacecraft, CAT scanners, and so on, the bulk of digital computers still perform tasks that require rigid repetition of fixed sequences without complaint or fatigue.

Unfortunately, though, this tireless idiot savant ability is now being applied in ways that degrade the lifestyle, peace of mind, and even sanity of ordinary citizens aiming to make a simple living in running a business or even getting a decent night's sleep. The sheer, tireless, machine insensitivity of computers has given us junk faxes, computer-generated auto-dialed telemarketing messages that make our phones ring at all hours, bills that threaten legal action unless payment of one cent is not made immediately, junk electronic mail that overflows our electronic mail boxes, and junk paper mail that fills our real mail boxes while simultaneously wasting precious paper.

Every time we receive a credit card statement we can almost guarantee a flyer that matches our consumer tastes. Now police officers routinely key cars' number plates into their Mobile Data Terminal to see what pops up, and they can even arrest and detain us until the outstanding warrant for a twenty-year-old parking offense is dug out of some county filing cabinet.[54] Unfortunately, as far as the arresting officers are concerned, we could be cop killers or double parkers, but the system labels us as criminals until humans can sort out the significance. And that lack of ability to discriminate is the point.

Furthermore, beneath the routinization of simple processes lies the belief that just because it is cheaper, it is more effective or efficient. Is a twenty-year-old parking ticket really worth an hour or two of a policeman's time—let alone the inconvenience and indignity of the arrested parties, who must sweat it out in the lock-up while waiting for some indication of what offense will be charged? If the arresting officers knew the details of the warrant, and if they were given a choice, would they elect to keep patrolling and assist in the prevention of crime rather than extract an old parking fine? Yet because someone somewhere decided to have all outstanding warrants put on the database, without applying any judgment to what that decision might mean in practical terms, what ensues is a farce that is only ended when human judgment prevails.

Here—in the bulk mail-outs, phone calls, nonsense billings, arrests for ancient oversights, and other standardized, judgment-free treatments— we see perhaps the greatest threat to our privacy: the removal of our right to be treated as an individual human being and not as a Social Security number, a number plate, a credit history, or an insurance record. Such numbers have no rights. They are targets, raw data, or database fields, and they are to be sorted, matched, mailed to, called, approved, denied, updated, bought, and sold. They don't need sleep, fear embarrassment, get angry, feel cold or hungry, forget things, or make mistakes. If they did, human judgment would be called for to deal with them, and that is incompatible with the routinized, standardized repetition that digital processing makes possible.

This instrumental treatment of human beings is at the heart of the privacy issue. Nothing is as naked as a number. It differs from the next number only by a single digit and deserves to be treated no differently from other digits in its range. Unless we protect our right to individuality, our right to the quality of differentness—even uniqueness—then all our efforts to restrict invasive monitoring, data logging, eavesdropping, and so on will amount to nothing. If we regard ourselves as numbers, as fodder for computation, then there is no impediment to the growing invasion of privacy.

Therefore, we need to ponder the larger issue of what the application of computing to social processes means for the rights and freedoms of ordinary citizens. How can we ensure that our lives are not a litany of database errors? How can we ensure the proper functioning of a democratic society and the adequate control of criminal elements and yet still maintain a society relatively free of surveillance? How can we provide jobs with the participative, trusted, and profitable involvement of workers without resorting to high levels of invasive monitoring? Perhaps the final answer is that nothing in life can be guaranteed, but that the first step toward the resolution of any problem is to be aware of it. All else follows from this realization, and fostering that awareness, at least in part, is one of the aims of this book.

7

Artificial Intelligence and Expert Systems

A Nevada woman, Julie Engle, underwent routine surgery in a hospital. The operation was completed without complication. However, soon afterward, Engle was administered pain relief by a computerized dispensing machine. Unfortunately, the system mistakenly instructed hospital staff to pump more than 500 milligrams of pain-relieving drugs into Engle's body, and within thirty minutes of the successful completion of the operation, she went into a coma. Five days later, she was pronounced brain dead. Engle had been secretary to Salt Lake City lawyer Vibert Kesler, who immediately launched a damages suit against the hospital for incorrect and irresponsible use of a medical expert system.[1]

If this kind of tragedy can occur with a comparatively simple application of artificial intelligence, imagine what might happen with some of the more complex applications planned for AI and expert systems. For example, the FBI is developing Big Floyd, an expert system designed to catch drug smugglers and to target potential terrorists and other possible miscreants. The U.S. Treasury Department wants to identify money-laundering banks, the Environmental Protection Agency wants to catch polluters, the IRS wants to find tax cheats, the Secret Service wants to target potential assassins, and the FBI's National Center for the Analysis of Violent Crimes is keen to identify potential serial killers, arsonists, and rapists. The application of expert systems is looked upon by all these agencies as one way in which their aims can be achieved by using the vast amount of personal, financial, and census data now contained in various U.S. databases.[2]

What Is Artificial Intelligence?

Definitions of artificial intelligence, or AI, vary quite considerably and more often than not tend to emphasize the peculiar (and sometimes pecuniary) interests of the expert or researcher offering the definition. Briefly, though, AI consists of two branches of research: one branch attempts to shed light on the nature of human intelligence by simulating it, or components of it, with the eventual aim of replicating it (or even surpassing it); the other branch attempts to build expert systems that exhibit intelligent behavior regardless of their resemblance to human intelligence. The latter school is particularly concerned with the construction of intelligent tools for assisting human beings in complex tasks such as oil exploration, medical diagnosis, chemical analysis, and fault identification in machinery. Other activities that fall under these two branches of endeavor include attempts to build systems with visual perception, systems that understand natural language, systems that demonstrate machine-learning capacities, systems that can manipulate objects (e.g., robotics), systems that can provide intelligent tuition, and systems that play games.

Artificial intelligence emerged as an academic discipline at a Dartmouth College, New Hampshire, conference in 1956. The term was invented by John McCarthy, the developer of one of AI's most popular programming languages, LISP. Much of the earliest work in AI was concerned with the construction of programs to play games in an intelligent fashion. Indeed, programs now have been constructed that can beat more than 99 percent of all human players in games such as tic-tac-toe (noughts and crosses), checkers, and especially chess.

Chess has highlighted some of the major differences in the way that humans and machines solve demanding intellectual tasks, and chess has also fueled criticism of other forms of problem solving using artificial intelligence. For example, while computers are forced to consider all possible moves from a given position, humans appear to be able to take a chess pattern and rapidly identify a handful of powerful moves. In other words, computers solve chess problems by the application of brute computational power (and, even then, the total combination of moves—10^{120}—is beyond them), while humans are able to exclude millions of disadvantageous moves at a glance.

It appears that this ability depends very much upon experience in the recognition of meaningful chess patterns. In a classic experiment, one of the high priests of AI, Herbert Simon, showed that meaningful chess positions were much more easily remembered by chess experts than by novices, but that when positions were essentially random, no differences in recall existed between novices and experts.[3] From this we can conclude that at least part of human expertise in chess lies in the ability to take a meaningful chess position (one that resembles known patterns of offense and defense) and focus on the few lines of development that are likely to improve the position. Computers, on the other hand, are unable at present to adopt this approach and must tediously calculate the worth of each possible sequence of future moves.

Yet this brute computational approach to chess playing has had its successes, and the very best chess programs can offer serious challenges to even the world's chess champion. And as computers become inevitably faster and researchers more experienced in the inadequacies of their software, it is likely that this gap between machines and the best of human players will close. Some research groups now believe that the best human player might be beaten within a decade, given the enormous gains in computational power that are appearing on the horizon.[4] Already, the title of world checkers champion held by Marion Tinley is under threat from a computer. At a recent competition, Tinley won 4–2 against the program known as Chinook. The other thirty-three games were drawn, but what is most revealing about the play-off is the fact that since the year of 1954, Tinley had lost only five games to human opponents.[5]

Part of the reason why humans are so capable in information reduction and, indeed, why they behave so intelligently across such a multitude of tasks and situations is that they have actively experienced the world and have accumulated a great deal of background or commonsense knowledge that assists them. For example, in navigating around a room, it is obvious that I know an enormous number of things about the physical properties of the world: doors, walls, and objects are solid and cannot be walked through, although doors can be if they are open; I know about gravity and objects falling if I knock them; I have enormously powerful perception that gives me depth and distance cues under great variations in lighting, including an understanding of the nature of glass; I know what purposes stairs fulfill and why they are designed the way they are as well as the hazards associated with using them.

Clearly, for a constant environment, this kind of knowledge can be provided for a computer, as shown by MIT's Terry Winograd in his block world known as SHRDLU—an environment of blocks, pyramids, and other shapes that can be manipulated by a computer on command.[6] The real difference, however, is that the knowledge I use to navigate a room represents only a miniscule fragment of the knowledge I have of the world in all of its physical, social, cultural, historical, political, economic, and scientific forms. In Winograd's block world, the smallest changes in the environment require extensive changes to the program, yet ordinary human beings deal with the world in a totally fluent, adaptable, and quite amazing manner when compared to the most adaptable and intelligent of machines.

One answer to this problem—namely, the commonsense knowledge that we have and that computers don't—has been to construct systems that attempt to learn from experience. Yet this, too, has met with disappointing levels of success.[7] We do not know in advance what a program needs to possess in terms of knowledge if it is to demonstrate real intelligence. Further, allowing a computer to interact with the world in order to acquire such knowledge often seems to fall foul of the sheer size of the knowledge that needs to be accumulated, as well as the difficulties of storing it in an appropriate form for it to be used again. Even more fundamentally, we don't understand what learning is (because much of learning also involves discarding unnecessary information—that is, forgetting), let alone what kinds of knowledge should be learned and how it should be structured.

Given a moment's thought, the existence of these difficulties makes a great deal of sense. As infants, human beings spend several years acquiring the kind of experiential knowledge they need in order to physically interact with the world and to manipulate it (and themselves) in an intelligent manner. Furthermore, it appears that, to some extent, we are designed to develop in this way. That is, we are constructed in a fashion that predisposes us to learn language and develop intellectually during years of experience. For example, children have an innate ability to acquire language; indeed, it is quite easy for children to learn several languages before puberty. Yet after this point has been reached, it becomes extremely difficult for individuals to acquire multiple languages (as any adult language learner can attest).

In addition, the evidence from cases of feral children (those raised by wild animals, such as wolves) shows that without exposure to language in these prepubescent years, individuals are incapable of developing human language at all. It is almost as if the human body regards puberty as the turning point to adulthood before which everything we need to survive (intellectually and perhaps even physically) should have been developed. After that point, the system loses its flexibility and locks up, taking the young adult through life with whatever intellectual capacities have or have not developed. It therefore remains a moot point whether researchers in AI can ever simulate this kind of experiential acquisition of knowledge, especially given the advantages that humans obviously have in their evolved predisposition to intellectual development.

What Is Intelligence?

The lessons learned from these efforts have also raised interesting questions about the nature of human intelligence and, indeed, exactly where the dividing line between intelligent and unintelligent behavior lies (or even if such a line exists). Several critics of AI, for example, have claimed that the brute computational approach to chess playing outlined previously could hardly be called intelligent. On the other hand, proponents of AI argue that the criterion of intelligence is constantly (and unfairly) redrawn by critics as soon as that criterion has been reached.[8] For example, at one stage arithmetical ability was regarded as a hallmark of intelligence, yet now that computers can calculate millions of times faster than any human that has ever lived, this is no longer regarded as a requirement of intelligence. Similarly, chess playing was once regarded as a demanding intellectual activity, yet now that computers can easily defeat the vast majority of chess players (though not all), this, too, seems to be losing its status as a litmus test of intelligence.

This argument begs the question of exactly what intelligence is and whether or not it can exist in nonhuman forms. After all, if at least one branch of AI aims to create intelligence (human or not) in a computational form, then surely a necessary first step is to define the parameters of that goal. Again, critics have argued that AI is a form of modern alchemy that is based on the latest metaphor of the mind, or at least its physical manifestation as the brain. In the days of Descartes, the brain was thought to be composed of hydraulic lines and pistons (then, the most powerful of technologies); later it was regarded as a telephone exchange (again, the most sophisticated of technologies of the time); and, now that the computer has gained supremacy as the ultimate technology of our age, not unexpectedly the brain is regarded as an information-processing engine—a computer with nonsilicon circuits. Thus critics of AI believe that the brain and hence the mind are unlikely to be under-stood in computational terms because there is little evidence that AI is based on anything other than the most recent technological metaphor of mind. For them, whatever achievements have occurred in AI are pathetic parodies compared to the richness, power, and fluency of the intelligence that every average human being displays in the course of daily life.

Despite this, many AI researchers are adamant that human intelligence is a symbol-manipulating activity that can be simulated in toto or at least in part by computational means. In other words, as intelligent beings, we have internal symbols or processes that have external referents and associated meanings, and by manipulating those symbols in rule-governed ways, we come to exhibit meaningful behavior in a dynamic environment. Yet one of the most powerful arguments against this view is John Searle's so-called Chinese Room scenario.[9]

Searle, a philosopher and long-time sceptic of the claims for artificial intelligence, proposes the following thought experiment: suppose that a man is inside a room that has a gap under the door and through this gap he receives sheets of paper from someone outside. No other form of communication is possible. The sheets of paper have Chinese symbols written on them, and the task for this individual is to translate those symbols into some other language, such as English. To do this, he looks up at a table on the wall and writes down the equivalent of the Chinese symbol in the required language. He then passes these papers under the door to the person waiting outside.

Now Searle's claim is that although the man in the room has manipu-lated symbols such that Chinese language has been translated into Eng-lish language, in no sense could the man be said to understand Chinese. He has simply followed rules in order to change one particular input format into a desired output format—and this is essentially what digital computers do. (Searle rightly ignores the difficulties associated with actually achieving such a performance level; this is assumed for the sake of the argument.) Hence, any claim that rule-governed symbol manipulation can allow a computer to understand language, or, more broadly, exhibit intelligence, is totally without foundation. Humans may manipulate symbols, but in communicating or demonstrating intelligence in other ways they must be doing other things as well. It is these other things that AI has not come to grips with.

Another approach to identifying what intelligence is, and therefore how we might approach the creation of it, was proposed in the 1950s by one of the founding fathers of computing, Alan Turing. Turing's Test, as it has been termed, has appeared in corrupted and in incorrect forms in numerous places. We therefore have opted to use the original representation of the test as proposed by Turing himself. To begin, imagine a game between three players, A, B, and C. A and B sit together in a room, unseen by C, who converses with them via typewritten messages (modern forms of this scenario could include VDTs). A is a man and B is a woman, but C's sex is immaterial. C has to identify which of his interlocutors is A and which is B. In addition, A's role is to confuse C, and B's role is to minimize C's confusion. The question that Turing asks is: What will happen when a machine takes the place of A in this game? The suggestion made by Turing is that any machine capable of taking A's place without C knowing it must have a strong claim to intelligence. By simplifying the scenario somewhat, many others have generally inferred that any machine that can convince a human that it, too, is human must be capable of thinking.

Yet Turing's test is not without ambiguity. In particular, it does not tell us for how long the human must be convinced that the program, machine, robot, or whatever is intelligent. For example, it has been claimed by some that a number of conversational programs satisfy the Turing test—at least for a while. These include Joseph Weizenbaum's Eliza and Doctor programs[10]—the latter simulating a Rogerian psychotherapist—and Kenneth Colby's Parry program,[11] which simulates a paranoid schizophrenic. Indeed, during the development of the Doctor program, Weizenbaum's secretary asked him to leave the room while she conversed with the therapist. Therefore, it appears that the extent to which machines are able to simulate human conversational intelligence is subject to a very human and subjective process—judgment.

Of course, neither Searle's nor Turing's test provides a great deal of assistance in determining just what intelligence is and therefore how it may (or may not) be recreated in either human or nonhuman forms. Searle's argument goes some distance in this direction, however, by arguing that intelligence is essentially the property of human brains. To get to this point, Searle argues the following: The man in the Chinese room is following instructions just as a computer does—indeed, the instructions constitute a program—and like any computer program, these instructions will yield identical results regardless of the physical mechanisms used to execute them. That is, we could replace the man with a complex system of pattern-matching video cameras or with an electromechanical device that runs templates over the symbols until one matches and then returns the relevant English translation. In principle, we could construct a computer out of beer cans (yes, it would work), and the Chinese translation program could be made to execute on such a machine.

This principle is one of the very foundations of AI: programs are formal representations and are therefore executable on any form of computational equipment. Furthermore, because AI proponents argue that the brain is a form of computational device, the program that executes within the brain (the product of which is our mind) must be able to be executed on other forms of computational machinery, such as digital computers. Thus, in order to replicate the mind, all we need do is discover the nature of the program that executes within the brain; we can then run it on a digital computer and replicate a mind. However, Searle's scenario is a strong criticism of this principle, which essentially disregards the physical architecture on which a program executes. In his view, our mental states are an outcome of the physiology of the brain. The mind is not a program that can be executed on any computer whether it be composed of beer cans, silicon, or neurons; instead, our mind emerges as a result of the particular neurophysiological properties of our brain.

That statement is not as ridiculous as it may sound. Searle is not saying that our intelligence cannot be recreated. Indeed, a common but incorrect representation of Searle's argument claims that he believes that only brains or organic mechanisms can become conscious. This carbon chauvinism, as it has been called, is not true of Searle's approach, but it is true that any mechanism that is causally equivalent to the brain (that is, in the way that it produces thinking) would be capable of producing comparable mental states. In other words, as systems theorists would have it, thinking, or the mind, is an emergent property of the brain as a physical organ in action.[12] A good analogy is to argue that whirlpools, steam, ice, raindrops, snowflakes, and sleet are phenomena that emerge from (or are caused by) the physical properties and characteristics of the water molecule. Similarly, Searle might argue, minds emerge from the peculiar structural, electrophysiological, and chemical qualities and processes of the human brain. By extrapolation, we might also infer that other animals also may have minds or at least possess mental states that are a byproduct of their own peculiar neurophysiological characteristics.

Lastly, because for many commentators language is the hallmark of intelligence, we need to devote some further attention at this point to the enormous difficulties language poses for efforts to understand it computationally. Again, as with our ability to navigate around a room, in understanding language we bring to bear an enormous amount of experience in hearing it, producing it in a variety of forms, and developing it formally through our education systems. Hence when I utter the sentence, "I can't bear it any longer," we immediately understand the context. One knows from experience that I'm not talking about a large, hairy and sometimes dangerous mammal, nor am I talking about the fruitfulness of a tree or the load-carrying capacity of a steel girder.

Such multiple meanings could, of course, be encoded in computational form (although this would be tedious and difficult), but other forms of language remain intractable for computers. For example, if I said "I have never failed any student in second-year mathematics," the implication is, of course, that I have taught such a course and that I have done so for some considerable length of time. Also, if I were to say, "I can't sit for the examination. My doctor has provided me with a medical certificate," the implications are that my illness prevents me from sitting the examination, that the medical certificate is a form of evidence for this claim, and that possibly some alternative assessment arrangements may be made or that the absence of an exam mark will be considered in the context of my illness.

Yet, for a computer, the second sentence, "My doctor has provided me with a medical certificate," might just as well be "I like eating chocolate." The inferences we draw are based upon our immense background and commonsense understanding of the world. As a further example, the sentences "The porridge is ready to eat" and "The tiger is ready to eat" are syntactically identical but semantically disparate. In order to understand these sentences, too, one needs considerable background information about what tigers and porridge are and the whole host of properties that we know they do and don't possess. Obviously, one conjures up thoughts of breakfast, and the other, thoughts of predation.[13] Unfortunately, as yet, computers do not have the necessary experiential context to understand such sentences, although there is hope that in the future some mechanism might allow us to efficiently represent such knowledge (massive and inconsistent though it might be) or gain it in an experiential (learned) manner similar to the way humans acquire it.

As a criticism of this approach, however, it is clear that, at least for human language, much of it depends on its anthropocentric basis—that is, the complex experience we have of being human and interacting with the world from inside a human body and within a human society and culture.[14] For example, when I say "He was heavy hearted," I don't mean that he has an inability to support his own heart or that his heart is made of lead. Even a human who had never heard this expression could probably decipher its meaning, having experienced the physiological or at least physical symptoms that depression or sadness brings. Similarly, comprehending "an iron fist inside a velvet glove" requires an understanding of what a fist represents (anger, repression, violence) as well as the physical and metaphorical properties of velvet (softness to the touch, delicate nature, etc).

This is not to say that some restricted subsets of language with identified meanings in fixed contexts (such as legal or economic contexts) cannot be understood by machines—quite the opposite. But it does imply that what we term natural language is natural to us as humans and is determined to a very large extent by the nature of human beings as physical and physiological, social and emotional entities. It also implies that without a similar physiological and experiential basis, computational efforts to understand language by application of syntax and grammar alone cannot approach the experience of language as it exists for humans.[15]

Expert Systems

In essence, expert systems are programs that encapsulate an expert's or several experts' knowledge of a particular knowledge domain in a computer-processable form. From this knowledge base, inferences may then be drawn that may equal or (hopefully) exceed the quality of similar inferences made by human experts.

Other definitions of an expert system that have been offered at different times include the following:

"An expert system is a computer system that uses a representation of human expertise in a specialist domain in order to perform functions similar to those normally performed by a human expert in that domain."
"An expert system is a computer system that operates by applying an inference mechanism to a body of specialist expertise represented in the form of 'knowledge.'"[16]

Such systems have been applied to many problem areas—for example, the analysis of chemical compounds (Dendral),[17] the diagnosis and treatment of infectious diseases (Mycin),[18] the configuration of computer systems for shipment (XCON),[19] and identifying likely areas for mineral exploration and mining (Prospector).[20] Yet, in some senses, expert systems have been around for many years in one form or another as sophisticated programs; the difference is that the knowledge base encapsulated in an expert system is not just the programmer's, but the structured understanding of acknowledged experts in a particular problem domain. Indeed, for the most part, expert systems are collections of rules that have been extracted from an expert by a knowledge engineer and they very often, although not exclusively, take the form of IF . . . THEN statements. For example, suppose that we wanted to construct an expert system for fault diagnosis of jet engines (and such systems do exist), then some of the rules we might identify could include the following:

IF the engine stalled in flight,
  AND the aircraft's wing was at a high or excessive angle of attack at low speed,

AND the engine subsequently restarted at a normal angle of attack,
THEN the engine may have suffered a compressor stall as a result of inadequate airflow into the engine caused by the aircraft being in a near-stall condition.

Similarly, in the case of a medical diagnostic system such as Mycin,

IF the infection requiring therapy is meningitis,
  AND the type of infection is fungal,
  AND organisms were not seen on the stain of the culture,
  AND the patient is not a compromised host,
  AND the patient has been in a region where coccidiomycoses are endemic,
  AND the race of the patient is black or Asian or Indian,
  AND the cryptococcal antigen in the csf was not positive,
THEN there is suggestive evidence that the cryptococcus is not one of the organisms that might be causing the infection.[21]

Of course, IF-THEN rules are not the only form in which knowledge can be stored in an expert system's knowledge base. Other forms include semantic networks, frames, and predicate logic, yet the essential nature of expert systems in applying deductive (and often inductive) methods to a body of knowledge remains unchanged. We should also note that the real benefit of expert systems occurs in applications of much greater complexity than this and that a number of such systems are able to supply the appropriate intervention, therapy, or repair procedures for the particular case in hand. In order to achieve this success, expert systems not only use a knowledge base and an inference engine to operate on that knowledge, but they also usually provide an explanatory interface that justifies their conclusions by explaining the system's line of reasoning with relevant probabilities for each of the conclusions it draws. Furthermore, much of the hard work involved in constructing an expert system is not so much at the programming level (although that can be very difficult) but in the extraction of rules from human experts by the knowledge engineer. Very often, experts do not consciously know the rules they use, and the knowledge engineer has to be skilled in identifying a rule component when it appears in an expert's explanation. Furthermore, experts' rules and knowledge often conflict, not only across experts but even in the same expert. Therefore, resolving such clashes is also part of the knowledge engineer's task.

Given the growth in the development of and the use of expert systems, particularly now that shells (software environments) for building such systems are quite common, perhaps it is appropriate to ask some questions about expert systems and their relationship to AI. For example, are expert systems intelligent? Are they part of artificial intelligence in any meaningful sense? Clearly, expert systems are part of the branch of AI that is concerned with the construction of intelligent tools, regardless of whether that intelligence resembles human intelligence. Perhaps, then, we should regard expert systems as smart tools, not possessing intelligence in any real sense (although again, we should be cognizant of whether we are redefining the criteria for intelligence) but simply assisting in the performance of tasks that humans find difficult and that take many years of acquiring sufficient expertise to solve. If this is the case, then perhaps expert systems inclusion under the label AI is a misnomer that is inappropriately applied to what effectively represents just another arm of computer science or information systems.

We need to contrast this claim with that made by people such as Donald Michie of the University of Edinburgh, Scotland, who argues that expert systems can provide syntheses of knowledge bases that represent new forms of knowledge that do not not have any human analog (for example, in the categorization of multiple heart arrhythmias that humans find difficult to diagnose).[22] If this is so, then perhaps expert systems do constitute a form of intelligence. Yet, again, we need to judge whether such new knowledge forms are in any way different from mathematical transformations applied to satellite weather data (which show different features of the climate) or chemical stains applied to cell cultures, which again yield new features or phenomena.

In more recent years, deeper criticisms have emerged regarding the real and widespread commercial utility of expert systems. Although many firms and research bodies have begun to develop expert systems, there appears to be a large gap between experimentation and actual, profitable usage by workers and managers. A 1989 Japanese survey found that of 388 expert systems under development, only 120 were working systems and 40 of these were the product of a single firm. In Australia, a similar survey revealed that since 1987 there had been a significant decline in the number of firms undertaking expert system work and that the original expectations of expert systems were unrealistic.[23] Other writers, such as Diane Berry and Anna Hart, have echoed the observation that there are relatively few expert systems in working practice, given the amount of work and the level of expectations placed upon them.[24]

Deeper misgivings that echo criticisms of conventional AI have been articulated by H. M. Collins, a British sociologist. Collins argues that the most appropriate tasks for computers are those that are narrowly defined, that require clearly constrained information and endless repetition. In other words, when we define a task so narrowly that we can perform it with much less than our full human capacities of judgment and knowledge, then it is appropriate for a machine. Intentional behavior—the kinds of acts people perform—requires vast contextual knowledge, a knowledge "soup," that sits upon a hierarchy of human interaction and socialization. Just as with AI's attempts to replicate human intelligence, in Collins's view expert systems will always encapsulate narrow, grainy knowledge bases with no foundation of intentionality or common sense.[25]

Legal Problems

Despite these misgivings, according to a recent report, at least half the U.S. corporations listed in the *Fortune 500* are currently developing expert systems either for their internal use or for commercial sale. This finding seems to suggest that many major companies in the United States have considerable faith in the future of expert systems. But despite this apparent confidence, there are substantial legal problems with expert systems that need to be resolved before we are likely to see more widespread application of these systems. For example, the Medical Software Consortium, a St. Louis supplier of medical systems, baulked at becoming involved in a joint NASA-U.S. Army project to develop an autonomous intensive care stretcher with expert diagnostic capabilities. For them, the potential for lawsuits was too daunting. This perception is becoming common given the eight-fold increase in product liability cases, for instance, that occurred between 1974 and 1986, when 13,595 such cases were filed.[26] Moreover, it seems that no company wants to be the test case for an expert system product liability suit, and everyone in the industry is concerned about how such a case would affect product liability insurance costs.

According to some sources, in certain cases government agencies have applied the same measures to software that they use to help regulate human experts. In 1986, for example, the Internal Revenue Service allegedly began treating software used to generate income tax returns in the same way that it deals with humans involved in tax preparation: if such a program makes a mistake, then it's liable.[27] However, this conclusion raises a major problem that is not resolved by such rulings—namely, just who is liable (because a system obviously cannot be). To help answer this question and to examine its complexities, we cite a scenario and the associated interpretation by one expert in the area, Richard M. Lucash.

Suppose that a chemical company, Chemcorp, obtains an expert system from a computer company, Syscorp. The purpose of the system is to control a process at one of Chemcorp's plants. Imagine that part of the system's task is to control the temperature of this process and that a defect in the system causes the plant to explode, thereby damaging the plant, causing injuries to workers and bystanders, and resulting in financial losses to Chemcorp because of shipping delays. In accordance with general practice in the software industry, Syscorp will have signed a contract with Chemcorp specifying that the system would have to meet certain performance standards and defining Syscorp's obligations if such standards were not met. These obligations might include repair of the system within the warranty period and reimbursement of financial loss. However, most such contracts place a specified limit on the software company's liability, and so, in this scenario, Chemcorp would have to bear some proportion of the costs resulting from the malfunction. Furthermore, Syscorp would be relieved of liability if the cause of the fault could be traced to Chemcorp or some other party—for example, if the system was not used as directed.

Moreover, Syscorp's contracts with other suppliers or contractors (say, chip or software companies) could further affect attribution of liability. In general, most of the elements of this chain, from designers to suppliers and subcontractors, would carry some form of insurance to protect themselves. Hence, for those parties who have contractual arrangements among themselves, attribution of liability is an ordered process, and in this sense expert systems and any other form of computer system are not differentiable. However, for those parties who are not linked by contractual arrangements, such as the bystanders injured in Chemco's explosion who now seek compensation, a different set of procedures applies—those pertaining to negligence and defective production.

It needs to be pointed out that negligence in the legal framework we are discussing is somewhat different from malpractice. Negligence means a failure to act as a reasonable person would under the same circumstances, whereas malpractice is a failure to demonstrate the minimum level of competence required by a profession. Judgments of malpractice in the United States turn on the extent to which an event could be foreseen, whether the work was primarily for the benefit of the client (and not other unknown parties who could be affected by it), and whether or not extending the professional's liability to the situation in hand would discourage others from entering the profession.

As Lucash argues, perhaps the most interesting case that has generalizable implications for all expert systems is when a professional uses an expert system containing the codified knowledge of another professional. For example, imagine that a doctor uses an expert system and, as a result of the system's faulty knowledge, the patient dies. In these circumstances, clearly the doctor who supplied the knowledge could foresee that it would be used by other doctors, yet, at the same time, an attribution of liability here could effectively discourage any doctor from helping to construct such expert systems. In these circumstances, Lucash suggests that experts require software companies to indemnify them against liability for errors or other inadequacies in the knowledge they supply. Certainly, the doctor using this system could be liable, especially if it was discovered that he failed to exercise a professional judgment or that he used the system contrary to manufacturer's instructions. As a point of interest, though, a doctor may also be liable if he failed to use such a system should it have been available, especially if it could be demonstrated that it would have improved patient care.

Given the preceding framework, clearly it is senseless to attribute liability to a system, although there are legal mechanisms in the United States by which product liability can be invoked. The doctrine of strict liability requires that one who sells a product in a defective condition—that is, unreasonably dangerous to the user—is subject to liability for the physical harm caused to the ultimate user. Injured parties thereby can claim compensation from the manufacturer or any other party in the chain of distribution. This provision removes the need to demonstrate that the manufacturer or distributors acted negligently. Only the defect that rendered the product unreasonably dangerous need be demonstrated.

However, this doctrine is problematical when applied to expert systems. First, the doctrine applies only to physical harm to persons or property. Some applications of expert systems will not involve this (e.g., a faulty prospecting program). Second, the doctrine does not apply to services (where expert systems have enormous application), only to products, basically because professional services are subsumed under the malpractice provisions. And when a combination of goods and services is provided (as with many expert systems), a court must look to whether the primary purpose of the transaction was to provide a product or a service. Applying these rules to a computer system, it appears that strict liability would not be imposed when the injured party is not a user of the system, because that user was primarily obtaining a service. Hence, in our example of the medical expert system, the patient was obtaining a service, and when the patient's next-of-kin sues the doctor for malpractice, the doctor may wish to seek compensation from the manufacturer through product liability. But this action probably would be disallowed because product liability is usually limited to cases in which the injured party is a consumer only.[28]

Other legal authorities have commented on the complexities involved in attributing liability in the case of expert systems. But, generally speaking, all parties involved in the development and use of expert systems may be exposed to some degree of legal risk. The knowledge engineer who implements the system risks overlooking important factors or misinterpreting the judgments of the domain experts on whom he or she relies. The domain expert defines the rules interpreted by the system and can make errors of omission or commission that create exposure to risk. The user might cause damage or injury by misinterpreting the outputs of the expert system; even failure to use an expert system—by a physician or lawyer, for example—might expose the potential user to a charge of passive negligence if it can be shown that the expert system could have avoided the damages or injuries that were incurred.[29]

Thus, the application of existing law to expert systems is not without problems. Yet, given the nature of our legal system and its foundation on precedent, it is unlikely that such inconsistencies and ambiguities will be resolved before the first test cases have worked their way through the courts. We can only speculate as to what the outcome might be.

Newer Developments

Despite these serious legal problems, expert systems are one of the more successful technologies to emerge from recent research into artificial intelligence. Although their widespread application still represents more of a promise than an obvious reality, as a number of commentators have noted, some expert systems clearly provide valuable service.[30]

Other initiatives in AI have tended to be mostly smoke and mirrors. The Japanese Fifth Generation Project, for example, launched with great fanfare in 1981, aimed to significantly advance the development of AI and parallel processing by 1991. More specifically, the project was expected to create systems that could understand natural language and speech, interpret the visual world, tap large databases, and solve complex problems by the application of inductive and deductive inference. Experts disagree on the exact state of play with the Fifth Generation Project— and, indeed, on the nature and aims of the project in the first place—but most accept that progress has been disappointing and that no major breakthroughs were achieved. The project's main effect was to galvanize Western governments into action; it led directly to the establishment of the MCC consortium in the United States and the Esprit project in Europe, for instance.[31]

A more promising line of research, included under the rubric of connectionism, aims to create intelligent machines by building neural networks. These networks consist of thousands of processing units, each analogous to a neuron in the brain, that are interconnected by links that are analogous to the synaptic connection between neurons.[32] Each link has a weight, or a connection strength, and a system's knowledge is encoded in the link weights and in the interconnection pattern of the system. Some units serve as input units and others as hidden units (they are connected to other units and thus cannot be seen from either the input or the output channels). Such networks have demonstrated the ability to learn by being given particular inputs and associating them with desired outputs. Furthermore, neural nets can exhibit associative recall in that they are able to produce a complete pattern of output once they are given a fraction of a particular pattern's input. A final interesting property of this technology is the extent to which it is fault tolerant (in something like the way the brain continues to function despite daily cell deaths and developmental decline).

To date, most neural nets have been simulated using very large Von Neumann architecture machines, but such simulations have been very slow in execution. There is hope, however, that with the development of massively parallel machines, neural networks will improve dramatically. David Waltz has estimated that if the present thousandfold increase in computing power every ten years continues, then, aided by connectionist models, a computer with the processing power of the human brain could be built for around $20 million (at today's prices) by the year 2012. In addition, if the decline in the cost of memory continues at its present rate (around a factor of ten every five years), then a machine with the connectionist memory capacity of the brain might be constructed for a cost of about $20 million (at today's prices) by the year 2017.[33] However, other writers, such as Jacob Schwartz, have been at pains to point out the enormous differences between what is known about the functioning of the brain and what we can reasonably expect from extrapolating existing developments in connectionism.[34] Although many researchers are optimistic that connectionist models may help diminish this gap, the issue remains an empirical question.

At another level, connectionism provides an interesting contrast to earlier work conducted within the symbolic-processing rubric, because in many ways their advantages and disadvantages are the mirror reverse of each other. Whereas the symbol-processing approach provided strong hypotheses based on theoretical approaches to cognition and human information processing, connectionism remains an extremely empirical or trial-and-error field, with researchers experimenting with different approaches on flimsy a priori grounds. Whereas symbol processing made concrete assertions about the structure of knowledge and information and how to access it, knowledge in a connectionist network is nothing more than a set of weights between nodes. This kind of knowledge representation is quite impoverished in the sense that it is difficult to see how higher-order concepts or principles can be built or represented in such an architecture. While a connectionist model might learn to discriminate quickly between faulty and faultless items on an assembly line, one wonders how such visual behavior could be enmeshed in higher-order cognition such as language. And this problem arises precisely because we do not yet understand how a simple weightage of inputs and outputs can possibly represent the kinds of knowledge structures that humans appear to use in their everyday activities.[35]

On the other hand, connectionist models free the researcher from developing a knowledge structure in an a priori sense, with all the difficulties that that endeavor has historically involved. Networks learn the optimal set of link weights and in a sense establish their own (although impoverished) knowledge structures once they have stabilized. And possibly it is in such low-level pattern recognition applications that neural nets will have their first real-life successes. Recognizing words in human speech, better robot vision systems, noise filters, quality control systems, and other areas seem tailor-made for connectionist models.[36] Yet offering their behavior as a model of human or other intelligence perhaps is overstated at present.

In a rather dramatic turnaround from his earlier work, Terry Winograd (with Fernando Flores) has mounted a grave challenge to the idea that machines will ever understand natural language and has even questioned the fundamental principles underlying AI.[37] Winograd and Flores claim that most of the past and present discourse in artificial intelligence is based upon a misinterpretation of human cognition and language. They say that the rationalist tradition in Western science and technology assumes that reality has an objective existence that is independent of the observer. In this view, cognitive processes are involved in mapping this reality; by manipulating mental representations of it, we create consciousness or, at least, exhibit thought. Winograd and Flores invoke phenomenologists such as Martin Heidegger and the biologist of perception Humberto Maturana to argue that cognition does not so much represent reality as a dynamic interaction with it that determines what is perceived and how it is understood.

For example, if a stick is illuminated from one side with white light and from another with red light, one shadow appears red and the other green, even though no light normally falls within the range of the spectrum usually associated with green. In other words, they argue, our internal pattern of retinal states determines our perception (rather than the other way around), often with little correspondence to external reality. If we extend this to neuronal states, then cognition is essentially a series of perturbations (by the environment) of the nervous system, and the range of possible perturbations (i.e., the range of events that can possibly alter our cognition) and their effects are determined by an evolutionary or (in the case of learning) a historical process of interaction and selection. That is, in the case of the perception of green, we have evolved to perceive green in these circumstances of reality, and our cognitive interaction with green does not involve a direct mapping—a one-to-one correspondence—between what is out there and its representation in our minds.

Winograd and Flores thus argue that our cognition of color, for example, involves a structural coupling between our cognitive capacities to perceive color and the environment. In other words, the nervous system cannot be seen as a passive filter of reality but as a generator of phenomena that may have little correspondence to the external world. Instead, patterns of stimulation cause perturbations in our nervous system, which has adapted and learned to accept such perturbations (while rejecting others) for the purposes of survival and species development. To put it crudely, Winograd and Flores believe that our cognition is constructed from selected aspects of reality and that, in turn, evolution and historical interaction with the world determine how we perceive the world and deal with it.

This complex argument is not easy to understand or deal with, but it does identify and reinforce some of the major difficulties that AI has and will continue to experience. For example, it suggests that language is a constructed phenomenon, bound up in the nature of human experience and interaction with the world. This is a point that many AI thinkers would agree with. This argument also suggests that for computers to become intelligent in the way that humans are (or to assume intelligence in any form), they need to develop interactively with the environment, just as human beings do. In this case, presumably, computers could develop their own structural coupling and cognitive mechanisms for dealing with the world in the constructivist sense that human beings do. Clearly, though, just how this interactive development can be achieved, or whether it can ever be achieved, remains an open question. Nor is it yet clear how such claims stand in relation to the arguments of Searle that a mind has causal mechanisms that determine it and that computer programs (as they currently exist) do not have such properties. Despite all of this speculation, it is clear that Winograd and Flores have proposed a radical conceptualization of cognition that runs counter to the symbol manipulation hypothesis endorsed by most mainstream AI researchers. It remains to be seen what status this conceptualization will be accorded in the light of future theoretical and practical developments.

A more recent critic of the algorithmic basis of thought is Oxford University's professor of mathematics Roger Penrose. In his book *The Emperor's New Mind*, Penrose provides a dazzling display of quantum mechanics, neuropsychology, metaphysics, and cosmology to convince his audience that intelligence or consciousness emerges from aspects of quantum theory and the possible quantum behavior of biological neurons. Unfortunately, although he mounts a sustained and convincing attack on conventional approaches to AI, Penrose's deeper arguments require a level of mathematical investment that most readers simply cannot provide. Hence, it is difficult to evaluate such claims when a substantial training in physics and mathematics is required as a prerequisite.[38]

Ethical Issues: Is AI a Proper Goal?

The promotion of artificial intelligence and the arrival of expert systems provide a rich source of ethical dilemmas for computer professionals and users. For example, given the extent to which AI has been funded from military sources, should we question the entire ethical basis of such a discipline? Or, because so much research of all kinds is funded by the military, is AI simply guilty of being more successful in this regard? We also need to be very careful about the credence that is placed on claims made by the so-called artificial intelligentsia as they go about pork-barrelling their projects. So many of their utterances over the years have proved to be hype, hot air, and bulldust that most AI watchers have learned to take AI predictions about future developments in the area with several large measures of salt.

But even the more practical and seemingly down-to-earth proposals have disturbing ethical aspects. For example, is it not dangerous to support, as Donald Michie does, the use of expert systems to make judicial judgments, administer our cities, and perhaps even replace our governments? Michie even has been known to state that such systems would have to be taught how to lie, because that is how real (and presumably good?) administrators work. You can't tell everyone the truth just because they ask for it, or so the argument runs. Indeed, Michie and Rory Johnston seriously believe that expert systems will one day solve the problems of unemployment, pollution, crime, war, overpopulation, and terrorism.[39] What faith should we place in such claims? Are they just another technocrat's folly, never to see the light of day? Commentators such as William Ascher have clearly pointed out the limitations of expert systems in political and administrative applications because of their comparatively narrow knowledge base and the difficulty in encapsulating the high-order concepts involved.[40]

Furthermore, what is the real value of claims by AI enthusiasts that we need to provide third world countries with expert systems for medical diagnosis, agricultural advice, and geological analysis because these countries lack substantial human expertise in such areas?[41] Is this suggestion yet another techno-fix that attempts to remedy the symptoms without addressing the causes? Perhaps we could argue (as many scholars have) that the reasons for these inadequacies can be traced to exploitation by the developed world (through irresponsible loan practices, trade cartels, cash crop economies perpetuated by Western involvement, etc.) and that the appropriate strategy for third world countries is to eliminate these problems rather than attempt to bootstrap economies by technological means. After all, what use is an expert system in a country that doesn't have a regular power supply, the parts or people to maintain it, or the expertise to tailor the system to local conditions and needs? Of what benefit is expert system advice that improves, say, agricultural output, if that output merely help pays off a foreign debt that was incurred buying weapons for a civil war brought about by colonial powers deciding that disparate racial groups should become a country? What purpose is there to an agricultural surplus that goes into the pockets of a political elite maintained by a power bloc that happens to need bases or a strategic buffer zone? From such an analysis, perhaps we inevitably are led to the conclusion that the most appropriate line of attack for solving the problems of these countries lies at a nontechnological level rather than through a computerized technological fix.

These issues might seem a long way from our home territory of AI and expert systems, and to a large extent they apply to almost any technology, but the point is that those whom we have termed the artificial intelligentsia have often exercised enormous influence and have commanded considerable resources. If they and their disciplines represent yet another technological talisman for resolving historically intractable problems, then perhaps all of us need to point out the human dimensions of the kinds of problems addressed previously. Perhaps, too, we should bear in mind that many distinguished experts in particular fields regularly make fools of themselves by transgressing the boundaries of what they understand.

At another level, we might also question the ethics of other proposed applications of AI. For example, the fascination that Joseph Weizenbaum's conversational Eliza and Doctor programs generated has led to a number of suggestions that AI be used to assist in the counseling of emotionally disturbed individuals. Given the present state of the art in AI, this proposal is somewhat ridiculous, and it appears even more so when one considers the theoretical and philosophical impediments to machines understanding natural human language that we have already outlined. Perhaps of even greater importance, though, is not just whether AI is a possible goal, but whether AI is a proper goal of human endeavor.

For example, one might argue that the counseling of emotionally disturbed people demands that the counselor have some insight into the nature of emotion and sentiment, not just at an abstract, symbol-manipulating level, but as a fellow human being who can empathize with the emotions of the individual.[42] Joe Weizenbaum has had a considerable amount to say about such questions. In his book *Computer Power and Human Reason: From Judgement to Calculation,* Weizenbaum outlines some potential goals of AI that he believes are immoral. For example, the wiring of sensors to the visual cortexes of blind people is something that he regards as morally obscene. Similar ventures include plans to hook up a machine to the corpus callosum (the main nerve trunk between the brain's hemispheres) of a person so that the machine could monitor nerve fiber traffic and learn from it.[43] Critics such as Weizenbaum may find such suggestions morally repulsive, but, on the other hand, similar experimental work has provided enormous benefits for some afflicted individuals. For example, the replacement of the human cochlea with a "bionic ear" has been pioneered by Australian researchers and has undoubtedly saved some people from the prospect of lifelong deafness.

But there are still other ways in which AI could be seen as an improper goal for society—in the kinds of developments imagined by science fiction writers such as Isaac Asimov.[44] Perhaps the most fundamental question of all is, Do we really need to replace humans by intelligent machines? Do the demands for productivity require that smart computers of some description replace thousands of workers? Should we, say, replace typists with scanning machines that recognize different handwriting? The counterargument may be best represented by an anecdote. A union leader looking over a quarry site bemoans the fate of his workers. He approaches the quarry owner and says, "If it wasn't for those steam shovels, we'd be employing 500 men with shovels." The owner replies, "And if it wasn't for your 500 men with shovels, we'd be employing 10,000 men with thimbles." Perhaps the message of this anecdote is not just that technological change demands changes in the nature of work, but that work can also be dangerous, dirty, and degrading to human beings. In that case, perhaps the design of work for human beings in conjunction with intelligent technology is what we require. Beyond that, the job-reducing potential of technology needs to be managed more effectively by the provision of training programs, incentive schemes, and appropriate government policies.

Quite apart from its consequences for employment, there is also an argument that AI is demeaning to human beings because it degrades the human condition. For example, it has been proposed by experts in robotics that "the specifically human characteristics of emotion, free will, moral responsibility, creativity and ethical awareness can be accommodated by the doctrine of robotic man."[45] Historically, most cultures have come to regard human beings as apart from animals and as the supreme pinnacle of creation or evolution. Humanists, in particular, have felt uncomfortable with the notion of consciousness as a mechanical process or, indeed, as any process that can be decomposed, understood, and recreated. For them, this reductionist viewpoint denies human beings their mystery or the possibility of an essence or soul that exists beyond the physical plane.

On the other hand, AI proponents such as Margaret Boden argue that this reaction arises because we have a limited (and perhaps demeaning) view of machines that stems from nineteenth-century images of clock-work and gears. She argues that such preconceptions do not encompass the potential richness and subtlety that machines can possess.[46] Yet J. David Bolter, in his book *Turing's Man,* argues that the metaphor of the computer leads us to view humanity in finite terms, as opposed to the infinite view of human consciousness popular during medieval and renaissance periods.[47]

Returning to our original line of argument, there may be at least one way in which AI could be unambiguously (in our minds) considered an improper goal for society. It may be intrinsically tainted because of its funding base and clear links with the military establishment, especially of the United States. For example, through funding from DARPA, ar-tificial intelligence researchers have embarked upon a huge spending spree to develop key weapons or weapons-related systems that form part of the Strategic Computing Initiative (SCI). These systems include an intelligent pilot's assistant that can help a fighter pilot under the stress of high-g maneuvers to plan target approaches, exits, and evasive actions and to monitor threats in a hostile aerial environment. Similarly, re-searchers have begun to develop prototypes of autonomous reconnais-sance vehicles that would head out into enemy territory, evade enemy attacks, and transmit tactical information back to a computerized head-quarters. Researchers are also investigating how to build expert systems that could assist generals in making correct decisions in the face of the enormous complexity, conflicting reports, and lightning speeds that char-acterize modern conflicts.[48] In more recent years, $30 billion has been spent on the U.S. Strategic Defense Initiative (Star Wars), a considerable amount of which has been devoted to developing autonomous or intel-ligent systems.[49] Critics once estimated the eventual cost of the program at $100 billion—at a time when the likelihood of superpower conflict was at its lowest for half a century.

We must ask, is it ethically responsible—in other words, is it a proper goal—for us to expend enormous amounts of money on such prospects? In particular, given the extreme difficulty we have in getting machines to do even the most basic of intelligent acts, what are the chances that such programs can succeed? And if they cannot succeed, surely they must be seen as an improper and wasteful enterprise. For example, it is still extremely difficult to get computers to see and intelligently deal with invariant objects that exist in a fixed environment, such as in a factory. In comparison, the problems of getting a machine to recognize objects in a dynamic environment (where, for example, a tank may take on twenty or thirty different forms) with camouflage, rain, poor visibility, and different seasons (which change foliage patterns and landscapes) boggle the imagination. Photograph interpreters, for example, often find it difficult to interpret the prints they receive from reconnaissance cameras on aircraft.

Given that human beings are extremely adept at interpreting their visual world (and have had millions of years of practice), do we really believe that a twenty-ton intelligent monster blundering around a forest can run into tank and aircraft mock-ups and distinguish them from the real thing? Of course, the visual input could be relayed to remote humans for interpretation, but this destroys any claims for intelligence (and perhaps further funding). Furthermore, such vehicles are supposed to conduct their activities in a hostile environment, so they must make their decisions in real time. They can't sit for hours calculating whether the obstacle in front of them is an antitank trap, a natural culvert, or an old latrine trench. If they delay, someone will destroy them. And here we come to the bottom line: how could such machines be cost effective in any sense? Incorporating millions of dollars of computing machinery into an armored shell with tracks and sensors to many people seems tantamount to saying, "Here is a lot of money . . . please burn it for us." If such projects face such enormous practical difficulties, should they be funded at all? There is little doubt among many commentators that without the constant military funding that it has received over the last thirty years or so, AI would almost certainly be just a quaint academic curiosity that few people would have heard of and even fewer would take seriously.[50]

Conclusion: The Limits of Hype

In an address to the Operations Research Society of America on 14 November 1957, the Nobel Prize laureate Herbert Simon stated, "Within ten years [by 1967] a digital computer will be the world's chess champion, unless the rules bar it from competition." He also went on to state, "Within ten years, a digital computer will discover and prove an important mathematical theorem and within ten years a digital computer will write music that will be accepted by critics as possessing considerable aesthetic value." Futurologists such as I. J. Good and Ed Frenkin of MIT's project MAC also claimed around that time that within a few short years we would have ultraintelligent machines able to reprogram themselves and become hundreds of times smarter than people.[51]

By 1970 Marvin Minsky of MIT was willing to be more specific. "In from three to eight years we will have a machine with the general intelligence of a human being," he declared.[52] In 1987 Hans Moravec from Carnegie Mellon University publicly stated that "in an astonishingly short time, scientists will be able to transfer the contents of a person's mind into a powerful computer, and in the process make him, or at least his living essence, virtually immortal." Even more astonishing, Professor Moravec went on to say, "Natural evolution is finished. The human race is no longer procreating, but designing its successors."[53] And as recently as 1992, Intelligent Computer Systems of Rockville, Maryland, announced their goal of developing a learning and thinking machine (LTM) similar to HAL, the superintelligent computer featured in Stanley Kubrick's movie *2001: A Space Odyssey.*[54]

There is little doubt that other disciplines have been guilty of exaggeration, but it is difficult to see how any of these could rival the kinds of hyperinflated claims and grandiose predictions that regularly tumble from the mouths of AI aficionados. Quite simply, there are obvious monetary advantages to be gained from maintaining a wall of pro-AI propaganda. Or, as AI gadfly Harvey P. Newquist III once put it, "In the late 70s and early 80s, everyone with a Ph.D. in Lisp programming from M.I.T., Carnegie-Mellon or Stanford formed a company, and there was enough venture capital floating around at that time to fund everyone with a business plan longer than an index card."

Hard-line critics such as the Dreyfus brothers regularly have ridiculed the inflated claims made by AI exponents.[55] They argue that part of the motivation for AI hyperbole lies in the large monetary incentives that are placed before AI researchers, not only in terms of large research grants that buy machines and research assistants (plus prestige, conferences in exotic places, and international lecture tours) but also in terms of private companies developing intelligent software products.

There is nothing wrong with attempting great feats (where would Silicon Valley be otherwise?), but in the face of monstrous theoretical and applied difficulties, one would expect AI enthusiasts to be a little more cautious and conservative in their predictions. Of course, many so-called AI companies provide useful goods and services in robotics, vision systems, and even expert systems, but the claims of a great many do not live up to reality.[56]

For example, Hubert Dreyfus has recently revised his twenty-year-old book *What Computers Can't Do* (now retitled *What Computers Still Can't Do*), and he has concluded that what he terms Good-Old-Fashioned-AI has clearly failed. After examining the trail of AI's claims and failures, Dreyfus finds it amazing that we ever believed it would be possible to build "a device that could capture our humanity in a physical symbol system." Nor does the recent emphasis on connectionist models shift Dreyfus from his position. "The key problems of endowing a computer with commonsense knowledge loom just as large," he says.[57]

In an earlier review of the Dreyfus brothers' book, *Mind over Machine*, sociologist and social critic Theodore Roszak joined in the attack against AI with the following devastating summary: "Defenders of AI are apt to dismiss the Dreyfus' critique as old hat. It may be. But AI is also old hat, still repeating the same unfounded claims, working with many of the same discredited assumptions after failing again and again to perform as advertised. AI's record of barefaced public deception is unparalleled in the annals of academic study."[58] Roszak goes on to say, in relation to AI's potential application in Star Wars and other complex military systems, that we should be mindful of the Dreyfus' characterization of AI as "snake oil," a "money grab," and a "genuine stupidity." For these critics, informing the public about the seamy side of AI is an obligation that may prevent the dangerous application of an immature and over-rated grab bag of technologies.

8

Computerizing the Workplace

It looks as if humans will be replacing robots for some straightforward work in modern factories. A psychologist told this cautionary tale at the British Association's conference in Bristol. Dr. Toby Wall of Sheffield University said engineers had been asked to design a new factory to make bicycle pedals based on an existing shopfloor with two parallel conveyor tracks. The engineers lined one conveyor with the latest computer-controlled machine tools making the parts and the other with computer-controlled assembly machines for the pedals. At the end, they positioned a robot to pick up finished parts and place them on the track. The system worked. But eventually the engineers removed the robot at the end of the line and put a human operator in its place. The reason, they explained, was because the task "made such little use of the robot's potential and capabilities."[1]

Where Will the Jobs Come From? Computers and the Quantity of Work

Work still remains central to the lives of millions of people. Despite frequent predictions of paid employment's early demise due to the imminent arrival of the leisure society, people who are lucky enough to be employed appear to be working harder than ever. According to a recent Harris survey, the amount of leisure time enjoyed by the average U.S. citizen shrunk by a staggering 37 percent between 1973 and 1989. Over the same period, the average working week, including travel-to-work time, grew from under 41 hours to nearly 47 hours. A recent international survey found that managers work 20 percent longer than they did a decade ago (63 percent put in more than 46 hours), take fewer and shorter vacations, spend more time away on work-related trips, and suffer much higher levels of stress. U.S. Bureau of Labor Statistics (BLS) figures also show that the proportion of Americans holding down two jobs is increasing, and more seem to be doing more work at home and taking part-time or temporary jobs.[2]

According to Juliet Schor, author of *The Overworked American* (1991), average leisure time in the United States has shrunk to just 16.5 hours per week. Moreover, Americans have worked an extra 9 hours a year for the past twenty years, with the result that the average work year in the United States is now almost a month longer than it was back in the halcyon days of 1969. Other U.S. opinion polls also have shown a marked preference among respondents in recent years for longer hours and higher incomes over more leisure and less pay—a reversal of the previous practice of trading income for leisure. Much the same thing seems to be happening in European countries such as Germany, where the sacred weekend is being sacrificed for weekend working in some industries, and in Australia, where twenty-four-hour working is being reintroduced, for example, in the coal industry. The Japanese, of course, continue to work longer hours than anybody else; they put in six weeks a year more than Americans and a huge fourteen weeks a year more than the French and Germans, and they rarely take anything more than very short holidays.[3]

The impact of new technologies in the workplace is an issue that has caused controversy throughout history. The most famous example is the Luddites, who went around the north of England in 1811–1812 smashing new textile machinery that they thought would decimate employment in the textile industry (it didn't). When the microchip first came to public attention in 1978–1979, equally dire predictions were made about the impact of this latest new technology on employment levels across manufacturing industry and commerce. There were even calls (in Holland) for a new tax on automation and calls in some quarters for the outright rejection of microprocessor-based technology in the workplace because of its job-destroying potential. In the context of rapidly rising unemployment in OECD countries, especially those of Europe, these concerns seemed reasonable, and the debate on computerization was largely structured in terms of its employment impact.

Then, in the late 1980s, the employment debate was put on the back burner for three main reasons. First, the introduction of computers into the workplace was much slower and messier than expected because of a host of financial, technical, human, and organizational problems (including oversell by the computer industry). The employment impact was correspondingly less severe and less obvious, while trade union opposition to new technology—with one or two exceptions, such as Fleet Street in London—was negligible to nonexistent. Second, the unemployment rate ceased to increase at such an alarming speed and, indeed, was falling steadily in many OECD countries. In the United States, the rate remained remarkably low on average. Third, the realization, particularly in the United States and in Europe, that the baby boom generation's entry into the work force was largely complete and that the arrival of the baby bust generation in the 1990s might see some shortages of labor developing helped take some of the heat out of the employment debate.

In a major U.S. report that reflected the way in which guarded optimism replaced pessimism in discussions of the employment impact of computers, Richard Cyert and David Mowery argued that there was no evidence to support fears of mass unemployment caused by technological change. Some contributors to their authoritative 1987 study *Technology and Employment: Innovation and Growth in the US Economy*, which was commissioned by the U.S. National Academy of Science, suggested that new technology ultimately would create more jobs than it would destroy, although they said that there would be lengthy and painful periods of adjustment for certain groups of workers. Other contributors to the volume repeated the familiar orthodox refrain that job losses would be more likely to result from the slow adoption of new technology rather than the too-rapid adoption. They advocated boosting education and training to speed the pace of change.[4]

In the early 1990s, the computers and employment debate is very much back on the agenda. As unemployment climbs or remains stubbornly high in most OECD nations, people again are asking, Where will the jobs come from in the future? In the United States, the famed Great American Job Machine, which created 31 million jobs in the 1970s and 1980s, appears to have ground to a halt. In the 1990–1992 recession, nearly 2 million jobs were lost as a result of downsizing, restructuring, and displacement—the favorite euphemisms for firing people. In most instances in which reorganization or computerization took place, the number of positions available usually declined. In the 1990s small companies, which had been responsible for much of the job creation in the 1980s, aren't creating jobs the way they used to. Many companies are shrinking their staff to a nucleus of core employees and intend only to hire part-time workers when and if demand picks up. Some analysts are now suggesting that the U.S. economy is undergoing a sea change and that employment will never recover to the levels prevailing in the halcyon days of the 1950s and 1960s.[5]

There is little doubt that the computerization of factories and offices has led to the steady erosion of employment opportunities, particularly for less-skilled manual workers and for clerical workers. An important British government-backed survey of about 2,000 workplaces, *Workplace Industrial Relations and Technical Change,* found that computers were replacing workers on a considerable scale, but in the medium rather than the short term. Author W. W. Daniel says that the introduction of new technology led to increases in manning in about one case in ten of those studied but to decreases—and often substantial decreases—in about one case in five. Although there were important variations between sectors, workplaces using advanced technology to replace manual workers saw the biggest decreases when observed over a four-year period. Job losses were also greater in the private as opposed to the public sector. However, most of the employment reductions took place through natural attrition over a period of time rather than through redundancies in the short term.[6]

Job losses have been particularly severe in traditional manufacturing industries, where competition from Japan and the newly industrialized countries (NICs) and the process of deindustrialization have made matters much worse. Old-style smokestack industries like steel and cars in Rust Bowl states like Pennsylvania, Indiana, Ohio, and Michigan will never again employ the thousands who used to toil in their huge manufacturing plants. While the U.S. economy generated 18 million new jobs between 1982 and 1989, there was a net loss of jobs in manufacturing of more than half a million; and in the 1990–1992 recession, 1.1 million manufacturing jobs were eliminated almost overnight. Among the hardest hit were food, rubber, electrical equipment, and autos. Manufacturing employment in future will be small-scale, high-tech, and dispersed across the North American continent. By the year 2000, employment in manufacturing industry as a proportion of the total U.S. labor force could be as low as 10 per cent. Precisely the same trends are being witnessed in Europe, but not in Asia.[7]

Job generation in the high-tech sector is impressive, but the high-tech sector remains small relative to aggregate employment. Even in the

United States, high-tech industries account for a mere 3 percent of the nonagricultural workforce, and this figure will grow to only about 4 percent by 1995. To illustrate the problem still further, it has been pointed out that the U.S. automobile industry still employs twice as many people as the entire high-tech sector. In the late 1980s the Bureau of Labor Statistics forecast that high-tech industries in the United States would generate between 750,000 and 1 million jobs by 1995, but this gain would still be less than half the jobs lost from U.S. manufacturing industry in the period 1980–1983 and less than the total of manufacturing jobs lost in 1990–1992. The majority of jobs in the future will be in low-tech or no-tech occupations such as cashier, receptionist, waiter, maid, hospital orderly, janitor, and security guard.[8]

A major study by Stanford University's Henry Levin and Russell Rumberger concluded that "neither high-technology industries nor high-technology occupations will supply many new jobs over the next decade. Instead, future job growth will favor service and clerical jobs that require little or no postsecondary schooling and that pay below average wages." They calculated that employment in jobs related to high-tech would grow by 46 percent in 1995 but that this increase would account for no more than 6 percent of all new jobs created in the U.S. economy.[9]

Likewise, two studies in 1988 and 1991 by consultants in Massachusetts confirmed that high-tech job creation is somewhat problematical. The 1988 study covered 18,000 information technology, biotechnology, and telecommunications companies across the United States. Of these, only 40 percent increased employment over the previous year, and the average gain was 7.2 percent. Although some companies recorded employment gains of 50 percent or more in one year, the majority of companies reduced employment. Based on these findings, the study predicted a modest overall employment gain for the whole high-tech sector in the 1990s of around 3 percent a year. The 1991 study of 22,000 small high-tech companies across the United States found that they had recorded an average gain in employment of 10.6 percent since 1989, but the total number of jobs added—140,000—was a drop in the ocean compared with the jobs lost from manufacturing over the same period.[10]

The 1990–1992 recession hit the high-tech sector badly. According to the American Electronics Association (AEA), in 1991 alone the U.S. electronics industry suffered a net loss of 90,000 jobs (out of a total of

2.35 million) and, for the first time since 1985, employment in software companies did not grow. Worse was to follow in 1992, when all the major computer companies announced further massive cutbacks. At its peak in 1986, IBM employed 410,000 worldwide, but with the axing of a further 40,000 jobs in 1992, IBM's payroll was down to 300,000 by early 1993—a 25 percent drop in five years. Digital announced that a further 18,000 of its workers would be laid off—out of a total already down to 110,000. Unisys closed seven of its fifteen plants and sacked 25,000 workers in 1991–1992, bringing the total reduction in its payroll since the merger of Sperry and Burroughs in 1986 to 54 percent. In addition, Wang, Amdahl, Cray, Hewlett-Packard, Compaq, Sun, and Apple all announced major downsizing and restructuring programs. One interesting phenomenon was that while traditional high-tech centers such as Silicon Valley and Route 128 were doing very badly, new job-creating technology hot spots were emerging around places such as Austin, Texas; Boise, Idaho; and Salt Lake City, Utah.[11]

One trend that could reduce job generation in the U.S. high-tech sector even further is the growing tendency of U.S. companies to export routine data-processing jobs to countries with cheap labor by using the latest satellite and telecommunications technology. Just as U.S. auto makers are setting up high-tech manufacturing plants across the border in Mexico, so corporations like Travelers, New York Life, and McGraw-Hill are sending data across the Atlantic for processing in Ireland, where some 3,000 "back-office" programming, data-entry, and claims-processing jobs have been created. As *Business Week* gleefully reported, "With unemployment at 20 percent, wages for Ireland's well-educated workers are rock-bottom." Indian programmers also are being used extensively by U.S. and European companies. For example, Britain's London Transport gave the job of developing a new timetable for the London underground railway system to a Delhi company. India currently is building a high-quality satellite link to boost this transnational trade in offshore programming.[12]

While there is wide agreement about the high-tech sector's inability to create large numbers of jobs in the future, there is fierce debate about the service sector's continuing ability to generate jobs and about the nature and quality of service sector employment. With 75 percent of the total U.S. work force of around 105 million now in the service sector, and with service sector employment growing at an annual rate of about 9 percent in the 1980s, the future of service sector employment is clearly an important issue.

There are three major debates about the future quantity of service sector employment that have become intertwined. First, the assumption that jobs in the knowledge, or information, industries will continue to grow as they have in the past has been questioned by various researchers. For example, in their book *The Knowledge Industry in the United States: 1960–1980,* Michael Rubin and Mary Huber show that the knowledge sector of the U.S. economy—education, R&D, communications, information services, and so on—grew only from 29 percent of U.S. GNP in 1958 to 34 percent in 1980. What's more, its growth rate had slipped since 1972 to roughly the same as the rest of the economy.[13] This finding seems to negate the earlier work of Marc Porat and, especially, Fritz Machlup, whose book *The Production and Distribution of Knowledge in the United States* (1962), started all the theorizing about future information societies and postindustrial societies—a notion popularized in particular by Daniel Bell in *The Coming of Post-Industrial Society* (1973).

Second, the idea that the service sector can continue to create jobs while the manufacturing sector steadily withers away has been challenged by academics such as Berkeley's Stephen Cohen and John Zysman, who argue forcefully in *Manufacturing Matters: The Myth of the Post-Industrial Economy* that the United States does not have a postindustrial economy, nor is it ever likely to have one, and, furthermore, it had better not try to acquire one. Pointing out that manufacturing in the United States has maintained its share of GNP (if not employment) over the past forty years and that the majority of the U.S. work force is still involved in goods production of some kind, Cohen and Zysman say that it is a mistake to view the process of social development as so many inevitable stages of progress up from agricultural society to industrial society and thence to postindustrial society.[14]

Moreover, Cohen and Zysman argue, the higher-paid manufacturing jobs support many of the lower-paid service sector jobs. The service sector, therefore, cannot continue to expand ad infinitum without a strong, underlying industrial base. And because manufacturers are more tradable than services (a recent House of Lords report in the United

Kingdom concluded that no more than 20 percent of services are tradable overseas), the United States cannot succeed or survive as a world power without being successful as an exporter of manufactured goods. Consequently, they say, the notion that the United States should somehow accept deindustrialization as inevitable, give up on manufacturing entirely, and rely on importing cheaper manufactured goods from the NICs is not only misleading but dangerous. Shifting production overseas will further damage U.S. industry by robbing it of the latest in products and production and design technology. This process is sometimes referred to "hollowing out."

A quite different perspective on the service sector is provided by Dartmouth College's James Brian Quinn, Jordan J. Baruch, and Penny Cushman Paquette, who point out that many service industries are coming to resemble manufacturing industries with their centralized, large-scale, capital-intensive facilities, standardized output (for example, through franchising), and automated distribution techniques. Moreover, service sector pay is fast catching up with manufacturing wages, and more services are being exported. These trends mean, they say, that a U.S. economy dominated by services can continue to support real increases in income and wealth for a long time. Indeed, they predict that most of the economic growth, the opportunities for entrepreneurship, and the applications of information technology will arise in the service sector over the next twenty years. The real danger, they say, is that business and governments will misinterpret the trends and waste money trying to shore up troubled Rust Bowl manufacturing industries.[15]

Third, the industrialization of the service sector that Quinn and his colleagues describe also may put pressure on service sector job creation once computer technology penetrates in a big way. For example, David Roessner of the Georgia Institute of Technology argues that clerical employment in the U.S. banking and insurance industries peaked about 1990 and will decline throughout the 1990s. Even under the most conservative assumptions, he says, absolute reductions in clerical employment of 22 percent in insurance and 10 percent in banking are expected by 2000. U.S. Department of Labor statistics released in 1992 confirmed that employment in services has been static at around 67 million since 1990. A U.K. study of 247 large companies for the Confederation of

British Industry suggested that up to 750,000 white-collar jobs would have to go from inefficient British firms if they are going to be able to compete with efficient U.K. and U.S. companies. Most of the companies in the survey made "the control of personnel costs" (getting rid of people) the most important way of increasing short-term profitability, and the most favored method of doing this was computerization.[16] While doubts have been raised about the quantity of jobs likely to be created in the service sector, there has been growing criticism of the quality of many new service sector jobs. Service sector jobs are generally less well paid, and they offer fewer fringe benefits. Of the 18 million jobs in services created in the 1980s, nearly 5 million paid less than $250 a week (at 1992 prices). This finding means that a quarter of the U.S. work force is now in low-wage jobs. A further 4 million of the jobs created in the 1980s were part-time jobs or temporary jobs, typically taken by married women, that offer no health care, life insurance, or pension entitlements. The United States now has 19 million part-time workers, representing nearly one-fifth of the entire workforce. Four-fifths of these part-timers work in sales, clerical, service, or unskilled labor occupations that are basically low-paid, dead-end jobs. The number of temporary jobs also grew five-fold between 1982 and 1988 to total 1 million. These employees typically are paid less, receive fewer benefits, and, of course, have no job security.[17]

Some say this trend toward part-time and temporary working is creating a new group of second-class citizens, variously called "contingent" as opposed to "regular" workers (in the United States) or "periphery" as opposed to "core" workers (in Europe). Core workers are "functionally flexible": in return for security and decent conditions, they are expected to do whatever the company commands. Periphery workers are "numerically flexible": they are hired to do a specific job when trade improves and fired when no longer required. The contingent work force in the United States is growing rapidly and now amounts to over one quarter of the entire U.S. work force. Critics say that the widespread use of contingent workers may do wonders in the short term for a company's bottom line, but it does little for stress and anxiety levels and employee morale.[18]

The biggest labor market problem in the 1990s seems to be the lack of decent, well-paid, middle-class jobs such as those enjoyed by the 1960s skilled blue-collar worker, who was usually the family's sole breadwinner. In many instances, the 1990s young couple now takes home less money together than did the 1960 father alone. This "shrinking middle" means that the 1990s work force increasingly is becoming polarized between highly paid professionals on the one hand and low-paid unskilled workers on the other. The decline of solid manufacturing jobs is largely to blame for this development. For many aerospace and defense workers, the 1990s peace dividend unfortunately has come to mean the pink slip, and these jobs have yet to be replaced.[19]

Finally, just as continued growth of the service sector may not generate a proportionate number of jobs because of computerization or industrialization of that sector, so, too, there are fears that any recovery in manufacturing will not be accompanied by significant employment growth. Economists call this phenomenon jobless growth, a paradox that comes about because new capital investment and the resulting improvements in productivity reduce the demand for labor even as output is increased.

Two recent studies seem to confirm this view. First, David Howell suggests that the increasing use of robots will displace large numbers of jobs in manufacturing industry, although the impact will be concentrated in a small number of industries and occupations, and the magnitude of the impact will be fairly small compared with the effects of economic cycles. Most of the jobs lost—or, rather, job opportunities eroded—in this way will be unskilled and semiskilled rather than scientific and technical, he says. Second, a British study of the world clothing industry argues that increasing automation will reduce employment in that industry by as much as 30 to 40 percent (or 1 million jobs in the United States and Europe) over the next ten years. In particular, they say, the use of flexible manufacturing systems (FMS) and computer-based systems in finishing, inspection, and production control after the mid-1990s will severely erode employment opportunities.[20]

The message from these studies is clear: we cannot assume that a computer-based economy automatically will provide enough jobs for everyone in the future. Computer professionals should be aware of this pressure on employment when designing and implementing systems that will reduce job opportunities for those most in need of them.

What Kind of Jobs? Computers and the Quality of Work

As a good-will gesture, Irv Klein and Jonah Kaufman hired several mentally handicapped adults to work in their 13 McDonald's restaurants on Long Island, New York, last year. The experience was so successful they recruited 34 more. The franchise owners found the new hires to be reliable, hardworking individuals.

With unskilled workers in dwindling supply, service companies are increasingly looking to the mentally retarded to man mops and grills. The fast-food industry, where the annual employment turnover rate is 200%, welcomes their loyalty. Of the 40 mentally handicapped adults hired by McDonald's on Long Island, only four have left. Says Kaufman: "These people never come in late and are rarely sick."

Kentucky Fried Chicken employs 28 mentally handicapped workers at company-owned restaurants in Virginia and is stepping up recruitment in Georgia and Kentucky. Flo Barber, a company human resources director, points out that these workers don't mind the chores that teenagers often find boring.

Marriott Corp. . . . says the productivity of retarded employees is the same as that for nondisabled workers.[21]

While computer professionals should be aware that computerization usually decreases the quantity of work available, they should be equally concerned about the implementation of systems that may degrade the quality of working life. This can happen through (1) deskilling the work force by reducing the control, responsibility, and job satisfaction of skilled operators, (2) increasing the stress, depersonalization, fatigue, and boredom experienced by employees, and (3) creating health and safety hazards for the work force, such as eyestrain, tension headaches, backache, and perhaps even miscarriages and birth defects. Each of these possible dangers of computerization in the workplace is considered in turn.

In its most recent form, the argument that automation deskills workers goes back to the publication in 1974 of Harry Braverman's seminal *Labor and Monopoly Capital: The Degradation of Work in the Twentieth Century*, a book that generated a great deal of new speculation about technology and the labor process and attracted a group of followers who became known as the labor process school of thought. Essentially, the labor process theorists argue that every attempt to introduce new technology and redesign jobs is really an attempt by profit-motivated employers to increase their control over the work force in order to exploit them further. Skilled workers are always a threat to management, so the argument goes, because they are in a position to set their own pace of work and thus can effectively control the work process. This labor process theory is basically an updated version of the old Marxist idea that the workplace is a battleground between capital and labor, a forum where the class struggle is fought.

Very much in the Bravermanian tradition, Harley Shaiken argues in *Work Transformed: Automation and Labor in the Computer Age* that computers deskill workers and thus degrade the quality of working life. He contends that managers don't like skilled workers because they are semiautonomous; managers therefore seek to remove skill from workers and transfer it to machines. In manufacturing plants, this transfer of skills to machines creates more jobs for less-skilled machine minders but fewer jobs for skilled workers. Moreover, he says, despite the promise that new technology can improve the quality of working life, many of the new jobs being created in futuristic factories are as tedious, fast-paced, and stressful as old-style assembly line jobs. Shaiken's views find support in the work of, for example, David Noble in the United States and Mike Cooley, among others, in the United Kingdom.[22]

The contrary view on automation is probably best exemplified by Larry Hirschhorn, who argues in *Beyond Mechanization: Work and Technology in the Post-Industrial Age,* that the notion that computers deskill workers and degrade work is the opposite of the truth. First, he points out that "robots can't run factories." The proven unreliability (see chapter 5) of most IT equipment, he says, actually increases the dependence of managers on their skilled work force and not vice versa. Second, if robots can't run factories, then neither can the traditional manager. "The new technologies introduce new modes of machine failure, new flaws in the control systems themselves, and new challenges to the design of jobs. In such settings, workers must *control the controls.*"[23] In consequence, human resource specialists must develop new forms of work design that foster cooperative rather than adversarial behavior, he says. Without a "vigilant, committed and curious" work force, he predicts that major system failures such as Three Mile Island will occur with increasing regularity. Managers cannot command workers to behave in new ways. They must transcend inherited patterns of authority and win over the work force so that they take a new interest in, and responsibility for, their actions. Far from deskilling the workforce, computer technology demands that employers of the future constantly improve staff quality through learning and retraining if they are to survive and prosper.

Support for Hirschhorn comes from the British survey *Workplace Industrial Relations and Technical Change*. This study found that manual manufacturing jobs involving the operation of new technology were generally associated with substantially more interest, more skill, more responsibility, and more variety than the old-style jobs they replaced. Both the managers and the shop stewards (union representatives) in the survey seemed to agree on this, although both also appeared to agree that the impact of computerization was slightly negative in terms of its effect on autonomy (as measured by the level of supervision), control over the pace of work, and how the job was done. In the case of office jobs, a similar consensus between managers and shop stewards emerged that new technology was associated with higher levels of interest, skills, responsibility, and variety, but there was a modest divergence of opinion on autonomy, the pace of work, and how the job was done. In the last three dimensions, shop stewards saw the impact of computers as modestly negative, while managers saw it as marginally positive.[24]

Between the proponents and opponents of deskilling is a fairly large and growing group of agnostics who steer a middle course between the somewhat crude conspiracy theories of the labor process school and the naive Panglossian view that all technology changes are for the best in this, the best of all possible worlds. For example, in summarizing a British symposium, *Information Technology in Manufacturing Processes*, Graham Winch says that there was a consensus that employers are not by any means simply motivated by a desire to control their work force. The choice of new technology is dictated by competitive market pressures and traditional managerial ideologies as much as power relations in the workplace. Some deskilling may occur, but this need not necessarily be so: "There is no single tendency towards de-skilling or re-skilling," he writes.[25]

Bellcore researchers Robert Kraut, Susan Dumais, and Susan Koch, after studying the impact of a computerized record system on the working lives of customer service representatives in a large utility company, argue that the process of computerization is far more complex than the idealized rhetoric and simplistic models of deskilling or upskilling imply. On the one hand, they found that office technology reduced job pressure and increased "the happiness and mental health" of the primary users. On the other hand, they say that the new record system made the service representatives' jobs less satisfying and deskilled the jobs by making them less complex, interesting, and challenging. The technology also decreased work satisfaction and involvement with work colleagues. They therefore conclude that monolithic or unidirectional models of technological impact are incorrect. "These data demonstrate the oversimplicity of earlier work portraying office automation in either starkly negative or positive terms."[26] Likewise, two British academics who have written extensively on technology management, David Buchanan and David Boddy, reject the view that computerization necessarily leads to either deskilling or reskilling. In *Managing New Technology*, they argue forcefully that computers can be used to complement "distinct and valuable" human skills rather than to replace them. There is no inevitable or uniform impact or effect of new technology on the nature of work, and it is misleading even to think in terms of impacts. "Bored and inefficient employees are the result of decisions about how their work is organized," they write.[27]

A number of other authors and researchers also have made the point that a particular type of technology does not determine what form of work organization will be adopted or what quality of work life will be achieved. They argue that the use of technology is a matter of strategic choice and often a matter of negotiated choice (between management and the work force). For example, in his study of the impact of computers in offices, *New Office Information Technology: Human and Managerial Implications*, Canadian professor Richard Long concludes that paper-using organizations can use new technology either to enhance human abilities and skills, increase user discretion and autonomy, and generally improve the quality of worklife or to do the exact opposite. For example, the controversial practice of computer monitoring can be either beneficial or detrimental to employee discretion and satisfaction, depending upon how it is implemented. Computer professionals need to recognize that "new office systems are not just technical systems, but behavioural systems which depend for success on the effective integration of both their social and technical components."[28]

Rob Kling and Suzanne Iacono emphasize the role of choice in office computerization and argue that specific interventions can lead to either increased flexibility in work life and streamlined work groups or regimented work organization and muddled work procedures. Kling and Iacono don't agree with the optimists or the pessimists, whose views on the quality of office work life are seen as overly deterministic. These authors don't expect to see any single form of office of the future emerging, but a variety of forms, depending upon managerial philosophies. Stephen Lepore, Rob Kling, Suzanne Iacono, and Joey George argue that the quality of office work life is contingent upon work force participation in the computer implementation process. This factor, they say, is more important than the technical character of the computing equipment.[29]

At the same time, Ian McLoughlin and Jon Clark have introduced a new argument that computerization generates contradictory imperatives that both deskill manual work tasks but at the same time upskill mental tasks associated with the operation of new technology. In *Technological Change at Work,* McLoughlin and Clark argue from their case studies of the introduction of new technology in various organizations that computers and information technology exercise an independent influence on work tasks and skills. In rejecting what is seen as the technological determinism of both the labor process and the negotiated choice theorists, they say (compare Hirschhorn) that computers by nature "generate more complex tasks which require mental problem-solving and interpretative skills and abilities and an understanding of system interdependencies" and that they "involve a fundamentally different relationship between the user and the technology compared to mechanical and electro-mechanical technologies."[30]

This account of computerization finds an echo in the work of Shoshana Zuboff, who argues that information technology is characterized by a fundamental duality. On the one hand, she says in her book, *In the Age of the Smart Machine,* that computers can be used by employers to replace people by following the traditional nineteenth-century labor-substitution logic. On the other hand, the capacity of computers to generate vast amounts of information about the underlying processes of production and administration enables employers to educate or "informate" their work force so that they can do their jobs better. "The informated organization," she writes, "is a learning institution . . . learning is a new form of labor."[31]

In a recent article, Zuboff spells out more clearly what she means by informating. "On the one hand, intelligent technology can be used to automate, but even as this occurs the technology has the capacity to translate those automated activities into data and to display those data. Information technology symbolically renders processes, objects, behaviours, and events so that they become visible, knowable, and shareable in a new way. The word I have coined to describe this second function is 'informate.' Information technologies can *informate* as well as *automate*. 'To informate' means to translate and make visible; 'informating' occurs as processes, objects, behaviours, and events are translated into and made visible as explicit information."[32]

But as Rob Kling and Charles Dunlop point out, Zuboff provides few illustrations of informating in her published work. While her "catchy and vivid imagery" has attracted a great deal of attention, the concept of informating has proved hard to operationalize for many kinds of work, they say. It seems to have been inspired, they say, by closed-loop process control systems in which blue-collar workers can become more analytical when they obtain new data about their work. The concept certainly has acquired a moral force through its images of empowerment, but "unfortunately the body of writing about informating seems to be driven much more by zeal to inspire managers with a new vision than by an interest in exploring the value, boundaries and problematics of the concept."[33]

No doubt these academic arguments about the precise impact of computers on the quality of work will continue, but it does seem that while the pessimists are being proved correct on the reduction in the total quantity of work, the optimists seem to be more correct on the question of quality. However, that is not to say that it has all been plain sailing for computerization in the workplace.

The Dangers of the Techno-Fix: Stress in the Modern Workplace

A number of recent studies have suggested that stress in the modern workplace is costing billions of dollars in lost working hours and reduced productivity. In the United States, for example, the Office of Technology Assessment (OTA) has estimated that stress-related illnesses cost businesses between $50 billion and $75 billion per year. Polls show that three-quarters of Americans now say their job causes them stress. Workers' compensation claims based on job stress have more than doubled in the United States since 1980 and now account for approximately 15 percent of all occupational disease claims. In California, work stress claims increased seven times between 1980 and 1988, and most insurers don't bother to fight the claims—nearly 80 percent of cases are settled out of court for an average of $7,450.[34]

In their book *Unhealthy Work: Stress, Productivity and the Reconstruction of Working Life,* Robert Karasek and Tores Theorell say that the increasing number of jobs involving computers is raising levels of stress at work. The data entry clerk picking 18,000 keystrokes hour after hour on a meaningless blur of documents and the auto worker wrestling with a set of misprogrammed, hydra-headed robotic welding machines are cited as examples of bad high-tech, high-strain jobs. The prevalence of such bad jobs is leading to the increased incidence of anxiety, depression, and coronary heart disease brought on by too much stress, they say. In *The Electronic Sweatshop,* Barbara Garson argues that computers are transforming the office of the future into a kind of stressed-out factory of the past.[35]

In Britain, a Department of Education and Science report estimated that stress in offices was costing the U.K. economy millions of pounds a year and found that those in closest contact with new technology were most at risk. The author of the report, Sue Cox, writes that automation often is seen as the solution to a messy office problem. But automating a mess only creates an automated mess, she says. Her report found that many workers were inadequately trained for new technology and that they needed help in coping with the stress arising out of change. Stress in the modern office led to loss of job satisfaction, low morale, absenteeism, and poor management–labor relations.[36]

Some recent commentators have even resurrected the concept of *technostress,* first popularized by Silicon Valley psychologist Craig Brod in his book of the same name published in 1984. Brod says that he first became aware of the problem of technostress when one of his clients described his wife as a peripheral. It is clear that Brod and his modern-day followers include this syndrome and almost anything else under the umbrella of technostress—including phenomena such as the irrational fear of new technologies, workplace alienation, speed-ups, information overload, the social dislocation caused by computerization, projecting individual needs onto computers, the depersonalization of the workplace, fatigue, and burn-out.[37]

It seems that Japanese employers deliberately set out to increase levels of stress in order to maximize productivity. In a study of the famous Toyota-General Motors NUMMI (New United Motors Manufacturing Inc.) car plant at Fremont, California, Mike Parker and Jane Slaughter argue that even the much-vaunted Japanese team concept of management is based on boosting stress. This is achieved by the regular speeding-up of production lines, the process of *kaizen,* or continuous improvement, and the constant testing of the production system to breaking point. Even the just-in-time (JIT) parts production system has been introduced, they say, to ensure that workers do not build up buffer stocks in order to take a rest. It's therefore not surprising that even the highly selected employees of U.S.-based Japanese car plants (or transplants) are starting to complain of burn-out.[38]

Whether it be Mazda at Flat Rock, Michigan, or Nissan at Smyrna, Tennessee, or Bridgestone at LaVergne, Tennessee, the message from the transplants seems to be the same: Japanese companies achieve their higher productivity levels by making people work harder and faster. Strip away the rhetoric of teamwork, partnerships, and wellness programs, and the reality of life in a Japanese car plant is a grueling pace of work, few rest periods, and a certain ruthlessness in dealing with employees who fall down on the job. As Harley Shaiken puts it, "There are two faces to the Japanese system. One is increased efficiency, better quality, and consulting the workers. But the other is increased pressure, stress, and tightly-strung manufacturing."[39] When employees fall ill, for instance, other members of the work team are expected to take up the slack; Japanese plants do not carry relief workers.

This linking of stress and the contemporary workplace is a growing theme in management literature. As Boddy and Buchanan put it,

The concern with work organization in the late 1980s and into the 1990s is thus based on pressures arising from stiffer trading conditions in domestic and international markets, from the realization that stress has more impact on job performance than dissatisfaction, and from the introduction of new computing and information technologies which lead to a rethink of work flows and work roles in manufacturing and administration. A de-skilled, unmotivated, uncommitted and inflexible workforce is not competitive when careful attention to costs, quality and delivery schedules is fundamental to capturing and retaining changing and unpredictable markets. The effective management of human resources has for these reasons become even more of a key factor in sustaining competitive advantage and work organization has for these reasons become a crucial management consideration.[40]

Another issue causing considerable controversy at present is that of the computerized monitoring of employees. According to a recent Office of Technology Assessment (OTA) report to the U.S. Congress, between 25 and 30 percent of U.S. clerical employees are now under surveillance in this way.[41] In the past, employees were monitored directly by progress-chasers, foremen, and supervisors. But these days monitoring can be done surreptitiously by microchip. Computer monitoring can take the form of the silent monitoring of phone calls to and from customers (or "service observation"), the timing of customer calls, checking up on private calls, and the measurement of keystrokes performed by word processor operators or data entry clerks. Computerized monitoring is constant, reliable, and cheap. Supervisors are no longer limited by what they can observe with their own eyes. A complete record of employee performance exists in the print-out.

Supporters of computer monitoring point out that it can be particularly useful in training new employees who deal with the public. Because managers are under ever-increasing pressure to improve productivity and competitiveness, computer monitoring also can be used to provide clear, accurate performance measures that help eliminate waste and enable the right people to get promoted. It also enhances the ability of managers to motivate employees. In addition, many companies also have suffered from industrial espionage and employee thefts. Because of the growing sophistication of manufacturing processes and office information systems, mistakes are more costly and computer systems are more prone to employee sabotage. In the United States, in particular, a dramatic increase in drug use at work—not to speak of the spread of AIDS—has, it is said, forced employers to take more interest in the behavior and private lives of employees.

Critics charge that computerized employee monitoring represents an intolerable invasion of privacy and a blatant disregard of human rights. It undermines trust, reduces autonomy, and fails to measure quality rather than quantity. They say that the practice causes stress and ill-health. For example, a recent University of Wisconsin study of 762 telephone operators found that monitored employees were more likely to suffer from headaches, back pain, severe fatigue and exhaustion, extreme anxiety, shoulder soreness, and stiff or sore wrists. Perhaps most damning of all, say the critics, computer monitoring is counterproductive because employee morale declines—and, with it, productivity.[42]

In an important study of the phenomenon, Canadian researchers Rebecca Grant, Christopher Higgins, and Richard Irving looked at the effect monitoring had on employee attitudes in the claims-processing division of a large insurance company, where they compared the behavior of monitored employees with that of unmonitored employees. They found that monitoring degraded the quality of the product offered to the customer and the work environment of employees. Whereas 85 percent of unmonitored employees rated work quality (customer service and teamwork) as the most important factor in their jobs, 80 percent of monitored employees said production quantity was most important. According to the researchers, monitoring promoted this bureaucratic behavior: monitored employees not unreasonably perceived that if a work task was not being counted, then it didn't count. But they did not necessarily see this to be a fair measure of an employee's worth. They also realized that customer service was sacrificed and that tasks requiring special attention were sidelined as a result of monitoring. Those who had internalized the new standards were happier in knowing what was expected of them. Those who felt the new quotas eliminated the intrinsic satisfaction of providing good service commented on the stress of being watched all the time.[43]

What is to be done about the growth of computer monitoring? MIT's Gary Marx and Sanford Sherizen have proposed a code of ethics to control the use of monitoring and to safeguard privacy. Their proposed guidelines include the following:

1. Apply to monitoring the same protection that applies to preemployment background checks—that is, permit only information to be collected that is directly relevant to the job.

2. Require employers to provide employees with advance notice of the introduction of monitoring as well as appropriate mechanisms for appeal.

3. Require people to verify machine-produced information before using it to evaluate employees.

4. Provide workers with access to the information themselves and provide mechanisms for monetary redress for employees whose rights are violated or who are victims of erroneous information generated by monitoring systems.

5. Apply a statute of limitations on data from monitoring. The older the data, the less its potential relevance and the greater the difficulty employees have in challenging it.[44]

Peter G. Neumann has also identified a number of other quality-of-work issues specifically associated with computerization. For example, he suggests that computers can bring out personal anxieties and phobias, which are often exacerbated when people are told that "the computer" is to blame rather than its designers or operators. Computers can increase fatigue and boredom, he says, because so many tasks associated with computers are highly repetitive, such as data entry, tape library maintenance, and audit trail watching. Computers can lead to a reduced ability of people to control systems and to the placing of unquestioning, blind trust in technology. "Because of factors such as enormous complexity and poorly-conceived human interfaces, people often have great difficulties understanding and controlling computer-based applications—especially in real time. The opportunities for accidental misuse or intentional abuse are greater. When something goes wrong, the problems are often very difficult to diagnose."[45]

But perhaps the most important consideration of all from the ethical point of view is that computers increase the sense of depersonalization. "Interactions with computers tend to depersonalize both the user community and the application itself. The resulting sense of anonymity can inspire a lack of respect for the system and its resources, and a diminished sense of ethics, values, and morals on the part of the affected people. The depersonalization can increase the temptations to commit misdeeds, diminish human initiative, and cause the abdication of decision-making responsibility. The sense of ethical behaviour seems much more diffuse, even though in principle it should be no different from ethical behaviour in general."[46] Neumann says that, while there are obvious quantitative differences between computer technology and other technologies, collectively these seem to make a qualitative difference.

Health and Safety Issues: Video Display Terminals and the Repetitive Strain Injury Debate

Computerization has allegedly created or exacerbated a number of environmental, health, and safety problems in the modern workplace. For example, there is serious concern about air quality in large office buildings, not only because of inadequate air-conditioning systems but also because of the widespread use of synthetic materials and substances in new IT equipment that release strange cocktails of chemicals into the atmosphere. After years of complaints, rumors, absenteeism, and high turnover, epidemiologists have now identified something called sick building syndrome (SBS) that results in drowsiness, headaches, eye irritation, sore throats, and so on. SBS is caused by a lack of fresh air and the accumulation of fungi, bacteria, dust, and debris in ventilation ductwork. The air-conditioning systems of high-rise office buildings have been found to contain fiberglass, asbestos, pollen, spores, carbon dioxide, tobacco smoke, formaldehyde from resins, ozone from photocopiers, toluene from cleaning fluids, and trichloroethane from office supply fluids, among other irritants and suspected carcinogens.

According to the U.S. Environmental Protection Agency, between 20 and 35 percent of U.S. office workers suffer from poor air quality at work, and as many as 150 million working days are lost each year in the United States through illness and absenteeism because of sick buildings. Consultants in the United Kingdom report that half of all British offices are sick to some degree and that 80 percent of British workers have suffered from sick building ailments. The World Health Organization (WHO) estimates that one-third of all new and remodeled office buildings in the world are sick. Levels of indoor pollution are frequently 100 times higher than outdoors and can even rise to 1,000 times higher. The recommended standards for air-conditioning are widely ignored.[47]

Further aggravating the situation are problems with the design of offices and office furniture, such as the modern fashion for open-plan arrangements. These usually reduce the amount of space available per employee. They also decrease privacy, efficiency, and job satisfaction and increase levels of annoyance and thus stress. Poorly designed seats, tables, and work stations, which do not conform to ergonomic principles, have been blamed for eyestrain, headaches, neck and shoulder ache, and wrist and elbow disorders. In the United Kingdom in 1992, new guidelines for ergonomic offices had to be introduced by the Health and Safety Commission following a spate of complaints from employee representatives.[48]

Considerable controversy has surrounded the growing use of video display terminals (VDTs). These were first introduced in the 1960s, but it was not until the 1970s that they became common in workplaces. Now there are about 20 million in daily use in the United States alone, and millions more are being added to the world stock of VDTs every year. But as their use has become more widespread, so have the allegations that VDTs cause eyestrain, headaches, backaches, stiff necks, and sore wrists. More serious complaints are that low-level radiation from VDTs can cause cataracts, miscarriages, and even birth defects. In management, labor union, and feminist circles, the alleged health and safety hazards of VDTs have become a big issue.

Yet, on both sides of the VDT debate, it is remarkable how little is known about VDT safety, despite a string of reports and studies that have appeared in the last decade. The first was the U.S. National Institute for Occupational Safety and Health (NIOSH) report, published in 1980, which stated that there was "cause for concern" about possible physical and psychological hazards arising out of prolonged VDT use. At the three major sites studied, VDT workers reported more instances of eyestrain and stiff necks as well as higher levels of stress, irritability, depression, and anxiety. But the NIOSH report left open the question of whether the high levels of stress reported and the associated psychological problems were caused by the nature of the job or by the use of VDTs or both.

The consensus of a 1981 National Academy of Sciences (NAS) conference was that the application of ergonomics in the form of better lighting, improved seating, and more appropriate screen technology would only go part way toward solving both the physical and psychological problems of VDT users and that job stress was a major causal factor. But a 1983 National Research Council (NRC) report appeared to conclude the opposite: that most of the physical problems associated with VDT work could be cured by ergonomics. "Our general conclusion," said study group chairman, Edward Rinalducci, "is that eye discomfort, blurred vision and other visual disturbances, muscular aches and stress reported among VDT workers are probably not due to anything inherent in VDT technology."[49]

The NRC findings did nothing to quell further speculation that VDTs were a problem—particularly from labor unions and feminist groups in the United States such as 9 to 5, the National Association for Working Women. In 1985 a Japanese study of 13,000 workers reportedly found a high level of miscarriages, premature births, and stillbirths among VDT operators, while a Swedish study of 10,000 programmers concluded that there were no statistically significant differences between the pregnancies of women who had experienced low, medium, and high levels of exposure to VDTs. Likewise, Kenneth Foster of the University of Pennsylvania found no connection between the use of VDTs and reproductive problems, nor did he believe that any strong connection was likely to exist. A Canadian government study of 51,885 births and 4,127 abortions found that congenital defects in infants were not related to whether women had used a VDT during their pregnancy. Yet more studies in the United Kingdom, Canada, Sweden, and Australia and a major new NIOSH study in the United States published in 1991 all appeared to clear VDTs of causing miscarriages and birth defects.[50]

Meanwhile a Japanese study by Professor Satoshi Ishikawa of Kitazato University found that 90 percent of VDT users reported eyesight problems, 17 percent suffered from eyeball degeneration, 27 percent reported stiff shoulders and necks, and 13 percent complained of insomnia. Swedish researchers reported a link between electromagnetic radiation from computer terminals and foetal deaths and deformities in pregnant mice, while a U.S. Office of Naval Research group reported a significant increase in abnormalities among chicken embryos exposed to low-frequency magnetic fields. A University of Maryland study also suggested a link between the electrostatic (as opposed to electromagnetic) radiation emitted from VDTs and the appearance of some types of dermatitis. In 1989 Cal-OSHA, California's Occupational Safety and Health Administration, came out with a report compiled by two dozen experts who failed to agree on whether new regulations were necessary to govern the use of VDTs, other than periodic rest breaks and regular eye tests.[51]

One of the most extensive studies of VDT hazards to emerge in recent years was conducted by the Kaiser-Permanente Medical Care Program in Oakland, California. The study followed 1,600 women clerical workers who had become pregnant and found that expectant mothers who had spent more than twenty hours per week at terminals were more than twice as likely to suffer a miscarriage as other clerical employees. However, the difference was not statistically significant. Job-related stress and poor working conditions for the VDT users could not be ruled out as intervening variables, said the researchers. Nevertheless, the director of the study, Edmund Van Brunt, was quoted as saying that he believed the research did indicate an association between VDT use and miscarriage, and it was this alleged link that was widely reported in the media around the world. With indications that some pregnant women were quitting their jobs on the spot as a result of the Kaiser-Permanente study, the report's authors were forced to retract—or at least to repeat the statistical qualifications. Michael Polen, one of the three authors, told *Fortune* magazine; "I regret that our study has increased the level of fear, and I think that's unwarranted. All we can say for sure is that we need more studies."[52]

Further evidence contained in the 1991 NIOSH report and a report from the National Radiological Protection Board (NRPB) in the United Kingdom in 1992 once again appeared to clear VDTs as such of causing damage to human health. But this evidence did not stop less-esteemed authorities from claiming from time to time that VDTs were responsible for such things as brain damage, bone damage, and the deformation of contact lenses. In particular, so-called electroscientists such as Paul Brodeur, author of *Currents of Death,* in the United States and Roger Coghill, author of *Electropollution,* in the United Kingdom made a series of outlandish claims in the period 1990–1992, including the suggestion that low-frequency radiation from VDTs was causing AIDS by helping break down the human body's immune system.[53]

A major event in the history of VDT health and safety occurred in 1987 when Suffolk County, a suburban area on Long Island, New York, passed a bill that for the first time would regulate the use of VDTs in the workplace. The controversial bill, sponsored by Democrat John Foley, was enacted one year later in 1988, after a thirteen-to-five vote and a stormy passage; the county chief executive, Patrick Halpin, used his veto over the bill under pressure from the county's business community, who had threatened to pull out of the area. The proposed act would apply to businesses operating more than twenty VDTs and would provide for fifteen-minute breaks every three hours for employees who used the terminals for more than twenty-six hours a week. In addition, employers would pay for 80 percent of the cost of eyeglasses and annual eye tests, and by 1990 all new VDT equipment installed in Suffolk County would have to feature adjustable chairs, detachable keyboards, and nonglare screens.

The Suffolk County measure finally became law in January 1989, but it was subsequently struck down in December 1989 by the New York State Supreme Court after it had been challenged by four large employers in the county. In the same month, outgoing New York City mayor Ed Koch vetoed a similar bill that would have applied much the same provisions to New York City workers and employers. However, in December 1990 the city of San Francisco passed a law regulating the use of VDTs in the city. Under the law, firms employing more than fifteen workers would have to supply antiglare shields, wrist rests, and adjustable chairs. Workers on VDT shifts of more than four hours would be entitled to a fifteen-minute break every two hours. The San Francisco law was heralded by labor and womens' groups around the nation, but it, too, was struck down. The San Francisco Superior Court in February 1992 ruled that only the state of California and not individual cities had the power to regulate worker safety. It was back to square one for the VDT watchdogs.[54]

If VDTs have proved a controversial addition to the modern office, then so-called repetitive strain injury (or RSI) is creating an even greater amount of controversy. For centuries, manual workers such as cobblers, blacksmiths, bricklayers, upholsterers, cotton-twisters, glass cutters, and meatpackers have suffered from strained ligaments and joints, which have sometimes necessitated that they quit their jobs. One such painful affliction is carpal tunnel syndrome, a nerve block involving the carpal ligament in the palm of the hand. For years, too, writers have complained of writer's cramp and sports lovers have suffered from epicondylytis, or tennis elbow, and tenosynovitis, or golfers' wrist, from overindulgence in their favorite sport. But in recent years there has been growing evidence that the excessive use of computer keyboards is greatly increasing the incidence of what is now known as RSI.

The term RSI seems to have originated in Australia, where it has been used to describe a variety of painful and disabling afflictions that appear to be caused by repetitive movements of the hands and arms. The three key ingredients seem to be a degree of force, repetition, and a fast pace of work. Keyboard operators seem particularly vulnerable because they can make up to 45,000 keystrokes per hour—often without a break. Typists, at least, move the carriage return and feed more paper into the typewriter so that their fingers received a bit of variety and relief. Fast repetition can irritate or inflame tendons (tenosynovitis or tendinitis) and lead to unpredictable and excruciating pain. One study of RSI among musicians found that the cramped circumstances of a flat rather than sloping orchestra pit during a five-hour Wagner opera led to an outbreak of RSI, which local doctors initially attributed to a possible disease of the muscles that had spread from musician to musician.[55]

An epidemic of RSI now seems to be sweeping the United States and Europe. In 1981 only 18 percent of all workplace injury cases in the United States involved RSI-type problems. But RSI claims amounted to 48 percent of all cases by 1988 and to a staggering 56 percent of the 185,000 cases reported in 1990. Most of the cases involved people who worked at computer keyboards, such as journalists, supermarket check-out workers, telephone operators, and data entry clerks. In 1992 a U.S. District Court judge in New York consolidated forty-four lawsuits against major computer makers into one case, while journalists around the United States inundated the courts with suits against Atex, suppliers of equipment to many newspapers. In the United Kingdom, beginning in 1990, the British courts started awarding damages to RSI victims when they found against the Inland Revenue, Book Club Associates, and British Telecom in three celebrated cases.[56]

Australia suffered a strange epidemic of RSI in the 1980s, beginning in 1981 with nearly 100 reported cases, rising to about 200 cases in 1983, and reaching a peak of over 900 cases in 1984, only to disappear—or, rather, decline steadily—from around 750 cases in 1985 to less than 200 in 1987. Most of the complainants were women office workers in government employment whose jobs involved spending long hours on computer keyboards. For example, of 560 reported cases in Western Australia prior to 1985, 22 percent involved data-processing operators,

19 percent were word-processing operators, 18 percent were secretary stenographers, and 12 percent were typists.[57]

In attempting to find the cause of Australia's RSI epidemic, Sara Kiesler and Tom Finholt of Carnegie-Mellon University, Pittsburgh, have suggested that poor ergonomic design of equipment is associated with RSI, while work practices such as speed-ups, heavier workloads, greater monotony, fewer rest breaks, nonstandard hours, and so on are also related to RSI. In particular, they say, those using keyboards for prolonged, rapid, and repetitive tasks such as data entry or word processing seem more prone to RSI than computer programmers and computer scientists who use keyboards in a more leisurely and varied way. But this finding could mean either of two things: that RSI sufferers get sick from physically doing the job or that they get sick from having such a boring, dead-end, monotonous, and low-status job. Yet RSI not only varies between countries, as the Australian experience indicates, it also appears to vary between workplaces within Australia, where similar types of people are doing similarly boring and repetitive jobs using similar equipment.[58]

The key question, therefore, is, Why did RSI suddenly in the 1980s become a problem of epidemic proportion in Australia? Kiesler and Finholt put forward four main reasons. First, there is historical precedent for RSI-type compensation claims in Australia and a long history of union involvement in workers' health issues. Second, RSI became a cause célèbre of Australian unions and feminist groups as soon as new technology started being introduced into Australian offices in the early 1980s. Third, RSI received official validation from the Australian medical establishment, who seemed quite confident in diagnosing it early (it is also compensatable with or without physical symptoms being present). Fourth, the Australian media followed the RSI story in some detail, thereby communicating the medical facts to a wider audience. Put these four factors together, say Kiesler and Finholt, and RSI rapidly became a socially legitimate disease that was perfectly respectable to have. It also provided an alternative to continued boring, repetitive work in an unpleasant, stressed environment. It was, they say, "a legitimate ticket out of the pink ghetto" for hundreds of women clerical workers.

"We do not intend to suggest that RSI is a scam to promote the practice of medicine or that Australian workers use RSI claims to defraud their employers," Kiesler and Finholt write. "We believe that they legitimately have symptoms of RSI. We speculate that if the work environment were better and if jobs were more satisfying, RSI complaints would not be as important. The epidemic in Australia ostensibly involves RSI, but we hypothesize that it is really related to bad work conditions and an unfulfilling work life. The ambiguous nature of RSI makes it the perfect candidate for many workers as they seek an approved exit from the computing pool while preserving benefits and some salary."[59]

Kiesler and Finholt therefore conclude that RSI is an extreme example of how the social, organizational, and political context of work and technological change defines and influences the nature of health problems. Illnesses and injuries like RSI do not occur in a vacuum, they say. They are created by society.

The Productivity Paradox: Improving the Payoff from Information Technology

A major lesson of the IT story so far is that the productivity payoff from computerization has been somewhat disappointing. In manufacturing, commerce, government, and elsewhere, productivity gains have often been hard to discern, despite massive spending on IT equipment. In the 1990s CEOs and IT managers have become much more circumspect about the claims for productivity gains made by computer vendors and much more careful about the way they spend money. There is no blank check for IT anymore.

The facts of what is being called the "IT productivity paradox" are simply stated. While manufacturing productivity in the United States grew at a healthy 4.1 percent a year in the 1980s, white-collar productivity only rose by a negligible 0.28 percent a year, despite the expenditure of huge sums of money on office technology and labor-saving equipment. In areas such as banking, insurance, and health care, productivity has declined in recent years. In his book *The Business Value of Computers*, former Xerox executive Paul Strassman found no link between IT spending and productivity in 292 companies studied. He even found a negative relationship between productivity and spending on management information systems (MIS). A major study by MIT's Management in the 1990s Research Program, published as *The Corporation of the 1990s: Information Technology and Organizational Transformation,* also concluded, "The evidence at the aggregate level does not indicate any improvements in productivity or profitability. Only a very few firms are demonstrably better off."[60]

Some clues as to why we have an IT productivity problem can be found in academic studies carried out in recent years. The first comes from the world of banking. Banks and financial institutions were among the first to automate their operations; some electronic funds transfer (EFT) systems date back to the 1950s. Thus Richard Franke reasoned that it should be possible to monitor the beneficial impact of computerization in the financial sector over a reasonable time period. But what he found was—to put it mildly—surprising. Franke reports that the adoption of computers by the U.S. financial industry has been associated with massive increases in fixed capital, but not with proportionate increases of output either in total or per unit of labor. In fact, while capital productivity in U.S. banks rose steadily in the quarter century to 1957, it began to decline steadily after 1958 with the onset of computerization. This decline in capital productivity continued for another quarter century. Productivity was particularly poor in the 1970s, yet by 1980 no less than a full half of all bank fixed capital expenditure went on computers and peripherals. Expected increases in capital and labor productivity and decreases in the growth of labor and capital inputs did not materialize.

However, says Franke, further analysis did indicate the beginnings of an improvement in productivity in the 1980s, and this trend may suggest that the financial industry is at last learning how to get the benefits out of automation. Drawing a parallel with the Industrial Revolution of eighteenth-century Britain, where it took a full fifty years for the economic benefits of technological transformation to become apparent, Franke believes that a similar thing might be happening with the current technological revolution. He therefore concludes that the IT revolution has been characterized so far more by technical success than by economic success. The adoption of computer technology initially leads to decreased capital productivity and profitability, he says, and it takes time before the necessary changes in work organization can be successfully implemented to take advantage of the new technology. "According to this assessment," he writes, "it will be early in the 21st century when the accumulated experience in producing and using the equipment of the second technological revolution leads to the more effective utilization of human and capital resources and to major increases in output. . . . Only with time can enterprises adjust to become productive."[61]

A more recent look at IT in the banking industry by *The Economist* came to similar conclusions. *The Economist* reports that U.S. banks increased their spending on IT from $5 billion in 1982 to $14 billion in 1991, but they have little to show for it: "Information technology has been a headache for banks of all descriptions. They have spent heavily on it, for it allows them to cut costs and it drives the design and delivery of their financial products. Yet it is expensive—and easy to get wrong. Few bankers can point to truly happy results from what they have spent already. . . . All this explains why many banks are rethinking how they use IT. . . . America's bankers (and Europe's) are now wishing they had spent their money better." Despite the massive spending, nearly 90 percent of bank payments, *The Economist* found, still involved the use of paper, and this figure was only expected to decline to between 70 and 80 percent by 2000.[62]

As for manufacturing industry, studies confirm this pessimistic view of the productivity payoff from IT spending. For example, Tim Warner says that while U.S. companies spent a huge $17 billion on robots, CAD-CAM (Computer-Aided Design–Computer-Aided Manufacturing) systems, and FMS (Flexible Manufacturing Systems) in 1987 alone, the annual increase in U.S. manufacturing productivity has been far below that of Japan and South Korea and even lower than that of Britain, France, and Italy. Warner looked in some detail at the three main ways in which IT has been deployed on the factory floor: FMS, or flexible manufacturing systems; CAD systems; and computerized information and control systems. These, in turn, were looked at in the context of four North American case studies. In each case, the company concerned had a problem (such as an inferior product, declining market share, slow response times, etc.) that it had attempted to rectify by the adoption of IT—or, as Warner puts it, "throwing computer power at the problem."

But, says Warner, in every case this solution was the wrong one. Heavy expenditure on a high-tech fix merely compounded the problem. Far more could have been achieved, he says, by, for example, redesigning products in order to reduce the number of parts. Again, managing the work flow in factories in a more intelligent way could have achieved very considerable savings. The point is that such changes affect the internal environment: automation, he says, is and must always be secondary. Warner points out that the Japanese have achieved large increases in productivity through the use of just-in-time (JIT) systems, which do not involve the use of high technology. And there are many other conventional improvements to work organization that should be considered before the use of information technologies. "A naive faith in technological silver bullets," he writes, "diverts manufacturers from the hard task of rebuilding their operations from the ground up. . . . Rather than reducing waste, an information technology approach adds to it by burdening an already inefficient system with the cost of computation," declares Warner.[63]

A fine example of the dangers of the high-tech fix was the incredible case of General Motors in the 1980s. Under CEO Roger Smith, GM spent a staggering $80 billion on robots and other manufacturing systems in the space of a few years. This amount was more than the annual GNP of many countries. But many GM plants as a result became overautomated with expensive, unreliable machines, and GM's market share continued to slide because so much else was wrong with the design and reliability of GM's cars, not to mention the design of the work process and employee morale in GM's plants. A similar problem occurred with Nissan's ill-fated Clayton plant in Victoria, which closed after massive expenditure on IT had saddled Nissan Australia with a huge interest bill.[64]

A third batch of studies has focused on productivity in the office, where lavish spending on computers is also being questioned. Recent research by the Brookings Institution think tank and by investment bankers Morgan Stanley has also found it hard to discern any improvements in office productivity, yet capital expenditure on computers zoomed in the late 1980s. While it is possible to find many individual success stories, and while it is evident that many commercial sectors are now wholly dependent on computers to service their customers, demonstrating the economic benefits in macro terms is much more difficult.[65]

Indeed, IT in the office has imposed new costs on employers. Documents that once went through one draft now go through a large number of redrafts, each one taking time and money to produce—and, incidentally, boosting the consumption of paper (so much for the forecasts of the paperless office). Employees often spend hours playing what-if games on their spreadsheets ("spreadsheet junkies") or generating electronic junk mail ("e-mail addicts") and endless faxes ("fax potatoes"). The time gained by the automation of routine tasks is often wasted on busywork (pretending to look busy) or futzing (fiddling around with your software), and expensive equipment lies underused for long periods, especially when it has been purchased for display purposes on executive desks in a modern version of Thorstein Veblen's conspicuous consumption. And because software is superceded so often, secretarial staff regularly have to spend many hours being retrained, whereas in the past learning to type was a once-in-a-lifetime task. In these and a thousand other ways, the benefits of computerization can be dissipated.

There are many other possible explanations of the IT productivity paradox. Some have suggested that we are not measuring the right factors when we evaluate productivity. For example, improvements in product quality, corporate image, customer service, and general convenience attributable to IT may not be taken into account. Conventional cost-accounting techniques, which focus on the cost of inputs such as labor, raw materials, and overheads also may not be fair to new technology: again, intangibles such as greater flexibility to put new products into production, improved turn-around times, and lower inventory costs are not included. But the most common explanation of all is that managers have generally failed to properly manage the implementation of IT systems. They have frequently failed to integrate IT with business strategy, the work process, human resource management, and budgeting.

In fact, there are fifty-seven varieties of the poor management hypothesis. Hundreds of articles in the management journals and scores of books have now been devoted to the question of how to manage IT so as to achieve some sort of productivity payoff and to improve competitive advantage. Every month or so, it seems, some management guru comes out with a new panacea that will allegedly solve the IT productivity problem. Thus in recent years we have been treated to quality circles, reengineering the work process, high-performance work systems, lean production systems, the learning organization, self-managed work teams, groupware, and so on. All these are laudable ways of working smarter, and some companies have achieved some spectacular results with them, but none of them seem to have done the trick so far for aggregate productivity.

However, there is a growing awareness that human factors and quality of work issues play a major role in determining the success or failure of IT systems. A major study of 2,000 U.S. companies by the Rand Corporation found that 40 percent of new office systems had been failures. Yet less than 10 percent of the failures were attributed to technical difficulties; the majority of the failures were attributed to human and organizational problems.[66] Companies are rediscovering that people, not machines, are their most valuable resource and that they can best improve their competitive performance by getting humans and technology to work together in harmony. Many managers are realizing what better managers figured out years ago: you need to get the people side of the equation right if you want to get the most out of the latest technology. This strategy is more profitable for the employer and much better for the employees.

In his study of U.K. banks, Steve Smith showed that conventional automation had not been very successful either in economic or social terms. It had failed to boost efficiency, it had disrupted work systems, and it had alienated the work force from the banks and from each other. He wrote, "Technologists have underestimated the value and importance of skill, knowledge, flexibility and career. . . . Contrary to scientific management, efficiency actually improves and control is made easier if the 'labor process' is coherent as possible. There should be a presumption in favor of skills, pride in the job, staff flexibility, apprentice-based careers and intuitive knowledge."[67]

One path to a better future may lie in the development of more human-centered systems—that is, systems that seek to retain and enhance human skills, control, and discretion, rather than taking them away from employees. Instead of splitting jobs into innumerable minor tasks, a more human centered approach is to give workers more knowledge of, and responsibility for, the entire work process—and this type of job design is made easier by IT. Human-centered systems, therefore, seem to make both economic and social sense.

9

Hypothetical Scenarios for Classroom Discussion

Debates about particular cases can be valuable tools for illustrating ethical dilemmas. Simple right or wrong answers are rarely sufficient, and the validity of all viewpoints must be considered before making a decision. The following hypothetical cases are intended to illustrate the complex web of actions and motivations that often exist in computer-related situations. And although at times these cases might appear somewhat contrived, bear in mind that truth has a persistent habit of being even stranger than fiction.

Instructors may wish to utilize these scenarios in different ways. They could form the basis of active role plays or simply provide perspectives from which students can argue the merits of different ethical positions and actions. Alternatively, they could be used as take-home assignments for class review or grading. In addition, students could be asked to plot out the elements of the scenarios with a variety of methodologies and notations. For example, flow charts could be used to represent the chain of interdependencies and the reasoning behind particular individual decisions. The limited information base and perspective of each actor also could be added to the other actors' perspectives. Finally, students could be asked to make an overall ethical judgment or statement, with a detailed justification of their viewpoint. Note, however, that grading the judgment itself is impossible, because there is no objective basis for determining the superiority of given ethical positions. However, the completeness and quality of the argument, its presentation, and its clarity can be graded easily.

Scenario 1

This scenario illustrates the classic conflict between greater and lesser evils and the means by which a particular noble end is achieved. As an ethical problem, it might be examined in the context of utilitarianism, although other theories also have some applicability.

A systems analyst is working for a major multinational corporation, Megatronics International Inc. The company's interests include mining, agribusiness, petrochemicals, international finance, third world manufacturing, tourism, and property development. After some time, the systems analyst begins to become aware of the extent to which this corporation is involved in illegal and unethical activities. For example, information from his systems suggests that money laundering and tax avoidance are being practiced regularly by Megatronics.

In addition, the analyst has become aware of the extent to which the company derives most of its profit from manufacturing plants in less-developed countries. These plants achieve massive profits and cost very little to operate in terms of salaries, plant modernization, working conditions, or pollution controls. He investigates one particular country, Lower Tse Tse, and discovers that its military dictatorship has entered willingly into a highly exploitative agreement with Megatronics. The deal provides poverty wages with no pollution restrictions to the local employees, thereby causing widespread sickness in the surrounding villages. Meanwhile, the government and its cronies receive large kickbacks and bribes, cars, private aircraft, and expensive homes courtesy of Megatronics.

These discoveries disturb the systems analyst greatly, and the more he digs, the more he comes to appreciate the extent and scope of Megatronics' unethical and illicit activities. After some late-night work, he manages to break the crucial security codes and examines a number of confidential documents. Not long after, an envelope appears on his desk containing several thousand dollars in cash. The implication the analyst draws from this is that his activities have been noticed and that an effort is now being made to buy his silence by those higher up in the organization.

Not knowing whom it should be returned to, the systems analyst stores the cash and refuses to spend it. Meanwhile, the security system is changed and all substantial files are regularly encrypted. Only authorized individuals are allowed access to certain files, and these are reencrypted after they have been worked on.

Now this man faces a dilemma: he knows that he is being watched and that his future employment (and perhaps even his health) may be in jeopardy. He also knows that it would be almost impossible to bring the company to account by calling in the authorities. His knowledge of the system tells him that all audit trails would disappear within a few minutes. So he plots his own justice by planning an elaborate theft of company funds.

First, he manages to obtain his supervisor's password by peering over her shoulder one day. Then, finding an isolated terminal, he logs into her account and begins siphoning off funds received from third world manufacturing installations. Then, after establishing a bank account for himself in Switzerland, he transfers all monies to this account, tenders his resignation, and flies to Europe to collect the money.

Finally, in an act of poetic justice, he contacts Greenpeace and Amnesty International and presents them with several million dollars with which to assist their efforts in Africa. In particular, the analyst asks that they focus on Lower Tse Tse. After several years, the glare of international attention from these groups helps bring about the downfall of the Lower Tse Tse dictatorship and ends the exploitative arrangements with Megatronics. A new contract is drawn up and the people begin to enjoy more of the fruits of their labor.

Scenario 2

This scenario encapsulates the kinds of problems raised by software developers trying to protect their products from piracy. It compares different viewpoints of what software is worth and hence how it should be protected. You must decide which parties are on shakiest ground, ethically speaking.

A computer science student, fresh out of graduate school, takes one of her completed projects and conceives of a brilliant redesign that would turn it into a revolutionary software product. She therefore sets up a small business for herself and dedicates twelve months to the redevelopment of the software, now and then taking on short commercial programming contracts to help pay the rent.

At the conclusion of the twelve-month period, our computer scientist feels somewhat resentful at having sacrificed most of a year's salary in order to undertake her pet project, so she reasons that she must maximize her returns from sale of the software. Having worked hard on developing a high-quality product, she believes that she should be appropriately rewarded in financial terms.

The thought of thousands of people pirating her software sends her into a state of apoplexy, and she therefore devises a scheme to take vengeance upon anyone who would illicitly copy her package. Her protection feature allows each user to make one backup copy of her disks, but any attempt to copy more not only corrupts the source disks but wipes clean any hard disks or floppies accessible by the system. Having done that, an icon appears on the screen depicting a pirate with a parrot on his shoulder. The parrot squawks, "Pieces of eight . . . pieces of eight . . . you should have paid me pieces of eight!"

Of course, the story does not end there. Dozens of individuals are caught this way, and they plot their revenge as well. They scour the Arpanet and public domain bulletin boards to find any electronic mail addresses owned by the computer scientist. They also hack into Mastercard, Visa, and other credit-lending companies and run up enormous bills on her behalf. They deluge her with abusive electronic mail and tie up her telephone by using her own telephone billing cards to call her number incessantly. Then they doctor her electricity bills, tenant history, and credit ratings. In short, they make her life a complete misery.

Eventually, both sides of the dispute settle down to a (fairly) civilized debate about the ethical dimensions of what each side has done. The computer scientist charges her attackers with fraud, forgery, theft, and harassment. Of course, the attackers collectively accuse her of the same offenses. The principle issue, however, and perhaps the central one in any software piracy case, is the differing values placed on the software by the manufacturer or developer and the purchaser. The pirates duplicate software because they claim it is ridiculously overpriced, while the developer claims to have spent years of effort getting the software right and should be compensated accordingly.

Scenario 3

In this scenario, issues of deception and consent are raised. Again, noble aims seem to be intended, but the methods by which they are achieved are questionable.

A medical researcher who is interested in epidemiology (the study of the origins of epidemics) wishes to use a benign computer virus to help verify some of his theoretical models of how diseases spread. (In the early days of computer viruses, such studies allegedly were carried out.[1] Although this scenario is not based on this material, the idea is used to illustrate the general issues that might or might not arise in such a study.)

The virus the researcher uses alerts users to the fact that their computer has been infected and also informs them that the virus is benign and will spontaneously self-destruct or disappear in a week. The alert message also asks users not to eradicate the virus (because it isn't doing any harm) and to continue with the normal program sharing and trading (illegal though it might be) that they normally engage in. The virus also asks the computer owners to write to the researcher (free of charge) to provide him with the information he needs to help study and model the epidemiological characteristics of the virus. This information, among other things, might include the location of the computer, the time the computer became infected (approximately), and the most likely source of infection. The aim of the research project is to see how fast and along what paths the virus is communicated and to determine whether this pattern of development bears any relationship to the way in which typical human diseases spread through a human population.

There are some laudable aims to this project. The researcher's ultimate goal is to more clearly understand the nature of human epidemics so that (presumably) they might be more easily brought under control. Therefore, in the final analysis, the researcher is concerned with saving human lives. The methods used, however, might be thought to be unethical for a variety of reasons. To begin with, whether or not the virus is harmless, it does consume resources that are not owned by the virus's creator (memory, user's time and attention, etc.). Moreover, the virus may rely upon the illegal software-copying activities of many computer users in order to propagate itself. Further, although the medical researcher's aims are clearly in the medical domain, it is possible that this information could be used in applications quite outside this sphere. For example, those concerned with software piracy could see this information as a rough metric of the rate of software piracy and use it to enforce legislation of a particular sort (for example, by placing a tax on all computer media to compensate software authors for the average rate of piracy that their work is likely to experience).

In addition, if these data have some bearing upon our understanding of how human epidemics develop, then other agencies, such as germ warfare establishments, also may be able to apply the data obtained to their research, so that more effective forms of germ agent dispersal and disease transmission are developed. Furthermore, in none of these applications, not even in the original epidemiological study, has the permission of the information supplier been sought. Indeed, the computer users, almost by definition (given the nature of this project), have been roped in without their consent. They may choose not to participate further, but to some extent they have already become involved without their prior, conscious, and considered consent.

In many ways, this situation resembles involuntary experimentation that could occur in almost any field. How would you feel if a psychological research institute bought TV advertising time, simulated the announcement of a nuclear attack (just as Orson Welles simulated radio coverage of an alien invasion), and then asked people to respond to them by describing their reactions and feelings? In this case, too, the prior consent of individuals was not sought, although they may have some choice about further participation. It is most unlikely that any such experiment would ever be officially endorsed, let alone conducted, in Western nations. It is clearly too unethical, not only bringing about possible psychological damage and extreme stress but also being based on deception of the potential participants.

It is obvious that in the case of our hypothetical virus experiment at least some degree of deception must be involved if the study has any chance of succeeding. That is, unless the virus were disguised in some way or attached to another (presumably useful) program, it is unlikely that many users would purposely attempt to acquire it.

Furthermore, it is not difficult to see that many computer users could become suspicious of the real nature of such a project. When they respond, all they are responding to is a name and an associated address. The apparent aims of the project may seem noble, but what if this weren't the real nature of the project? Although it may seem far-fetched, in recent years a number of papers have appeared that depict the real possibility of computer viruses being used as a military weapon. Imagine for a moment that, say, the U.S. military creates a virus that is attached to a very useful public domain utility program, then loads it onto thousands of disks and distributes it to bulletin boards and networks. Inevitably, the software will reach certain Middle Eastern countries either through disks mailed there or through the trade of information that is a normal component of dialogue and international relations. Of course, rather than sabotage their own networks, the American devisers of the virus have made sure that it will be triggered only by a Muslim computing environment (for example, by known operating characteristics of their machines or the presence of large numbers of text files in Arabic).

Although this type of sabotage constitutes an act of war, this kind of war has been going on between technological powers for more than forty years. For example, among other dangerous activities, U.S. submarines, ships, and aircraft regularly played dangerous games with those of the former Soviet Union, often in the Arctic Circle and often bringing about minor collisions and other forms of damage. For the isolated computer user faced with responding to our researcher's request, it is possible (although remotely) that he or she is participating in a study (by some secret security agency) that will determine if and how a campaign of viral warfare could become feasible. Indeed, the most paranoid of us could conceive of a situation in which the medical research request is a clever cover and in which responding is an unnecessary diversion. Perhaps the real information is gathered by the virus anyway and is accumulated as it is passes from one system to the next. The real project would be completed when the agency begins to collect disks from isolated locations and begins its analysis of transmission rates and transmission paths, as well as forms of viral protection and defense.

Scenario 4

Here we consider the constraints that professionals face in handling complex, unpredictable projects with many variables. Quite often in such

*cases, information is incomplete or even unobtainable. People are falli-
ble, and events sometimes transform a minor detail into an awesome
problem. Furthermore, problems often compound and magnify each
other, so that a chain of events or decisions provides a seamless trail
where it is difficult to identify the crucial error and hence to find where
responsibility lies.*

A group of civil engineers is involved in a major construction project.
Their duties include liaison with the architects and builders and the
provision of advice on appropriate structural materials for different parts
of the building. The major tool they use to provide this advice is a
software package that analyzes stresses on materials by using CAD-CAM
to produce plans and a small expert system containing expertise on the
physical properties of building materials such as steel, ducting, concrete,
and insulation.

However, the stress analysis system has a bug that produces arithmetic
errors in some calculations. (The reader might note that a rather famous
bug in IBM systems had a similar property.) The engineers do not notice
the odd values produced by the system and, unfortunately, these incorrect
calculations are used as a basis to construct the new building. Indeed, it
is impossible for the engineering team to check the calculations by other
means because they are too complex, too numerous, and too time-
consuming to fit within project deadlines.

Furthermore, the expert system that is part of the package contains
incorrect information. Specifically, the steel being used in parts of the
building is an alloy that has very good corrosion properties but a slightly
diminished ability to bear load compared to conventional steels. Unfortunately, the expert who provided the knowledge for the expert system
did not fully understand the difference in load-bearing ability with this
particular alloy, and hence this factor is not taken into consideration in
calculating the stresses to which the building will be subjected. Yet in
selling the package to engineers and architects, the developers of the
system have promoted it as being the safest in the world.

Halfway through the construction process, the building is unable to
support the loads being placed upon it. A crane on the uppermost floor
crashes through several floors and kills a number of workers in the
process. An analysis of the disaster shows that the arithmetic bug and
the misunderstanding of the structural properties of the steel alloy inter-

acted to bring about the failure. Had more conventional materials been used, the errors in the calculations would not have been of any consequence, but when combined with the weaker structural properties of the alloy, the calculations were inappropriate.

In these circumstances, who has the greater ethical responsibility for the accident? The engineers, who failed to recognize that the stress values were incorrect? The developers and commercial backers, whose tight schedules made checking the stress calculations impossible? The software developers, who supplied a faulty product? Or the so-called expert, whose knowledge of the properties of building materials was inadequate? In considering these questions, one might want to consider the kinds of defenses that each of these individuals or groups might offer.

The engineers might argue that checking the calculations was impractical given the deadline. The developers might counter that they had a responsibility to their shareholders and their investment. They were assured by the architects, engineers, and designers that automation of the design and engineering process would save time and cut costs. The developers would argue that it's not their fault that this new technology did not make the grade.

The software developers might argue that the arithmetic bug would have been of little consequence had more conventional construction materials been used. In any case, they would say, "everyone knows" that all software has bugs and that no complex system can be said to be entirely free of error, so the users of the system should have been aware of this fact. Therefore the software company might blame the engineers for not attempting to check at least some of the calculations, as this step would have revealed the presence of an error.

Ultimately, though, the developers might blame the construction materials expert they consulted. His job was to provide them with the facts and rules that needed to be encapsulated into the expert system contained in the stress analysis package. If this person's knowledge of building materials and their structural properties had been more adequate, they might maintain, then the arithmetical errors would have been inconsequential. As it was, in combination with the errors of calculation, this gap in understanding precipitated the disaster. Hence, because the expert provided inadequate knowledge, the software developers would hold that he caused the accident.

For his part, the materials expert might claim that all human knowledge is inadequate and incomplete. Moreover, much of any expert's knowledge of facts and of rule-based behavior is contradictory. Furthermore, he might argue that no one individual can be expected to know everything or to keep up with every change in such a fast-moving complex area. The software company should have realized this and incorporated knowledge gained from other sources. It also should have built more checks and controls into the software.

The software company might argue that it is not in the business of building perfect systems, because this is both practically and theoretically impossible for the scale of systems it markets. No amount of further knowledge, no amount of further checks and validations, can guarantee that the software is correct. These procedures may help, but they are not a sufficient condition for providing perfect systems. Users must reconcile themselves to the fact that in the real world systems do fail, despite the best of efforts, methodologies, and procedures. But, the software developer might claim, this problem is exacerbated by users who place blind faith in technology, developers who abbreviate the design and engineering process, and consultants who are unrealistic in representing the state and accuracy of the knowledge they possess.

Scenario 5

Individual rights are routinely in conflict with the rights of others and of society as a whole. The right to bear arms that is enshrined in the U.S. constitution is in conflict with the right of others to live in a threat-free environment, while the right of the public to know can conflict with the individual's right to privacy. Such privacy considerations have increased with the exponential growth in data storage, analysis, and distribution. But can an individual's right to privacy and even to a decent quality of life override the interests or rights of society?

It is 2005 and the spread of the AIDS virus has continued along its predicted path, almost unchecked by educational campaigns, safe sex, and the identification of high-risk groups. Like most clinical tests, the test for the HIV virus is not error-proof, and misdiagnosis does occur, however great the odds against it.

Unfortunately, double testing of blood from a blood bank did not identify it as being infected, and, as a result of an emergency transfusion, you now carry HIV antibodies. That is, you are antibody positive and are expected eventually to display the symptoms of the full-blown AIDS syndrome. Of course, the AIDS virus is unlike any other epidemic in one very important sense: individuals take several years to die from it. Most other major epidemic diseases—smallpox, cholera, and so on—kill people very quickly so that quarantining people is usually both a short term and a very effective epidemiological control; people either survive the short quarantine period and are prevented from infecting others during the infectious period, or they die. However, with AIDS, the prospect of quarantining people for up to ten years while they progress through the stages of the disease appears to be unacceptable, and, hence, infected individuals must live within society and suffer varying degrees of fear, discrimination, rejection, and alienation.

In 2005 the government has begun conducting compulsory AIDS-testing programs to help predict the course of the epidemic and to determine the impact of various initiatives. Test results are said to be totally confidential, and in order to prevent avoidance of the test, Social Security numbers, tax returns, and databases of all kinds are used to track down individuals and to present them (forcibly, if necessary) for testing. Of course, as a law-abiding citizen you present yourself, you are diagnosed as antibody positive, and the outcome is logged onto a government database system. However, you are confident that because the outcome of the test is confidential, you will be able to lead a fairly normal life, you follow safe sex practices to protect others, and you hope that in the time that you have left a cure or at least better treatments will be found.

With the growth of AIDS as one of the more common terminal diseases, however, an increasing number of people have been lying to insurance companies about their infection, and upon reaching a terminal stage, they kill themselves in car accidents and other apparently nonsuicidal forms of ending it all. In this way, victims' families are securing massive insurance payouts, and the insurance companies are feeling the pinch. However, in the interests of individuals' rights, the government prohibits insurance companies from demanding an AIDS test on an insurance applicant. It is sufficient that the government know who is infected, and the public release of such information is considered socially destabilizing.

Nevertheless, insurance companies are desperate to discover such information so that they can offer competitive premiums without such a high degree of risk. Two options are open to them: to somehow gain access to government files or else to obtain the same information through alternative sources. Like insurance companies everywhere, the U.S. companies hate risk, so they choose to do both. Through the tried and trusted method of bribery through a third party, some of this information is obtained. The remainder is gained by indirect means. Medical insurance companies note the kinds of treatments that patients receive and, by looking for patterns in these ailments, quickly determine the chances that particular policy holders and applicants might have AIDS. This information is sold to other insurance companies as well.

Furthermore, in order to secure lower premiums for their businesses, employers are encouraged to monitor workers' use of sick leave, any gossip about sexual preferences, and any drug usage. These reports, too, are added to the information mosaic gathered by the insurance companies. Lastly, landlords and other employers also are eager to obtain access to these records. In the case of landlords, they don't want to provide accommodation to an AIDS victim because, given the hysteria over AIDS, they may not be able to rent their premises again. In the case of employers, they don't want to invest heavily in training and providing a career structure for an individual if that person is likely to die before the investment is recouped. Furthermore, being an AIDS victim makes a person susceptible to blackmail, and that risk cannot be tolerated for employees entrusted with heavy responsibilities and financial powers.

What kind of quality of life do you think you can expect from this point on? Remember that federal and state employees of all kinds might have access to information about you, from police and ambulance personnel to doctors, lawyers, parole officers, and tax officials. Could their services or actions be modified as a result? And if similar information were available to anyone sufficiently interested to interrogate insurance databases (for a fee, of course), then what does this imply for the kind of life that you are likely to lead? Do you have a right to privacy in this regard or does the public have the right to know of a potential threat in its midst? Does computer-based storage of this information increase the risk of threats to individuals at the price of providing governments and health authorities with the information they need to combat the spread of AIDS?

Scenario 6

Ethical judgments require us to define our terms and concepts. In this scenario, we are dealing with the concept of justice itself and the ways in which computer technology might affect its process and quality. Again, we are placing in conflict our responsibilities toward the individual and the integrity and functioning of the state. Computers seem to be one of a handful of technologies—like nuclear technology and biotechnology— that place these issues into sharp relief.

It is 2005 again. Among its many other problems, the United States is wracked with intolerable levels of criminal activity and violence. Much of this unrest is the aftermath of crack—the cheap cocaine derivative that has now been on the streets for more than twenty years. However, there are other contributory factors, including high levels of unemployment for a large percentage of the black community, slum conditions, inadequate education for the poor, and a health system that operates on a cash basis only.

Among the most pressing problems is a situation that threatens to make a mockery of the Bill of Rights and the United States' claim to being a great democracy. This problem lies in the numbers of persons who are incarcerated and awaiting trial. These individuals, although technically innocent until proven guilty, are nevertheless spending periods in jail of up to a year before appearing in court. The sheer number of cases being dealt with by the criminal justice system has become impossible to handle; as a result, periods of remand have become ridiculously long, with innocent citizens being deprived of long periods of their lives without compensation. Moreover, as a result of these extended periods of incarceration, more and more people are emerging from jail as AIDS carriers, without having a history of high-risk activity. Although often found innocent, they have nevertheless been given a kind of life sentence by the penal system.

To help solve this problem, the federal government authorizes dramatic changes to court procedures in all states in order to accelerate the rate at which cases are heard and resolved. One of these changes includes the development and application of an expert system for determining the length of sentence in the event of a conviction. (Already, such proposals are being made by legal authorities.[2]) The system includes the entire history of U.S. court cases, their findings and associated sentences, and the laws in the individual states.

In essence, once a guilty verdict has been returned by a jury, the system immediately determines the maximum and minimum sentences prescribed for the crime under the relevant state's laws. It then consults what its designers have termed its internal conscience. Here, the system matches the pattern of the characteristics of the crime as closely as possible with a database of benchmark cases for which one hundred independent judges have provided sentences after having read the details of the case. Once the crime has been matched and the mean sentence calculated from its conscience, the standard deviation of these sentences is calculated (in other words, a measure of the variability of the recommended sentences is found). A statistical test is performed to determine if the mean sentence arrived at by the conscience is lower than the maximum sentence and, if it is, then this mean sentence is imposed.

Is anything wrong with this system in an ethical sense? After all, it prevents a judge from taking a day or two before imposing sentence and therefore it must help the throughput of cases. This benefit in itself must assist those who are still awaiting trial. Furthermore, under this system, sentences are determined by a much larger cross-section of judges than most courts would allow. Surely this remote judicial forum would be much more fair and balanced than one that allows an ill-tempered judge with indigestion to vent his discomfort by imposing the maximum sentence?

However, imagine that of those one hundred judges who were consulted to provide the conscience of the system, five of them are borderline psychotics who have been known to impose maximum sentences for crimes that particularly disturb their already-disturbed psyches. For other, equally serious crimes that do not offend their prejudices, they have been known to systematically impose rather trivial sentences—the minimum allowable by law. Furthermore, at least another five of these same one hundred judges are on the verge of senility: too revered to be fired or to have their judgment questioned, but effectively incompetent to have a jury before them.

In this case, at least 10 percent of the program's conscience is either unbalanced or simply incompetent. Given the average age of senior judges, these figures probably are not unrealistic. Even so, about 90 percent of the conscience has been based upon the reasoning of sound, experienced individuals (we hope), and perhaps we should be satisfied with that percentage. Indeed, even if only 90 percent of these people are reasonably competent, if appropriate numbers of females and those from various ethnic backgrounds and religions are included, then this should be a much fairer judicial forum than the one-person lottery we currently experience.

However, if this system were centralized, with courtrooms all over the country consulting it as required, then we effectively have a standardized system for dispensing sentences. But do we also have a system with standardized defects? Will all flashers invariably offend the psychotic judges and receive very long or even maximum sentences, whereas in our present system, through sheer luck of the draw they would have been treated more leniently?

Obviously, some percentage of the population that commits crimes that enrage the small number of psychotic judges on the panel always will be unfairly treated, even if only marginally, although the margin might be quite large if all of the unsystematic judges also happen to coincide in returning a hefty sentence. Perhaps this outcome is no different from our present circumstances. After all, some ethnic groups and sections of society are overrepresented in our jails, and, like all human beings, individual judges are susceptible to prejudice.

Therefore, if both systems are biased in some form, are we replacing one inadequate system by another? Is it better to allow chance to determine some aspects of the judicial forum? Or is it better to allow (perhaps small, perhaps large) biases to be dispensed in a more standardized fashion?

Moreover, we might argue that sampling one hundred judges simply replicates the status quo, which, as we noted previously, is clearly not without bias. Perhaps even a thousand judges would not be sufficient to provide what we might call a fair system. Where do we find an adequate number of black female judges or judges from humble origins? Where do we get enough judges who can relate to the circumstances that impoverished, addicted, or abused people find themselves in? Clearly we could go to excessive lengths to provide a perfect system: reformed alcoholic or drug-addicted judges to try cases involving substance abusers, Vietnam veterans to judge other Vietnam veterans, and so on.

Certainly the present system doesn't provide this level of fairness (and perhaps it shouldn't be expected to), but perhaps it does provide the human context in which trials occur. Remote evaluation of case notes does not provide this context, and certainly one could argue that no amount of fine pattern matching can come close to understanding the idiosyncrasies and human texture that distinguishes almost any case from any other.

Hence we come to several rather fundamental questions, beginning with the following: What are the ethical dimensions of such a scenario? Is a faster, less faulty machine-administered system of justice better than a slower, more faulty human-administered one? Should justice be administered by individuals who are permitted to experience the nuances of a real case, or by the recorded judgments of individuals who remotely consider case details and rely upon group stability to guarantee fairness? In any case, would our anticipated system simply replicate the status quo, which we may already assume to be unjust? Or inevitably, are we forced to mete out justice in the best way we can—faulty or not, biased or not, human or not?

At this point we ask what we probably should have asked ourselves at the outset: What is this system designed to achieve? Or, in essence, what is the problem we hope to solve? Are we attempting to achieve a better system of justice? If so, then we had better ask ourselves what we think justice really is. We might be surprised to find that even on this rather fundamental point, not much agreement can be found.

Is the problem simply what we originally specified—that the judicial process is too slow? Or is there more to the problem than this? Is the problem really that many people's lives are so empty or squalid that they resort to substance abuse in order to make their lives that much more bearable? Is it that, as a society, we have failed to provide the social conditions necessary for people to hope and to raise their horizon beyond the next meal, the next day, or the next fix? Perhaps these are the problems we should be attempting to solve. If so, then our expert system is only an attempt to solve a superficial manifestation of these problems.

The contemporary literature in the philosophy of technology labels such phenomena "techno-fixes"—that is, attempts to concoct a superficial technological solution to what is essentially a human problem.[3] Another example of a techno-fix might be the use of artificial insemination in captivity in order to preserve endangered species. Clearly, the real problem that endangered species face is not a lack of reproductive vigor; rather, it is the destruction of habitat through human pollution, population pressure, or predatory behavior. Hence, any attempt to fix such a problem through technological means represents a superficial effort at best, because the solution addresses the symptoms of the problem rather than the root causes.

Should computer professionals be forced to think through the ethical basis, origins, and implications of the work they undertake (even if society or governments do not)? Should they accept money to solve pseudoproblems or to create high-tech fixes for the symptoms of more fundamental problems? Should they be made aware of the extent to which their work relies upon value judgments, not only in design and implementation terms (is this software feature a good/bad/useful/complicated/cost-effective one?) but also in terms of the values embedded in the design specification and those that are implicitly held by the client or sponsor?

Scenario 7

Consider the following hypothetical scenario. It is designed to illustrate many of the common problems that software designers (and their clients) encounter during the development of a new information system. In addition, it addresses ethical issues relating to the quality of work life and relationships between employers and their employees.

Liverwurst Literature Inc. was a small but successful publishing company that derived its major source of income from subscriptions to a range of magazine titles. With the entry of a major foreign company into the market, however, Liverwurst decided that it needed to expand its operations to remain competitive, and so it looked at the range of changes that would have to be implemented in order to boost its competitiveness. The company quickly found that its existing subscription-processing system was inadequate to meet the anticipated levels of processing. As a result, management decided that a new computer-based system was needed to overcome the limitations of the existing, largely manual system, which was clearly out of the Dark Ages.

Before considering the computerized system and its development, it is important to understand how the manual system operated.

Original System

The steps in the original system were:

1. Incoming mail was directed to the mail clerk, who sorted out the payments received. The remaining items were divided into orders and nonorders (i.e., complaints, changes of address, etc.). At this stage, items were manually counted and totaled to serve as a control for subsequent steps. These later steps were handled by staff working in the subscriptions department.

2. The first task in the subscriptions department was to sort the orders by transaction type (new, continuing, gift, etc.) and code them accordingly. Batches of each transaction type were assembled for the next stage of processing, the data-processing stage.

3. A manual card file system was used to carry out the major data-processing tasks. The data entry section filled in the order cards and verified them; they were then passed to the data-processing clerk who typed them into a file on a microcomputer, sorted them, and printed out the list of orders. What the data-processing phase produced was an initial set of bills, mailing labels, notices, and subscriber cards. This phase also detected any invalid inputs.

4. Subscriber cards resulting from the third stage of the process were then taken and manually inserted into the alphabetically ordered card file boxes. This file was periodically used as a basis for the production of monthly mailing labels, annual renewal notices, and so on.

A schematic representation of the system follows.

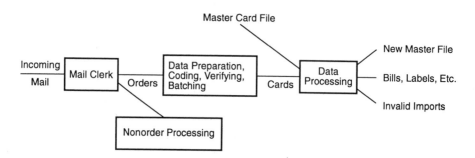

This labor-intensive system became increasingly slow, expensive, unreliable, and unable to keep up with the seasonal peaks in subscription processing. Delays and customer complaints prompted the management to follow the lead of many larger-circulation periodicals and to automate their subscription processing.

Nevertheless, the system had several positive aspects. First, it required a high level of operator involvement. Workers felt they had a level of expertise that made the system work despite its problems. They felt that the company required and valued their skills. In addition, workers were highly familiar with the system and knew where problems were likely to occur. Hence, their fault diagnosis was surprisingly quick. Workers had a good grasp of the functionality of the system. Its physical layout provided them with a good mental model of how it worked.

The skill and involvement of the workers can be explained in large part by the extent to which the existing procedures had been codesigned by the workers. Many of the original codesigners still worked for Liverwurst and were able to provide specialist advice or important information when needed. Consequently, a great deal of relevant expertise and specialist knowledge relevant to the system were already in house.

Finally, although the existing system was heavily routinized, so that most workers performed repetitive piecework, nevertheless the physical form of the system provided direct, observable feedback to all workers on the amount of work that had been completed that day and how much was left to be processed. It was also possible for workers to predict a lag in the processing so that they could take a quick break or help another worker who had an excessive amount to do. Thus, some amount of autonomy and choice existed.

The Development Process

Because the company did not have the appropriate computer skills to develop the new system, management opted to employ a team of consultants who appeared to have a good track record in software development. The consultants' previous training and experience were focused on deriving program solutions from clearly formulated programming problems. In the case of Liverwurst Literature, they analyzed the situation, identified the parts that could benefit from a programming solution, and applied that solution to the problem.

Being mindful of the cost ceiling that the company had given them, the consultants decided that adapting an existing off-the-shelf-solution would be most cost effective. That is, they believed that customizing this package to meet the unique needs of Liverwurst was the most efficient way of implementing the required system. Their approach focused on processing the data and took a top-down form:

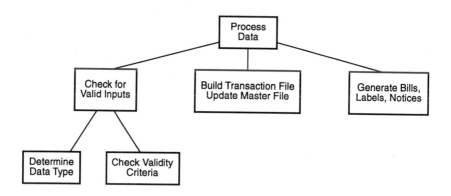

The software solution fitted into the original system in the following way:

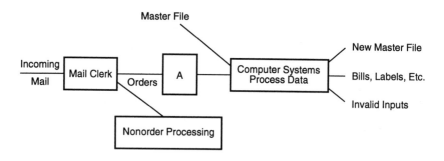

In this new configuration, *A* is a program to add the new entries to a master file held on a disk.

In the process of developing this system, the consultants did look at the existing system, but they did not analyze its strengths and deficiencies either from a pure processing point of view or from a worker's point of view. They did not attempt to compare existing computer-based systems in similar applications with the system they intended to provide. They did not have any formal or informal discussions with workers as to how the existing system could be improved or how the anticipated system could best be grafted onto the current one. They did not attempt to validate the system with the workers as it was being developed. Their attempts at requirements specification were not comprehensive. Their testing procedures in the early stages of development were inadequate, and several bugs proved impossible to eliminate without rebuilding the code from scratch. As a result of this, a key member of the programming team resigned in midproject, principally because she believed her warnings in regard to specification and testing had not been heeded. This person was the most knowledgeable in the team, and her departure meant that whatever likelihood there had been of delivering a bug-free product was now gone.

The Outcome

When the product eventually was delivered, it proved necessary to place the system over several floors because some of the printers and card readers were too noisy to be placed near the clerical workers, and acoustic baffles were too expensive. As a consequence of this, workers frequently had to travel from one floor to another to obtain output or input. They also were unable to see if other workers were overloaded. The system did not provide any statistics to workers (only to the analysts), and, hence, there was little feedback on how much had been accomplished and how much of the day's processing was left.

As part of their contract, the consultants agreed to be involved in a teething period in which the bugs in the system would be ironed out and operators would be trained. However, this period was very short, and only the simplest problems with the system were rectified while the trainers and analysts remained in house. By the time of their departure, the expertise of the operators had increased markedly, but the range and complexity of the problems they faced became enormous. The operators soon found that telephone diagnoses were little help.

In addition, the error-checking and input-validation procedures involved in the new system were inadequate. A trivial error would often cause the program to reject entire batches of input or cause an update run to stop completely. When this happened, the transaction input listing had to be found and manually checked for errors. This labor also involved another cumbersome process of updating the transaction file.

Faced with this problem, the management imposed additional levels of control on the manual-processing steps that preceded the computer processing. This procedure required the use of more complicated input forms and control sheets to handle exceptional conditions. These changes resulted in the need for more, not less, personnel, increased costs, more delays, and reduced staff morale.

The workers began expressing the view that whereas previously they had a good model of the system and how it worked, the training carried out by the consultants had not provided such a model for the new system. Hence, the ability of operators to predict failures, to diagnose faults, and to cover for weaknesses or bottlenecks was not part of the new system.

The physical layout of the previous system had given them feedback on work progress and had allowed them to have some control over their own work routines, but they now had little understanding of how the day's work was progressing or when they might be able to assist another worker. This problem was exacerbated by the location of the system over several floors.

Workers expressed the view that their skills had been downgraded and that their new tasks required little initiative, no thought, and even less skill or involvement in the goals of the enterprise. While they recognized that old skills had to be discarded and new ones learned, they also pointed out that if they had been involved in the system design from the start, they could have designed tasks and work roles that would have preserved some autonomy, responsibility, and pride in their skills.

In sum, because of these technical and work force difficulties, for the new system as a whole:

Costs went up rather than down.
Reliability and quality of service went down.
More clerical people were required.
Employee morale went down.
Employee turnover went up.

Cases like this do happen, perhaps more frequently than many of us are willing to admit. Obviously, there are issues of considerable ethical significance here, including system designers' responsibilities to both their clients and their users, who may have conflicting goals. For workers, the quality of their work life and their job satisfaction may be just as important as the salary packages they receive. For employers, however, efficiency and competitiveness translate into profitability (and employment).

The major issue, therefore, is how to maximize profitability and corporate efficiency without creating an unbearable working environment for employees. One possible solution would be to incorporate workers into the design process, system implementation, and fine tuning. After all, the experts in these matters are often the workers.

In addition, we should question the after-delivery practices of the consulting company and its responsibilities in delivering a quality product through a reliable and professional development process. Without such professional practices, many commentators question whether the software industry can truly take on the status of a profession in the manner that, say, law and medicine have. Fly-by-night companies, shoddy products, and ridiculous disclaimers are more in the realm of shady businesses than a profession of educated and intelligent people. If computer professionals wish to be accorded the status of other professions, then their social awareness and ethical values must be upgraded substantially.

Scenario 8

Technological possibilities open up ethical issues that are often different only in scale rather than in principle. However, ethical codes are subject to fashion and convention. In disciplines such as psychology and the life sciences, certain experiments that were conducted two decades ago could not be conducted today because of ethical constraints. Given these shifting sands, how is a professional to behave? Does ethical theory provide any guidance in such circumstances?

Dr. Otto Schimmel is a psychotherapist with degrees from reputable universities in the United States and Britain. He is a native of the tiny East European country of Upper Gransk and maintains a small psychological counseling practice in its capital city. After ten years of treating patients with phobias, obsessive-compulsive disorders, marital problems, and other assorted afflictions of modern living, Dr. Schimmel suddenly discovers the world of bulletin boards and the UUCP network. Even from Upper Gransk, a PC network allows him to communicate throughout Transylvania, Rumania, and Bulgaria and from there to the rest of the world.

As a resourceful individual, the good doctor recognizes that a huge, well-educated, middle-class audience is at his fingertips. Electronic mail can reach him from almost anywhere, and a notice can reach hundreds of thousands of people around the world for little more cost than a local telephone call. Schimmel quickly invents the notion of "e-mail therapy" and begins to think about the logistics of such a notion. These considerations include key questions such as how to ensure payment, avoid hoax patients, and so on.

First, he posts a note on several Internet news groups advertising his therapeutic services. He lists his qualifications and experience and the basis on which the therapy will be conducted. To enroll in therapy, Schimmel asks that prospective patients provide key personal details, such as name, date of birth, address, e-mail address, educational background, marital history, employment history, present income, and a brief outline of their problems. Schimmel then indicates by e-mail whether he is willing to accept an individual as a patient (based on the nature of the problem and the patient's capacity to pay). For example, any borderline psychotics are quickly rejected, and any charity cases (students, etc.) are also discouraged from enrolling.

Once a patient has been accepted, Schimmel requests a deposit in the form of an international money order made out to his business account or, if patients are unwilling to make a deposit, he asks them to evaluate his first half-dozen sessions and if they have been of no benefit, the patient can leave the therapeutic relationship without incurring any costs.

Hoax patients are easily identified by the personal data they supply. A friend of Schimmel's has access to international credit agency files (despite the fact that there is nothing worth buying in Upper Gransk) and can quickly determine whether the patient is a real person and what their credit-worthiness is. Pranksters have their e-mail bounced back to them once their addresses are added to an e-mail kill file.

In the process of therapy, the psychotherapist receives e-mail from patients, looks at his records, and responds to the e-mail with comments, further questions, requests for clarification, and so on. Most of the problems he handles are minor neuroses, relationship problems, and other difficulties that often stem from individuals having too much money and too much time on their hands (and Schimmel is keen to help them out in this respect). In short, the problems that Schimmel chooses to deal with are quite minor—often just lonely people with few people they can talk to or trust.

Although Schimmel is aware of the ethical dimensions involved, he believes that the scheme has a number of clear benefits. Firstly, his location in Upper Gransk means that he is not constrained by any code of ethics because Upper Gransk has no local or national professional body of psychotherapists with a code of ethics. No local laws prevent him from conducting psychotherapy in this manner, and no privacy laws constrain his use of the private data he receives and stores.

Conducting psychotherapy by e-mail has certain benefits. The partial anonymity of the electronic link means that patients are more willing to be honest, are less inhibited by the expectation of interpersonal condemnation in someone's presence, and are perhaps even more willing to begin the therapeutic relationship because of the remoteness of the therapist. Otherwise, how does such a relationship differ from one conducted by ordinary mail? Is face-to-face contact really necessary for psychotherapy to work or to be ethically responsible? Are codes of conduct adopted by professional bodies in particular countries binding on similar professionals in other countries? Can Schimmel be guided by any relevant ethical principles or theories? Finally, is it ethical to use a UUCP connection for profit-making purposes, or does anything go?

Scenario 9

This scenario draws attention to ethical and professional issues involved in possible programmer or system designer licensing and to the ethical basis of the software development industry.

John and Mary Anybody are newlyweds with bright, shiny visions of a dream home built with their hard-earned cash. Like many people, the Anybodys aren't satisfied with a prefabricated cookie-cutter design for their home. They want split levels, spiral staircases, skylights, and other features that require a skilled professional architect. With the help of the

Yellow Pages, they look under "Architects" and call a number of them in order to find one they think they can work with.

Eventually, after many meetings, John and Mary settle on Norman Nonlinear, whom they like and who has many impressive certificates hanging on the walls of his office. Together they design the dream home. Norman moves shapes around a board, draws perspectives, and eventually drafts the design. In this mythical locale, building design standards don't exist and builder and architect licensing doesn't exist, so that effectively architectural design is a free-for-all. If you have a few certificates in building, plumbing, or whatever you can call yourself an architect and design and build anything—no matter how big—from scratch.

With much gusto, Norman hires workers from all quarters to begin construction. The soil isn't tested, so the wrong kind of foundation is laid. Drainage is poor because the flood-prone nature of the property has never been recorded. The roof is far too heavy for the walls, so they begin to crack, windows fall out, and doors stick. Nothing in the house is level. Some of the plumbing remains unconnected to the mains because the components are nonstandard, and even the fuse box frequently is overloaded because too many power points are on each line. The toilet is located right next to the kitchen, so several doors have to be installed in order to eliminate odors. Finally, one toilet often fails to flush because the upper floor is too high for the local water pressure to reach it. In sum, the building is a nightmare of structural and design problems that are impossible to rectify—they are embedded too deeply in the design itself. It would be better to tear down the house and start again.

As it turns out, Norman Nonlinear, although a very nice guy, has no qualifications or experience to undertake such a task—the legal system simply allows him to. Although he has some certificates in plumbing and carpentry and has designed and built a few garages, he has no experience in larger design and certainly could not be expected to design a project as nonstandard and complex as this one. But on the other hand, designing and building a large house is just like designing and building a big garage—right?

Does any of this tale sound familiar in the context of software design? It should. Cost overruns, outright system development failures, and poorly implemented designs are chronic in the software business, to say the least. Because of these widespread problems, the issue of programmer licensing has been raised several times in recent years, with support and condemnation coming from different quarters.[4] Some commentators have argued that it would be impossible to evaluate development competence because of the vastly different paradigms and applications that exist in computing. Some developers apply object-oriented methodologies, some restrict themselves to large database applications or network communications. Others create machine code for low-level instruments, and so on. The same objections could be applied to, say, surgeons, who use vastly different techniques to treat vastly different problems, yet they manage to certify themselves as ear, nose, and throat specialists, and so on.

In a similar vein, we might ask, Why should computing be any different from any other profession with regard to licensing and registration? Doctors, lawyers, pharmacists, and so on all have their activities regulated so that not just anyone can be called an attorney or, in this scenario, an architect. Would we be happy if the surgeon performing our heart bypass merely had a basic medical degree and some varicose vein surgery under her belt? Then why do we allow anyone with a basic computer science degree (or less) to handle any software project of any complexity? When we drive, we expect others to be licensed and competent. We expect civil engineers to be similarly certified. We expect air traffic controllers to have appropriate training and to be weaned into more complex control situations as their judgment and experience increase. Yet we allow inexperienced software developers to build software that drives everything from ambulance scheduling software to nuclear reactor control systems.

In the end, a system of apprenticeship might be required. Just as surgeons are introduced to specific techniques and exposed to more and more difficult cases by their surgical instructors so, too, might software designers be apprenticed to experienced designers in specific application areas. Yet it could be that the world of computing applications is too idiosyncratic and too different from one organizational context to the next for it to provide discrete skills and knowledge that could be suitable for licensing examination and certification. Nevertheless, whatever the outcome of the licensing debate, there is a growing feeling that the unregulated, barnstorming days of programming may be over.

Scenario 10

This last scenario raises issues that many undergraduates already are familiar with or will be as the Internet reaches the farthest points of the globe. An international, publicly funded resource such as the Net would appear to have accountability inherent in its functioning, yet this does not appear to be the case. Indeed, the Net is the arena of daily worldwide abuses that are fascinating both for their technological character and their resistance to eradication.

The Internet is a vast collection of mainframes, minicomputers, and PCs that are connected by a variety of physical transmission links (coaxial, fiber optic, microwave, satellite) and communications protocols such as TCP/IP and UUCP (Unix-to-Unix Communications Protocol). The result is that large numbers of corporations, small businesses, government agencies, military sites, research laboratories, and private individuals now have the ability to exchange electronic mail, software, news, and files. It is even possible for them to connect to and interact in real-time with massive public databases such as the Library of Congress, community bulletin boards, and commercial indexers of scientific and academic literature such as DIALOG. But, in effect, the Internet (or Net, as it is more usually known) is really indescribable because it is largely unregulated (or self-regulated, at best) and conforms to few conventions or standards beyond the technical requirements needed to add a site to its sprawling, international connections. A very clear and accessible introduction to the Net can be found in *Zen and the Art of the Internet,* which is available (awkwardly enough) from many Internet sites and university computer centers.

Because the Net was never designed in an a priori sense—that is, like topsy "it simply growed" as more and more nodes were added to it—there is little central control or administration, and for many years it has been a fascinating source of practical and ethical dilemmas over its means of operation, over the information it carries, and over what constitutes acceptable user behavior and legitimate usage. Although many Net users have made the effort to write ad hoc guides to etiquette (or "Nettiquette"), very few of the news groups that circulate around the world on the Net are moderated or controlled in their content and, in effect, almost any user has the power to create new news groups or to send almost anything around the world to the hundreds of thousands of people who may be prepared to read it or view it. Furthermore, a whole hierarchy of alternative Internet news groups exists, and the range of their aims and contents is limited only by the human imagination.

Many writers have waxed lyrical about the scope, potential, and power of the Net. Some, such as the Electronic Frontier Foundation's John Perry Barlow, have identified it as the natural enemy of tyranny—a communications medium beyond the control of authoritarian governments because the Net is a spontaneous, haphazard anarchy. (One wonders what happened to Voice of America, BBC World Service, and other long-standing radio broadcasts.) But there is more to the vision than this: somehow, according to Barlow, the mere connection of thousands of individuals will lead to a liberating, spiritual, edifying experience of global proportions.

Despite this noble portrayal, the reality of the Net is much more base and disturbing. Although the sheer daily volume of data on the Net is staggering—some have described it as having 500 telephones in your kitchen—it doesn't take long for most new users to decrease the scope of their reading and limit themselves to the few groups that form their central interests or that they find to be most useful to them in terms of the quality of their content. Unfortunately, a great deal of what the Net carries is unmitigated garbage: off-the-cuff ideas, rabid diatribes, ideological vendettas, public arenas for personal abuse, or adolescent, trivial junk. Flame (or abuse) wars are so common that news-reading software contains "kill file" features that screen news items that have been posted by a particular person or that are about a particular topic.

Although it might seem noble to have an international forum to discuss ideas, ideologies, proposals, and projects—an intellectual's electronic forum—sadly, the Net as a whole seldom lives up to that ideal. In reality, the Net has a very large proportion of news groups that discuss scores of obscure, ridiculous, trivial, obscene, narrow, or patently silly issues. For example, a Dan Quayle fan club thrived for a while, as do groups that distribute pornographic images, discuss human sexuality (including aberrant and abhorrent practices), make recommendations on the latest pornographic movies, electronically publish unpublished (and often unpublishable) poetry, and cover topics and recreations that have little relevance to any commercial, scientific, or serious activity.

It is even possible to engage in the computer equivalent of phone sex by reading the news group alt.personals. Users who post to this news group are assigned an anonymous e-mail identifier, and any correspondence to them is routed via the machine that assigns the anonymous tag. As a result, dozens of solicitations for sex, get togethers, and assorted "good times" appear daily in the news group, and a roaring, anonymous exchange of fantasies, four-letter words, and even dates and addresses occurs. What started out as a well-intentioned way for lonely people to send mail to each other and perhaps one day meet—a computer-based lonely hearts club—has been turned into a source of terminal-based sex and soliciting. And, unfortunately, the story of alt.personals is very much the story of the Internet as a whole. What began as a well-intentioned experiment, an international communications democracy, has quickly sunk into an anarchy of abuse, electronic graffiti, and sexual deviance.

Furthermore, the amazing connectivity of the Net has been commandeered to assist in free-ranging software piracy and the international exchange of pornographic images and animations cut from blue movies. Typically, these pirates identify a site and log into it through the legitimate anonymous FTP log-in that many Internet sites provide to facilitate access to the software they legitimately store. Having gained access anonymously, the pirates upload their files to a hidden directory they create and proceed to swap the latest software or to trade pornographic pictures and movies. In fact, the capabilities of the Internet help these pirates to find other pirate-infested sites and to contribute to the free trade.

For example, a number of Internet sites act as servers for a system known as Archie. Archie interrogates the majority of Internet sites and builds a database of files and the sites which hold them. Just as legitimate users can interrogate Archie to find, for example, sites holding the latest release of the GNU C compiler, pirates can also look for pirated commercial software hidden deep on the disks of unsuspecting Internet sites. Obviously, the piracy eventually will be discovered and the files deleted by responsible system administrators, with clear warnings made visible to guard against further piracy. However, many thousands of sites have exactly the same vulnerability, and even if it were possible for system administrators to identify the Internet addresses (or possibly e-mail addresses) of the pirates, it is unlikely that any significant action would be taken against them. The evidence is too flimsy, too difficult to collect, too easy to manipulate, and, in the end, the administrators are too busy to deal with the extra hassle. Often the administrator simply refuses all further anonymous log-ins, thereby removing access to possibly thousands of Internet users who might need copies of that site's software.

Beyond this abuse, even casual Net usage reveals blatant copyright violations that occur with mind-numbing regularity—and not just software copyright. Quite often, literary and scientific work is reproduced in its entirety—sometimes with the author attribution and copyright notice attached—with no apparent understanding that such reproduction is a violation of the rights of the author and publisher. Month after month, Monty Python scripts, chapters from Douglas Adams novels, published scientific papers, and other material floats around the Net. And even though much of this activity is genuinely well-intentioned or naively innocent—"just sharing the great book I read on the weekend"—nevertheless, the capabilities of the Net allows copyright violations, within seconds, on a scale that thousands of printing presses or photocopiers could never approach.

Lastly, the Net offers a huge number of ways to perpetrate more mundane pranks, annoyances, and abuses. Flame wars often lead to people filling their opponent's mailbox with hundreds of four-letter-word messages. Anonymous e-mail is not difficult to create, and the "test" news group of the Net even allow the various methods to be experimented with. Computer account passwords are routinely stolen, and embarrassing messages are posted around the world to the obvious dismay of the real account holder. And despite its alleged claim to noncommercial status, the Net advertises hundreds of items for sale every day, and commercial services of almost every kind are advertised freely.

This last point raises an often-asked question: Who pays for Internet and why don't they stop these abusers? Unfortunately if the answer to these questions were as simple as adding up the bottom line, then changes would have happened long ago. In part, the Internet, or at least the major transmission routes that run the length of the United States, are paid for by the U.S. government. Similarly, many international sites and their communications links are paid for with taxpayers' money. However, a huge amount of Internet traffic is carried by commercial institutions and private individuals armed with little more than a phone line and a modem. Because the Net is a store and forward system, such that one site feeds many local sites that, in turn, feed their local sites, even if the major backbone sites were removed, the Net would continue to exist, although with slower propagation. Furthermore, while many sites block the receipt and retransmission of news groups they consider to be objectionable, this impediment has little effect on their ultimate spread, and as far as many governments are concerned, what they are paying for is the communications bandwidth, not the cost of each byte transmitted. That is, the major links are leased lines, and the price paid for their rental is based on capacity. In a sense, the capacity is already bought and paid for, irrespective of whether it sits idle or is used to carry pornography or terminal sex. Hence, some abusers feel no qualms about consuming bandwidth that might otherwise be unused.

But beyond these funding issues lie the very difficult, practical problems of controlling the multitude of abusive behaviors that occur on the Net. Offensive news groups that have been terminated by authorities can easily be recreated or substituted with mailing lists that e-mail the same material around the world. And the problems of monitoring e-mail with its possibility for encryption are so nightmarish that they hardly bear thinking about. Even distinguishing pornographic images, for example, from software binaries is impossible until the data has been assembled and accessed with the appropriate viewer or player. There is no way that this task can be automated to assist human intervention.

More mundane problems such as commercial advertising, junk mailing, and excessive flaming are even more problematic because they rely on the ethical judgment of individual users. Although guides to ethical Net behavior may be helpful, they are pointless if the bulk of users chooses to ignore them. Because abusive behavior is unlikely to be punished, one can understand why mere moralizing is ignored by thousands of Net abusers. Finally, regulation and control of network submissions and e-mail is an onerous and thankless task that few people are willing to undertake. In the case of e-mail, it is physically impossible to deal with its volume, let alone its content. And even with successful moderation of a news group, disgruntled abusers are free to set up their own news group or mailing list or else engage in the myriad of other abusive behaviors that the Net allows.

You might like to discuss this interpretation of the Internet and compare it with more glowing accounts. Would sensitizing Net users to ethical issues cut down abuse? Would severe punishments and making an example make a difference? In the end, does it matter?

Appendix A

ACM Code of Ethics and Professional Conduct

On October 16, 1992, ACM's Executive Council voted to adopt a revised Code of Ethics.
The following imperatives and explanatory guidelines were proposed to supplement the Code as contained in the new ACM Bylaw 17.

Commitment to ethical professional conduct is expected of every voting, associate, and student member of ACM. This Code, consisting of 24 imperatives formulated as statements of personal responsibility, identifies the elements of such a commitment.

It contains many, but not all, issues professionals are likely to face. Section 1 outlines fundamental ethical considerations, while Section 2 addresses additional, more specific considerations of professional conduct. Statements in Section 3 pertain more specifically to individuals who have a leadership role, whether in the workplace or in a volunteer capacity, for example with organizations such as ACM. Principles involving compliance with this Code are given in Section 4.

The Code is supplemented by a set of Guidelines, which provide explanation to assist members in dealing with the various issues contained in the Code. It is expected that the Guidelines will be changed more frequently than the Code.

The Code and its supplemented Guidelines are intended to serve as a basis for ethical decision making in the conduct of professional work. Secondarily, they may serve as a basis for judging the merit of a formal complaint pertaining to violation of professional ethical standards.

It should be noted that although computing is not mentioned in the moral imperatives section, the Code is concerned with how these funda-

Reprinted from "ACM Code of Ethics and Professional Conduct," *Communication of the ACM*, vol. 36, no. 2, February 1993, pages 100–105.

mental imperatives apply to one's conduct as a computing professional. These imperatives are expressed in a general form to emphasize that ethical principles which apply to computer ethics are derived from more general ethical principles.

It is understood that some words and phrases in a code of ethics are subject to varying interpretations, and that any ethical principle may conflict with other ethical principles in specific situations. Questions related to ethical conflicts can best be answered by thoughtful consideration of fundamental principles, rather than reliance on detailed regulations.

1. General Moral Imperatives.

As an ACM member I will . . .

1.1 Contribute to society and human well-being This principle concerning the quality of life of all people affirms an obligation to protect fundamental human rights and to respect the diversity of all cultures. An essential aim of computing professionals is to minimize negative consequences of computing systems, including threats to health and safety. When designing or implementing systems, computing professionals must attempt to ensure that the products of their efforts will be used in socially responsible ways, will meet social needs, and will avoid harmful effects to health and welfare.

In addition to a safe social environment, human well-being includes a safe natural environment. Therefore, computing professionals who design and develop systems must be alert to, and make others aware of, any potential damage to the local or global environment.

1.2 Avoid harm to others "Harm" means injury or negative consequences, such as undesirable loss of information, loss of property, property damage, or unwanted environmental impacts. This principle prohibits use of computing technology in ways that result in harm to any of the following: users, the general public, employees, employers. Harmful actions include intentional destruction or modification of files and programs leading to serious loss of resources or unnecessary expenditure of human resources such as the time and effort required to purge systems of computer viruses.

Well-intended actions, including those that accomplish assigned duties, may lead to harm unexpectedly. In such an event the responsible person or persons are obligated to undo or mitigate the negative consequences as much as possible. One way to avoid unintentional harm is to carefully consider potential impacts on all those affected by decisions made during design and implementation.

To minimize the possibility of indirectly harming others, computing professionals must minimize malfunctions by following generally accepted standards for system design and testing. Furthermore, it is often necessary to assess the social consequences of systems to project the likelihood of any serious harm to others. If system features are misrepresented to users, coworkers, or supervisors, the individual computing professional is responsible for any resulting injury.

In the work environment the computing professional has the additional obligation to report any signs of system dangers that might result in serious personal or social damage. If one's superiors do not act to curtail or mitigate such dangers, it may be necessary to "blow the whistle" to help correct the problem or reduce the risk. However, capricious or misguided reporting of violations can, itself, be harmful. Before reporting violations, all relevant aspects of the incident must be thoroughly assessed. In particular, the assessment of risk and responsibility must be credible. It is suggested that advice be sought from other computing professionals. (See principle 2.5 regarding thorough evaluations.)

1.3 Be honest and trustworthy Honesty is an essential component of trust. Without trust an organization cannot function effectively. The honest computing professional will not make deliberately false or deceptive claims about a system or system design, but will instead provide full disclosure of all pertinent system limitations and problems.

A computer professional has a duty to be honest about his or her own qualifications, and about any circumstances that might lead to conflicts of interest.

Membership in volunteer organizations such as ACM may at times place individuals in situations where their statements or actions could be interpreted as carrying the "weight" of a larger group of professionals. An ACM member will exercise care to not misrepresent ACM or positions and policies of ACM or any ACM units.

1.4 Be fair and take action not to discriminate The values of equality, tolerance, respect for others, and the principles of equal justice govern this imperative. Discrimination on the basis of race, sex, religion, age, disability, national origin, or other such factors is an explicit violation of ACM policy and will not be tolerated.

Inequities between different groups of people may result from the use or misuse of information and technology. In a fair society, all individuals would have equal opportunity to participate in, or benefit from, the use of computer resources regardless of race, sex, religion, age, disability, national origin or other such similar factors. However, these ideals do not justify unauthorized use of computer resources nor do they provide an adequate basis for violation of any other ethical imperatives of this code.

1.5 Honor property rights including copyrights and patents Violation of copyrights, patents, trade secrets and the terms of license agreements is prohibited by law in most circumstances. Even when software is not so protected, such violations are contrary to professional behavior. Copies of software should be made only with proper authorization. Unauthorized duplication of materials must not be condoned.

1.6 Give proper credit for intellectual property Computing professionals are obligated to protect the integrity of intellectual property. Specifically, one must not take credit for other's ideas or work, even in cases where the work has not been explicitly protected, for example by copyright or patent.

1.7 Respect the privacy of others Computing and communication technology enables the collection and exchange of personal information on a scale unprecedented in the history of civilization. Thus there is increased potential for violating the privacy of individuals and groups. It is the responsibility of professionals to maintain the privacy and integrity of data describing individuals. This includes taking precautions to ensure the accuracy of data, as well as protecting it from unauthorized access or accidental disclosure to inappropriate individuals. Furthermore, procedures must be established to allow individuals to review their records and correct inaccuracies.

This imperative implies that only the necessary amount of personal information be collected in a system, that retention and disposal periods for that information be clearly defined and enforced, and that personal information gathered for a specific purpose not be used for other purposes without consent of the individual(s). These principles apply to electronic communications, including electronic mail, and prohibit procedures that capture or monitor electronic user data, including messages, without the permission of users or *bona fide* authorization related to system operation and maintenance. User data observed during the normal duties of system operation and maintenance must be treated with strictest confidentiality, except in cases where it is evidence for the violation of law, organizational regulations, or this Code. In these cases, the nature or contents of that information must be disclosed only to proper authorities. (See 1.9)

1.8 Honor confidentiality The principle of honesty extends to issues of confidentiality of information whenever one has made an explicit promise to honor confidentiality or, implicitly, when private information not directly related to the performance of one's duties becomes available. The ethical concern is to respect all obligations of confidentiality to employers, clients, and users unless discharged from such obligations by requirements of the law or other principles of this Code.

2. More Specific Professional Responsibilities.

As an ACM computing professional I will . . .

2.1 Strive to achieve the highest quality, effectiveness and dignity in both the process and products of professional work Excellence is perhaps the most important obligation of a professional. The computing professional must strive to achieve quality and to be cognizant of the serious negative consequences that may result from poor quality in a system.

2.2 Acquire and maintain professional competence Excellence depends on individuals who take responsibility for acquiring and maintaining professional competence. A professional must participate in setting standards for appropriate levels of competence, and strive to achieve those standards. Upgrading technical knowledge and competence can be achieved in several ways: doing independent study; attending seminars, conferences, or courses; and being involved in professional organizations.

2.3 Know and respect existing laws pertaining to professional work ACM members must obey existing local, state, province, national, and international laws unless there is a compelling ethical basis not to do so. Policies and procedures of the organizations in which one participates must also be obeyed. But compliance must be balanced with the recognition that sometimes existing laws and rules may be immoral or inappropriate and, therefore, must be challenged.

Violation of a law or regulation may be ethical when that law or rule has inadequate moral basis or when it conflicts with another law judged to be more important. If one decides to violate a law or rule because it is viewed as unethical, or for any other reason, one must fully accept responsibility for one's actions and for the consequences.

2.4 Accept and provide appropriate professional review Quality professional work, especially in the computing profession, depends on professional reviewing and critiquing. Whenever appropriate, individual members should seek and utilize peer review as well as provide critical review of the work of others.

2.5 Give comprehensive and thorough evaluations of computer systems and their impacts, including analysis of possible risks Computer professionals must strive to be perceptive, thorough, and objective when evaluating, recommending, and presenting system descriptions and alternatives. Computer professionals are in a position of special trust, and therefore have a special responsibility to provide objective, credible evaluations to employers, clients, users, and the public. When providing evaluations the professional must also identify any relevant conflicts of interest, as stated in imperative 1.3.

As noted in the discussion of principle 1.2 on avoiding harm, any signs of danger from systems must be reported to those who have opportunity and/or responsibility to resolve them. See the guidelines for imperative 1.2 for more details concerning harm, including the reporting of professional violations.

2.6 Honor contracts, agreements, and assigned responsibilities   Honoring one's commitments is a matter of integrity and honesty. For the computer professional this includes ensuring that system elements perform as intended. Also, when one contracts for work with another party, one has an obligation to keep that party properly informed about progress toward completing that work.

A computing professional has a responsibility to request a change in any assignment that he or she feels cannot be completed as defined. Only after serious consideration and with full disclosure of risks and concerns to the employer or client, should one accept the assignment. The major underlying principle here is the obligation to accept personal accountability for professional work. On some occasions other ethical principles may take greater priority.

A judgment that a specific assignment should not be performed may not be accepted. Having clearly identified one's concerns and reasons for that judgment, but failing to procure a change in that assignment, one may yet be obligated, by contract or by law, to proceed as directed. The computing professional's ethical judgment should be the final guide in deciding whether or not to proceed. Regardless of the decision, one must accept the responsibility for the consequences. However, performing assignments "against one's own judgment" does not relieve the professional of responsibility for any negative consequences.

2.7 Improve public understanding of computing and its consequences   Computing professionals have a responsibility to share technical knowledge with the public by encouraging understanding of computing, including the impacts of computer systems and their limitations. This imperative implies an obligation to counter any false views related to computing.

2.8 Access computing and communication resources only when authorized to do so Theft or destruction of tangible and electronic property is prohibited by imperative 1.2—"Avoid harm to others." Trespassing and unauthorized use of a computer or communication system is addressed by this imperative. Trespassing includes accessing communication networks and computer systems, or accounts and/or files associated with those systems, without explicit authorization to do so. Individuals and organizations have the right to restrict access to their systems so long as they do not violate the discrimination principle (see 1.4).

No one should enter or use another's computing system, software, or data files without permission. One must always have appropriate approval before using system resources, including .rm57 communication ports, file space, other system peripherals, and computer time.

3. Organizational Leadership Imperatives.

As an ACM member and an organizational leader, I will . . .

3.1 Articulate social responsibilities of members of an organizational unit and encourage full acceptance of those responsibilities Because organizations of all kinds have impacts on the public, they must accept responsibilities to society. Organizational procedures and attitudes oriented toward quality and the welfare of society will reduce harm to members of the public, thereby serving public interest and fulfilling social responsibility. Therefore, organizational leaders must encourage full participation in meeting social responsibilities as well as quality performance.

3.2 Manage personnel and resources to design and build information systems that enhance the quality of working life Organizational leaders are responsible for ensuring that computer systems enhance, not degrade, the quality of working life. When implementing a computer system, organizations must consider the personal and professional development, physical safety, and human dignity of all workers. Appropriate human-computer ergonomic standards should be considered in system design and in the workplace.

3.3 Acknowledge and support proper and authorized uses of an organization's computing and communications resources Because computer systems can become tools to harm as well as to benefit an organization, the leadership has the responsibility to clearly define appropriate and inappropriate uses of organizational computing resources. While the number and scope of such rules should be minimal, they should be fully enforced when established.

3.4 Ensure that users and those who will be affected by a system have their needs clearly articulated during the assessment and design of requirements. Later the system must be validated to meet requirements. Current system users, potential users and other persons whose lives may be affected by a system must have their needs assessed and incorporated in the statement of requirements. System validation should ensure compliance with those requirements.

3.5 Articulate and support policies that protect the dignity of users and others affected by a computing system Designing or implementing systems that deliberately or inadvertently demean individuals or groups is ethically unacceptable. Computer professionals who are in decision-making positions should verify that systems are designed and implemented to protect personal privacy and enhance personal dignity.

3.6 Create opportunities for members of the organization to learn the principles and limitations of computer systems This complements the imperative on public understanding (2.7). Educational opportunities are essential to facilitate optimal participation of all organizational members. Opportunities must be available to all members to help them improve their knowledge and skills in computing, including courses that familiarize them with the consequences and limitations of particular types of systems. In particular, professionals must be made aware of the dangers of building systems around oversimplified models, the improbability of anticipating and designing for every possible operating condition, and other issues related to the complexity of this profession.

4. Compliance with the Code.

As an ACM member I will . . .

4.1 Uphold and promote the principles of this Code The future of the computing profession depends on both technical and ethical excellence. Not only is it important for ACM computing professionals to adhere to the principles expressed in this Code, each member should encourage and support adherence by other members.

4.2 Treat violations of this code as inconsistent with membership in the ACM Adherence of professionals to a code of ethics is largely a voluntary matter. However, if a member does not follow this code by engaging in gross misconduct, membership in ACM may be terminated.

This Code and the supplemental Guidelines were developed by the Task Force for the Revision of the ACM Code of Ethics and Professional Conduct: Ronald E. Anderson, chair, Gerald Engel, Donald Gotterbarn, Grace C. Hertlein, Alex Hoffman, Bruce Jawer, Deborah G. Johnson, Doris K. Lidtke, Joyce Currie Little, Dianne Martin, Donn B. Parker, Judith A. Perrolle, and Richard S. Rosenberg. The Task Force was organized by ACM/SIGCAS and funding was provided by the ACM SIG Discretionary Fund.

Appendix B
Computing Curricula 1991

A Summary of the ACM/IEEE-CS Joint Curriculum Task Force Report

Introduction

ACM first published recommendations for undergraduate programs in computer science in 1968 in a report called "Curriculum '68." The report was produced as an activity of the ACM Education Board, which since then has been providing updates to recommendations for computer science programs as well as recommendations for other academic programs in computing.

In 1984 it was recognized by Education Board Chair Robert Aiken that there was a need for a fresh look at undergraduate computer science curricula. The discipline had matured considerably during the previous decade, but there had been enough changes in both subject matter and pedagogy to create a need to update the recommendations that had been published in 1979. One problem was that while many programs had sprung up in response to local demand, the implementors did not have a good feel for the discipline and the programs were too narrow, often lacking depth as well as breadth. It was decided that a good starting point for reconsideration of degree programs in computer science would be to establish a working definition of the discipline.

At about the same time, informal discussions took place between members of the Education Board and members of the IEEE Computer Society regarding the possibility of joint work in the curriculum area. Both societies had published curriculum recommendations independently, but it was recognized that there was a great deal of overlap in interests and considerable commonality between the recommendations of the two groups. Furthermore, joint recommendations from the two societies were likely to have a much greater impact than recommendations from only one of the two.

Reprinted from "Computing Curricula 1991," *Communications of the ACM*, vol. 34, no. 6, June 1991, pages 69–84.

Consequently, a task force of distinguished computer scientists was formed in 1985 by ACM, in cooperation with the Computer Society, to establish a definition of the discipline and to make recommendations for an introductory course sequence that would provide a foundation for curricula in the discipline. The task force, chaired by Peter Denning, published its report in December 1988. It was decided to complete the task of developing recommendations for the entire undergraduate curriculum by forming another task force jointly with the Computer Society; this was done in February, 1988.

The Joint ACM/IEEE-CS Curriculum Task Force published its report in March, 1991. A summary of the report is provided in the following article, and the entire report can be ordered through the ACM Order Department (Order Number 201910). The report represents the efforts of the task force to present current thinking on goals and objectives for computing curricula. Recommendations and comments were solicited from the computer science and engineering community through several sessions and extensive discussions at national conferences, through specific requests to experts in various areas, and through the establishment of a group of 120 reviewers.

This report is significant in that it not only represents an update of curriculum recommendations to meet changing needs, but it represents a unified set of recommendations from the two major societies of the discipline for computing curricula in a variety of academic contexts, including programs in liberal arts, sciences, and engineering. The report provides new perspectives on the importance and role of laboratories in the curriculum, and the importance and role of social, ethical, and professional issues in the curriculum. It also reinforces the importance of theoretical foundations (including mathematics), the development and application of communication skills, and the inclusion of significant design experiences, including working in teams, in a program.

The report is in some sense more difficult to use for assistance in curriculum development than were previous reports. It does not provide a single set of sample courses, or a sample curriculum. The report recognizes that there are many effective ways to organize a curriculum, even for a particular set of goals and objectives: it emphasizes the specification of a minimal set of subject matter that should be included in all programs along with guidelines for organizing the subject matter into courses and incorporating additional material and pedagogy to complete a curriculum. Several examples of curricula for different design objectives are provided. While the task force was sympathetic to the desirability of developing a concise set of curriculum guidelines, it was decided that there is still a need for diversity and well-intentioned experimentation in computing curricula; it is hoped the report will encourage this.

Reports of this type invariably create controversy, and there have indeed been objections to the report expressed by some of the reviewers as well as by others. Hopefully there will be lively debate about the recommendations of the report and about additional recommendations that were not included. Many efforts are under way to implement the report's recommendations, and the results of those efforts will be useful in evaluating the recommendations.

A great deal of thanks goes to the members of the task force who contributed so much time and effort toward the completion of the report and also to the reviewers who provided comments and suggestions. The task force was cochaired by Allen Tucker, representing ACM, and Bruce Barnes, representing the Computer Society of the IEEE. The other members are listed as coauthors of the summary report that follows this introduction. The ACM Education Board is pleased to present this report and to sincerely thank all members of the task force for a lot of hard work and an important contribution to undergraduate education in the discipline of computing.

A. Joe Turner, *Chair, ACM Education Board*

This article is a summary of the report *Computing Curricula 1991* [4], which is published as a separate document by the Association for Computing Machinery (ACM) and the Computer Society of the IEEE (IEEE-CS). The purpose of this article is to provide a sufficiently complete snapshot of that report's content so that readers will have a clear sense of its scope, methodology, and general recommendations. While a complete curriculum design document is not presented here, the full report does have that goal. Readers who are interested in using these recommendations as a basis for curriculum design will therefore need to obtain a copy of the full report itself.

In the spring of 1988, the ACM and the IEEE-CS formed the Joint Curriculum Task Force. The charter of the Task Force was to present recommendations for the design and implementation of undergraduate (baccalaureate) curricula in the discipline of computing. Throughout this article, the term *computing* is used to encompass the labels "computer science," "computer science and engineering," "computer engineering," "informatics," and other similar designations for academic programs. Programs in related areas, such as information systems, were not considered by the Task Force.

These recommendations supersede the separate curriculum recommendations [2, 3, 7] of the ACM and the IEEE-CS. Since those recommendations were published, significant changes have been made to the introductory courses [9, 10]. The evolution of accreditation guidelines [1, 5, 11], alternative model curricula [8], and the recent report *Computing as a Discipline* [6] all testify to the rapid and fundamental changes that have taken place. A strong motivation for making such a joint effort at this time thus comes from the fact that the discipline and its pedagogy have changed significantly in the last several years.

Another motivation for this work comes from the growing recognition that, despite strong and fundamental differences among institutions offering undergraduate programs in computing, these programs share a substantially large curriculum in common. Any curriculum recommendations that attempt to speak for the entire discipline must not only identify this shared subject matter, but also suggest ways in which it can serve as a basis for building undergraduate programs in different kinds of institutions. This work thus serves the interests of a wide constituency: in effect, the faculties of all undergraduate programs that offer concentration programs in computing, whether they occur in colleges of engineering, liberal art colleges, or other academic contexts.

Objectives and Overview

The report *Computing Curricula 1991* has the following primary objective: to provide curricular guidance for implementing undergraduate programs in the discipline of computing. The curriculum recommendations are based upon goals for programs and upon a definition of the discipline.

As a second means for attaining this objective, the report's guidelines are based on a comprehensive definition of the discipline, provided in the report *Computing as a Discipline* [6]. This definition was chosen because:

• it is up-to-date and widely available;
• it was developed by a task force of widely respected scholars in a cooperative effort between the ACM and the IEEE-CS; and
• it provides a detailed and comprehensive specification of the subject matter of the discipline.

When used as a basis for curriculum design, this definition provides a conceptual and organizational context from which a common collection of subject matter for all undergraduate programs can be drawn. In the present article, this shared collection of subject matter is called the *common requirements*. That definition also provides the conceptual context from which the advanced and supplementary subject matter can be drawn. This article is presented in the following major parts:

• A set of curricular and pedagogical considerations that govern the mapping of the common requirements and advanced/supplemental material into a complete undergraduate degree program. These considerations include the roles of laboratories, programming, mathematics and science, professionalism, a new notion called recurring concepts, and other educational experiences that combine to make up an entire undergraduate degree program in computing.

• A collection of subject matter modules called knowledge units that comprise the common requirements for all undergraduate programs in the field of computing.

• A collection of advanced and supplementary curriculum material that provides depth of study in several of the subject areas. The coverage of this material will vary in accordance with differing overall degree requirements of different types of institutions.

Because these curriculum recommendations are intentionally flexible, they do not prescribe a single set of courses for all undergraduate programs in computing. Instead, they provide guidelines that allow individual departments to design their own programs according to local objectives and constraints.

Relationship with Previous Curricular Recommendations

The curricular guidelines in the report *Computing Curricula 1991* are influenced by a number of prior curricular efforts that preceded it, including the ACM guidelines [3], the IEEE-CS guidelines [7], and other alternative guidelines (e.g., [8]). This section summarizes the major similarities and differences between the present report and its predecessors.

These prior reports influenced the report in the following major ways:

• The report *Computing as a Discipline* advocated the integration of laboratory work with classroom lectures, affirmed the importance of design in the curriculum, and proposed a breadth-first approach for the introductory courses in the curriculum.

• The 1983 IEEE-CS report contained in-depth descriptions of important topic areas for computer science and engineering, included laboratory material to support the lecture topics, and used modules and submodules as a basis for organizing subject matter and constructing courses.

• The 1978 ACM report provided detailed course descriptions for undergraduate programs in computer science, and established a prominent role for programming in the curriculum.

While the report *Computing Curricula 1991* also promotes broad discipline coverage for all programs, it offers alternative ways of achieving such breadth. Some alternatives include a breadth-first approach to the introductory courses while others include a more traditional approach. More generally, the present report has significantly broader overall goals than does the *Computing as a Discipline* report. The present report addresses the curricular needs of a broader range of institutions and programs in computing than does the 1983 IEEE-CS report or the 1978 ACM report. Its subject matter is also more current and it casts the role of programming and design in a different light. Overall, it attempts to integrate theory, abstraction, design, and the social context of computing into the curriculum in more compelling ways.

In summary, the report is influenced by its predecessors, yet it is quite different in scope and objectives from any one of them. It reflects the rapid and dramatic evolution of the discipline of computing and its pedagogy that has taken place during the last several years. It is holistic, attempting to reach a wider constituency than any of its predecessors. It is intentionally designed to encourage curriculum innovation and evolution, enabling educators to respond in a timely fashion to future changes in the discipline rather than to simply update earlier models.

Undergraduate Program Goals/Graduate Profiles

Undergraduate programs in computing share common attributes, values, and curricula, and so do their graduates. The following discussion reflects the Task Force's view or these shared attributes and values that serve as a basis for the curriculum recommendations that follow.

Undergraduate programs should prepare graduates to understand the field of computing, both as an academic discipline and as a profession within the context of a larger society. Thus, graduates should be aware of the history of computing, including those major developments and trends—economic, scientific, legal, political, and cultural—that have combined to shape the discipline during its relatively short life.

The first goal for undergraduate programs, therefore, is to provide a coherent and broad-based coverage of the discipline of computing. Graduates should develop a reasonable level of understanding in each of the subject areas and processes that define the discipline, as well as an appreciation for the interrelationships that exist among them.

A second goal for undergraduate programs in computing is to function effectively within the wider intellectual framework that exists within the institutions that house the programs. These institutions vary widely in their respective missions. Some of them emphasize breadth of study over depth, while others emphasize the opposite. Some are rigid in the overall balance between requirements and electives, while others are more flexible.

Third, different undergraduate programs place different levels of emphasis upon the objectives of preparing students for entry into the computing profession, preparing students for graduate study in the discipline of computing, and preparing students for the more general challenges of professional and personal life.

Fourth, undergraduate programs should provide an environment in which students are exposed to the ethical and societal issues that are associated with the computing field. This includes maintaining currency with recent technological and theoretical developments, upholding general professional standards, and developing an awareness of one's own strengths and limitations, as well as those of the discipline itself.

Fifth, undergraduate programs should prepare students to apply their knowledge to specific, constrained problems and produce solutions. This includes the ability to define a problem clearly; to determine its tractability; to study, specify, design, implement, test, modify, and document that problem's solution; and to work within a team environment throughout the entire problem-solving process.

Finally, undergraduate programs should provide sufficient exposure to the rich body of theory that underlies the field of computing, so that students appreciate the intellectual depth and abstract issues that will continue to challenge researchers in the future.

Underlying Principles for Curriculum Design

As noted earlier, the report *Computing as a Discipline* presented a comprehensive and contemporary definition of the discipline of computing. This definition provides a conceptual basis for defining a new teaching paradigm, as well as undergraduate curriculum design guidance for the discipline. The definition includes a specification of the subject matter by identifying nine constituent subject areas and three processes that characterize different working methodologies used in computing research and development. That specification is used in significant ways in this article.

From the subject matter of the nine areas of the discipline, this article identifies a body of fundamental material called the *common requirements,* to be included in every program. The curriculum of each program must also contain substantial emphasis on each of the three processes, which are called *theory, abstraction,* and *design.* In addition, this article identifies a body of subject matter representing the social and professional context of the discipline, also considered to be essential for every program. Finally, a set of concepts that recur throughout the discipline, and that represent important notions and principles that remain constant as the subject matter of the discipline changes, are an important component of every program.

The Nine Subject Areas

Nine subject areas are identified in *Computing as a Discipline* as comprising the subject matter of the discipline. Each of these areas has a significant theoretical base, significant abstractions, and significant design and implementation achievements. While these subject area definitions cover the entire discipline, they each contain certain fundamental subjects that should be required in all undergraduate programs in computing; this fundamental subject matter is identified later as the common requirements for all programs. On the other hand, certain parts of these subject areas are less central and are therefore not included in the common requirements. These topics are left for the advanced components of the undergraduate or graduate curriculum.

Thus, in some cases, major components of a subject area that appear in its title are not included in the common requirements. For example, the common requirements do not contain subject matter on symbolic computation. However, the subject area title "Numerical and Symbolic Computation" from *Computing as a Discipline* is retained, both in the interest of continuity and because additional subject matter will appear in the advanced components of computing curricula. For instance, symbolic computation appears among the advanced and supplemental topics that are described in an upcoming section, even though it does not appear among the common requirements.

The nine subject areas are:

- Algorithms and Data Structures
- Architecture
- Artificial Intelligence and Robotics
- Database and Information Retrieval
- Human-Computer Communication
- Numerical and Symbolic Computation
- Operating Systems
- Programming Languages
- Software Methodology and Engineering

More detailed discussion of these areas can be found in the report *Computing as a Discipline,* as well as the full report *Computing Curricula 1991* itself.

The Three Processes: Theory, Abstraction, and Design

Because computing is simultaneously a mathematical, scientific, and engineering discipline, different practitioners in each of the nine subject areas employ different working methodologies, or processes, during the course of their research, development, and applications work.

One such process, called *theory,* is akin to that found in mathematics, and is used in the development of coherent mathematical theories. An undergraduate's first encounter with theory in the discipline often occurs in an introductory mathematics course. Further theoretical material emerges in the study of algorithms (complexity theory), architecture (logic), and programming languages (formal grammars and automata). The present curriculum recommendations contain a significant amount of theory that should be mastered by undergraduates in all programs.

The second process, called *abstraction,* is rooted in the experimental sciences. Undergraduate programs in computing introduce students to the process of abstraction in a variety of ways, both in classes and in laboratories. For example, the basic von Neumann model of a computer is a fundamental abstraction whose properties can be analyzed and compared with other competing models. Students are introduced to this model early in their undergraduate coursework. Undergraduate laboratory experiments that emphasize abstraction stress analysis and inquiry into the limits of computation, the properties of new computational models, and the validity of unproven theoretical conjectures.

The third process, called *design,* is rooted in engineering and is used in the development of a system or device to solve a given problem. Undergraduates learn about design both by direct experience and by studying the designs of others. Many laboratory projects are design-oriented, giving students firsthand experience with developing a system or a component of a system to solve a particular problem. These laboratory projects emphasize the synthesis of practical solutions to problems and thus require students to evaluate alternatives, costs, and performance in the context of real-world constraints. Students develop the ability to make these evaluations by seeing and discussing example designs as well as receiving feedback on their own designs.

In all nine subject areas of computing, these three processes of theory, abstraction, and design appear prominently and indispensably. A thorough grounding in each process is thus fundamental to all undergraduate programs in the discipline.

Social and Professional Context

Undergraduates also need to understand the basic cultural, social, legal and ethical issues inherent in the discipline of computing. They should understand where the discipline has been, where it is, and where it is heading. They should also understand their individual roles in this process, as well as appreciate the philosophical questions, technical problems, and aesthetic values that play an important part in the development of the discipline.

Students also need to develop the ability to ask serious questions about the social impact of computing and to evaluate proposed answers to those questions. Future practitioners must be able to anticipate the impact of introducing a given product into a given environment. Will that product enhance or degrade the quality of life? What will the impact be upon individuals, groups, and institutions?

Finally, students need to be aware of the basic legal rights of software and hardware vendors and users, and they also need to appreciate the ethical values that are the basis for those rights. Future practitioners must understand the responsibility they will bear, and the possible consequences of failure. They must understand their own limitations as well as the limitations of their tools. All practitioners must make a long-term commitment to remaining current in their chosen specialties and in the discipline of computing as a whole.

To provide this level of awareness, undergraduate programs should devote explicit curricular time to the study of social and professional issues. The subject matter recommended for this study appears in the knowledge units under the heading *SP: Social, Ethical, and Professional Issues.*

Recurring Concepts

The discussion thus far has emphasized the division of computing into nine subject areas, three processes, and its social and professional context. However, certain fundamental concepts recur throughout the discipline and play an important role in the design of individual courses and whole curricula. *Computing as a Discipline* refers to some of these concepts as *affinity groups* or *basic concerns throughout the discipline.*[1] The Task Force refers to these fundamental concepts as *recurring concepts* in this article.

Recurring concepts are significant ideas, concerns, principles and processes that help to unify an academic discipline. An appreciation for the pervasiveness of these concepts and an ability to apply them in appropriate contexts is one indicator of a graduate's maturity as a computer scientist or engineer. Clearly, in designing a particular curriculum, these recurring concepts must be communicated in an effective manner; it is important to note that the appropriate use of the recurring concepts is an essential element in the implementation of curricula and courses based upon the specifications given in this article. Additionally, these concepts can be used as underlying themes that help tie together curricular materials into cohesive courses.

---

1. Page 9 of [6].

Each recurring concept listed in this article

- Occurs throughout the discipline,
- Has a variety of instantiations,
- Has a high degree of technological independence.

Thus, a recurring concept is any concept that pervades the discipline and is independent of any particular technology. A recurring concept is more fundamental than any of its instantiations. A recurring concept has established itself as fundamental and persistent over the history of computing and is likely to remain so for the foreseeable future.

In addition to the three characteristics given above, most recurring concepts

- Have instantiations at the levels of theory, abstraction and design,
- Have instantiations in each of the nine subject areas,
- Occur generally in mathematics, science and engineering.

These additional points make a strong assertion concerning the pervasiveness and persistence of most of the recurring concepts. Not only do they recur throughout the discipline, they do so across the nine subject areas and across the levels of theory, abstraction and design. Furthermore, most are instances of even more general concepts that pervade mathematics, science and engineering.

The following is a list of 12 recurring concepts that are identified as fundamental to computing. Each concept is followed by a brief description.

Binding: the processes of making an abstraction more concrete by associating additional properties with it. Examples include associating (assigning) a process with a processor, associating a type with a variable name, associating a library object program with a symbolic reference to a subprogram, instantiation in logic programming, associating a method with a message in an object-oriented language, creating concrete instances from abstract descriptions.

Complexity of large problems: the effects of the nonlinear increase in complexity as the size of a problem grows. This is an important factor in distinguishing and selecting methods that scale to different data sizes, problem spaces, and program sizes. In large programming projects, it is a factor in determining the organization of an implementation team.

Conceptual and formal models: various ways of formalizing, characterizing, visualizing and thinking about an idea or problem. Examples include formal models in logic, switching theory and the theory of computation, programming language paradigms based upon formal models, conceptual models such as abstract data types and semantic data models, and visual languages used in specifying and designing systems, such as data flow and entity-relationship diagrams.

Consistency and completeness: concrete realizations of the concepts of consistency and completeness in computing, including related concepts such as correctness, robustness, and reliability. Consistency includes the consistency of a set of axioms that serve as a formal specification, the consistency of theory to observed fact, and internal consistency of a language or interface design. Correctness can be viewed as the consistency of component or system behavior to stated specifications. Completeness includes the adequacy of a given set of axioms to capture all desired behaviors, the functional adequacy of software and hardware systems, and the ability of a system to behave well under error conditions and unanticipated situations.

Efficiency: measures of cost relative to resources such as space, time, money, and people. Examples include the theoretical assessment of the space and time complexity of an algorithm, the efficiency with which a certain desirable result (such as the completion of a project or the manufacture of a component) can be achieved, and the efficiency of a given implementation relative to alternative implementations.

Evolution: the fact of change and its implications. This involves the impact of change at all levels and the resiliency and adequacy of abstractions, techniques and systems in the face of change. Examples include the ability of formal models to represent aspects of systems that vary with time, and the ability of a design to withstand changing environmental demands and changing requirements, tools and facilities for configuration management.

Levels of abstraction: the nature and use of abstraction in computing; the use of abstraction in managing complexity, structuring systems, hiding details, and capturing recurring patterns; the ability to represent an entity or system by abstractions having different levels of detail and specificity. Examples include levels of hardware description, levels of specificity within an object hierarchy, the notion of generics in programming languages, and the levels of detail provided in a problem solution from specifications through code.

Ordering in space: the concepts of locality and proximity in the discipline of computing. In addition to physical location, as in networks or memory, this includes organizational location (e.g., of processors, processes, type definitions, and associated operations) and conceptual location (e.g., software scoping, coupling, and cohesion).

Ordering in time: the concept of time in the ordering of events. This includes time as a parameter in formal models (e.g., in temporal logic), time as a means of synchronizing processes that are spread out over space, time as an essential element in the execution of algorithms.

Reuse: the ability of a particular technique, concept or system component to be reused in a new context or situation. Examples include portability, the reuse of software libraries and hardware components, technologies that promote reuse of software components, and language abstractions that promote the development of reusable software modules.

Security: the ability of software and hardware systems to respond appropriately to and defend themselves against inappropriate and unanticipated requests; the ability of a computer installation to withstand catastrophic events (e.g., natural disasters and attempts at sabotage). Examples include type-checking and other concepts in programming languages that provide protection against misuse of data objects and functions, data encryption, granting and revoking of privileges by a database management system, features in user interfaces that minimize user errors, physical security measures at computer facilities, and security mechanisms at various levels in a system.

Trade-offs and consequences: the phenomenon of trade-offs in computing and the consequences of such trade-offs; and the technical, economic, cultural and other effects of selecting one design alternative over another. Trade-offs are a fundamental fact of life at all levels and in all subject areas. Examples include space-time trade-offs in the study of algorithms, trade-offs inherent in conflicting design objectives (e.g., ease of use versus completeness, flexibility versus simplicity, low cost versus high reliability and so forth), design trade-offs implied in attempts to optimize computing power in the face of a variety of constraints.

In constructing curricula from the overall specifications of the Task Force, curriculum designers must be aware of the fundamental role played by recurring concepts. That is, a recurring concept (or a set of recurring concepts) can help to unify the design of a course, a lecture, or a laboratory exercise. From the instructor's perspective (and also from the student's perspective), a course is rarely satisfying unless there is some "big idea" that seems to hold disparate elements together. We see the use of recurring concepts as one method for unifying the material this way.

At the level of the entire curriculum, the recurring concepts also play a unifying role. They can be used as threads that tie and bind different courses together. For example, in introducing the concept of *consistency* as applied to language design in a programming language course, the instructor might ask students to consider other contexts in which consistency played an important role, such as in a previous software design or computer organization course. By pointing out and discussing the recurring concepts as they arise, instructors can help portray computing as a coherent discipline rather than as a collection of unrelated topics.

From Principles to Curriculum

An undergraduate curriculum in computing should provide each graduate with a reasonable level of instruction in all of the subject areas identified above. This allows each graduate to achieve a *breadth* of understanding across the entire discipline rather than just in a few of its parts. Breadth is ensured in the present guidelines by way of the common requirements.

The undergraduate curriculum should also provide the reasonable *depth* of study in some of the nine subject areas of the common requirements. While the particular way in which subject area depth is achieved will vary among different types of programs, it is essential that depth of study be achieved in one way or another. Depth is ensured in the present guidelines by way of the *advanced/supplemental topics* (see following discussion).

Among the three processes—theory, abstraction, and design—it is fair to assume that some undergraduate programs emphasize more theory than design, while others emphasize more design than theory. However, the process of abstraction will normally be prominent in all undergraduate curricula. Theory, abstraction, and design are included throughout the common requirements, and are reinforced by the integration of laboratory work with subject matter in a principled and thorough way.

To support the development of maturity in the mathematical and scientific aspects of computing, an undergraduate curriculum should also include certain mathematics and science subject matter to complement the subject matter in the discipline itself. Similarly, to support the development of maturity in the scientific and engineering aspects of the discipline, the present guidelines recommend that students regularly engage in laboratory work and other educational experiences.

An overview of a complete undergraduate program in computing can be summarized as shown in Figure 1. This summary provides a general level of guidance for implementing undergraduate programs in the discipline. There, the need to recognize different institutional contexts and programmatic goals is accommodated by the box in that figure labeled *Other Degree Requirements.*

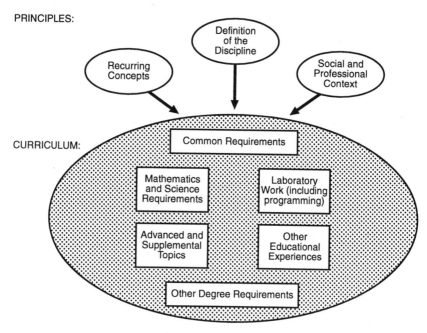

Figure 1
A Complete Curriculum and Its Underlying Principles

Assuring Breadth and Depth

To realize the breadth requirements, undergraduate programs should provide a broad selection of topics taken from all nine subject areas of computing. However, because different institutions will want to fulfill these common requirements in different ways, they are not presented as a single prescribed set of courses. Instead, the common requirements' topics are presented as a collection of *knowledge units*. These can be combined in various ways to form different sets of courses, or *implementations*, in different undergraduate settings. Further discussion of constructing courses out of knowledge units appears later, and many examples are given in the full report itself.

To realize the depth requirements, different institutions will offer additional requirements and electives in accordance with their overall educational missions, faculty size, and subject area expertise. The full report describes a number of advanced and supplemental topics that provide depth of study in the nine areas of the discipline of computing.

The Role of Programming

The term *programming* is understood to denote the entire collection of activities that surround the description, development, and effective implementation of algorithmic solutions to well-specified problems. While this definition is not to be construed to mean simply "coding in a particular programming language or for a particular machine architecture," it does necessarily include the mastery of highly stylized skills in a particular programming language or languages. Thus, fluency in a programming language is an essential attribute of the mastery of programming. On the other hand, programming is not to be construed so broadly as to subsume all of the activities involved in software methodology and engineering. The latter is a much broader notion and includes, for example, the development of specifications and the maintenance of software.

Programming occurs in all nine subject areas in the discipline of computing. It is part of the design process, it is used to implement the models that occur in the abstraction process, and sometimes it even occurs in the process of probing a theoretical result. Thus, the role of programming in the undergraduate curriculum is also multidimensional; students develop programs during the design of software, they exercise and modify programs during other laboratory experiments, and they read programs in the normal course of studying subject matter in textbooks and the published literature. In this latter sense, programming is an extension of the basic skills that students and professionals normally use in day-to-day communication.

Mastery of programming can be accomplished in several ways during an undergraduate's career. First, a substantial portion of the common requirements' laboratory work contains programming as an essential part. For example, the knowledge unit *SE1: Fundamental Problem Solving Concepts* requires laboratory work in which students design, implement, and exercise programs in a modern programming language. Second, undergraduate texts in the various subject areas teach and use conventional programming techniques throughout their presentations of subject matter. Lectures in courses throughout the curriculum also use well-established styles of programming to explain or clarify algorithmic concepts. Third, the computing literature is replete with programs and examples of programming methodology, and undergraduates become familiar with this literature during their studies. Instructors should take care to present examples of good programming style for students to study and emulate.

Thus, undergraduates should develop an early understanding of programming. They should continue to actively engage in the mastery and use of programming paradigms and languages throughout their coursework, homework, and laboratory exercises.

It should be noted here that the common requirements do not assume that students will have any experience with programming before taking their first course in the discipline. However, increasing numbers of students do gain such experience in secondary school. Many feel the amount of attention traditionally paid to the syntax of a programming language in the first course is excessive, and ought to be replaced with a more balanced introduction to the discipline.

For these reasons, *PR: Introduction to a Programming Language* is defined as a separate knowledge unit, but is not a *required* part of the common requirements. That is, most programs will be able to introduce a programming language in conjunction with other knowledge unit material, especially the one named SE1, during the scheduled laboratory periods that accompany the first course. For those programs that do require a more careful treatment of this topic, the optional knowledge unit *PR: Introduction to a Programming Language* can be added to the common requirements to fulfill this need.

The Role of Laboratories

The report *Computing as a Discipline* makes a clear statement about the purpose and structure of laboratory work in the undergraduate curriculum; this article expands upon that statement by identifying in more detail how these very important laboratory activities can be integrated into an undergraduate curriculum. An undergraduate curriculum in computing is ideally comprised of an integrated program of lectures and laboratory experiences. The learning process occurs as a result of interaction among students, instructors, and the subject matter.

Laboratories demonstrate the application of principles to the design, implementation, and testing of software and hardware systems. Laboratories also emphasize techniques that utilize contemporary tools and lead to good experimental methods, including the use of measuring instruments, diagnostic aids, software and hardware monitors, statistical analysis of results, and oral and written presentation of findings. The laboratories should augment the instruction that takes place in the lectures by having clearly stated objectives that complement the lectures.

The laboratory exercises included in the *Suggested Laboratories* part of each knowledge unit provide a diverse set of learning experiences. Some involve the execution of hardware, software, or simulators to observe some phenomenon, either by data collection or by visualization. Others are designed to increase student expertise in software methodology through the development of alternative design and implementation techniques. Still others are similar to science experiments because they involve hypothesis formation and testing. These types of laboratory experiences combine to increase student problem-solving ability, analytical skill, and professional judgment.

In the presentation of laboratories among the knowledge units, two distinct types of laboratory work are offered. These are called *open* laboratories and *closed* laboratories. An open laboratory is an unsupervised assignment that may involve the use of a computer, software, or hardware for its completion. Students can complete an open laboratory at their own convenience as it does not require direct supervision. Conventional programming assignments are often done in an open laboratory setting.

A closed laboratory is a scheduled, structured, and supervised assignment that involves the use of computing hardware, software, or instrumentation for its completion. Students complete a closed lab by attending a scheduled session, usually 2–3 hours long, at a specific facility. Supervision is provided by the instructor or a qualified assistant who is familiar with the details of the assignment. The specialized equipment, software, and supervision offered by closed laboratories makes them more desirable than open laboratories in certain situations. Closed laboratories are particularly important in situations where the assignment relies on instructor-student interaction or a team effort among students to complete the work. For example, the use of software tools that facilitate the production of large-scale software, CAD programs, or other packages of considerable complexity normally require the initial guidance and advice of an expert.

Whether the lab is open or closed, the facility should be staffed by a knowledgeable person during all scheduled laboratory hours. Staffing ensures immediate feedback and guidance during times when students are working independently on laboratory assignments.

The designation *open* or *closed,* along with the laboratories themselves, should be used as suggestions, or statements of preference by the Task Force, rather than prescriptions for all programs to follow. That is, some laboratories that are designated as closed may be done as open laboratories and vice versa. This choice may depend on how the particular lab experience and objectives fit into the curriculum as well as the available facilities in a particular institutional setting.

Whether open or closed, a laboratory assignment should always be carefully planned by the instructor. Descriptions that include clear statements of purpose, methodology, and results should be carefully prepared for the students. Laboratory assignments should be realistically designed, so that an average student can complete the work in the allotted time. It is particularly important to make sure that adequate facilities are available to support the goals of each laboratory assignment.

Completion of a laboratory assignment should be accompanied by a written or oral report by the student. Written reports should reflect a disciplined and mature writing style, in addition to the successful completion of the laboratory work itself. It is expected that there will be homework in addition to laboratory assignments, and this work should also be well-integrated with the subject matter of the lectures.

Other Educational Experiences

Beyond the subject matter of the curriculum, undergraduates in computing should have additional experiences that will help them develop the capacity for critical thinking, problem solving, research methods, and professional development. These experiences can be incorporated into the classroom lectures, laboratories, and extracurricular activities of the undergraduate program. These additional experiences generally fall into three categories:

1. working as part of a team
2. written and oral communication
3. familiarization with the profession

For further discussion of these requirements, readers are encouraged to consult the full report.

The Common Requirements

The common requirements form the basis for a curriculum in computing by providing a platform of knowledge that is considered essential for all students who concentrate in the discipline. These are not the only topics that should be covered, yet they contain the basic body of knowledge that should be part of every curriculum. The common requirements are expressed here as *knowledge units* rather than complete courses, to allow different programs to package the subject matter in different ways. Such variations will occur because different institutions and types of programs will have different pedagogical priorities, educational goals, and general constraints within which they implement the common requirements.

While every knowledge unit is considered to be essential, the depth and breadth of coverage for each topic therein will not be the same. For example, the knowledge unit *AL6: Sorting and Searching* recommends that various sorting and searching algorithms be covered in six lecture hours and associated laboratory work. However, this is only about two weeks' time. Thus, only a few of the multitude of sorting techniques can be covered in any appreciable depth—perhaps insertion sort, heap sort, and quicksort— while various other sorting techniques can be covered in a more surveylike fashion. Instructors will inevitably make tradeoffs between depth and breadth of coverage, given the constraints of the number of lectures in a knowledge unit, in the same way they do now with current textbooks. Furthermore, some knowledge units offer only a broad level of coverage of a topic (see, for instance, the knowledge units designated as PL1, OS1, or AI1). Additional depth in these subjects can be obtained only by exceeding the coverage recommended by the common requirements, either in the coverage of the knowledge unit, or in an advanced course.

Organizing the Common Requirements: The Knowledge Unit

In the following discussion, a *knowledge unit* is understood to designate a coherent collection of subject matter that is so fundamental within one of the nine subject areas of the discipline listed earlier, or within the area of social, ethical, and professional issues (SP), that it should occur in every undergraduate curriculum. While the subject matter of a knowledge unit is often related to other knowledge units in the common requirements by way of a prerequisite structure, it can nevertheless be introduced within any of several alternative course structures.

For easy cross-referencing among the knowledge units, Table 1 gives the two-letter tags used to identify each of the nine subject areas, the additional area of social and professional context (SP), and the optional introduction to a programming language (PR).

Table 1. The Subject Areas and Tags

Subject Area	Tag
Algorithms and Data Structures	AL
Architecture	AR
Artificial Intelligence and Robotics	AI
Database and Information Retrieval	DB
Human-Computer Communication	HU
Numerical and Symbolic Computation	NU
Operating Systems	OS
Programming Languages	PL
Introduction to a Programming Language (optional)	PR
Software Methodology and Engineering	SE
Social, Ethical, and Professional Issues	SP

The collected knowledge units are organized by subject area. Each knowledge unit within a subject area is identified by the tag for that subject area. For example, the knowledge units in the area of Algorithms and Data Structures are identified by the tags AL1, AL2, AL3, and so forth.

The following sample knowledge unit illustrates the presentation style for knowledge units:

AL6: Sorting and Searching

Comparison of various algorithms for sorting and searching, with focus on complexity and space versus time trade-offs.

Recurring Concepts: complexity of large problems, consistency and completeness, efficiency, trade-offs and consequences.

Lecture Topics: (six hours minimum)
1. $O(n^2)$ sorting algorithms (e.g., insertion and selection sort): space-time complexity: best, worst cases
2. I($n \log n$) sorting algorithms (e.g., quicksort, heapsort, mergesort); space-time complexity: best, worst cases
3. Other sorting algorithms (e.g., Shell sort, bucket sort, radix sort)
4. Comparisons of algorithms
5. Serial search, binary search and binary search tree; space-time complexity: best, worst cases
6. Hashing, collision resolution

Suggested Laboratories: (closed) Corroboration of theoretical complexity of selected sorting and searching algorithms by experimental methods, identifying differences among best, average, and worst case behaviors.

Connections:
  Related to: AL5, AL8
  Prerequisites: AL4
  Requisite for: AI2, OS7, PL9

Table 2 offers a complete list of the titles of the knowledge units that comprise the common requirements. While these titles suggest something about the knowledge units' contents, a detailed presentation of each one is given in the full report [4].

The Advanced and Supplemental Curriculum

A complete curriculum will include not only the common requirements, but also certain additional material. This advanced and supplemental

Table 2. Summary of the Common Requirements

AL:	**Algorithms and Data Structures (approximately 47 lecture hours)**

AL1: Basic Data Structures
AL2: Abstract Data Types
AL3: Recursive Algorithms
AL4: Complexity Analysis
AL5: Complexity Classes
AL6: Sorting and Searching
AL7: Computability and Undecidability
AL8: Problem-Solving Strategies
AL9: Parallel and Distributed Algorithms

AR: Architecture (approximately 59 lecture hours)

AR1: Digital Logic
AR2: Digital Systems
AR3: Machine-Level Representation of Data
AR4: Assembly-Level Machine Organization
AR5: Memory System Organization and Architecture
AR6: Interfacing and Communication
AR7: Alternative Architectures

AI: Artificial Intelligence and Robotics (approximately nine lecture hours)

AI1: History and Applications of Artificial Intelligence
AI2: Problems, State Spaces, and Search Strategies

DB: Database and Information Retrieval (approximately nine lecture hours)

DB1: Overview, Models, and Applications of Database Systems
DB2: The Relational Data Model

HU: Human-Computer Communication (approximately eight lecture hours)

HU1: User Interfaces
HU2: Computer Graphics

NU: Numerical and Symbolic Computation (approximately seven lecture hours)

NU1: Number Representation, Errors, and Portability
NU2: Iterative Approximation Methods

OS: Operating Systems (approximately 31 lecture hours)

OS1: History, Evolution, and Philosophy
OS2: Tasking and Processes
OS3: Process Coordination and Synchronization
OS4: Scheduling and Dispatch
OS5: Physical and Virtual Memory Organization
OS6: Device Management
OS7: File Systems and Naming
OS8: Security and Protection
OS9: Communications and Networking
OS10: Distributed and Real-time Systems

Table 2.—*Continued*

PL: **Programming Languages (approximately 46 lecture hours)**

PL1: History and Overview of Programming Languages
PL2: Virtual Machines
PL3: Representation of Data Types
PL4: Sequence Control
PL5: Data Control, Sharing, and Type Checking
PL6: Run-time Storage Management
PL7: Finite State Automata and Regular Expressions
PL8: Context-Free Grammars and Pushdown Automata
PL9: Language Translation Systems
PL10: Programming Language Semantics
PL11: Programming Paradigms
PL12: Distributed and Parallel Programming Constructs

SE: **Software Methodology and Engineering (approximately 44 lecture hours)**

SE1: Fundamental Problem-solving Concepts
SE2: The Software Development Process
SE3: Software Requirements and Specifications
SE4: Software Design and Implementation
SE5: Verification and Validation

SP: **Social, Ethical, and Professional Issues (approximately 11 lecture hours)**

SP1: Historical and Social Context of Computing
SP2: Responsibilities of the Computing Professional
SP3: Risks and Liabilities
SP4: Intellectual Property

---

material gives each individual student an opportunity to study the subject areas of the discipline in depth. The curriculum should provide depth of study in several of the nine subject areas beyond that provided by the common requirements. Students normally achieve that depth by completing several additional courses in this part of the curriculum. The number of such courses will vary in accordance with institutional norms. The sample implementations in the appendix of the full report illustrate these kinds of variations.

The topics in the following list should be considered as areas where courses may be developed to provide in-depth study in advanced undergraduate and graduate courses. Other topics beyond these are important as well, but will vary with the particular interests and expertise of the faculty in individual programs. However, these topics tend to be so significant to the discipline at this time that several of them ought to appear among the advanced courses offered by any undergraduate program.

Advanced Operating Systems
* Advanced Software Engineering
Analysis of Algorithms
* Artificial Intelligence
Combinatorial and Graph Algorithms
Computational Complexity
* Computer Networks
* Computer Graphics
Computer-Human Interface
* Computer Security
* Database and Information Retrieval
Digital Design Automation
Fault-Tolerant Computing
Information Theory
Modeling and Simulation
Numerical Computation
* Parallel and Distributed Computing
Performance Prediction and Analysis
Principles of Computer Architecture
Principles of Programming Languages
* Programming Language Translation
Real-Time Systems
Robotics and Machine Intelligence
Semantics and Verification
Societal Impact of Computing
* Symbolic Computation
* Theory of Computation
* VLSI System Design

Several of the topics in this list are marked with an asterisk (*). This denotes that a more complete description is given in the full report *Computing Curricula 1991*. Those descriptions are intended to give more concrete information that will assist in developing courses in these topic areas.

Mathematics and Science Requirements

An understanding of mathematics and science is important for students who concentrate their studies in computing.

Mathematical maturity, as commonly attained through logically rigorous mathematics courses, is essential to successful mastery of several fundamental topics in computing. thus, all computing students should take at least one-half year[2] of mathematics courses. These courses should cover at least the following subjects:

Discrete Mathematics: sets, functions, elementary propositional and predicate logic, Boolean algebra, elementary graph theory, matrices, proof techniques (including induction and contradiction), combinatorics, probability, and random numbers

Calculus: differential and integral calculus, including sequences and series and an introduction to differential equations

It should be noted that some of the discrete mathematics topics should be treated early in the curriculum, since they are needed for some of the basic knowledge units.

The half-year mathematics requirement should also include at least one of the following subjects:

Probability: discrete and continuous, including combinatorics and elementary statistics

Linear Algebra: elementary, including matrices, vectors, and linear transformations

Advanced Discrete Mathematics: a second course covering more advanced topics in discrete mathematics

Mathematical Logic: propositional and functional calculi, completeness, validity, proof, and decision problems

Many implementations will have additional mathematics requirements beyond this minimum set. For example, professionally oriented programs will normally require five or six mathematics courses. Students who wish to pursue graduate study in computing are often well-advised to take more mathematics.

Science is important in computing curricula for three reasons. First, as well-educated scientists and engineers, graduates of computing programs

---

2. We mean the equivalent of one-half academic year of full-time study. Typically, this would be four or five semester-long courses.

should be able to appreciate advances in science because they have an impact on society and on the field of computing. Second, exposure to science encourages students to develop an ability to apply the scientific method in problem solving. Third, many of the applications students will encounter after graduation are found in the sciences.

For these reasons, all computing curricula should include a component that incorporates material from the physical and life sciences. Ideally, courses in this component are those which are designed for science majors themselves.

Programs intended to prepare students for entry into the profession should require a minimum of one-half year of science. This normally includes a year-long course in a laboratory science (preferable physics) and additional work in the natural sciences.

Building a Curriculum

Overall Design Considerations

A curriculum for a particular program depends on many factors, such as the purpose of the program, the strengths of the faculty, the backgrounds and goals of the students, instructional support resources, infrastructure support and, where desired, accreditation criteria. Each curriculum will be site-specific, shaped by those responsible for the program who must consider factors such as institutional goals, opportunities and constraints, local resources, and the prior preparation of students.

Developing a curriculum involves a design process similar to others with which computer scientists and engineers are familiar. A successful implementation will grow from a well-conceived and well-articulated specification of the purpose of the curriculum, the context in which the curriculum will be delivered, and other external opportunities and constraints. As with systems, the success of the implementation of a curriculum depends on the care with which it is designed.

All curriculum designs, including but not limited to computing curricula, should be guided by certain principles. First, the purpose of a curriculum is to educate students. The curriculum design therefore should focus on providing a way for students to gain the desired knowledge, expertise and experience by the time they graduate. The outcome expected for students should drive the curriculum design.

Second, a curriculum is more than a set of isolated courses. There are unifying ideas and goals that span the whole curriculum. This article has included the discussion of recurring concepts as an indicator of those ideas that should be pervasive in a computing curriculum.

Third, there are many ways for students to learn beyond the standard lecture delivery format. Laboratories, in particular, present many opportunities for innovation. Faculty members should apply creative energy to developing alternative instructional methods.

Fourth, every environment has constraints that must be considered. A curriculum plan must not be overly optimistic nor overly restrictive, but should be realistic, both for students and for faculty. For example, a curriculum plan that requires a student to take four computing courses during the last term of the senior year invites a variety of problems.

Fifth, computing is more than just a collection of facts and algorithms. It is a dynamic, vital discipline that offers many challenges and interesting problems, exciting results, and imaginative applications. The curriculum should try to impart this sense of excitement to students; the material may be difficult, but it need not be dull.

Designing a computing curriculum adds another set of special concerns. The rapid change in the discipline itself demands that a computing curriculum be dynamic, not static. It must be built so that it can evolve along with the subject matter. All curricula should be evaluated periodically to see that they are meeting their goals; computing curricula should be evaluated for content to be sure they are up-to-date. Many departments also face changes that are caused by changing infrastructure, such as their organizations, enrollments, and funding levels.

Another concern in computing curricula comes from the fluid nature of theory in the discipline. As computing is based on artifacts in addition to physical laws, many of its "fundamentals" are subject to constant reinterpretation and reevaluation. Thus, the theory of computing evolves more rapidly than does theory in other sciences.

Computing, however, has one great advantage for curriculum designers. It provides frequent opportunities for accomplishing multiple goals through one instructional experience. Activities can be leveraged for several purposes. For example, a discussion of loops or recursion can simultaneously introduce the concept of searching by the use of appropriately chosen examples.

Designing Courses from Knowledge Units

The knowledge units enumerated earlier and described in the full report specify the scope of topics that all computing students should study. The lecture hours associated with each knowledge unit give an approximate indication of the depth to which these topics should be covered; we intend this to represent the minimum coverage that a typical program should ensure. The prerequisite structure suggests that some sequencing is required in the composition of courses out of knowledge units, but the size of the units allows many organizational options. Additionally, material in a knowledge unit may be split and covered at different times and in different courses, if deemed appropriate.

The knowledge units do not need to be covered completely in what would be identified as a set of "core courses," as long as they are all covered in one required course or another. Furthermore, some parts may be covered either in a standard class setting or in a laboratory setting. Thus, the knowledge units of the common requirements can be combined in various ways to form courses. In this activity, one may use the following guidelines:

• Knowledge units should be combined so that the composite subject matter forms a coherent body of topics for an undergraduate. In some cases, one or more of the recurring concepts can provide the "glue," while in other cases one of the nine subject areas can provide a basis for course organization.

• The combined set of courses that comprise an implementation should have a prerequisite structure that is consistent with the prerequisite structure that exists among their constituent knowledge units.

• The combined set of courses that comprise the implementation should cover all of the knowledge units that make up the common requirements. As specified here, these total about 271 lecture hours, which is equivalent to about seven one-semester courses.[3] This total does not include time spent in scheduled laboratory work, nor does it include the advanced and supplementary coursework that provides depth of study for all majors.

Implementations may, of course, exceed this minimum by assigning additional depth of coverage or topic selections beyond those that are suggested in the common requirements.

---

3. When the optional 12-hour knowledge unit *PR: Introduction to a Programming Language* is incorporated into the curriculum, the total number of lecture hours increases to about 283.

The following are two sample courses, an introductory course entitled "Problem-solving, Programs, and Computers" and another course entitled "Data Structures and Algorithms," that result from combining selected knowledge units under the foregoing guidance. The first of these courses takes knowledge units (KUs) from a number of different subject areas, and has "consistency and completeness" as a recurring concept. The second of these courses has all of its knowledge units taken from a single subject area.

Problem Solving, Programs, and Computers

Topic Summary: This course has three major themes: a rigorous introduction to the process of algorithmic problem solving, an introduction to the organization of the computers upon which the resulting programs run, and an overview of the social and ethical context in which the field of computing exists. Problem-solving rigor is guaranteed by a commitment to the precise specification of problems and a close association between the problem-solving process and that specification. For example, the identification of a loop is closely tied to the discovery of its invariant, which in turn is motivated by the problem specification itself.

Computer organization is introduced by way of a simple von Neumann machine model and assembler, upon which students can develop and exercise simple programs. Elements of the fetch execute cycle, runtime data representation, and machine language program structure are thereby revealed.

This course contains 40 lecture hours of KU topics, and is taught as a four-credit-hour course. A scheduled weekly laboratory is used to teach programming language syntax and machine organization, as well as to support student programming exercises.

Prerequisites: An introduction to logic, as would usually be found at the beginning of a discrete mathematics course (that can be taken concurrently)

Knowledge units: AL3 (3/3), AL6 (2/6), AR3 (2/3), AR4 (7/15), NU1 (1/3), NU2 (2/4), PL1 (2/2), PL3 (2/2), PL4 (1/4), SE1 (11/16), SE5 (4/8), SP1 (3/3)[4]

Data Structures and Analysis of Algorithms

Topic Summary: This course covers data structures and algorithms in some depth. Topics covered include data structures, a more formal treatment of recursion, an introduction to basic problem-solving strategies, and an introduction to complexity analysis, complexity classes, and the theory of computability and undecidability. Sorting and searching algorithms are presented in the light of the

---

4. In the list of knowledge units that accompany a particular course description, the notation p/q means that p lecture years are used out of a total of q hours that are available from the knowledge unit. Thus, when p = q the entire knowledge unit is used in that course.

presentation of problem-solving strategies and complexity issues. Finally, parallel and distributed algorithms are introduced briefly.

This course is taught in three lectures and a two-hour laboratory per week. It contains 33 lecture hours devoted to KU topics and their laboratories.

Prerequisites: "Computing II"

Knowledge units: AL1 (9/13), AL3 (2/3), AL4 (4/4), AL5 (4/4), AL6 (3/6), AL7 (3/6), AL8 (6/6), AL9 (2/3) The full report contains many more examples of course descriptions that are appropriate in a variety of institutional settings.

Integrating the Curriculum into a Course of Study

The computing curriculum will have to be developed to meet institutional requirements and should take advantage of institutional strengths. Ultimately, the computing curriculum will be integrated into a complete four-year course of study.

Some suggestions for steps to start building a curriculum are:

- Identify goals of the program, focusing on student outcomes.
- Identify strengths of the faculty.
- Identify constraints of the local situation.
- Establish a plan and schedule for design, implementation, evaluation, modification, and transition.
- Design and implement the curriculum components.

Related Concerns

The report *Computing Curricula 1991* addresses the relationship between its recommendations with each of the following topics. For further details, readers are encouraged to consult the report itself.

- Faculty and Staff
- Laboratory Resources
- Service Courses and Joint Degree Programs
- Library Support
- Relationship with Accreditation, Placement Tests, and Achievement Tests

Summary

This article summarizes a specification for implementing undergraduate programs in computing, as opposed to a single curriculum. This approach is required because of the need to serve a large and diverse constituency. The ultimate success of this approach will therefore depend strongly upon the creative energies of faculty members at the various institutions that support undergraduate programs in computing.

This specification acknowledges the primary importance of the following elements in undergraduate computing curricula: nine major subject areas; theory, abstraction and design; recurring concepts; the social and professional context; mathematics and science; language and communication; and integrated laboratory experience. Successful undergraduate programs that follow from this specification will pay close attention to each of these elements in their implementations.

The appendix of the full report *Computing Curricula 1991* contains the following 12 sample curricula that are provided as "proofs of concept" for this specification.

· Implementation A: A Program in Computer Engineering
· Implementation B: A Program in Computer Engineering (Breadth-First)
· Implementation C: A program in Computer Engineering (Minimal Number of Credit-Hours)
· Implementation D: A Program in Computer Science
· Implementation E: A Program in Computer Science (Breadth-First)
· Implementation F: A Program in Computer Science (Theoretical Emphasis)
· Implementation G: A Program in Computer Science (Software Engineering Emphasis)
· Implementation H: A Liberal Arts Program in Computer Science (Breadth-First)
· Implementation I: A Program in Computer Science and Engineering
· Implementation J: A Liberal Arts Program in Computer Science
· Implementation K: A Liberal Arts Program in Computer Science (Breadth-First)
· Implementation L: A Program in Computer Science (Theoretical Emphasis)

Acknowledgments

The Task Force wishes to thank the following persons who generously served as reviewers for this work in its various stages: Narenda Ahuja,

Donald J. Bagert, Jr., James C. Bezdek, Nathaniel Borenstein, Richard J. Botting, Donald Bouldin, Albert W. Briggs, Jr., J. Glenn Brooksheer, Wai-Kai Chen, Lucio Chiaraviglio, Neal S. Coulter, Steve Cunningham, Ruth Davis, Peter J. Denning, Scot Drysdale, Larry A. Dunning, Peter Durato, J. Philip East, Adel S. Elmaghraby, John W. Fendrich, Gary A. Ford, Edwin C. Foudriat, Donald L. Gaitros, David Garnick, Judith L. Gersting, Sakti P. Ghosh, Ratan K. Guha, Stephen T. Hedetnieme, Thomas T. Hewett, Jane Hill, Stuart Hirshfield, James A. Howard, John Impagliazzo, Greg Hones, Charles Kelemen, Willis King, Robert L. Kruse, Yedidyah Langsam, Eugene Lawler, Burt Leavenworth, R. Rainey Little, Dennis Martin, Fred J. Maryanski, Jeffrey J. McConnell, Daniel D. McCracken, Catherine W. McDonald, John McPherson, David G. Meyer, Victor Nelson, Chris Nevison, Robert Noonan, Jeffrey Parker, Margaret Peterson, Paul Purdom, Arthur Riehl, David C. Rine, Rockford J. Ross, Richard Salter, G. Michael Schneider, Greg Scragg, Mary Shaw, Daniel P. Siewiorek, David L. Soldan, Harry W. Tyrer, Annelieses von Mayrhauser, Z.G. Vranesic, Henry Walker, F. Garnett Walters, John Werth, Terry Winograd, Charles W. Winton, Charles T. Wright, Jr., and Grace Chi-Dak N. Yeung.

It should be noted that not all of the reviewers agree with all of the recommendations in this article or the full report. However, all comments were carefully considered by the Task Force throughout this report's development. Additional thanks are due to Kathleen A. Heaphy for proofreading and editorial comments on various drafts of the report itself.

References

1. Accreditation Board for Engineering and Technology, Inc. Criteria for Accrediting Programs in Engineering in the United States. Dec. 1988.

2. ACM Curriculum Committee on Computer Science. Curriculum 68: Recommendations for the undergraduate program in computer science. *Commun. ACM 11*, 3 (Mar. 1968), 151–197.

3. ACM Curriculum Committee on Computer Science. Curriculum 78: Recommendations for the undergraduate program in computer science. *Commun. ACM 22*, 3 (Mar. 1979), 147–166.

4. ACM/IEEE-CS Joint Curriculum Task Force. *Computing Curricula 1991.* Feb. 1991.

5. Computing Sciences Accreditation Board. Criteria for Accrediting Programs in Computer Science in the United States. Jan. 1987.

6. Denning, P.J., Comer, C.E., Gries, C., Mulder, M.C., Tucker, A.B., Turner, A.J., and Young, P.R. Computing as a discipline. *Commun. ACM 32*, 1 (Jan. 1989), 9–23.

7. Educational Activities Board. The 1983 Model Program in Computer Science and Engineering. No. 932. Dec. 1983.

8. Gibbs, N.E., and Tucker, A.B. Model curriculum for a liberal arts degree in computer science. *Commun. ACM 29*, 3 (Mar. 1986), 202–210.

9. Koffman, E.P., Miller, P.L., and Wardle, C.E. Recommended curriculum for CSI, 1984: A report of the ACM curriculum task force for CS1. *Commun. ACM 27*, 10 (Oct. 1984), 998–1001.

10. Koffman, E.P., Stemple, D., and Wardle, C.E. Recommended curriculum for CS2, 1984: A report of the ACM curriculum task force for CS2. *Commun. ACM 28*, 8 (Aug. 1985), 815–818.

11. Mulder, M.C., and Dalphin, J. Computer science program requirements and accreditation— an interim report of the ACM/IEEE computer society joint task force. *Commun. ACM 27*, 4 (Apr. 1984), 330–335.

Notes

Chapter 1

1. Sources for the ozone hole: *The New York Times,* Science section, 29 July 1986, page C1; the Blackhawk crashes: B. Cooper and D. Newkirk, *Risks to the Public in Computers and Related Systems,* on Internet, compiled by Peter G. Neumann, November 1987; Therac-25 and other radiation therapy cases: Jonathan Jacky, "Programmed for Disaster—Software Errors Imperil Lives," in *The Sciences,* September–October, 1989; Jonathan Jacky, "Risks in Medical Electronics," *Communications of the ACM,* vol. 33, no. 12, December 1990, page 138; "Patients Die After Radiation Mix-Up," *The Guardian,* London, 23 February 1991; John Arlidge, "Hospital Admits Error in Treating Cancer Patients," *The Independent,* London, 7 February 1992; Patriot missile: *New York Times,* 21 May 1991, and *Patriot Missile Defense: Software Problem Led to System Failure at Dhahran, Saudi Arabia,* U.S. General Accounting Office, February 1992; Hubble trouble: *Software Engineering Notes,* vol. 17, no. 1, January 1992, page 3.

2. AT&T phone outages, January 1990 and September 1991: *Software Engineering Notes,* vol. 15, no. 2, April 1990, and vol. 16, no. 4, October 1991, pages 6–7; *Time,* 30 September 1991; *Fortune,* 13 January 1992; A320 crashes: "Airbus Safety Claim 'Cannot Be Proved,'" *New Scientist,* 7 September 1991, page 16, and successive reports in *Software Engineering Notes,* esp, vol. 13, 14 and 15; Osprey crashes: *Flight International,* 18–24 September 1991; *New Scientist,* 15 August 1992; YF-23 and other fly-by-wire glitches: *Software Engineering Notes,* vol. 16, no. 3, July 1991, pages 21–22; Lauda crash: various reports in *Software Engineering Notes,* vol. 16 and 17.

3. "The 'Dirty Power' Clogging Industry's Pipeline," *Business Week,* 8 April 1991; Naruko Taknashi et al., "The Achilles Heel of the Information Society: Socioeconomic Impacts of the Telecommunications Cable Fire in the Setagaya Telephone Office, Tokyo," *Technological Forecasting and Social Change,* vol. 34, no. 1, 1988, pages 27–52; Beavers and dead cows: AP report in *Software Engineering Notes,* vol. 17, no. 1, January 1992; Foxes: *The Riverine Grazier,* Hay, New South Wales, Australia, 10 April 1991; Trawlers: *The Australian,* 16 April 1991; New Jersey and others: *Software Engineering Notes,* vol. 16, no. 2, April 1991, page 4, and vol. 16, no. 3, July 1991, pages 16–17.

4. "Saboteur Tries to Blank Out Oz," *The Australian,* 23 November 1987, page 1; "Laid-Off Worker Sabotages Encyclopaedia," *San Jose Mercury News,* 5 September 1986.

5. "Thieves Destroy Data on Chernobyl Victims," *New Scientist,* 22 September 1990; "Exxon Man Destroys Oil Spill Documents," UPI report in *The Australian,* 4 July 1989; "'Losing' a Warehouse," *Software Engineering Notes,* vol. 16, no. 3, July 1991, page 7.

6. "Inhabitant of Amsterdam Lies Dead in Apartment for Half a Year," *Software Engineering Notes,* vol. 16, no. 2, April 1991, page 11; "Defence of the Data," *New Scientist,* 19 January 1991, and "Theft of Computer Puts Allies' Plan at Risk," report from *The Times* (London) in *The Australian,* 14 March 1991.

7. "Poindexter Deleted 5,000 Computer Notes," Reuters and AP reports in *The Weekend Australian,* 17–18 March 1990; "Terminally Dumb Substitutions," *Software Engineering Notes,* vol. 15, no. 5, October 1990, page 4.

8. James H. Paul and Gregory C. Simon, *Bugs in the Program: Problems in Federal Government Computer Software Development and Regulation* (Subcommittee on Investigations and Oversight of the House Committee on Science, Space and Technology, U.S. Government Printing Office, Washington, DC, September 1989); Shawn McCarthy, "Dye Fears Computer Sabotage," *Toronto Star,* 31 October 1990; *Computers at Risk: Safe Computing in the Information Age* (National Academy Press, Washington, DC, 1991).

9. Peter J. Denning (ed.), *Computers Under Attack: Intruders, Worms and Viruses* (ACM Press/Addison-Wesley, Reading, MA, 1990), page iii; Lance J. Hoffman (ed.), *Rogue Programs: Viruses, Worms and Trojan Horses* (Van Nostrand Reinhold, New York, 1990), page 1.

10. Reports in *Business Week,* 7 November 1988, 3 April 1989, 15 June 1992, and 27 July 1992; *The Australian,* 4 August 1992.

11. Peter G. Neumann, "What's in a Name?" *Communications of the ACM,* vol. 35, no. 1, January 1992, page 186; *Software Engineering Notes,* vol. 14, no. 5, July 1989, page 11; vol. 16, no. 3, July 1991, pages 3–4; and vol. 17, no. 1, January 1992, pages 12–13; *Business Week,* 18 June 1990, 18 May 1992, and 8 June 1992; Marc Rotenberg, "Protecting Privacy," *Communications of the ACM,* vol. 35, no. 4, page 164; *The New York Times,* 4 May 1990, page A12; *The Los Angeles Times,* 8 January 1991; *Computing Australia,* 20 August 1990; Langdon Winner, "A Victory for Computer Populism," *Technology Review,* May–June 1991, page 66.

12. "Expert Systems Fail to Flourish," *The Australian,* 22 May 1990; Harvey P. Newquist III, "Experts at Retail," *Datamation,* 1 April 1990, pages 53–56; Dianne Berry and Anna Hart (eds.), *Expert Systems: Human Issues,* (MIT Press, Cambridge, MA, 1990); Roger Penrose, *The Emperor's New Mind* (Oxford University Press, New York, 1989).

13. Reports in *Business Week,* 19 August 1991, 15 June 1992, 13 July 1992; *Fortune,* 4 November 1991, 24 February 1992, 24 August 1992; Barbara Goldoftas, "Hands That Hurt: Repetitive Motion Injuries on the Job," *Technology Review,* January 1991, pages 43–50.

14. Deborah C. Johnson, *Computer Ethics* (Prentice-Hall, Englewood Cliffs, NJ, 1985) page 3; John Ladd, "Computers and Moral Responsibility: A Framework for an Ethical Analysis," in Carol C. Gould (ed.), *The Information Web: Ethical and Social Implications of Computer Networking* (Westview Press, Boulder, CO, 1989), pages 218–220.

15. Peter G. Neumann, "Computers, Ethics and Values," *Communications of the ACM,* vol. 34, no. 7, July 1991, page 106; Leslie S. Chalmers, "A Question of Ethics," *Journal of Accounting and EDP,* vol. 5, no. 2, Summer 1989, pages 50–53.

16. See Deborah C. Johnson, op. cit., 1985, chapter 1; and M. David Ermann, Mary B. Williams, and Claudio Gutierrez (eds.), *Computers, Ethics and Society* (Oxford University Press, New York, 1990), part 1.

17. Deborah C. Johnson, op. cit., 1985, chapter 2; Deborah C. Johnson and John W. Snapper (eds.), *Ethical Issues in the Use of Computers* (Wadsworth, Belmont, CA, 1985) part 1; Donn B. Parker, Susan Swope, and Bruce N. Baker (eds.), *Ethical Conflicts in Information and Computer Science, Technology, and Business* (QED, Wellesley, MA, 1990), parts 2, 4, 5, and 6.

18. Donn B. Parker et al., op. cit., 1990, page 5; Charles Dunlop and Rob Kling (eds.), *Computerization and Controversy: Value Conflicts and Social Choices* (Academic Press, San Diego, CA, 1991), pages 656–657; D. Dianne Martin and David H. Martin, "Professional Codes of Conduct and Computer Ethics Education," *Social Science Computer Review,* vol. 8, no. 1, Spring 1990, pages 96–108.

19. John Ladd, "The Quest for a Code of Professional Ethics: An Intellectual and Moral Confusion," in Deborah C. Johnson and John W. Snapper (eds.), op. cit., 1985, page 813.

20. Peter G. Neumann, "Certifying Professionals," *Communications of the ACM,* vol. 34, no. 2, February 1991, page 130.

21. "Computing Curricula 1991: A Summary of the ACM/IEEE-CS Joint Curriculum Task Force Report," *Communications of the ACM,* vol. 34, no. 6, June 1991, pages 69–80.

22. Donald Gotterbarn, "Computer Ethics: Responsibility Regained," *Phi Kappa Phi Journal,* Summer 1991, page 31.

23. Peter G. Neumann, "Computers, Ethics, and Values," *Communications of the ACM,* vol. 34, no. 7, page 106.

Chapter 2

1. From reports in *Software Engineering Notes,* vol. 13, no. 2, April 1988, page 5; *The Australian,* 24 May 1988.

2. Jay S. Albanese, "Tomorrow's Thieves," *The Futurist,* September–October, 1988, page 25; Hugo Cornwall, *Datatheft: Computer Fraud, Industrial Espionage and Information Crime* (Heinemann, London, 1987), page xi.

3. "Cybercrime Casebook Grows," *The Times* report in *The Australian,* 7 April 1992; "Counting the Cost of Computer Chaos," *New Scientist,* 8 February 1992; PA report in *The Australian,* 9 April 1991; August Bequai, *Technocrimes: The Computerization of Crime and Terrorism* (Lexington Books, Lexington, MA, 1987). See also Patricia Franklin, *Profits of Deceit: Dispatches from the Front Lines of Fraud* (Heinemann, London, 1991) and Bryan Clough and Paul Mungo, *Approaching Zero: Data Crime and the Computer Underworld* (Faber & Faber, London, 1992).

4. "Feds Crack Down on Criminals," *Computing Australia,* 17 July 1989; *The Guardian,* 29 August 1990; *Computing* (UK), 30 January 1992.

5. Albanese, op. cit.; Tom Forester, *High-Tech Society* (Basil Blackwell, Oxford, UK, and MIT Press, Cambridge, MA, 1987), pages 219–222 and 261–268; *The Los Angeles Times,* 11 February 1989; *Computer Talk* (UK), 4 May 1992; *The Weekly Telegraph,* 27 August–2 September 1992.

6. Reports in *Business Week,* 11 February 1991 and 13 July 1992; *New Scientist,* 8 June 1991; *The New York Times,* 28 August 1991; and *The Australian,* 20 April 1992.

7. *The Los Angeles Times,* 18 October 1989; *The Columbus Dispatch,* 20 February 1992; *Computer Talk,* 5 November 1990 and 29 July 1991.

8. *The New York Times* News Service, 27 March 1987, cited in *Software Engineering Notes,* vol. 12, no. 2, April 1987, pages 8–9; *New York Newsday,* 7 March 1991.

9. *The New York Times,* 25 April 1991; *Business Week,* 1 July 1991.

10. UPI report in *The Straits Times* (Singapore), 1 July 1991.

11. *The New York Times,* 8 October 1990; *The San Francisco Chronicle,* 18 December 1991.

12. *Software Engineering Notes,* vol. 14, no. 1, January 1989, page 16; vol. 14, no. 2, April 1989, page 16; vol. 16, no. 2, April 1991, page 16.

13. *The San Francisco Chronicle,* 5 November 1991; *The Sacramento Bee,* 4 October 1991.

14. R. Doswell and G. L. Simmons, *Fraud and Abuse of IT Systems* (National Computing Centre, Manchester, UK, 1986), pages 32–35; Hugo Cornwall, "Criminal Myths," *Computer Talk,* 10 February 1992, page 11.

15. *The Australian,* 1 September 1987.

16. *The Los Angeles Times,* 18 April 1989; *Computing Australia,* 22 May 1989.

17. Rob Kling, "When Organisations Are Perpetrators: Assumptions about Computer Abuse and Computer Crime," in Charles Dunlop and Rob Kling (eds.), *Computerization and Controversy: Value Conflicts and Social Choices* (Academic Press, San Diego, CA, 1991), pages 676–692.

18. *The Financial Times,* 22 October 1984.

19. *PC Week,* vol. 4, no. 21, 26 May 1987; *Business Week,* 1 August 1988 and 3 July 1989; Jeffrey A. Hoffer and Detmar W. Straub, "The 9 to 5 Underground: Are You Policing Computer Crimes?" *Sloan Management Review,* Summer 1989, pages 35–43.

20. *The Australian,* 5 January 1988 and 26 April 1988; *The Independent* (London) 30 October 1986; *Computer Talk,* 8 July 1991.

21. *Computer Talk,* 25 February 1991; *New Scientist,* 8 February 1992.

22. Jeffrey A. Hoffer and Detmar W. Straub, op. cit.; Detmar W. Straub and William D. Nance, "Discovering and Disciplining Computer Abuse in Organisations: A Field Study," *MIS Quarterly,* vol. 14, no. 1, March 1990, pages 44–55.

23. Hugo Cornwall, op. cit., page 46.

24. *Business Week,* 1 August 1988, page 53; Detmar W. Straub and William D. Nance, op. cit., page 51.

25. *The Financial Times,* 22 October 1984; Hugo Cornwall, op. cit., page xiii.

26. *The Financial Times,* 3 January 1986; *The Australian,* 1 September 1987.

27. *The Australian,* 11 July 1988; *Information Week,* 11 July 1988, cited in *Software Engineering Notes,* vol. 13, no. 3, July 1988, page 10.

28. *The Financial Times,* 2 September 1986; *The Australian,* 15 September 1987; *Software Engineering Notes,* vol. 13, no. 3, July 1988, page 10; *Computer Talk,* 10 July 1989.

29. *Computer News* (UK), 15 January 1987.

30. *The Wall Street Journal,* 18 May 1987; *Computing Australia,* 10 August 1987.

31. *Computer Weekly* (UK), 13 December 1990; *The Sunday Times* report in *The Australian,* 26 May 1992; *Computer Talk,* 4 May 1992; *Weekly Telegraph,* London, 27 August–2 September 1992.

32. *Los Angeles Times,* 11 February 1989; *Software Engineering Notes,* vol. 17. no. 2, April 1992, page 13; *Computer Talk,* 17 June 1991.

33. *The Chicago Tribune,* 15 August 1986; "Are ATMs Easy Targets for Crooks?" *Business Week,* 6 March 1989.

34. *Digital Review,* 6 April 1987, page 75; AFP report in *The Australian,* 2 November 1992.

35. *Evening Outlook* (Santa Monica, CA), 4 February 1988; *The Boston Globe,* 17 August 1989; *Software Engineering Notes,* vol. 17, no. 2, April 1992.

36. *Computer Talk,* 11 March 1991; *The Australian,* 13 August, 13 October, and 28 October 1992.

37. *Business Week,* 11 February 1991 and 13 July 1992; *The New York Times,* 28 August 1991; *Software Engineering Notes,* vol. 16, no. 3, July 1991, page 14 and vol. 17, no. 2, April 1992, page 15.

38. Leslie D. Ball, "Computer Crime," in Tom Forester (ed.), *The Information Technology Revolution* (Basil Blackwell, Oxford, UK, and MIT Press, Cambridge, MA, 1985), page 534, reprinted from *Technology Review,* April 1982; *Software Engineering Notes,* vol. 13, no. 2, April 1988.

39. Ball, op. cit., pages 534–535.

40. Cornwall, op. cit., page 102.

41. *The Independent,* 14 October 1990; *Computer Talk,* 9 December 1991; *Software Engineering Notes,* vol. 15, no. 3, July 1990, page 10.

42. *Software Engineering Notes,* vol. 15, no. 1, January 1990, page 16; *The Los Angeles Times,* 5 November 1991.

43. *Software Engineering Notes,* vol. 11, no. 2, April 1986, page 15.

44. Keith Hearnden, "Computer Criminals Are Human, Too," in Tom Forester (ed.), *Computers in the Human Context* (Basil Blackwell, Oxford, UK, and MIT Press, Cambridge, MA, 1989), pages 415–426.

45. Hearnden, op. cit., page 420; Ball, op. cit., page 536; Cornwall, op. cit., page 135; and AAP report in *The Australian,* 14 March 1989.

46. *Software Engineering Notes,* vol. 14, no. 5, July 1989, page 12; *The Courier-Mail* (Brisbane), 12 September 1991.

47. *Computing Australia,* 23 July 1990.

48. J. Buck BloomBecker, "Introduction to Computer Crime," in J. H. Finch and E. G. Dougall (eds.), *Computer Security: A Global Challenge* (Elsevier, North-Holland, 1984); J. Buck BloomBecker, *Spectacular Computer Crimes* (Business One Irwin, Homewood, IL, 1990).

49. Other useful taxonomies of computer crime have been provided by Donn B. Parker, *Fighting Computer Crime* (Scribner's, New York, 1983) and Detmar W.

Straub and Cathy Spatz Widom, "Deviancy by Bits and Bytes: Computer Abusers and Control Measures" in Finch and Dougall, op. cit.

50. Hearnden, op. cit., pages 420–421.

51. Katherine Hafner et al., "Is Your Computer Secure?" *Business Week,* 1 August 1988; *The Washington Post,* 18 September 1988; *The Chicago Tribune,* 17 September 1987; *Software Engineering Notes,* vol. 16, no. 4, October 1991, page 22.

52. System Security Study Committee of the National Research Council, *Computers at Risk: Safe Computing in the Information Age* (National Academy Press, Washington, DC, 1991); UPI report in *The Australian,* 27 February 1990; *Computer Talk,* 8 July 1991; Peter G. Neumann, "Insecurity About Security?" *Communications of the ACM,* vol. 33, no. 8, August 1990, page 170. See also Maurice V. Wilkes, "Revisiting Computer Security in the Business World," *Communications of the ACM,* vol. 34, no. 8, August 1991, pages 19–21.

53. *Computer Talk,* 10 February 1992.

54. Michael Cross, "How Fred Lets the Fraudsters In," *The Independent* (London), 30 October 1986.

55. Kenneth Rosenblatt, "Deterring Computer Crime," *Technology Review,* vol. 93, no. 2, February–March 1990, pages 35–40.

56. Richard Larson, "The New Crime Stoppers," *Technology Review,* vol. 92, no. 8, pages 27–31; *Computing Australia,* 14 May 1990; *The Australian,* 14–15 March 1987; *The Financial Times* (London), 24 July 1986; *Computing Australia,* 15 June 1987; *New Scientist,* 20 November 1986.

57. *Evening Standard* (London), 7 February 1992; *Software Engineering Notes,* vol. 17, no. 2, April 1992, page 9; *The Guardian* (London), 6 December 1991. See also Clive Davidson, "What Your Database Hides Away," *New Scientist,* 9 January 1993.

Chapter 3

1. *Palo Alto Times Tribune,* 7 February 1988, cited in *Software Engineering Notes,* vol. 13, no. 2, April 1988; Katherine M. Hafner et al., "Is Your Computer Secure?" *Business Week,* 1 August 1988, page 53.

2. *Fortune,* 22 April 1991, pages 77–80; *Time,* 10 June 1991, pages 36–38.

3. *Business Week,* 18 May 1992; *The Australian,* 7 November 1989.

4. Katherine M. Hafner et al., op. cit., page 54.

5. Hugo Cornwall, *Datatheft: Computer Fraud, Industrial Espionage and Information Crime* (Heinemann, London, 1987), pages 127–128.

6. Wire service reports in *The Australian,* 9 April 1991, 14 May 1991, 16 June 1992, and 13 October 1992.

7. *Computer Talk* (UK), 19 August 1991 and 9 December 1991; *New Scientist,* 14 December 1991.

8. Mary Jo Foley, "A Small Software Firm Takes on Uncle Sam—and Wins," *Datamation,* 15 April 1988; AP and UPI reports in *The Australian,* 15 August 1991 and 18 August 1992.

9. AP and UPI reports in *The Australian,* 23 July 1991; *New Scientist,* 27 July 1991; *The Australian,* 11 September 1990, 14 May 1991, and 29 October 1991.

10. Reuter report in *The Australian*, 31 July 1990; *Technology Review*, vol. 95, no. 2, February–March 1992, pages 15–16; *South China Morning Post* report in *The Australian*, 31 December 1991; *Business Week*, 22 April 1991, 3 February 1992, and 18 May 1992; *The Australian*, 18 June 1991, 25 August 1992, and 17 October 1992.

11. Pamela Samuelson, "Digital Media and the Law," *Communications of the ACM*, vol. 34, no. 10, October 1991, pages 23–28.

12. Anne W. Branscomb, "Who Owns Creativity? Property Rights in the Information Age" in Tom Forester (ed.), *Computers in the Human Context* (Basil Blackwell, Oxford, UK, and MIT Press, Cambridge, MA, 1989), reprinted from *Technology Review*, May–June 1988.

13. *Time*, 10 June 1991, pages 36–38.

14. *Fortune*, 22 April 1991, page 80; *Computing Australia*, 19 March 1990.

15. *Business Week*, 31 August 1987 and 22 May 1989; *The Australian*, 21 April 1987.

16. *The Australian*, 3 July 1990, 10 July 1990, and 11 August 1992; *Business Week*, 16 July 1990.

17. *The Australian*, 12 March 1991, 18 February 1991, and 21 April 1992; *Business Week*, 27 April 1992.

18. *The Australian*, 19 December 1989, 2 January 1990, and 27 March 1990.

19. *The Australian*, 29 November 1988.

20. Tom Forester, *Silicon Samurai: How Japan Conquered the World's IT Industry* (Blackwell, Oxford, UK, and Cambridge, MA, 1993) chapters 1 and 8; *The Australian*, 20 August 1991, 16 June 1992, and 23 June 1992; *Business Week*, 19 August 1991.

21. *Business Week*, 20 July 1992.

22. Anne W. Branscomb, op. cit., page 412; *The Australian*, 25 April 1989.

23. *Business Week*, 13 May 1991; *The Economist*, 22 August 1992.

24. Brian Kahin, "The Software Patent Crisis," *Technology Review*, vol. 93, no. 3, April 1990, pages 53–58.

25. *The Australian*, 10 April 1990, 17 September 1990, 15 October 1991, 13 February 1992, and 18 February 1992.

26. Reports from *The Economist* in *The Australian*, 13 March 1990 and 25 September 1990; *Business Week*, 7 May 1990; *New Scientist*, 22 June 1991.

27. Anne W. Branscomb, op. cit., page 414; *The Economist*, 22 August 1992; *Business Week*, 13 May 1991.

28. Dan Charles, "The Rights and Wrongs of Software," *New Scientist*, 29 September 1990, pages 34–38.

29. Deborah G. Johnson and John W. Snapper, *Ethical Issues in the Use of Computers* (Wadsworth, Belmont, CA, 1985), page 298; Paul Marett, "Legal Issues in Electronic Publishing," *Oxford Surveys in Information Technology*, vol. 4, 1987, pages 1–24.

30. Anne W. Branscomb, op. cit.; Paul Marett, op. cit.; Stuart R. Hemphill, "Copyrighting Technology: Are We Asking the Right Questions?" *High Technology Business*, August 1988.

31. Pamela Samuelson, "Why the Look and Feel of Software User Interfaces Should Not Be Protected by Copyright Law," *Communications of the ACM*, vol. 32, no. 5, May 1989, pages 563–572.

32. Richard M. Stallman, "Why Software Should be Free," page 7—freely copied off Internet, 1989; Dan Charles, op. cit., page 38; Simson L. Garfinkel, "Programs to the People," *Technology Review*, vol. 94, no. 2, February–March 1991, pages 53–60.

33. Anne W. Branscomb, op. cit., page 408.

34. *Business Week*, 19 May 1986; *The Economist* report in *The Australian*, 25 August 1992.

35. UPI report in *The Australian*, 10 November 1992.

36. Peter Gwynne, "Stalking Asian Software Pirates," *Technology Review*, vol. 95, no. 2, February–March, 1992, pages 15–16; *Business Week*, 18 May 1992; *The Australian*, 2 April 1991 and 28 April 1992.

37. Peter Gwynne, op. cit., page 15.

38. *The Australian*, 21 November 1989, 20 August 1991, and 24 March 1992; *Business Week*, 4 December 1989; *Rapport Asia* (Singapore), June 1991, page 5.

39. *Datamation*, 1 August 1989, pages 41–42; UPI report in *The Australian*, 28 May 1991.

40. Peter Gwynne, op. cit., page 15; Tom Forester, op. cit., chapter 8.

Chapter 4

1. "Conclusion of the HBO Captain Midnight Saga," *Software Engineering Notes*, vol. 11, no. 5, October 1986, pages 24–25.

2. *Software Engineering Notes*, vol. 13, no. 1, January 1988, page 7.

3. *Software Engineering Notes*, vol. 16, no. 1, January 1991, page 13.

4. "Enter the Technically-Competent Terrorist," *The Australian*, 8 April 1986; Perry Morrison, "Limits to Technocratic Consciousness: Information Technology and Terrorism as Example," *Science, Technology and Human Values*, vol. 11, no. 4, 1986, pages 4–16.

5. Dan Charles, "Can We Stop the Databank Robbers?" *New Scientist*, 26 January 1991, pages 12–13.

6. Ben Brock, "Hackers Beseige U.S. Voice-Mail," *The Australian*, 2 April 1991.

7. *Software Engineering Notes*, vol. 17, no. 2, April 1992, page 15.

8. Herbert Blankesteijn, "Dutch Phone Phreaks Dial the World for Free," *New Scientist*, 8 June 1991, page 19.

9. *The Australian*, 3 July 1989.

10. Mark Lewyn, "Phone Sleuths Are Cutting off the Hackers," *Business Week*, 13 July 1992, page 90.

11. Mark Lewyn, "Does Someone Have Your Company's Number?" *Business Week*, 11 February 1991, page 49; see other interesting cases in *Software Engineering Notes*, vol. 13, no. 4, October 1988, pages 14–16.

12. Peter G. Neumann, in *Software Engineering Notes*, vol. 9, no. 1, January 1984, pages 12–15.

13. Peter G. Neumann, op. cit.

14. Interested readers can find a much more detailed account of hacking in Katie Hafner and John Markoff's book, *Cyberpunk: Outlaws and Hackers on the*

Computer Frontier (Simon and Schuster, New York, 1991). The authors provide a very readable account of major hacking cases with a rich background on the individual hackers.

15. Stuart Gill, "Hi-Tech's Hubcap Thieves Are in It for the Buzz," *Computing Australia,* 26 October 1987, pages 33–34.

16. Eric S. Raymond (ed.) and Guy L. Steele, Jr., *The New Hacker's Dictionary,* (MIT Press, Cambridge MA, 1991).

17. *Software Engineering Notes,* vol. 12, no. 4, October 1987, page 9.

18. Sara Kiesler, Jane Siegel, and Timothy McGuire, "Social Psychological Aspects of Computer-Mediated Communication," *American Psychologist,* vol. 39, no. 10, 1984, pages 1123–1134.

19. Rosemarie Robotham, "Putting Hackers on the Analyst's Couch," *The Australian,* 31 January 1989, pages 30–34.

20. "NASA Hackers Weren't as Smart as It Seems," *Computing Australia,* 13 July 1987.

21. Brian Reid, "Lessons from the UNIX Break-Ins at Stanford," *Software Engineering Notes,* vol. 11, no. 5, October 1986, page 29.

22. "More on Nonsecure Nonlogouts," *Software Engineering Notes,* vol. 11, no. 5, October 1986, page 26.

23. Peter Lowe, "Still No Trace of High-Profile Hacker Author," *The Australian,* 10 February 1987.

24. I. S. Herschberg and R. Paans, "The Programmer's Threat: Cases and Causes," in J. H. Finch and E. G. Dougall (eds.), *Computer Security: A Global Challenge* (Elsevier, North-Holland, 1984) pages 409–423.

25. "Hacking Away at Shaky Security," *The Australian,* 26 January 1988; "Hackers Found Guilty After Cracking Duke's Code," *The Australian,* 29 April 1986; "Lords Clear British Hackers," *New Scientist,* 28 April 1988, page 25; "Hackers Appeal on Prestel Conviction," *Computing Australia,* 13 July 1987, page 13.

26. Peter Warren, "Unholy Alliance," *Computer Talk,* 22 October 1990.

27. Jay Peterzell, "Spying and Sabotage by Computer," *Time,* 20 March 1989; Richard Caseby, "Worried Firms Pay Hush Money to Hacker Thieves," *South China Morning Post,* 12 June 1989 (reprinted from *The Times*); and "Open Season for Hackers," *Computing Australia,* 18 September 1989.

28. *Software Engineering Notes,* vol. 15, no. 5, October 1990, page 12.

29. *The Daily Telegraph* (UK), 8 June 1990; Richard Siddle, "Freed Hacker in Lords Quest," *Computer Talk,* 8 April 1991; "Hacking Defined as Crime," *Computing Australia,* 16 July 1990; "Hacker Takes up the Challenge and Pays," *Computing Australia,* 4 June 1990; "Mad Hacker Jailed in UK Legal First," *The Australian,* 12 June 1990.

30. *Software Engineering Notes,* vol. 15, no. 2, April 1990, page 18.

31. Clifford Stoll, *The Cuckoo's Egg* (Doubleday, New York, 1990).

32. Dan Charles and Graeme O'Neill, "Hackers Plan Revenge for Police Clampdown on Computer Crime," *New Scientist,* 21 April 1990; Michelangelo Rucci, "Vic Pair Hacked into Top US Sites," *The Australian,* 27 March 1990.

33. Various reports from the Internet-circulated Computer Underground Digest, July 1992.

34. ""Harmless" Hacker under Jail Threat," *Computer Talk,* 7 October 1991; "Arrested Israeli 'Genius' Saw Hacking as a Challenge," *The Australian,* 10 September, 1991.

35. *Computer Talk,* 8 July 1991.

36. *Detroit News,* 10 May 1990.

37. Mark Lewyn, "Why the 'Legion of Doom' has Little Fear of the Feds," *Business Week,* 22 April 1991, page 62.

38. Dorothy Denning, "ATE vs. Craig Neidorf," *Communications of the ACM,* vol. 34, no. 3, March 1991, pages 23–43.

39. Dan Charles, "Crackdown on Hackers May Violate Civil Rights," *New Scientist,* 21 July 1990, page 8.

40. Richard Hollinger, "Hackers: Computer Heroes or Electronic Highwaymen?" *Computers and Society,* vol. 21, no. 1, 1991, pages 6–16.

41. J. F. Schoch and J. A. Hupp, "The Worm Programs—Early Experiences with Distributed Computation," *Communications of the ACM,* vol. 25, no. 3, 1982, pages 172–180.

42. A. K. Dewdney, "Computer Recreations," *Scientific American,* May 1984, pages 15–19, and March 1985, pages 14–19.

43. Fred Cohen, "Computer Viruses: Theory and Experiments," in J. H. Finch and E. G. Dougall (eds.), op. cit., pages 143–157.

44. Perry Morrison, "Computer Parasites: Software Diseases May Cripple Our Computers," *The Futurist,* March–April 1986, vol. 20, no. 2, pages 36–38; Lee Dembart, "Attack of the Computer Virus," *Discover,* November 1984, pages 90–92.

45. Anne E. Webster, "University of Delaware and the Pakistani Virus," *Computers and Security,* vol. 8, 1989, pages 103–105.

46. Kenneth R. van Wyk, "The Lehigh Virus," *Computers and Security,* vol. 8, 1989, pages 107–110.

47. Yisrael Radai, "The Israeli PC Virus," *Computers and Security,* vol. 8, 1989, pages 111–113.

48. *Software Engineering Notes,* vol. 15, no. 1, January 1990, page 13.

49. Julian Cribb, "Computer Virus Due to Strike in March," *The Australian,* 12 February 1992.

50. "Russian Viruses in Global Epidemic," *The Australian,* 3 November 1992.

51. "NewsTrack," *Communications of the ACM,* vol. 35, no. 6, June 1992, page 10.

52. "Cornell Virus Suspect Suspended for Violation," *The Australian,* 6 June 1989; "Cornell Suspends Student Hacker," *Computing Australia,* 12 June 1989; Tony Fainberg, "The Night the Network Failed," *New Scientist,* 4 March 1989, pages 36–42.

53. Ben Brock, ""Benign' Nature of Crime Spares Hacker from Prison," *The Australian,* 8 May 1990.

54. Lee A. Daniels, *The New York Times,* 25 February 1992.

55. Roland Tellzen, ""Malicious' New Strain of Viruses the Next Threat," *The Australian,* 29 May 1990.

56. Richard Jinman, "US Author Attacks Virus Spread Theory," *The Australian,* 5 June 1990.

57. Lance J. Hoffman (ed.), *Rogue Programs: Viruses, Worms and Trojan Horses* (Van Nostrand Reinhold, New York, 1990).

58. Nicholas Rothwell, "Computer AIDS: The Hitech Disease That Is Spreading Worldwide," *The Weekend Australian*, 4 June 1988; David Hebditch, Nick Anning, and Linda Melvern, *Techno-Bandits* (Houghton Mifflin, Boston, 1984).

59. "Operation Virus," *The Australian*, 18 November 1991; *Software Engineering Notes*, vol. 17, no. 2, April 1992, page 18.

60. Mark Lewyn, "'Killer' Viruses: An Idea Whose Time Shouldn't Come," *Business Week*, 23 July 1990.

61. Joe Dellinger, "Virus Protection Strategies," *Software Engineering Notes*, vol. 13, no. 1, January 1988.

62. Evan I. Schwartz and Jeffrey Rothfeder, "Viruses? Who You Gonna Call? 'Hackerbusters,'" *Business Week*, 6 August 1990, pages 48–49.

63. "What to Do about Computer Viruses," *Fortune*, 5 December 1988, page 16; "Local Crime Team Crack the Riddle of Big Red," *The Australian*, 14 April 1987.

64. "NewsTrack," *Communications of the ACM*, vol. 35, no. 2, February 1992, page 12.

65. John Charlton, "Dons Confounded by Spanish Virus," *Computer Talk*, 2 June 1991.

66. Bryan Boswell, "Fired Workers Take Revenge," *The Australian*, 7 December 1991.

67. *Software Engineering Notes*, vol. 17, no. 2, April 1992, page 19.

68. "Virus Hits Hospital Computers," *Los Angeles Times*, 27 March 1989.

69. Richard Siddle, "U.S. Virus Creator Unfit for Trial," *Computer Talk*, 9 December 1991.

70. "Defence Departments Team up for Virus/Hack War," *Computing Australia*, 19 November 1990; see also Richard Jinman, "Army Makes No Secret of Strong Need for Security," *The Australian*, 29 May 1990.

71. Peter Denning (ed.), *Computers Under Attack: Intruders, Worms and Viruses* (ACM Press/Addison-Wesley, New York, 1990).

72. "Viruses Give Legislators a Headache," *The Australian*, 13 March 1990.

Chapter 5

1. John Arlidge, *The Independent* (London), 7 February 1992.

2. Richard Saltos, *The Boston Globe*, 20 June 1986, page 1.

3. Jonathan Jacky, "Risks in Medical Electronics," Inside Risks column, *Communications of the ACM*, vol. 33, no. 12, 1990, page 138.

4. Peter Mellor, "Can You Count on Computers?" *New Scientist*, 11 February 1989.

5. G. R. Gladden, "Stop the Lifecycle, I Want to Get Off," *Software Engineering Notes*, vol. 7, no. 2, April 1982, pages 35–39.

6. E. Sibley, "The Evolution of Approaches to Information Systems Design Methodologies," in T. W. Olle, H. Sol and A. Verrin-Sturat (eds.), *Information Systems Design Methodologies: Improving the Practice* (Elsevier, North-Holland,

1986); see also J. A. Bubenko, *Information Systems Methodologies—A Research View* (SYSLAB Report no. 40, Systems Development and Artificial Intelligence Laboratory, University of Stockholm, Sweden, 1986); R. G. Canning, "Getting the Requirements Right," *EDP Analyzer,* vol. 15, no. 7, 1977, pages 1–14; B. P. Lientz and E. B. Swanson, *Software Maintenance Management* (Addison-Wesley, Reading, MA, 1980).

7. U.S. Government Accounting Office Report, FGMSD-80-4, 1979, as cited in *Software Engineering Notes,* vol. 10, no. 5, October 1985, page 6.

8. Roger Woolnough, "Britain Scrutinizes Software Quality," *Electronic Engineering Times,* 13 June 1988, page 19.

9. "Downtime Cost the US \$5.2bn Last Year," *The Australian,* 4 August 1992.

10. "American Airlines' Costly Glitch," *Business Week,* 27 July 1992; *The Australian,* 4 August 1992; *The Philadelphia Inquirer,* 6 January 1989, page 1; Charles Wright, "A New Way of Talking," *The Bulletin* (Australia), 4 August 1992, pages 68–69.

11. Tarek Vdel-Hamid and Stuart Madnick, "The Elusive Silver Lining: How We Fail to Learn from Software Development Failures," *Sloan Management Review,* vol. 32, no. 1, 1990, page 39.

12. "Central Postal/Banking Computer Failure in Japan," *Software Engineering Notes,* vol. 16, no. 3, July 1991, page 5.

13. Peter G. Neumann, "Survivable Systems," Inside Risks column, *Communications of the ACM,* vol. 35, no. 5, 1992, page 130.

14. "Don't Call Us . . .," *New Scientist,* 19 September 1992, page 7.

15. K. Lyytinen and R. Hirschheim, "Information Systems Failures—A Survey and Classification of the Empirical Literature," *Oxford Surveys in Information Technology,* vol. 4, 1987, pages 257–309; see also Charles Perrow, *Normal Accidents,* (Basic Books, New York, 1984); Peter Checkland, *Systems Thinking, Systems Practice,* (John Wiley, Chichester, England, 1981).

16. See Perry Morrison, "An Absence of Malice: Computers and Armageddon," *Prometheus,* vol. 2, no. 2, 1984, pages 190–200.

17. See Perry Morrison, ibid. as well as A. Chayes and J. Wiesner, *Underestimates and Overexpectations in ABM: An Evaluation of the Decision to Deploy an Anti-Ballistic Missile* (Harper and Row, New York, 1969), pages 122–123.

18. See *The Guardian Weekly,* 17 July 1988; *Sydney Morning Herald,* 4 August 1988, pages 1 and 11; James Coates and Michael Kilian, *Heavy Losses: The Dangerous Decline of American Defense* (Penguin, New York, 1986).

19. Admiral James Watkins, Chief of Naval Operations and Vice Admiral Robert Walters, Deputy Chief of Naval Operations, Department of Defense Authorizations for Appropriations for Fiscal Year 1985. *Hearings before the Senate Committee on Armed Services,* pages 4337–4379.

20. As reported in *Software Engineering Notes,* vol. 13, no. 4, October 1988, page 3.

21. "Patriot Games," *The Economist,* 10 October 1992, page 103; Marc Rotenberg, "Patriot Lapse: Software Failure," *Software Engineering Notes,* vol. 16, no. 3, July 1991, page 19; also *New Scientist,* 15 February 1992.

22. Steve Homer, "Battling on with Veteran Computers," *New Scientist,* 14 November 1992, pages 32–35.

23. Penelope Carrington, "Ship Makes List—The Hard Way," *The Seattle Times,* 5 August 1992, page D1.

24. B. Cooper and D. Newkirk, *Risks to the Public from Computer Systems,* Internet news group, November 1987.

25. Rodney Hoffman, "HERO—Hazards of Electromagnetic Radiation to Ordnance," *Software Engineering Notes,* vol. 16, no. 2, April 1991, page 18; "Electronic Blizzard Brings Down US Planes," *Monitoring Times,* May 1990, page 4.

26. John Lamb, "Computer Crashes and the Stranded Traveller—Air Traffic Control in Britain," *New Scientist,* 8 September 1988, page 65.

27. D. Black, *The Independent,* 24 September 1987; also reported by D. Kranzberg, *Software Engineering Notes,* vol. 12, no. 4, October 1987, pages 2–3.

28. Bruce Campion-Smith, "Glitches Stalling Updated Airport Radar," *The Toronto Star,* 3 August 1992.

29. *San Francisco Chronicle,* 25 October 1991.

30. *Boston Globe,* 6 October 1991.

31. Henry Spencer, "Concorde Tire Bursts: Risks When the Automatic System Fails," *Software Engineering Notes,* vol. 12, no. 4. October 1987, page 4.

32. The Sunday Times (London), 11 March 1990.

33. Peter G. Neumann, Inside Risks column *Communications of the ACM,* vol. 34, no. 5, October 1991, page 128; J. E. Hopcroft, & D. B. Krafft, "Toward Better Computer Science," *IEEE Spectrum,* December 1987, pages 58–60.

34. Tony Collins, *Computer Weekly,* 19 October 1989, page 1; *Computer Weekly,* 26 October 1989, page 9.

35. Carolyn Leitch, *The Toronto Globe and Mail,* 4 March 1992; Thomas McCarroll, "Futures Shock," *Time,* 29 June 1992, page 17.

36. M. Shaw, "A Sampler of System Problems and Failures Attributable to Software," compiled from a variety of sources in *Software Engineering Notes* (no other publication details available).

37. *Software Engineering Notes,* vol. 11, no. 2, April 1986, page 7.

38. *Electronic Design,* 15 September 1983.

39. "Smashing a Smasher," *Time,* 29 June 1992, page 21.

40. Henry Spencer, "Old Soviet Spacecraft Loss Attributed to Software," *Software Engineering Notes,* vol. 16, no. 3, July 1991, page 19.

41. *Software Engineering Notes,* vol. 10, no. 2, April 1985, page 6; *Software Engineering Notes,* vol. 11, no. 1, January 1986, page 9.

42. H. Bassen, J. Silberberg, F. Houston, W. Knight, C. Christman, and M. Greberman, "Computerized Medical Devices: Usage Trends, Problems and Safety Technology," *Proceedings of the 7th Annual Conference of IEEE Engineering in Medicine and Biology Society,* September 27–30, 1985, Chicago, Illinois, pages 180–185.

43. Elisabeth Geake, "Did Ambulance Chiefs Specify 'Safety' Software?" *New Scientist,* 7 November 1992, page 7; Charles Arthur, "Ambulance Computer System Was 'Too Complicated,'" *The Australian,* 14 November 1992; Christine McGourty, "999 Computer Is Closed Down Indefinitely," *The Weekly Telegraph,* no. 70, 17 November 1992, page 6; Monica Horten, "London Ambulance Tangled in Deaths Row," *The Australian,* 3 November 1992.

44. *The New York Times* Science Times Section, 29 July 1986, page C1.

45. As reported in *Software Engineering Notes,* vol. 12, no. 3, July 1987, page 15.

46. Tony Wray, "The Everyday Risks of Playing Safe," *New Scientist,* 8 September 1988, pages 61–64.

47. E. N. Adams, "Optimizing Preventing Service of Software Products," *IBM Journal of Research and Development,* vol. 28, no. 1, 1984, page 8.

48. David Parnas, "The Parnas Papers," *Computers and Society,* vol. 14, no. 9, 1985, pages 27–36; David L. Parnas, "Software Aspects of Strategic Defense Systems," *American Scientist,* vol. 73, no. 5, September–October 1985, pages 432–440.

49. Brenton R. Schlender, *Fortune,* 25 September 1989, pages 72–76.

50. Mark Bartelt, "Software Error at Bruce Nuclear Station," *Software Engineering Notes,* vol. 15, no. 2, April 1990, page 3; Tom Wilkie and Susan Watts, *The Independent,* 24 November 1991; Susan Watts, "Computer Watch on Nuclear Plants Raises Safety Fears," *The Independent,* 13 October 1991.

51. Mike Whitehorn, "An Object Lesson in Programming," *New Scientist,* 8 February 1992, pages 37–40.

52. "Something Rotten in the State of Software," *The Economist,* 9 January 1990, pages 81–84.

53. Evan Schwartz, "Turning Software from a Black Art into a Science," *Business Week,* 2 December 1991, pages 54–55; Brenton R. Schlender, op. cit.

54. Peter Mellor, "More Long Lived Bugs," *Software Engineering Notes,* vol. 16, no. 3, July 1991, page 27; E. N. Adams, op. cit.

55. Edward J. Joyce, "Is Error-Free Software Achievable?" *Datamation,* 15 February 1989, pages 53–56; Neil Gross, "Rails That Run on Software," *Business Week,* 2 December 1991, page 56.

56. David Parnas, op. cit.

57. Steven Levy, "Down by Law," *Macworld,* January 1992, pages 73–82.

58. Nancy Leveson, "Software Safety," SEI Curriculum Module SEI-CM-6-1.1, July 1987, Software Engineering Institute, Carnegie Mellon University; David Parnas, John Schouwen, and Shu Po Kwan, "Evaluation of Safety-Critical Software," *Communications of the ACM,* vol. 33, no. 6, 1990, pages 636–648.

Chapter 6

1. Evelyn Richards, "Proposed FBI Crime Computer System Raises Questions on Accuracy, Privacy—Report Warns of Potential Risk Data Bank Poses to Civil Liberties," *The Washington Post,* 13 February 1989.

2. Deborah Johnson, "Computers and Ethics," *National Forum,* Summer 1991, vol. 71, no. 3, pages 15–17.

3. Larry Reibstein and Lisa Drew, "Clean Credit for Sale: A Growing Illegal Racket," *Newsweek,* 12 September 1988, page 49.

4. Sundar Iyengar, "American Express Is Watching . . ." Internet *'Risks' Forum,* vol. 8, no. 66, 4 May 1986.

5. David Burnham, "Tales of a Computer State," *The Nation,* April 1983.

6. Jacques Vallee, *The Network Revolution: Confessions of a Computer Scientist* (And/Or Press, Berkeley, CA, 1982).

7. D. Dyer, "The Human Element," *'Risks' Forum,* vol. 1, no. 22, 16 October 1985; Peter G. Neumann, "What's in a Name?" Inside Risks column, *Communications of the ACM,* vol. 35, no. 1, January 1992, page 186.

8. David Burnham, op. cit.

9. Richard Lacayo, "Nowhere to Hide," *Time,* 11 November 1991, pages 40–43.

10. Peter Kimball, *The File* (Harcourt Brace Jovanovich, San Diego, CA, 1983).

11. Most incidents are reported in Peter G. Neumann, op. cit.; see also Rebecca Mercuri, "Report on the First Computers, Freedom & Privacy Conference," *'Risks' Forum,* vol. 11, no. 39, 4 April 1991; and James Rainey, *The Los Angeles Times,* 12 May 1989.

12. Evan I. Schwartz, "The Rush to Keep Mum," *Business Week,* 8 June 1992, page 33.

13. Richard Lacayo, "Nowhere to Hide," *Time,* 11 November 1991, pages 40–43.

14. *The Wall Street Journal,* 15 October 1991, page B1.

15. "Now Giving Credit Where It's Due," *Information Week,* 19 August 1991, pages 36–38.

16. Evan I. Schwartz, "It's Time to Clean up Credit Reporting," *Business Week,* 18 May 1992, page 28.

17. Jeffrey Rothfeder, "Looking for a Job? You May Be Out Before You Go In," *Business Week,* 24 September 1990.

18. *Software Engineering Notes,* vol. 17, no. 1, January 1992, page 12.

19. Albert B. Crenshaw, *The Washington Post,* 11 December 1991, page F1.

20. Jeffrey Rothfeder, "Is Nothing Private? Computers Know a Lot About You—And They're Quite Willing to Tell," *Business Week,* 4 September 1989, pages 32–37; see also Marc Rotenberg, "Prepared Testimony and Statement for the Record of Marc Rotenberg, Director, Washington Office, Computer Professionals for Social Responsibility (CPSR) on the Use of the Social Security Number as a National Identifier, before the Subcommittee on Social Security, Committee on Ways and Means, US House of Representatives," reprinted in *Computers and Society,* vol. 21, nos. 2, 3, and 4, 1991, pages 13–19.

21. Langdon Winner, "A Victory for Computer Populism," *Technology Review,* May/June 1991, page 66; *Software Engineering Notes,* vol. 16, no. 1, January 1991, pages 22–23; *Business Week,* 29 July 1991.

22. *Christian Science Monitor,* 1 August 1991, page 12.

23. Peter Coy, "Why All the Heavy Breathing over Caller ID?" *Business Week,* 18 June 1990, page 34; Marc Rotenberg, "VT Caller ID Decision," *Software Engineering Notes,* vol. 17, no. 2, April 1992, page 17.

24. Virginia Matthews, "Privacy Being Whittled away by Data Demand," *The Weekly Telegraph* (UK), no. 54, July 1992; "Caller Identity Phone Systems Under Scrutiny," *The Australian,* 6 July 1992.

25. Francis Gibb, "Data Act Sheds First Light on 'Secret' Personal Files," *The Australian,* 3 November 1987.

26. Greg Tucker, "Europe Grasps Nettle of Data Privacy Protection Legislation," *Computing Australia,* 19 September 1988, pages 24–29.

27. Duncan Campbell, "On and Off the Record," *Personal Computer World,* October 1988, page 146.

28. Peter Warren, "Data Protection's Paper Tiger," *Computer Talk,* 10 February 1992; Richard Siddle, "Crimes and Misdemeanours," *Computer Talk,* 3 June 1991.

29. Peter G. Neumann, op. cit., 1992; Ben Brock, "Libertarians Fear an Erosion of Privacy," *The Australian,* 16 April 1991.

30. Perry Morrison, "Limits to Technocratic Consciousness: Information Technology and Terrorism as Example," *Science, Technology and Human Values,* vol. 11, no. 4, 1986, pages 4–16; David Burnham, *The Rise of the Computer State* (Random House, New York, 1983).

31. Morrison, 1986, op. cit.

32. Charles Bruno, "The Electronic Cops," *Datamation,* 15 June 1984, pages 115–124.

33. David A. Banisar, "CPSR Files Suit Against FBI over Wiretap Proposal," *'Risks' Forum,* vol. 13, no. 81, 18 September 1992.

34. Curtis Jackson, "NSA and Encryption Algorithms," *'Risks' Forum,* vol. 2, no. 20, 2 March 1986; Dave Platt, "Data Encryption Standard," *'Risks' Forum,* vol. 2, no. 17, 28 February 1986.

35. From the text of a speech delivered by Chuck Hammill to *The Future of Freedom Conference,* November 1987, and reprinted in the Internet newsgroup, alt.society.futures, 21 September 1992.

36. John A. Adam, "Cryptography=Privacy?" *IEEE Spectrum,* August 1992, pages 29–34; and testimony of Professor David Farber before the Computer Systems Security and Privacy Advisory Board of the National Institute of Standards and Technology.

37. Gary H. Anthes, "DARPA Program to Battle War on Drugs, Terrorism," *Federal Computer Week,* 24 April 1989, vol. 3, no. 17, pages 1 and 53; Gary T. Marx, *Undercover: Police Surveillance in America* (University of California Press, Berkeley, CA, 1988).

38. Jonathan Markoff, "US Is Moving to Restrict Access to Facts about Computer Virus," *The New York Times,* 11 November 1988, page 12.

39. John Shattuck and Muriel Morrisey Spence, "The Dangers of Information Control," in Tom Forester (ed.), *Computers in the Human Context* (Basil Blackwell, Oxford, UK, and MIT Press, Cambridge, MA, 1989), reprinted from *Technology Review,* April 1988, pages 63–73; Bryan Boswell, "U.S. Military Seeks Control of Data," *The Australian,* 22 March 1988.

40. Philip Elmer-Dewitt, "Peddling Big Brother," *Time,* 24 June 1991; *Privacy Journal,* July 1990, vol. 16, no. 9, page 1.

41. Philip Elmer-Dewitt, op. cit.

42. A. N. Maiden, "Watching Big Brother," *Time* (Australia), 11 February 1991, pages 46–47.

43. Frank Devine, "The Underhanded Theft of Australia's Privacy," *The Australian,* 13 February 1992; Tracy Aubin, "Australia Card III: A Fait Accompli," *The Australian,* 14 September 1990, page 11; Tony Healy, "Database Akin to ID Card," *The Australian,* 23 January 1990.

44. K. Meyer, *'Risks' Forum,* vol. 13, no. 2, 25 September 1992.

45. Barry Fox and Jeremy Webb, "Britain Declines to Play the Health Card," *New Scientist,* 1 February 1992, pages 12–13.

46. Helen Meredith, "Bedlam Ensues as Europe Faces Human Rights Issue," *The Australian*, 6 March 1990; "Police Computer Fuels Fears of 'European Connection,'" *New Scientist*, 4 January 1992; David Lyon, "British Identity Card: The Unpalatable Logic of European Membership?" *The Political Quarterly*, vol. 62, no. 3, July 1991, pages 377–385.

47. Susan Gray, "Electronic Data Bases and Privacy: Policy for the 1990s," *Science, Technology and Human Values*, vol. 14, no. 3, 1989, pages 242–257; David Flaherty, "The Emergence of Surveillance Societies in the Western World: Toward the Year 2000," *Government Information Quarterly*, vol. 5, no. 4, 1988, pages 377–387.

48. Daizy Gedeon, "Local Group Keeps an Eye on Security," *The Australian*, 27 March 1990; Barry Fox, "Phonetappers Profit from Weak Radio Link," *New Scientist*, 5 September 1992, page 17.

49. Gary T. Marx and Sanford Sherizen, "Monitoring on the Job," in Tom Forester (ed.), op. cit.; George J. Church, "The Art of High-Tech Snooping," *Time*, 20 April 1987, pages 19–21; Oliver Baube, "EC Farms to Join Electronic Network," *The Australian*, 24 March 1992.

50. Gene Bylinsky, "How Companies Spy on Employees," *Fortune*, 4 November 1991; Stephen Koepp, "The Boss That Never Blinks," *Time*, 28 July 1986.

51. Geoffrey S. Goodfellow, "Electronic Surveillance," *'Risks' Forum*, vol. 1, no. 22, 16 October 1985.

52. David Stamps, "The IS Eye on Insider Trading," *Datamation*, 19 April 1990.

53. Katie Hafner and Susan Garland, "Privacy," *Business Week*, 28 March 1988.

54. Cristobal Martin, "A Simpler Risk of Computerized Warrant Systems," *'Risks' Forum*, vol. 13, no. 82, 25 September 1992; William D. Bauserman, *'Risks' Forum*, vol. 13, no. 81, 18 September 1992; Michael Kielsky, "Computerized Warrant Systems and Mobile Terminals," *'Risks' Forum*, vol. 13, no. 82, 25 September 1992.

Chapter 7

1. "AI in Medical Diagnosis and Aviation," *Software Engineering Notes*, vol. 11, no. 2, April 1986, page 5; "Dispute over Drug Death," *The Australian*, 8 September 1987.

2. Michael Schrage, *The Washington Post National Weekly Edition*, vol. 3, no. 40, 1986, page 6.

3. Herbert A. Simon, *Models of Thought* (Yale University Press, Yale, 1979).

4. Greg Wilson, "Chess Computers Make Their Move," *New Scientist*, 5 August 1989, pages 32–35.

5. Elisabeth Geake, "Playing to Win," *New Scientist*, 19 September 1992, pages 24–25.

6. Terry Winograd, "Understanding Natural Language," *Cognitive Psychology*, vol. 3, pages 1–191; Terry Winograd, *Understanding Natural Language* (Academic Press, New York, 1972).

7. John Haugeland, *Artificial Intelligence: The Very Idea* (MIT Press, Cambridge, MA, 1986).

8. Donald Michie and Rory Johnston, *The Creative Computer: Machine Intelligence and Human Knowledge* (Penguin Books, Harmondsworth, UK, 1985), pages 17–18.

9. John Searle, "Minds, Brains and Programs," in John Haugeland (ed.), *Mind Design* (MIT Press, Cambridge, MA, 1982); John Searle, "Minds, Brains and Science," *The 1984 Reith Lectures* (British Broadcasting Corporation, London, 1984).

10. Joseph Weizenbaum, *Computer Power and Human Reason: From Judgement to Calculation* (W. H. Freeman, San Francisco, 1976).

11. Kenneth Colby, F. Hilf, S. Weber, and H. Kraemer, "Turing-Like Indistinguishability Tests for the Validation of a Computer Simulation of Paranoid Processes," *Artificial Intelligence,* vol. 3, 1972, pages 199–221; Kenneth Colby, "Modeling a Paranoid Mind, with Open Peer Commentaries," *Behavioural and Brain Sciences,* vol. 4, 1981, pages 515–533.

12. W. Daniel Hillis, "Intelligence as an Emergent Behaviour; Or: The Songs of Eden," in Stephen R. Graubard (ed.), *The Artificial Intelligence Debate: False Starts and Real Foundations* (MIT Press, Cambridge, MA, 1988).

13. "Complex Barriers to Speaking Real English," *The Australian,* 14 April 1987.

14. Hubert L. Dreyfus and Stuart E. Dreyfus, *Mind over Machine: The Power of Human Intuition and Expertise in the Era of the Computer* (Basil Blackwell, Oxford, UK, 1986).

15. For some of the known physiological properties of brains, see, for example, David L. Waltz, "The Prospects for Building Truly Intelligent Machines," in Stephen R. Graubard (ed.), op. cit. 1988.

16. Alex Goodall, *The Guide to Expert Systems* (Learned Information, Oxford, UK, 1985).

17. Avron Barr and Edward A. Feigenbaum, *Handbook of Artificial Intelligence* (William Kaufmann, New York, 1981), vol. 2, pages 106–115.

18. Edward H. Shortliffe and Bruce Buchanan, "A Model of Inexact Reasoning in Medicine," *Mathematical Biosciences,* vol. 23, 1975.

19. Arnold Kraft, "XCON: An Expert Configuration System at Digital Equipment Corporation," in Patrick H. Winston and Karen A. Prendergast (eds.), *The AI Business* (MIT Press, Cambridge, MA, 1984).

20. Martin Fischler and Oscar Firschein, *Intelligence: The Eye, the Brain and the Computer* (Addison Wesley, Reading, MA, 1987).

21. Richard Forsyth, "The Anatomy of Expert Systems," in Masoud Yazdani and Ajet Narayanan (eds.), *Artificial Intelligence: Human Effects* (Ellis Horwood, Chichester, UK, 1984), pages 186–199.

22. Donald Michie, *On Machine Intelligence* (Ellis Horwood, Chichester, UK, 1986); I. Mozetic, N. Bratko, and N. Lavrac, "An Experiment in Automatic Synthesis of Expert Knowledge Through Qualitative Modelling," *Proceedings of the Logic Programming Workshop,* Albufeira, Portugal, June 1983.

23. Kester Cranswick, "Just Yesterday's Buzzword?" *Computing Australia,* 18 June 1990; Roland Tellzen, "Expert Systems Fail to Flourish," *The Australian,* 22 May 1990.

24. Dianne Berry and Anna Hart, *Expert Systems: Human Issues* (MIT Press, Cambridge, MA, 1990).

25. H. M. Collins, *Artificial Experts: Social Knowledge and Intelligent Machines* (MIT Press, Cambridge, MA, 1990).

26. Edward Warner, "Expert Systems and the Law," *High Technology Business,* October 1986, pages 32–35.

27. Edward Warner, ibid.

28. Richard M. Lucash, "Legal Liability for Malfunction and Misuse of Expert Systems," *SIGCHI Bulletin,* vol. 18, no. 1, 1986, pages 35–43.

29. Kathleen Mykytyn, Peter Mykytyn, and Craig Slinkman, "Expert Systems: A Question of Liability?" *MIS Quarterly,* vol. 14, no. 1, 1990, pages 27–38.

30. Robert R. Weaver, *Computers and Medical Knowledge: The Diffusion of Decision Support Technology* (Westview Press, Boulder, CO, 1991).

31. Edward Feigenbaum and Pamela McCorduck, *The Fifth Generation: Artificial Intelligence and Japan's Computer Challenge to the World* (Addison Wesley, Reading, MA, 1983); Karen Fitzgerald and Paul Wallich, "Next-Generation Race Bogs Down," *IEEE Spectrum,* June 1987, pages 28–33.

32. David L. Waltz, op. cit., 1988.

33. David L. Waltz, ibid.

34. Jacob Schwartz, "The New Connectionism: Developing Relationships between Neuroscience and Artificial Intelligence," in Graubard, op. cit., 1988.

35. Stephen Jose Hanson and David J. Burr, "What Connectionist Models Learn: Learning and Representation in Connectionist Networks," *Behavioural and Brain Sciences,* 1990, vol. 13, pages 471–518.

36. Maureen Caudill and Charles Butler, *Naturally Intelligent Systems* (MIT Press, Cambridge, MA, 1990).

37. Terry Winograd and Fernando Flores, *Understanding Computers and Cognition: A New Foundation for Design* (Ablex, Norwood, NJ, 1986).

38. Roger Penrose, *The Emperor's New Mind: Concerning Computers, Minds and the Laws of Physics,* (Oxford University Press, New York, 1990).

39. Donald Michie and Rory Johnston, op. cit., 1985.

40. William Ascher, "Limits of 'Expert Systems' for Political-Economic Forecasting," *Technological Forecasting and Social Change,* 1989, vol. 36, pages 137–151.

41. Edward Warner, op. cit., 1986.

42. Jeffrey Rothfeder, *Minds over Matter* (Prentice Hall, New York, 1985); Barbara Garson, *The Electronic Sweatshop: How Computers Are Transforming the Office of the Future into the Factory of the Past* (Simon and Schuster, New York, 1988).

43. Richard Pree, "The Human Mind Stored Forever," *The Australian,* 1 December 1987.

44. Isaac Asimov, Patricia Warrick, and Martin Greenberg (eds.), *Machines That Think* (Penguin, Harmondsworth, UK, 1985).

45. Geoff Simons, *Is Man a Robot?* (John Wiley, Chichester, UK, 1986).

46. Margaret Boden, "AI and Human Freedom," in Masoud Yazdani and Ajet Narayanan (eds.), op. cit., 1984.

47. J. David Bolter, *Turing's Man* (Pelican, Harmondsworth, UK, 1986).

48. Elizabeth Corcoran, "Strategic Computing: A Status Report," *IEEE Spectrum,* April 1987, pages 50–54.

49. Helen Meredith, "Twinkle Fades to Black," *The Australian,* 28 July 1992.

50. Tom Foremski, "Artificial Intelligence: Military Cash Keeps It in Line," *Computing Australia,* 21 September 1987.

51. Donald Michie and Rory Johnston, op. cit., 1985, page 71.

52. Igor Aleksander and Piers Burnett, *Thinking Machines: The Search for Artificial Intelligence* (Oxford University Press, Oxford, UK, 1986).

53. Richard Pree, op. cit., 1987.

54. NewsTrack column, *Communications of the ACM,* vol. 35, no. 4, April 1992, page 14.

55. Hubert L. Dreyfus, *What Computers Can't Do* (Harper and Row, New York, 1979); Hubert L. Dreyfus and Stuart E. Dreyfus, 1986, op. cit.

56. Alex Kozlov, "Rethinking Artificial Intelligence," *High Technology Business,* May 1988, pages 18–25; Lawrence Hunter, "AI's Limits," *Technology Review,* July 1988, pages 74–76; Helen Meredith, "Narrower Focus for Expert Systems," *The Australian,* 9 May 1989.

57. Hubert Dreyfus, *What Computers Still Can't Do: A Critique of Artificial Reason* (MIT Press, Cambridge, MA, 1992).

58. Theodore Roszak, "Smart Computers at Insecure Stage," *New Scientist,* 3 April 1986, pages 46–47.

Chapter 8

1. *The Financial Times* (London), diary section, undated.

2. George C. Church, "The Work Ethic Lives!" *Time,* 7 September 1987; "Americans Are Still Having a Love Affair with Work," *Business Week,* 18 January 1988; "You Must Be Very Busy," *Time,* 20 August 1990; international survey reported in *The Weekend Australian,* 3–4 March 1990; Anne B. Fisher, "Welcome to the Age of Overwork," *Fortune,* 30 November 1992.

3. James Graff, "Weekend Work," *Time,* 19 December 1988; Alan Goodall, "Holiday a Dirty Word in Japan," *The Australian,* 24 December 1988; Walter Kiechel III, "The Workaholic Generation," *Fortune,* 10 April 1989; Nancy Gibbs, "America Runs Out of Time," *Time,* 24 April 1989; Juliet B. Schor, *The Overworked American: The Unexpected Decline of Leisure* (Basic Books, New York, 1991); Barbara Killinger, *Workaholics: The Respectable Addicts* (Simon and Schuster, New York, 1992); OECD survey reported in *The Age* (Melbourne), 14 July 1990.

4. Richard M. Cyert and David C. Mowery (eds.), *Technology and Employment: Innovation and Growth in the US Economy,* Panel on Technology and Employment, Committee on Science, Engineering and Public Policy (National Academy Press, Washington, DC, 1987); see also Richard M. Cyert and David C. Mowery, "Technology, Employment and US Competitiveness," *Scientific American,* vol. 260, no. 5, May 1989, pages 28–35.

5. Louis S. Richman, "America's Tough New Job Market," *Fortune,* 24 February 1992; Ronald Henkoff, "Where Will the Jobs Come From?" *Fortune,* 19 October 1992.

6. W. W. Daniel, *Workplace Industrial Relations and Technical Change,* Report of the U.K. Workplace Industrial Relations Survey, cosponsored by the Depart-

ment of Employment, the Economic and Social Research Council, the Policy Studies Institute, and the Advisory, Conciliation and Arbitration Service (PSI/Frances Pinter, London, 1987), pages 278–282.

7. Brian O'Reilly, "The Job Drought," *Fortune,* 24 August 1992.

8. "America Rushes to High-Tech for Growth," *Business Week,* 28 March 1983; Ian Anderson, "New Technology Will Not Provide Jobs," *New Scientist,* 10 May 1984; Richard Brandt, "Those Vanishing High-Tech Jobs," *Business Week,* 15 July, 1985; "Is the US Becoming a Nation of Sales Clerks?" *Business Week,* 18 May 1987.

9. Russell W. Rumberger and Henry M. Levin, "Forecasting the Impact of New Technology on the Future Job Market," *Technological Forecasting and Social Change,* vol. 27, 1985, pages 399–417.

10. *Business Week,* 19 December 1988; *Fortune,* 4 November 1991.

11. *The Australian,* 2 June 1992, 6 October 1992, 20 October 1992, and 1 December 1992; *Business Week,* 19 August 1991, 19 October 1992, and 23 November 1992.

12. Harley Shaiken, "High-Tech Goes Third World," *Technology Review,* January 1988; *Business Week,* 21 March 1988 and 12 December 1988; *The Australian,* 28 November 1989; *Computer Talk* (UK), 9–22 September 1991.

13. Michael R. Rubin and Mary T. Huber, *The Knowledge Industry in the United States: 1960–1980* (Princeton University Press, Princeton, NJ, 1986).

14. Stephen S. Cohen and John Zysman, *Manufacturing Matters: The Myth of the Post-Industrial Economy* (Basic Books, New York, 1987).

15. James Brian Quinn, Jordan J. Baruch, and Penny Cushman Paquette, "Technology in Services," *Scientific American,* vol. 257, no. 6, December 1987.

16. J. David Roessner, "Forecasting the Impact of Office Automation on Clerical Employment, 1985–2000," *Technological Forecasting and Social Change,* vol. 28, 1985, pages 203–216; *Business Week,* 11 May 1992; *The Australian,* 7 April 1987, reprinted from *The Times,* London.

17. Sar A. Levitan and Elizabeth A. Conway, "Part-Timers: Living on Half-Rations," *Challenge,* vol. 31, no. 3, May–June 1988; Louis Uchitelle, "Reliance on Temporary Jobs Hints at Economic Fragility," *The New York Times,* 16 March 1988, page A1; and Michael A. Pollock, "The Disposable Employee Is Becoming a Fact of Corporate Life," *Business Week,* 15 December 1986; plus *Fortune,* 24 August 1992.

18. *Business Week,* 24 July 1989; *Time,* 18 September 1989.

19. *Business Week,* 19 August 1991; *Fortune,* 24 February 1992, 24 August 1992, and 16 November 1992.

20. David R. Howell, "The Future Employment Impacts of Industrial Robots," *Technological Forecasting and Social Change,* vol. 28, 1985, pages 297–310; Kurt Hoffman and Howard Rush, *Microelectronics and Clothing: The Impact of Technical Change on a Global Industry* (Praeger, New York, 1988).

21. "Hiring the Handicapped," *Fortune,* 26 September 1988.

22. Harley Shaiken, *Work Transformed: Automation and Labor in the Computer Age* (Holt, Rinehart and Winston, New York, 1985); Harley Shaiken, "The Automated Factory: Vision and Reality," in Tom Forester (ed.), *Computers in the Human Context* (Basil Blackwell, Oxford, UK, and MIT Press, Cambridge, MA, 1989); David F. Noble, *Forces of Production* (Knopf, New York, 1985);

Mike Cooley, *Architect or Bee?* (Langley Technical Services, Slough, UK, 1980); Stephen Wood (ed.), *The Degradation of Work?* (Hutchinson, London, 1982); David Knights, Hugh Willmott, and David Collinson (eds.), *Job Redesign* (Gower, Aldershot, UK, 1985).

23. Larry Hirschhorn, "Robots Can't Run Factories," in Tom Forester (ed.), op. cit., page 301; Larry Hirschhorn, *Beyond Mechanization* (MIT Press, Cambridge, MA, 1984). Even Shaiken comes close to conceding this point. See, for example, the last paragraph of his piece in Tom Forester (ed.), op. cit., page 299.

24. W. W. Daniel, op. cit., pages 151–166.

25. Graham Winch, "New Technologies, New Problems," in Graham Winch (ed.), *Information Technology in Manufacturing Processes* (Rossendale, London, 1983), page 7.

26. Robert Kraut, Susan Dumais, and Susan Koch, "Computerization, Productivity, and Quality of Worklife," *Communications of the ACM,* vol. 32, no. 2, February 1989.

27. David Boddy and David A. Buchanan, *Managing New Technology* (Basil Blackwell, Oxford, UK, 1986), pages 84–112.

28. Richard J. Long, *New Office Information Technology: Human and Managerial Implications* (Croom Helm, London, 1987); Richard J. Long, "Human Issues in New Office Technology," in Tom Forester (ed.), op. cit., pages 328–329 and 332.

29. Rob Kling and Suzanne Iacono, "Desktop Computerization and the Organization of Work," in Tom Forester (ed.), op. cit., page 351; Stephen J. Lepore, Rob Kling, Suzanne Iacono, and Joey George, "Implementing Desktop Computing, Infrastructure, and the Quality of Worklife," in *Proceedings of the International Conference on Information Systems* (IFIP, Boston, 1989).

30. Ian McLoughlin and Jon Clark, *Technological Change at Work* (Open University Press, Milton Keynes, UK, 1988), pages 116–117.

31. Shoshana Zuboff, *In the Age of the Smart Machine* (Basic Books, New York, 1988).

32. Shoshana Zuboff, "Informate the Enterprise: An Agenda for the Twenty-First Century," *National Forum,* the Phi Kappa Phi journal, Summer 1991.

33. Rob Kling and Charles Dunlop, "Key Controversies about Computerization and White Collar Worklife" in Ronald Baeker, John Buxton, and Jonathan Grudin (eds.), *Human–Computer Interaction* (Morgan-Kaufman, San Mateo, CA, 1992).

34. Curt Suplee, "The Electronic Sweatshop," *The Washington Post,* Outlook section, 3 January 1988, page B1; "Stress on the Job," *Newsweek* special report in *The Bulletin* (Australia), 25 April 1988, pages 40–45; *Fortune,* 31 July 1989.

35. Robert Karasek and Tores Theorell, *Unhealthy Work: Stress, Productivity and the Reconstruction of Working Life* (Basic Books, New York, 1990); Barbara Garson, *The Electronic Sweatshop: How Computers Are Transforming the Office of the Future into the Factory of the Past* (Simon and Schuster, New York, 1988).

36. Sue Cox, *Change and Stress in the Modern Office* (Further Education Unit, Department of Education and Science, London, UK, 1986).

37. Craig Brod, *Technostress: The Human Cost of the Computer Revolution* (Addison-Wesley, Reading, MA, 1984). It is worth noting that Bruce Charlton argues that stress has become a trendy catch-all concept that is frequently used

to describe both a stimulus and a response. We say that such-and-such causes stress and yet is caused by stress. He says the stress concept is so broad and so diffuse that it is more likely to confuse than to clarify: "It is a concept without value . . . a pseudo-explanation which provides a blind alley for rational thought. There is no reason for us to use the word," he declares (Forum, *New Scientist*, 29 June 1991, page 55).

38. Mike Parker and Jane Slaughter, "Management by Stress," *Technology Review*, vol. 91, no. 7, October 1988; Louis Kraar, "Japan's Gung-Ho US Car Plants," *Fortune*, 30 January 1989.

39. Joseph J. Fucini and Suzy Fucini, *Working for the Japanese: Inside Mazda's American Auto Plant* (Free Press, New York, 1990); *Time*, 14 September 1987; *Business Week*, 14 August 1989; *Fortune*, 30 January 1989.

40. David Boddy and David A. Buchanan, op. cit., page 105.

41. *Federal Government Information Technology: Electronic Surveillance and Civil Liberties* (Office of Technology Assessment, US Congress, Washington, DC, 1985); *The Electronic Superviser: New Technology, New Tensions* (Office of Technology Assessment, US Congress, Washington, DC, 1988).

42. Gene Bylinsky, "How Companies Spy on Employees," *Fortune*, 4 November 1991.

43. Rebecca A. Grant, Christopher A. Higgins, and Richard H. Irving, "Computerized Performance Monitors: Are They Costing You Customers?" *Sloan Management Review*, Spring 1988, pages 39–45.

44. Gary T. Marx and Sanford Sherizen, "Monitoring on the Job," in Tom Forester (ed.), op. cit., reprinted from *Technology Review*, November/December 1986. See also Michael W. Miller, "Computers Keep Eye on Workers and See If They Perform Well," *The Wall Street Journal*, Monday 3 June 1985, page 1.

45. Peter G. Neumann, "Are Risks in Computer Systems Different from Those in Other Technologies?" *Software Engineering Notes*, vol. 13, no. 2, April 1988, pages 2–4.

46. Peter G. Neumann, op. cit., page 3.

47. Faye Rice, "Do You Work in a Sick Building?" *Fortune*, 2 July 1990; *The Times* report in *The Australian*, 19 June 1990; *The Economist* report in *The Australian*, 16 May 1989.

48. *The Times* report in *The Australian*, 1 December 1992.

49. Tom Forester, *High-Tech Society* (Basil Blackwell, Oxford, UK, and MIT Press, Cambridge, MA, 1987), page 215.

50. Kenneth R. Foster, "The VDT Debate," in Tom Forester (ed.), op. cit., reprinted from *American Scientist*, vol. 74, no. 2, March–April 1986, pages 163–168; "VDUs and Health," *Futures*, June 1987, page 362; reports in *The Australian*, 19 September 1989, 20 February 1990, and 19 March 1991.

51. "VDTs 'Cause Eye Problems,'" *The Australian*, 1 December 1987; "Studies Underline Hazards of Computer Terminals," *New Scientist*, 13 August 1987, page 33; David Kirkpatrick, "How Safe Are Video Terminals?" *Fortune*, 29 August 1988; *Software Engineering Notes*, vol. 13, no. 4, October 1988, page 19; UPI report in *The Australian*, 20 June 1989.

52. Christine Gorman, "All Eyes Are on the VDT," *Time*, 27 June 1988; and David Kirkpatrick, op. cit., page 44.

53. Reports in *The Australian,* 22 August 1989, 29 August 1989, and 8 October 1991; *Computer Talk* (UK), 5 November 1990, 7 October 1991, and 6 April 1992; *Technology Review,* February/March 1991, pages 16–17.

54. Reports in *The Australian,* 30 June 1987, 21 June 1988, 17 January 1989, 2 January 1990, 1 January 1991, and 18 February 1992; *Time,* 7 January 1991.

55. Howard Bird, "When the Body Takes the Strain," *New Scientist,* 7 July 1990, pages 37–40; Barbara Goldoftas, "Hands That Hurt," *Technology Review,* vol. 94, no. 1, January 1991, pages 43–50.

56. Peter T. Kilborn, "Automation: Pain Replaces the Old Drudgery," *The New York Times,* 24 June 1990, page 1; *Business Week,* 13 July 1992; *The Australian,* 30 June 1992; *Computer Talk* (UK), 18 June 1990 and 25 March 1991.

57. Mark Ragg, "Plague of RSI Suddenly 'Disappears,'" *The Australian,* 7 September 1987; Mark Ragg, "Whatever Happened to RSI?" *The Bulletin,* 9 April 1991.

58. Sara Kiesler and Tom Finholt, "The Mystery of RSI," *American Psychologist,* December 1988, pages 1004–1015; see also "A Newsroom Hazard Called RSI," *Columbia Journalism Review,* January/February 1987.

59. Sara Kiesler and Tom Finholt, op. cit., page 1012.

60. Paul A. Strassman, *The Business Value of Computers* (The Information Economics Press, New Canaan, CT, 1990); Michael S. Scott Morton (ed.), *The Corporation of the 1990s: Information Technology and Organizational Transformation* (Oxford University Press, New York, 1991).

61. Richard H. Franke, "Technological Revolution and Productivity Decline: The Case of US Banks," in Tom Forester (ed.), op. cit., pages 281–290, reprinted from *Technological Forecasting and Social Change,* vol. 31, 1987, pages 143–154.

62. "Banks and Technology: Cure-All or Snake-Oil?" Special Report in *The Economist,* 3 October 1992.

63. Timothy N. Warner, "Information Technology as a Competitive Burden," in Tom Forester (ed.), op. cit., pages 272–280, reprinted from *Sloan Management Review,* vol. 29, no. 1, Fall 1987.

64. Report in *The Australian,* 28 May 1992.

65. See, for example, William Bowen, "The Puny Payoff from Office Automation," *Fortune,* 26 May 1986.

66. Cited by Richard J. Long, op. cit., page 327.

67. Steve Smith, "Information Technology in Banks: Taylorization or Human-Centered Systems?" in Tom Forester (ed.), op. cit. 1989, pages 377–390, reprinted from *Science and Public Policy,* vol. 14, no. 3, June 1987.

Chapter 9

1. A. K. Dewdney, "Computer Recreations," *Scientific American,* June 1985, pages 12–17.

2. Donald H. Berman and Carole D. Hafner, "The Potential of Artificial Intelligence to Help Solve the Crisis in Our Legal System," *Communications of the ACM,* vol. 32, no. 8, 1989, pages 926–938.

3. Perry Morrison, "Limits to Technocratic Consciousness: Information Technology and Terrorism as Example," *Science, Technology and Human Values,* vol. 11, 1986, pages 4–16; Alan Drengson, "Applied Philosophy of Technology: Reflections on Forms of Life and the Practice of Technology," *The International Journal of Applied Philosophy,* vol. 3, no. 1, 1986, pages 1–13.

4. See, for example, the range of articles contained in *Software Engineering Notes,* vol. 16, no. 1, January 1991, pages 25–31.

Index